Vicki Valosik

Britain's Olympic Women

Britain has a long and distinguished history as an Olympic nation. However, most Olympic histories have focused on men's sport. This is the first book to tell the story of Britain's Olympic women, how they changed Olympic spectacle and how, in turn, they have reinterpreted the Games.

Exploring the key themes of gender and nationalism, and presenting a wealth of new empirical, archival evidence, the book explores the sporting culture produced by British women who aspired to become Olympians, from the early years of the modern Olympic movement. It shines new light on the frameworks imposed on female athletes, individually and as a group, by the International Olympic Committee (IOC), the British Olympic Association (BOA) and the various affiliated sporting international federations. Using oral history and family history sources, the book tells of the social processes through which British Olympic women have become both heroes and anti-heroes in the public consciousness. Exploring the hidden narratives around women such as Charlotte Cooper, Lottie Dod, Audrey Brown and Pat Smythe, and bringing the story into the modern era of London 2012, Dina Asher-Smith and Katarina Johnson-Thompson, the book helps us to better understand the complicated relationship between sport, gender, media and wider society.

This is fascinating reading for anybody with an interest in sport history, Olympic history, women's history, British history or gender studies.

Jean Williams is Professor of Sport at the Institute of Sport and Human Sciences, University of Wolverhampton, UK. She is also a Non Executive Director at The Silverstone Motor Sport Museum.

Routledge Research in Sports History

The *Routledge Research in Sports History* series presents leading research in the development and historical significance of modern sport through a collection of historiographical, regional and thematic studies which span a variety of periods, sports and geographical areas. Showcasing ground-breaking, cross-disciplinary work from established and emerging sport historians, the series provides a crucial contribution to the wider study of sport and society. Available in this series:

A History of Chinese Martial Arts
Edited by Fan Hong and Fuhua Huang

The Early Development of Football
Contemporary Debates
Edited by Graham Curry

Sport, War and the British
1850 to the Present
Peter Donaldson

The Emergence of Football
Sport, Culture and Society in the Nineteenth Century
Peter Swain

Britain's Olympic Women
A History
Jean Williams

For more information about this series, please visit: www.routledge.com/sport/series/RRSH

Britain's Olympic Women

A History

Jean Williams

Routledge
Taylor & Francis Group
LONDON AND NEW YORK

First published 2021
by Routledge
2 Park Square, Milton Park, Abingdon, Oxon OX14 4RN

and by Routledge
52 Vanderbilt Avenue, New York, NY 10017

Routledge is an imprint of the Taylor & Francis Group, an informa business

© 2021 Jean Williams

The right of Jean Williams to be identified as author of this work has been asserted by her in accordance with sections 77 and 78 of the Copyright, Designs and Patents Act 1988.

All rights reserved. No part of this book may be reprinted or reproduced or utilised in any form or by any electronic, mechanical, or other means, now known or hereafter invented, including photocopying and recording, or in any information storage or retrieval system, without permission in writing from the publishers.

Trademark notice: Product or corporate names may be trademarks or registered trademarks, and are used only for identification and explanation without intent to infringe.

British Library Cataloguing-in-Publication Data
A catalogue record for this book is available from the British Library

Library of Congress Cataloging-in-Publication Data
A catalog record has been requested for this book

ISBN: 978-0-367-47321-1 (hbk)
ISBN: 978-1-003-03484-1 (ebk)

Typeset in Goudy
by Wearset Ltd, Boldon, Tyne and Wear

For Simon, and the little cat, Bubkiss.

For my Mum and Dad, who bought one of those great cabinet colour televisions in 1972, and gave me a typewriter for Christmas the same year. This book was probably inevitable from then on, eventually.

Contents

List of figures		ix
Acknowledgements		xi
	Introduction: Britain and the Olympic Movement	1
1	British Olympic pioneers 1900–1912: Chattie, Lottie and Jennie	12
2	The Olympic inter-war revival and the British Olympic Association: Gladys Carson and the 1924 Paris Games	62
3	The first all-female British Olympic team at Lake Placid, USA in 1932: Mollie, Joan, Cecilia and Megan	95
4	The 1936 Berlin Olympic Games: how gender and politics shaped the career of athlete Audrey Brown	113
5	Austerity and the second London Olympic Games in 1948: how Margaret Wellington swam to fame as 'The Peppy Kid'	140
6	Elizabeth II, Britain and Olympic Cold War rivalries: equestrian Pat Smythe and the New Elizabethans 1952–1960	171
7	Britain's Olympic Golden Girls and the changing media industry 1964–1984: the decline of amateurism and the rise of sports medicine	217

| 8 | Olympic legacies: lottery funding, professional sport, diversity and fame | 268 |

| | Appendix 1: Great Britain's female team at the 1964 Winter Olympics in Innsbruck, Austria and the 1964 Summer Olympic Games, Tokyo | 279 |

| | Appendix 2: Great Britain's Olympic women's team at the 1968 Mexico Summer Olympic Games and the Grenoble Winter Games | 284 |

| | Appendix 3: Great Britain's female team at the 1972 Summer Olympic Games in Munich, West Germany and the 1972 Winter Olympics in Sapporo, Japan | 290 |

| | Appendix 4: Great Britain's female team at the 1976 Summer Olympic Games in Montréal, Canada and the 1976 Winter Olympics in Innsbruck, Austria | 298 |

| | Appendix 5: Great Britain's female team at the 1980 Summer Olympic Games in Moscow, USSR and the 1980 Winter Olympics in Lake Placid, USA | 305 |

| | Appendix 6: Great Britain's female team at the 1984 Summer Olympic Games in Los Angeles, USA and the 1984 Winter Olympics | 312 |

| | *Bibliography* | 323 |
| | *Index* | 345 |

Figures

1.1	Four women tennis players after an exhibition match taken at the Roehampton Club in 1929	23
1.2	Lottie Dod at home with her brothers, Willy and Tony, with whom she played mixed matches and against rivals	31
1.3	Lottie Dod with Welford Park Archery Club	32
1.4	Lottie Dod at 85 years of age. 'The Old Lady Of The Courts'	36
1.5	Jennie Fletcher in 1912	41
1.6	Jennie Fletcher far right, with gold and silver medallists in the individual 100-metres freestyle	42
1.7	Image from Jennie Fletcher's scrapbook, showing a photographic portrait alongside her gold medal	45
1.8	The plaque of the winning medallists at the Olympic Stadium, Stockholm, listing Great Britain's victory in the 4 × 100-metres freestyle relay, alongside other international swimming greats	47
2.1	A.S.A. Championship Diving medals of Belle White, an Olympian of four games, the last in 1928, and a bronze medallist of 1912	68
2.2	Gladys Carson's head and shoulders photograph portrait taken at the 1924 Olympic Games; from Gladys Carson's scrapbook	75
2.3	Team Photograph Postcard of Britain's Olympic swimmers in 1924; from Gladys Carson's scrapbook	78
2.4	This somewhat controversial photograph of Gladys Carson and an annoyed male opponent was widely mediated; from Gladys Carson's scrapbook	81
2.5	Gladys Carson Hewitt's headstone showing the Olympic rings, which is not so unusual for proud British women Olympians and their families	84
4.1	Mary Lines, Britain's first big female track and field athletics star in the 1920s, a working class clerk for Schweppes, from London	118

Figures

4.2	Mary Lines practices the relay, a multiple world record holder, often overlooked in the record books, although her times are often referenced	119
5.1	Margaret Wellington at the 1948 London Olympic Games	144
5.2	A training photograph taken of Margaret Wellington, to refine her technique prior to the 1948 London Olympic Games	147
5.3	Flight and travel tickets. Invitations to overseas international competitions enabled Margaret, 'The Peppy Kid', to see the world and meet some of her heroes, including fellow athletes and movie stars	151
5.4	Margaret swam into her 80s, ideally in a 50-metre pool, with a lane reserved for her at the local swimming baths	154
5.5	The star of the 1948 London Olympic Games, Fanny Blankers-Koen, with four gold medals, here beating Britain's Dorothy Manley, a typist from Woodford Green	156
5.6	The actual swimming costumes that Margaret Wellington, Helen Yate and the British team wore in 1948 were the latest technology of the time, in finest silk and with the distinctive Jantzen diver logo	164

Acknowledgements

I would like to thank Simon, above all, for encouraging me to finish this book. Encouragement is of course a euphemism. My Olympic 'shelfie' is actually what used to be our wine rack, and he is keen that dozens of folders of committee minutes do not permanently become lodged where there should be something aged and interesting resting instead. He is of course, quite right.

The conviction that the stories of the amazing pioneering Olympian women deserve to be told in a collective biography has sustained such a large undertaking. Originally, I was advised that Britain's Olympic women sounded like a short journal article, rather than a book. At 120,000 words, I have had to curtail the story more than I would have liked, but each individual story is remarkable; collectively these women are inspiring. I would have loved to include more images too.

People often ask, why has this book taken so long? The Olympics are a huge topic. I have lost key family members and good friends during the writing of this book, which has meant that my hardiness for the project has waxed and waned over time. This has recently included my beloved little writing partner, the cat, who has snoozed without undue concern through my efforts on the laptop these last ten years. The Friday Afternoon Writing Club is 50 per cent down on its personnel, and finishing the manuscript has been less fun as a result. Some of it has even seemed like work.

I have been helped by a period of research leave from the University of Wolverhampton, for which I am very grateful. I would also like to particularly thank Simon Whitmore and his colleagues at Routledge, and Taylor and Francis for their help in completing the work. Simon was good enough to publish my first academic book in 2003 and so there is a nice symmetry to his being commissioning editor in this project so many years later.

Thankfully, my Dad and Mum both lived through World War II and knew quite a bit about resilience. Both were great sports enthusiasts, taking four of my siblings and me from swimming to football, to gymnastics and tennis with enormous patience, when it was clear that my most distinguished destiny was to win the occasional 'Most Improved Player'. I also had a galaxy of uncles and aunts who were active, hilarious and vital. When Dad purchased a colour TV for the 1972 Munich Olympic Games, I was inspired by Olga Korbut, who seemed much less fierce than Mary Peters, and the local gymnastics club tolerated my enthusiasm to BAGA level 2. My family have always been sporty, and we share our competitive spirit on high days and holidays, and so much love to 'the gang', which is now extending to a new generation, Ava, Jessica, Cameron, Millie and Amelia. I am also Godmother to Lilah, who is a joy.

I would also like to thank Joanna, with whom I created jjheritage.com as a consultancy business. It's been great fun professionally and personally. Jo and Graham have provided support and many cups of tea. Mick and Susan inspired Jo and me to take on sporting challenges. Lots of inspiration then, and consolation.

Many of us who write professionally about sport begin with a love of the subject, and end by loving the subject a little less. Sometimes a lot less. The gigantism, money, corruption, discrimination and politicisation of the Olympic Movement makes it easy not to love. Within those imperfect and often highly unpleasant structures though, women have carved out an unwanted and often unencouraged history for themselves as representatives of an ideal which is highly personal to them, and testament to their own agency. That story has yet to be told, and this book is just a beginning. I would particularly like to thank the Olympians' family members who shared stories. Precious sources deserve to be treated with great respect. I hope that I have returned the kindness that I have received.

Introduction
Britain and the Olympic Movement

The Olympic Games are the largest sports spectacle in the world and the most significant tournaments for women athletes in the twenty-first century. Spectators in the various stadia number the hundreds of thousands, and billions more follow the games on their televisions and through social media channels.[1] This now extends also to satellite organisations of the Olympic movement, including the World Anti-Doping Agency; the Court of Arbitration for Sport; the Olympic Congress and Commissions and the International Foundation for the Olympic Truce. There are separate Winter, Summer and Youth Olympic festivals with the International Olympic Committee (IOC) increasingly acting as an umbrella organisation for a wide range of sports bodies and tournaments, such as the International Paralympic Committee, which nevertheless remain separate and organise their own events.

The British have played a prominent part in modern Olympic tradition since a version of the ancient Pan-Hellenic games was reinterpreted in Athens in 1896, though no women competed in this first edition. The sheer diversity of women who have represented Britain since the first female competitors took part in the Paris Games of 1900 is remarkable. For example, the youngest female competitor in Olympic history was Cecilia Colledge who skated in the 1932 Los Angeles games at 11 years and 78 days. The eldest female competitor was also British. Lorna Johnstone first took part in the 1956 Stockholm dressage individual competition, appeared again in the 1968 Mexico individual and team events and finally performed in both at the 1972 Munich games, aged 70. That increasing numbers of women, in a widening range of disciplines, have changed the Games between 1900 and 2020 is obvious to even the most casual observer. However, the extent to which women have transformed the Olympic Games remains to be more fully understood.

Gender and nationalism are two of the crucial ways through which Olympism has been presented and understood: yet there has never before been a research monograph on British women in the Olympic movement more generally. A study such as this is therefore long overdue, given that internationalism and more recent globalisation, have mediated sportswomen from Britain as heroes, and anti-heroes, in a number of countries as a result of their Olympic performances. Cosmopolitan forces have also been at work, whereby overseas female Olympic rivals have registered on the British public consciousness, both as individuals and groups. These women serve both as comparators and competitors for audiences against which to judge the performance and behaviour of British representatives.

We know relatively little about women in the Olympic movement, for all the millions of words written on the subject. Baron Pierre de Coubertin, the anglophile French founder of the IOC, was partly inspired to do so by his admiration for the British male public school tradition and remained firmly opposed to female participation.[2]

The modern Olympic Movement, as Pierre de Fredy, Baron of Coubertin saw it was, from the outset, a determinedly masculine construction. Born in 1863 of an aristocratic family, the defeat of France by the Prussians in 1870 led to Coubertin's longstanding interest in improving the physical fitness of his fellow countrymen. Thomas Hughes had published *Tom Brown's Schooldays* in 1856. After reading a French translation, Coubertin made a pilgrimage to the chapel at Rugby school, where it was set, some years later in 1884. He took rather literally its depiction of Thomas Arnold, the former head-teacher from 1828 to 1842, as an advocate of sports for boys in helping to instil physical robustness and integrity. Arnold's focus had been more moral and academic than sporting, while *Tom Brown* had been a romanticised version of the author's childhood at the school. Fictionalised as it may have been, sport in *Tom Brown*, in Coubertin's selective reading at least, helped to make boys into men.

Pierre Coubertin had also visited 82-year-old Dr William Penny-Brookes and his Wenlock Games in 1890. From 1849 these had more of a regional, class-based inclusive purpose than public school sport and involved women in 'tea' races that were thought to be more respectable than the more widespread smock races as the light-coloured garments became opaque with perspiration.

Brookes described his purpose as the 'reinstitution of the games of their forefathers... to maintain that good feeling between the high and low, rich and poor, which happily for us, is the national characteristic of Old England'.[3] Penny-Brookes had attempted to hold a national London-based Olympics at the Crystal Palace as early as 1866.[4] John Astley Cooper's proposed Pan-Britannic festival of 1891 was another attempt at national competition intended to strengthen Anglo-Saxon links with the Empire and the United States, by invitation-only.

Nationalistic pride in British precursors to modern Olympic Games, such as the Cornish and Cotswold versions, led Ron Pickering, the teacher, coach and journalist to considerably overstate their importance:

> The influence of English rural sports, and the work of William Penny Brooks [sic] and Robert Dover, have been significant in the development of the Olympic Games philosophy. Almost half the events in the

Modern Games are historically connected to British rural sports. Therefore we have a certain arrogant claim and a responsibility to the development of the Modern Olympic Games.[5]

As Williams' work on the Cotswold Games shows, these events used 'Olympic' to denote high quality, respectable competition, even when not all of the behaviour on display conformed to these promises.[6] Penny Brookes was too unwell to attend the first 1894 international congress called by De Coubertin to create the IOC at the Sorbonne, but he fully supported its intent:

> The object is so noble, generous and philanthropic that I regard the inception and promotion by France as a great honour to your country and a great benefit to other nations, one which I hope they will recognise and gratefully accept.[7]

However, unlike the older man, Coubertin was to oppose the participation of women steadfastly all his life. Although the major force behind the games between the first Paris congress of the IOC in 1894 and his retirement as President of the IOC in 1925, his views did not prevail in his lifetime. They nevertheless continue to have a lasting influence.

The IOC still considers itself to be a patrimony and all nine of its presidents have been men: Demetrios Vikelas (Greece) 1894–1896; Baron Pierre de Coubertin (France) 1896–1925; Henri de Baillet-Latour (Belgium) 1925–1942; Sigfrid Edström (Sweden) 1946–1952; Avery Brundage (USA) 1952–1972; Lord Killanin of Dublin and Spittal (Ireland) 1972–1980; Juan Antonio Samaranch (Spain) 1980–2001; Jacques Rogge (Belgium) 2001–2013 and currently Thomas Bach.

Charles Herbert, Secretary of the British Amateur Athletic Association was one of two Britons of the 12 original members of the International Olympic Committee. The IOC was therefore a 'club for the boys' for almost 90 years, though Monique Berlioux was to be director from 1967 to 1985, followed, as Secretary-General, by Françoise Zweifel. It seems clear that women first tried to join the IOC in the 1930s. However, it was not until Avery Brundage's retirement as President, that the situation regarding women leaders changed: it took almost another 10 years before Pirjo Haggman and Flor Isava-Fonseca were appointed to the IOC in 1981.[8] Britain was consequently to have a female Prime Minister elected before it was to have an appointed International Olympic Committee representative. Mary Glen Haig was member number 340 when she was selected in 1982 as the third woman to be on the Executive Committee, and she served as an honorary member from 1993.

Approaching the history of women by looking mainly at the IOC as a set of institutions can therefore tell only a small part of a more interesting story. This book is therefore an unashamedly revisionist attempt to place British women centre-stage, and an international female tradition more generally, in the history of the Olympic Games. Women competitors became more central to the work of the IOC in the last quarter of the twentieth century, but it does not automatically follow that earlier female participants saw their Olympic experience as any more or less valuable. One of the most significant tensions in the discussion then, is the sporting culture produced by British women who looked to become Olympians, in relation to the frameworks imposed on female athletes, individually and as a group, by the IOC, the National Organising Committee (NOC) and the various affiliated sporting international federations. Interconnections and parallels are a key theme throughout.

The British Olympic Association (BOA), formed in 1905, used its centenary to produce *Chasing Gold* to chronicle 'the greatest achievements of British competitors in Olympic Summer and Winter Games from 1896 to 2004'.[9] It acknowledged that British women such as skater Jeanette Altwegg, swimmer Anita Lonsbrough and ice dancer Jayne Torvill were part of the story, as were athletes like Anne Packer, Mary Rand, Mary Peters, Sally Gunnell and Kelly Holmes. What though, of the other medallists; the 'probables' and the 'possibles' for selection; the nearly-winners and those who were just pleased to take part?

At the meeting to form the BOA in 1904, the council included representatives of archery; association football; athletics; cycling; fencing; gymnastics; life-saving; skating; rowing; rugby football and skiing, all of which had governing bodies or clubs.[10] At the fourth congress of the IOC that year, the patronage of the King for the event made the establishment of the British council a strong possibility.[11] In addition to royal interest, the British reception party included: C. B. Fry, W. G. Grace, Count Darnley, Lord Kinnaird and Herbert Gladstone, who was to go on to become Home Secretary in Asquith's government of 1910. The group took in receptions at the Lord Mayor of London's Mansion House, the Fishmongers' Corporation Hall at the entrance to London Bridge, Lord's, the Archers Hall, Windsor Palace, Horse Guards' Parade and a number of other select social gatherings. In modern day terms, it looked suspiciously like a bid-event for the games.

The provisional British Olympic Council formed in May 1905, with the Right Honourable Lord Desbrough of Taplow as Chair, also representing the Epée Club and the Royal Life Saving Society. Lord Montagu of Beaulieu, Colonel Sir C. C. Howard Vincent and Sir Lees Knowles provided titled support, as did Captain A. Hutton as President of the Amateur Fencing Association and Colonel H. Walrond of the Royal Toxophilite Society. The remaining founding members were: H. Benjamin of the Amateur Swimming Association; T. Britten of the National Cyclists Union; W. Fisher of the National Skating Association; R. Gridley of the Amateur Rowing Association; C. Herbert of the Amateur Athletic Association; G. Rowland Hill of the Rugby Football Union; E. Lawrence Levy of the Amateur Gymnastic

Association; E. Syers of the Ski Club of Great Britain; F. Wall of the Football Association and Theodore Cook of the Amateur Football Association, along with the Reverend de Courcy Laffan as Secretary. It was to be a long and gradual process to include more women in the organisation of the British Olympic Association, and the book highlights each incremental growth, as sporting administration became less a voluntaristic activity for the well-to-do white male with a private income, and more a job for trained professionals.

From its formation until the present day, the BOA has made a very distinctive contribution to the Olympic Movement. The three aims of its creation were to spread knowledge of the Olympic movement in Britain; to secure the weight and influence of British associations in the organisation of the Games, and to ensure the participation of 'properly accredited' representatives only at the Olympics and other Athletic Congresses.[12] In this last strategic objective, the BOA was not always successful.

Until 1983, women's participation in the Olympic Games was heavily influenced by a paradoxically male ideal of gentlemanly amateurism. That year, the IOC accepted a proposal from the International Amateur Athletics Federation (IAAF) that male and female participants should be recompensed for time spent competing that took them away from their work, allowed to earn money from sport-related sources such as endorsements, and that these earnings should be placed in a trust fund for their retirement. By 1980, after the Moscow Games, Juan Antonio Samaranch was elected to President of the IOC and wished to make it a world championship in all sports. Though he by no means succeeded, this necessarily meant accepting professionalism and a more commercialised future for the Games. Between 1896 and 1984 the Olympic Games were mainly amateur, although this was a contested ideology. From 1988 onwards, the scientific and technocratic principles of professional sport dominated Olympic spectacle.

The conflation of Britishness with Englishness that is, to a large extent, London-centred is clearly to be resisted. This was, however, an assumption made by many sportswriters in the press coverage of 1908 and 1948. Representing Great Britain at the Olympic Games has clearly been unlike representing Ireland, Wales, Scotland or England as a nation in other sporting events. The partition of Ireland into six northern counties, which remained within the United Kingdom, and the 26 of the Irish Free State (which became a republic in 1949) has added to the complexity of defining a Great Britain Olympic team. At the Paris Games of 1924, Ireland made its first appearance as an independent nation, though, as the Olympic Council of Ireland (OCI) have noted, many of the successes of Irish athletes have been credited to other teams.

Migration, immigration and naturalisation add other factors of identity and representation, as do regionalism, race, ethnicity and representation. So-called hyphenated identities of Black-British, British-Asian, British-Jew and British-Muslim have been an increasingly important part of a diverse population, as have other patterns of migration for economic and political reasons.

The ostensible multicultural inclusiveness is perhaps reflected in the title of *Team GB* for the Great Britain and Northern Ireland Olympic team. These changes are explored in a broadly chronological structure, with inflections of difference and diversity in British society, particularly after World War I and, more especially, after World War II.

Structure of the book and methodology

When I began this research in 2005, recently after London won the bidding process for 2012, neither the British Olympic Association nor the International Olympic Committee museum staff in Lausanne could tell me how many British women competitors there had been in the history of the modern games. I was intrigued, but not particularly surprised, by this lack of interest in the IOC and BOA's own history. *Britain's Olympic Women* is therefore intended as a contribution, not only to comparative research in Olympic studies, but also to the wider field of international sport and the gendered political economies of major cultural events. Crucially, the book argues that we cannot understand the role of Britain within the Olympic movement, without considering the pioneering role of women athletes. Similarly, we cannot understand the Olympic movement globally without understanding the role of women internationally, as integral to the ideals, practices and problems that comprise the IOC.

Definitions of who is to be included in what kind of Olympic tradition can be less than clear-cut. Who is not considered to be an Olympian is as telling as who is included, and by which conventions. Those unclear boundaries are explored by this work.

While broader social changes such as women's movement into the workforce after the two world wars might provide a background to the gradual increase in the number of women athletes, seeing sport as part of wider culture helps also to locate female activism as a struggle for resources. The growing gigantism of the Olympics and the aesthetics of the spectacle, have meant that women wanted access to what it represented at any one time. It is possible to argue that women have used the Olympics for their own purposes, even while acknowledging diverse chauvinism and various abuses that are an inherent part of the history of the Olympic Games.

Why would a female athlete *not* want to be applauded by an international, now global, audience when historically there have been fewer opportunities for her skill to be recognised than exist for sportsmen? Sport remains one of the most prominent examples of gendered labour markets in global society. The kudos and the fame are surely the point, when the amateur tradition has been so strong in preventing direct financial benefit from winning or taking part in the Olympics.

The book is a collective biography of women's key British women in the Olympic movement, including both British athletes and administrators.

Chapter One begins with the tennis stars Charlotte Cooper Sterry and Lottie Dod. This contrasts with the life and career of working class swimmer Jane 'Jennie' Fletcher. Chapter Two focuses on swimmer Gladys Carson and her experiences of the 1924 Paris Olympic Games. Gladys would go on to become a Home Economics teacher, and her life evidences a degree of upward social mobility. Chapter Three focuses on the Winter Olympics, which were held as a discrete tournament from 1924 onwards. The First All-Female British Olympic Team who went to the 1932 Winter Olympics held at Lake Placid, were all figure skaters and this chapter explores why this discipline was so crucial to the women's programme. Chapter Four concerns the career of Audrey Brown, who ran in the highly-politicised 1936 'Nazi' Summer Olympics. Chapter Five is the last to highlight the importance of swimming, and diving, to the women's Olympic schedule, discussing Margaret Wellington, and how it was actually Commonwealth success that helped her to travel extensively. Chapter Six looks at the confluence of Elizabeth II's Coronation as a young, fashionable head of state and the rise of equestrianism in 1950's Britain. The star was Pat Smythe, who was well established before her Olympic appearances.

Chapter Seven concerns the 'Golden Girls' of the 1960s, who were responsible for most of Britain's medals but often did not go on to develop a role in public life. However, increasingly, women athletes like Mary Peters, Tessa Sanderson (gold 1984) and, more recently, Kelly Holmes have used Olympic success as platforms for post-competition careers. In contrast, Mary Glen Haig who was a hospital administrator by profession, as well as an Olympic foilist, could be said to have used her public role to advance her career as an amateur Olympic administrator, at the highest level.

The conclusion looks at the continuity and change since the mainly amateur tradition of the Olympics before 1988. Using two shorter case studies of the rower Sarah Winkless and football player Eniola Aluko, the conclusion analyses what systems enable Britain to compete on an increasingly technocratic world sporting stage.

But a career in public life has not been an automatic transition, by any means. Other Olympians, like Sally Gunnell (gold in 1992) have found the transition to a media career more difficult to negotiate, while the extent of Sharron Davies' willingness to diversify 'brand SD' has led to a degree of notoriety. After her 1976 debut at the age of 13 and her 1980 Moscow silver medal for the 400-metres individual medley, Davies has presented and commentated, appeared as Amazon on the television show Gladiators, danced on ice, endorsed Bernard Matthews' poultry products, modelled, written books and developed her own website, to name but a few of her activities.[13] This also includes an Olympic comeback in 1992 in the 200-metres individual medley.

It is unlikely in the next 100 years that any British monarch will have such a pronounced effect on the BOA, IOC and the popularity of Olympic competition in Britain as Elizabeth II. Not least, Elizabeth acceded to the throne as such a young woman, beautiful, glamorous and a rare British female head of state. A New Elizabethan age was forecast, and sport was integral to Elizabeth's professional and private profile. Without an abdication, Charles, William and their heirs will seem to be older and more pedestrian.

The high media profile of Olympians Princess Anne (BBC Sports Personality of the Year in 1971 and an Olympic Competitor in 1976) and her daughter Zara Phillips (who failed to represent Britain in 2004 and 2008 because of injury to her horse Toytown, but who won the BBC Sports Personality of the Year in 2006 as Eventing World Champion) has also helped the cause of women's sport more broadly in Britain. In 2012, Zara carried an Olympic flame at Cheltenham Racecourse, on her horse Toytown. As a member of the Great Britain Eventing Team, Phillips won a silver medal at the 2012 Summer Olympics, and her medal was presented by her mother. One of the points made by the collective biography is that social class, ethnicity, regional affiliation and personal preference nuance the life chances of our women Olympians.

The material to tell the story of Britain's women Olympians has been obtained from the IOC Archive in Lausanne, the British Olympic Association Archive, at the time held at Wandsworth in London and several sports governing bodies. These include the Women's Amateur Athletic Association holdings at the University of Birmingham; the Amateur Swimming Association in Loughborough; British Judo and The All England Women's Hockey Association holdings at the University of Bath Special Collections and the British Judo Association in Walsall. Susan Bandy kindly shared her collection of material relating to Alice Milliat and the Fédération Sportive Feminine Internationale 'Women's Olympics' in 1922. Under the title of 'Women's World Games' they were held again in 1926, 1930 and 1934 but the materials continue to 1936.

I have used oral history interviews extensively in my research throughout my career. In looking at the lives and careers of women, this has been vital since the written record in archives rarely considers women in any great detail. Autobiographies and individual interviews have illuminated much of the official documentation because, though there has been both systematic and casual exclusion of women, there has also been a great deal of self-determination and achievement by women who have contested these processes.[14] In order to explain why all the self-discipline and effort has been worthwhile, the autobiographical and oral history elements make the often-overlooked point that individuals do particular things for very precise reasons. While I may be attempting to look at them collectively, as it were, British women Olympians are as alike and different as any set of individuals regardless of the interests of academics.

The lack of specific studies of women's Olympic involvement is a major weakness in our understanding of the role that they have played in sport more generally from the last decade of the nineteenth century to the present. In this proposed long twentieth century view of British women's involvement, it will be argued that sport has been more important to the lives of female athletes than has so far been recorded in social and cultural histories. The family history also makes the point that each woman had a legacy in her own circle, and many much more broadly.

For many female British Olympic athletes there has been a great deal of enjoyment and fulfilment in sport and beyond. If it is possible to be unequivocal about anything in writing this history, it is clear that the Olympic movement has not exactly been begging women to be involved this last hundred years or so. What is evident is that women have lobbied consistently for over a century for more of a role in Olympic tradition and that diplomacy continues. Indeed, it could be argued that women's sport outside the Olympic programme has been as at least, if not more, important than the internal dynamics of the IOC. Readers may be surprised that swimming was more important to the women's schedule of the Summer Olympics than track and field athletics between 1912 and 1936, when the Nazi regime politicised the 4 × 100-metres sprint relay to an unprecedented degree.

Many experienced academics will turn first to the Bibliography of a book to look at the architecture of the research, and to examine the type of sources that have been used. Academic publishers meanwhile are moving towards seeing individual chapters as valuable in their own right, with their own references. This project was always conceived as a book, because I wanted to show that different sports, and diverse individuals, had made a particular contribution to Olympic history. Some of these are less well covered sports, such as equestrianism, fencing, ice dance, skiing, tennis and new Olympic disciplines such as BMX cycling, women's football, snowboarding and so on.

So, due to the confines of space and time, there is a Select Bibliography at the end of the book, which focuses particularly on the archival sources, and the contemporary texts often written by, or about, women athletes. The secondary academic literature is there, for students who wish to follow-up references, at both the chapter level and for context in the Bibliography. The Select Bibliography focuses less on more recent academic texts, as readers are more likely to be aware of these, although where a text was particularly foundational or seminal, it has been included. The richness lies in the archival collections, even where these could be temporary, such as the Graham Budd Auction artefacts and in the contemporary publications, especially the under-used magazine *World Sports*. There were many adventure books aimed at girls, and sporting magazines, which assumed an informed female and male readership. The degree of segregation in the market for women's and men's magazines, often assumed today, therefore requires revision. Important pioneering journalists such as Pat Besford and Susan Noel, had sustained and high profile careers in the 1950s and 1960s, as did many Olympians who wrote for the media, such as Pat Smythe. There are many autobiographies and autobiographical articles on which to draw, to compile a collective biography.

This will surprise those used to the present Rupert Murdoch saturated media, where it is a convention to say that less than 5 per cent of sports media covers women's events. The 'tabloidisation' of the media under Murdoch has been a relatively recent change however, and before this, women were more present in the industry, and more present in coverage. So the emphasis in the bibliography is to resist a narrative of increasing 'progress' in relation to women's sport. Change is not necessarily progress, and advances, hard won, can also be overturned, and lost. More optimistically, the richness of the contemporary source material will, I hope stimulate more research into women's sports writing, which has a more diverse historical literature than is often acknowledged. After all, the first sporting text in the English language was written by a woman.[15] Probably.

Notes

1 Allen Guttmann *The Olympics: A History of the Modern Games* Urbana and Chicago: University of Illinois Press, 1992, second edition 2002 preface.
2 Pierre De Coubertin *Olympic Memoirs* Lausanne: International Olympic Committee, 1997 p. 142.
3 Sam Mullins *British Olympians: William Penny Brookes and the Wenlock Games* London: Birmingham Olympic Council in association with the British Olympic Association 1986 p. 10. Penny Brookes reportedly made the remarks at an address to the Hadley (Shropshire) Athletic Club in 1882 as reported by the *Shrewsbury Chronicle* 17 February 1882.
4 For other versions of these folk and regional games, see for example, William Hone (ed.) Joseph Strutt *The Sports and Pastimes of the People of England; including the rural and domestic recreations, may games, mummeries, shows, processions, pageants and pompous spectacles from the earliest period to the present time* London: Thomas Tegg, 1845 Wandsworth: British Olympic Association Library and Archive (hereafter BOA Archive, London).
5 Ron Pickering 'It's Not the Winning But the Taking Part' *History of the Olympic Games Pamphlet* 1972 BOA Archive, London.
6 Jean Williams 'The Curious Mystery of the Cotswold "Olimpick" Games: Did Shakespeare Know Dover...and Does it Matter?' *Sport in History Special Edition Sport and Literature* 29: 2 2009 pp. 150–170.
7 William Penny Brookes *Letter to De Coubertin 13 June 1894 Much Wenlock* Lausanne: International Olympic Committee Library and Archive (hereafter IOC Archive, Lausanne).
8 Mary Leigh 'The Enigma of Avery Brundage and Women Athletes' (unpublished paper Department of Physical Education, State University College at Brockport, undated) p. 9 United States File, IOC Archive, Lausanne.
9 British Olympic Association *Chasing Gold: Centenary of the British Olympic Association* London: Getty Images, 2005.
10 The British Olympic Association *The British Olympic Association and the Olympic Games* Surrey: G. Donald and Co. Ltd., 1987 pp. 7–11.
11 'La Reunion du Comité International Olympique a Londres 1904' *Revue Olympique* GB File IOC Archive, Lausanne.

12 British Olympic Association *Provisional Council Minutes April 1906* GB File IOC Archive, Lausanne.
13 Sharron Davies www.sharrondavies.com accessed 2 February 2019.
14 There are also a number of biographies of women Olympians such as Sharon Kinney Hanson's *The Life of Helen Stephens: The Fulton Flash* Carbondale: Southern Illinois University Press, 2004; but I've found fewer autobiographies of British women.
15 Jean Williams, 'Olympism and Pastoralism in British Sporting Literature' Sharon Harrow (ed.) *British Sporting Literature and Culture in the Long Eighteenth Century* London: Ashgate 2015 pp. 35–55.

Chapter 1

British Olympic pioneers 1900–1912
Chattie, Lottie and Jennie

Introduction

Early versions of the Games organised by the International Olympic Committee (IOC) after it was founded at the International Athletic Congress at the Sorbonne in 1894 were marked by the interplay of nationalistic discourse and friendly international competition.[1] The inaugural 1896 IOC Olympic Games was hosted at the restored Panathenaic Stadium in Athens, thanks due to the financial and moral support of Greek royal family; businessman George Averoff and public funding. The front cover of the programme was entitled *The Olympic Games BC776–AD1896*, and on the rear a collection of sporting paraphernalia hung like a wreath over a cycle race.[2] Importantly, the recreation of Hellenic Olympic tradition had allowed enough time for reinvention, reinterpretation and recreation of ideas and ideals, so that the modern Olympics reflected contemporary concerns more than being a replication of their historical antecedents.

The elitist overtones of Pierre de Coubertin's aspiration to create an aristocracy 'determined solely by physical superiority' was evident from the outset but was always contested.[3] Between the first Olympic Games in Athens in 1896 and the 1912 Stockholm Olympiad, the course of the movement was by no means a story of steady progress, and the enterprise was by no means assured. Commerce was absolutely integral to amateur sport. Although there were calls for all future Games to be held in Greece, plans had already been agreed to hold the Paris edition in 1900 alongside the Exposition Universelle.

There remains some debate about if, and how, women took part in the Olympic Games of 1896. Karl Lennartz has documented references to a woman who ran the marathon distance in March 1896 before the official Olympic marathon race for men and another within 24 hours of the sanctioned event.[4] But newspapers are problematic historical sources. Were 'Melpomene' and Stamati Revithi two separate women or the same person? So while important potential female pioneers might be traced to the earliest modern revivals of Hellenic culture, it is also important to remember that, from the outset, the first few Olympic Games were not merely sporting tournaments, cultural gatherings and artistic competitions, but also significant commercial enterprises.

In making the Olympic Games representative of modern sporting contests, the IOC stipulated that: 'The competitions are rigorously confined to amateurs'.[5] Britain's Charlotte 'Chattie' Cooper (married name Sterry); Charlotte 'Lottie' Dod; and Jane 'Jennie' Fletcher (married name Hyslop) were very much part of this amateur tradition, although other influences were just as significant such as class, geographical mobility, individual taste and life choices. The three case studies of very different amateur lives are the basis of this introductory discussion.

Olympic definitions built on an existing amateur tradition that was summarised by the attitude of Lottie Dod in this excerpt:

Foreword

By Lottie Dod

I have always been against commercialization of games because, regardless of the sporting spirit in which they may be played, continued advancement must be uppermost in mind to the exclusion of so much of the fun of it [sic]. But I'm given to understand the aim of this book is to help the young enthusiast to enjoy his or her games as well as try and win them – and the two ideals should be by no means incongruous. To these young people I would say 'Master your game but don't let it master you!'[6]

Professional sport had a long history. Amateurism was a more recent invention. By the later decades of the nineteenth century, the establishment of central governing bodies, codification of rules, national competitions, paying spectators and international audiences meant that professional sport sat alongside amateur ideals. Amateurism was fundamentally a wish to distance middle class sporting enthusiasts from working class specialists enforced by an elaborately superior bureaucracy. However, each sport defined amateurism slightly differently and it still remains a contested and constantly redefined ideal today.

The Amateur Swimming Association (ASA) definition of an amateur was a good example of the broad principle:[7]

An amateur is one who has never competed for a money prize, declared wager, or staked bet; who has never taught, pursued or assisted in the practice of swimming, or any other athletic exercise, as a means of pecuniary gain; and who has not, knowingly, or without protest, taken part in any competitions with anyone who is not an amateur.[8]

From the codification of modern sport, rules sought to protect those who wished to play for fun, against those who were good enough to earn a living through physical labour. At the 1912 Stockholm Olympic Games the most spiteful aspects of amateurism were displayed when native American Jim Thorpe subsequently had his pentathlon and decathlon medals withdrawn because he was paid to play baseball. While the British Olympic Association (BOA) considered his situation 'unfortunate' the notion that 'rules are rules' held sway. Here ethnicity and class were important factors in the discrimination. Thorpe's medals were posthumously returned in 1983. It remains unclear who benefitted from this rather tardy gesture. But the timescale does reflect how haughty the IOC has been throughout its history, and not just in its gender imbalance. There has been a long history of 'othering' contestants in what were ostensibly friendly sporting contests.

At the same time, until 1948 equestran events remained open only to those who held a senior rank in the military. Arguably, this was even more hypocritical, as these horsemen were professional in the sense of being paid to work with animals in the course of their daily duties. So amateurism was never a clearly defined ethos, often being referred to as the antithesis of professionalism, which in itself covered a range of activities. As Lincoln Allison indicated:

> For all the insistence by public school amateurs that the only true amateur is a 'gentleman', it is also true, in a clear and important sense, that working-class amateurism was a purer form than that of those for whom sport was an enhancer of curricula vitae.[9]

The 'shamateur' was notionally motivated by enthusiasm, but received covert financial reward, often in the form of 'expenses'. Administrators for the BOA had to be amateurs but they enjoyed very nice social events and travel as 'benefits in kind' because they saw this as a public service. Would we consider them today as shamateurs, who benefitted materially from their sporting endeavours? Perhaps. Most meetings were followed by a nice luncheon, at the very least and the general atmosphere of the BOA was of a gentlemen's club, until 1948 at least. Most serving members either had a private income or held occupations with sufficient time and status to allow them to dedicate considerable time to being committee-men.

Even so, this was not entirely a 'top-down' process and working class amateurs were a significant force in popularising many sports. Charlotte Cooper was part of the upper middle class tennis 'set', as was Lottie Dod. However, Cooper excelled only in tennis, mainly at Wimbledon, while Dod was the most celebrated British sporting all-rounder of her lifetime. Undoubtedly in British history, she can be considered so still today and has inspired many female Olympians to master more than one sport and discipline. Dod won her Olympic silver medal in 1908 in archery, for instance. In contrast, Jennie

Fletcher was a working class amateur swimmer. The large and complex issue of amateurism is a key theme of this chapter and of the book as a whole. The ideals, though often contravened, have had a lasting effect on the voluntarism that was the mainstay of British women's participation in the Olympic games in the twentieth century. The interconnections and parallels between amateurism and voluntarism have been almost entirely neglected in the academic literature, and so the fusion of these twin themes recurs across the chapters, even as the chronological structure shows how these could change over time.

Arguably, the Olympic movement would go on to globalise amateur ideals more than any other international sporting tournament until the late 1980s. At the same time, the mercantile aspects of exhibitions related to early Olympic Games concerned sporting administrators who wished to keep athletic excellence somehow pure from profit-making[10] Although the idea of a pure Olympic Games was a fiction from the outset, it was a persuasive invention, lasting almost a century. This chapter examines early examples of how the ethos was interpreted through Olympic competitions before World War I. Lottie Dod summarised the tensions at the heart of the expanding Olympic enterprise at this time:

> My lawn tennis days are many years behind me now, and I admit that I may be a little old fashioned in my views. While realising to get to the top of the tree nowadays players *have* to devote their lives to one game, the idea of it still strikes me as appalling! I sometimes wonder if they derive half the enjoyment out of sport we used to get.[11]

However, even before the First World War, Lottie Dod's views on amateur sport as pure of commercialisation would have been rather naïve, and perhaps deliberately so. She was, after all, fortunate enough to benefit from a considerable private income and had no need to work, or to marry, in her long life.

The case studies here are intended to challenge the academic consensus that Edwardian women's sport lacked committed pioneers. Female amateurism has often been neglected or assumed to be an aspect of youthful enthusiasm. However, this tends to homogenise female experience and diversity was much in evidence. As Joyce Kay has indicated, sport was believed to be synonymous with modernity in late Victorian and Edwardian Britain, so a variety of women took up the outdoor life, in one form or another, regardless of how emancipated they considered themselves.[12]

Early Olympic Games were indebted to the exhibition movement and shaped by commercial influences in how they were staged, although the sporting events were broadly amateur in ethos. The modern revival of Olympic Games, with their objective of a sporting and cultural 'bond of unity' also grew in an increasingly militarised world order. Intended as a quadrennial celebration of common ideals, and as an antidote to conflict between nation states, the Olympic Games were also embedded in wider mercantile processes, such as mass tourism and transnational global movement, as increasing numbers of people travelled in order to compete, spectate and officiate.

The gradual process of the inclusion of more sports and events in the Olympic programme for women was also profoundly shaped by amateur values, therefore. Existing transnational aspects of women's sport were highlighted from the Paris Games of 1900 onwards, showcasing greater female variety in national sporting cultures. In characterising the phases of the amateur ethos, Lincoln Allison suggested that establishment took place between 1863 and 1895, hegemony held from 1895–1961 and the decline came between 1961 and 1995.[13] Amateurism was not just a British obsession: the inclusion of women on the United States Olympic team in 1900 led to North American debates about how this affected definitions of amateurism across several national sports' governing bodies. Playing croquet, tennis, golf, equestrianism, ballooning and yachting all required access to considerable resources, not least time, and a certain social confidence to dress and conduct oneself in appropriate ways in public sporting contests. If middle class women, amateurs predominated among the first female Olympians in 1900; this was to change quickly and, by 1912, working class swimmers were an important part of Britain's medal hopes.

The formation of the BOA and its impact on the IOC

The religious zeal imbued within aspects of amateurism was much in evidence in the formation of a British Olympic Association during the time period covered by this chapter. The Principal of Cheltenham College, and a member of the IOC since 1897, Reverend Robert Stuart de Courcy Laffan, was central to the founding of the British Olympic Association.[14] As a representative of the Headmasters' Conference, Laffan considered the spiritual and moral benefits of physical exercise as central to the modern Olympic movement and amateur values fundamental to the way in which British sport was organised. Laffan was so dedicated to the Olympic movement that he missed only two meetings of the IOC in his 30 years as a member. He oversaw a sumptuously extravagant visit of the IOC to London in 1904, directly leading to the formation of the British Olympic Association. Robert Laffan became Honorary Secretary of the BOA until his death in 1927 and was particularly concerned that British views on the moral benefits of athletic competition should be well represented in the IOC.

At the meeting to form the BOA in May 1905, the council included representatives of the Amateur Athletics Association; the Amateur Fencing Association; the National Cyclists Union; the National Skating Association; The Amateur Rowing Association; the Rugby Football Union; the

Football Association; the Amateur Gymnastics Association; the Ski Club of Great Britain; The Amateur Swimming Association and The Royal Toxophilite Society.[15] Sir Lees Knowles represented the Cambridge University Achilles Club and the Right Honourable Montagu of Beaulieu attended in his own right, having particular enthusiasms in motor sport and field sports. The Right Honourable Lord Desborough of Taplow, who chaired this distinguished all-male meeting, was President of the Epée Club and acting President of the Life Saving Society. Desborough therefore became His Majesty's Government's First British Representative at Athens for the Olympic Games. Although the 1908 Olympic Games were already planned for in Rome, London would host festivities just three years after the BOA formed, when an earthquake forced the Italian organisers to withdraw.

From its formation until the present day, the BOA has made a very distinctive contribution to the Olympic Movement therefore, heavily inflected by the amateur aristocratic and upper class tradition of British sporting administration.[16] The objects of the BOA were:

a   To spread in Great Britain a knowledge of the Olympic movement.
b   To secure that the views of the British Associations shall have their due weight and influence in the organisation of the Olympic Games.
c   To ensure the participation, both in Olympic Games and in International Athletic Congresses, of representatives properly accredited by the great Athletic and Sporting Associations of Great Britain and by Educational Authorities interested in Physical Education; and to facilitate the attendance of such representatives.

Two-thirds of the British Olympic Council, which was appointed to oversee the work of the BOA, were from member sporting associations. The remaining third were to be elected at an Annual General Meeting. To open subscriptions as widely as possible, any amateur could become an individual member by paying 5 shillings annually or commute this to a Life Membership for £2, 2 shillings. Clubs could join for 10 shillings, while Associations and Unions paid £1, 1 shilling annually.[17]

Amateurism and voluntarism

While the class-based element of sporting amateurism as expressed by the BOA could, at times, be harmful to individual women's careers, the constant need for redefinition continued throughout the twentieth century. Women were not invited into the male domain of the IOC or the BOA, but they simply persisted in attempting to take part in Olympic competition and refused to go away. This need for clarity could provoke administrators to rigidly apply rules, but there remained gaps between the letter and the spirit of amateur values. For all its snobbishness, sporting amateurism was based in a much wider British voluntaristic tradition of public service, and Olympians, male and female, often viewed themselves as benefitting their home nation by competing.

The modern Olympic movement adapted and altered to accord with wider social change, and therefore its philosophies could shift. Roche has called the effect of social democracy and feminism on the wider Olympic movement, its ideology, rules and rituals 'alternative internationalism'.[18] It is the often-overlooked aspects of female international rivalries and nationalistic values that the chapter explores. As a relatively small sporting and cultural festival before World War I, selective aspects of Olympic tradition subsequently became reinvented, and an increased female schedule was a key reinterpretation of late Victorian sporting ideals.

As much as amateur sport made the upper middle class tennis players Charlotte Cooper and Lottie Dod famous, it also gave working class Jennie Fletcher opportunities that she would not otherwise have had. The benefits of Olympic voluntarism have rarely been considered as part of the literature. The first case study of Charlotte Sterry in the Paris Olympic Games of 1900 illustrates this point nicely.

Charlotte 'Chattie' Cooper and the Paris Olympic Games 1900

The Paris Exposition, held at the same time as the 1900 Olympic Games, featured a Palace of Optics and an illuminated Celestial Globe, both of which symbolised technological ambition and cultural modernity.[19] A 2008 edition of the *Journal of Olympic Studies* has considered how the 1900 Paris Olympic Games signalled new kinds of modernity invested in sporting spectacle.[20] Here sport was following a market-based exhibition movement.

Increased global communication and cosmopolitan tastes had been popularised since The Great Exhibition of the Industry of All Nations in 1851 had stimulated public discussion over the relative benefits of Free Trade policies and the influence of overseas design on British goods.[21] The Great Exhibition had been the grandest international display of manufactured products, held in the purpose-built Crystal Palace in Hyde Park. Followed by the Philadelphia World's Fair in 1876, the Paris Exposition in 1889 and the Chicago Columbian Exposition in 1893, subsequent trade fairs combined art, industry and science for overseas and domestic tourists. They were the first mega events and the next three Olympiads (Paris 1900, St Louis 1904 and London 1908) were held under the auspices of the much larger international shows or world fairs.[22] Sport was less significant than commerce in each case. The programme of Olympic Games would take some considerable time to regularise and particular women's sports and disciplines have sometimes been in, and then out of, the Olympic schedule.

From the inclusion of female athletes in the Paris edition in 1900, the Olympic Games highlighted some existing transnational aspects of women's sport and made them more visible. Although the numbers of female competitors was low, the media representation of sportswomen was very evident. By 1900, 'Women were emerging as a political and social force – they were getting jobs, travelling, motoring, cycling, joining clubs for their hobbies and becoming avid readers of magazines'.[23] Those who were not lucky enough to travel themselves, could read about the events in an increasing number of publications, thanks to generally improving levels of literacy and education.

Jean de Paleologu, better known for his commercial posters and illustrations in magazines like *Vanity Fair* as 'Pal', designed a striking poster for the Paris 1900 fencing competition featuring a woman, clad all in black but for a red heart, holding aloft foil, sabre and épéé.[24] This style of design drew on high art, commercial design and an increasing 'propaganda culture' using banners, posters and other multimedia promotional literature.[25] Similar designs with a red heart could be seen on slightly salacious Valentine cards of the period, and also featuring a woman in music hall posters, designed to arrest the attention of busy urban commuters for a few minutes.

In Paris, a total of over 1,000 competitors took part in widely ranging contests from 14 May to 28 October. It is not that surprising that some competitors did not know whether they were taking part in an 'International Games', 'World Championships' or the 'Grand Prix of the Paris Exposition'.[26] An earlier consensus that women participated in two sports (tennis and golf) at the Paris Olympic Games in 1900 has now been widely been revised. It now seems that between 23 and 42 women took part, depending on how accurate the official report was. The extended time-span gave scope for a considerable range of activities. At least five countries were represented in female events: Bohemia, France, Great Britain, Switzerland and the USA. But it remains difficult to be definitive.

The somewhat haphazard approach whereby the local organising committee set the schedule for each Olympic Games saw several women participants in Paris; some of whom were already famous and others of whom we know little. Tedder and Daniels hold, for example, that among the first women competitors in Paris in 1900 was Swiss-American sailor Countess Hélèn de Pourtalès.[27] She sailed the *Lérina* with her husband to victory on 22 May 1900; competed again on 23 June and finished second in a race two days later. In Tedder and Daniels' interpretation de Pourtalès therefore narrowly beat British tennis star Charlotte Cooper to become the first woman to win an Olympic first place. First place, rather than gold medal, because those who won in Paris received objects d'art, rather than a numismatic souvenir to mark their victory.

Conversely, Bill Mallon has argued that the croquet players Madame Brohy and Mademoiselle Ohnier may now be considered the first two women Olympic victors.[28] We have few details about French croquet players Filleaul Brohy, Marie Ohnier and Mademoiselle Després. Croquet competitions included women-only and open disciplines, so more research remains to be done on the imperfect records that exist. Mallon does not recognise Hélèn de Pourtalès as a competitor, though he acknowledges that she may have co-owned the vessel.

An Italian equestrian, Elvira Guerra, born in Russia, rode her horse *Libertin* in the Hacks and Hunter class but this was later declared not to have been an Olympic event.[29] Balloonist, Madame Maison, who sailed with her husband to fourth place in an endurance race, was similarly almost lost to the record. Mallon dismisses ballooning on the grounds that, like motor sport, it was a power-assisted performance.[30] This is equivocal since many events which stand in the record books as 'official' at the time have since been discontinued and the aviation, motor racing and other powered sports were extensively covered in the official report.

There is, however, broad consensus that the Paris Olympic golf competitions were very much society occasions.[31] Margaret Abbott was one of four 'Steamship Set' Americans competing against six French women. Another American citizen, Polly Whittier, represented the Golf Club de Saint-Moritz, Switzerland where she was also studying at the time.[32] A member of the Chicago Golf Club, formed by Scottish-American Charles Blair MacDonald in 1892, Margaret was coached by some of the best amateurs of the day and had established a notable reputation, especially winning the Dearing Cup in 1898.[33] At that stage there were over 25 golf clubs in France and 10 private Riviera courses at places like Deauville, so it was by no means unusual for Abbot and her circle to follow the cosmopolitan set and the sun to France for a game of golf. Having already established a series of victories in Chicago, Abbott was to become the first female US Olympic winner, with her compatriots, Pauline 'Polly' Whittier of Boston and Daria Pankhurst Huger Pratt from New York, winning second and third place, respectively.

In all, the official results of the *Prix de la ville de Compiègne* (championnat de dames) were:

Golf de Compiègne 3 October (9 holes)
1. Margaret Abbott (USA) 47
2. P. Whittier (USA) 49
3. D. Pratt (USA) 53
4. Mrs Froment Meurice (FRA) 56
5. E. Ridgway (FRA) 57
6. Mrs Fournier-Sarlovèze (FRA) 58
7. Mary Abbott (USA) 65
8. Baronness Fain (FRA) 65
9. Mrs Gelbert (FRA) 76
10. Mrs A. Brun (FRA) 80.

In the Official Report, it was reported that Margaret Abbott of Chicago won a gold plaque and a porcelain bowl; Pauline Whittier was awarded a silver-gilt tablet; third-placed Daria Huger Pratt received a silver panel; Mrs Froment Meurice from Paris got a silver bronze plate for fourth place and Mrs Henri Ridgway, representing the Deauville Golf Club, a bronze inscription for fifth.[34] Prize money was available for both the women's, male amateur and male open tournament, but it is not possible from the official report to detect how this was disbursed among the winning golfers.

Margaret Abbott had been born to wealthy parents in Calcutta, India in 1878.[35] Both her mother Mary, who finished seventh in Paris, and she, played mostly at Chicago Golf Club, along with her younger brother Sprague, but in 1900 Margaret was taking instruction at art school in Paris. Mary was widowed by 1900 and something of a Chicagoan society hostess and a literary editor. Relatively tall for her generation at 5 feet, 11 inches, Margaret was said to have a 'classy backswing' and was particularly strong when driving. However, a chronic knee ailment caused when falling from a bicycle when she was a child limited her physical mobility. After also going on to win a prestigious French title in 1900, Abbott continued to play golf in New York while raising four children with her husband, the writer Finley Peter Dunne. Welch suggests the records of her Chicago career were lost in a fire at the club-house in 1912.[36] Margaret Abbott was said to have been unaware that she held an Olympic title at her death in 1955 and would also be unconscious of the fact that she and her mother had made history by competing in the same event at the same time. The official report lists 19 competitors but we have only the names of the top 10 in the results, so estimates of the overall number of women at the 1900 Paris Olympics may well rise with more research.[37]

Some 13 years later, Daria Pratt would marry Prince Alexis of Serbia, who was in opposition to the ruling monarch King Aleksandar I. Greek Count Alexandros Mercati, the husband of her daughter Harriet Wright, born of a previous marriage, was in turn was a good friend of King Konstantinos I who had come eleventh in the men's golf in the Paris Olympics in 1900. Konstantinos I remained an IOC member until 1925. Daria Pratt retained the title Princess of Serbia, once widowed.[38]

The tennis competitions were not quite as illustrious, but were still comfortably upper middle class in tone. Like the track and field athletics and golf competitions, professionals competed in the men's tennis, as well as amateurs, but not in the same events. Again, like the golf, the tournament seems to have had its controversies, not least accusations of poor organisation, so far as *Lawn Tennis*, was concerned.

> A correspondent writes, the French Exhibition Tournament looks like being a failure; the whole committee having resigned rather than put up with hole and corner work. When men like Sandford, Masson, Voigt and Hough resign for this reason, it is a sure indication that there was no chance of this tournament being well done. In fact, the Exhibition people made impossible stipulations, amongst others that the tournament would

be played at Courbevoie where no spectators would come, and where the courts are not yet made. A Ladies Doubles competition seems to have been one of the casualties of the various re-scheduling changes, with the Exhibition managers preferring a professional emphasis, perhaps to draw in the crowds.[39]

In the event, for an entry fee of 10 Francs, the Olympic tennis tournament was scheduled to begin on Thursday 6 July, so that it would follow on from the English Championships at Wimbledon, and the Île de Puteaux was defended as a quality venue, and easily accessible for spectators, located 10 minutes' walk from the Gare Paris-Saint-Lazare, the second busiest station in Paris after the Gare du Nord. It may be that *Lawn Tennis* was inclined to interpret anything other than the Wimbledon Championships as an inferior tournament.

Regardless of these debates, Charlotte Cooper, born in 1870, became the first British female Olympic prize winner on 11 July 1900, after taking the women's singles tennis title from the perhaps leading female French player, Hélèn Prevost.[40] A letter from Mr C. A. Voigt of the Tennis Club de Paris, published in *Lawn Tennis* reported that the Ladies' singles winner had won 350 Francs, the runner-up having taken home 150 Francs and the mixed doubles winners had each taken 300 Francs.[41] This effectively halved an earlier proposal for the winner of the women's singles to take home 700 Francs, while the men's singles winner took home 1500 Francs.[42]

An entry of six female tennis players competed at the Île de Puteaux Club in Paris, of which Pierre De Coubertin was a member.[43] This was an international field, with third place tied by Marion Jones, probably the best lady player in the United States at the time, and Hedwig Rosenbaum of Bohemia.[44] Marion Jones had just become the first American woman to play at Wimbledon in June 1900 and her younger sister Georgina also competed in the Paris Olympics. Marguerite Fourrier of France completed the women's singles field.

Cooper also won the first Olympic mixed doubles title with Wimbledon star Reginald Doherty, better known as R. F. in tennis circles, making her a victor twice over. Cooper's double victory in 1900 reflected the strength in depth of British tennis at this time. This feat is recorded in the official report but not listed on the official IOC site.[45] There had previously been men's singles and doubles at the 1896 Olympic Games in which Britain's John Boland had taken two victories, along with Friedrich Traun of Germany. Rosenbaum and Jones were both credited bronze medallists with British partners Archibald Warden and Laurence Doherty, respectively, in the mixed doubles. 'Big Do' and 'Little Do', as the Doherty brothers were known, were virtually tennis royalty in 1900, winning the men's Olympic doubles together, and R. F., forfeiting the semi-finals in the men's singles where he was scheduled to play his brother. Like the golf, several competitors entered as individuals and not as state representatives and so some partnerships combined nationalities.

Figure 1.1 Four women tennis players after an exhibition match taken at the Roehampton Club in 1929. Chattie Cooper, a five-time Wimbledon Champion second on the left and Lottie Dod, also a five-time Wimbledon champion, is on the extreme right.

Source: The Dod Collection, Wimbledon Lawn Tennis Museum.

Biographical details on Cooper's co-competitors, like Hélèn Prevost, have been difficult to track, but Prevost won second place in the mixed doubles with a Scottish-born player of Irish descent, Harold Mahoney. Today, Prevost is therefore retrospectively considered a double silver medallist, in a team of mixed nationalities, not that unusual at the time. In the Handicap doubles, with her father André, Hélèn Prevost beat France's youngest competitor, Kate Gillou who was just 13 years of age, and her partner Max Germot, for the title. This is not today considered a medal event. André Prevost was at the time 40 years of age and took third place in the Olympic men's doubles with Georges de la Chapelle, sharing the title with Harold Mahoney and Arthur Norris. Several families would follow by winning multiple medals at Olympic Games, but this father–daughter combination at the same tournament remains quite unusual. André Prevost would finish runner-up to Paul Aymé in the French men's singles Championship in 1900, while Hélèn, uncontested, took the women's singles title.

In all, Cooper would go on to hold five singles successes at Wimbledon during her career (1895, 1896, 1898, 1901 and 1908) and this still maintains her place as one of the all-time greats at the All England Club. A journalist summarised her rise to fame in 1898:

> The present holder of the title first appeared in the list of classified lady players in the year 1892 when she was placed at 15.3 from Miss L. Dod, who was then lady champion. She has since that time risen rapidly to foremost place in the lawn tennis world, and although there may be one or two of her sex whose claims to be considered her equal would doubtless hold good, there is certainly no lady at present playing who would be entitled to take precedence of her. Her first championship meeting, when partnered by Mr H.S. Mahony she won the All England Mixed Doubles Championship, beating in the Challenge round the holders, and presently put the seal upon her fame by a victory in the All England Championship at Wimbledon. Since then she has always been in the forefront, and after losing her Irish championship in 1896 to Miss Martin and her English title last year to Mrs Hillyard has in the present year of grace succeeded in regaining both positions.[46]

Cooper played her club tennis at Ealing Lawn Tennis Club and is said to have ridden to Wimbledon with her racket clipped to a bracket on the front fork of her bicycle.[47] She was also a defeated finalist in the 1897, 1899, 1900, 1902, 1904 and 1912 singles tournaments. With Dorothea Douglass, Charlotte Sterry was a defeated women's doubles finalist in 1913, 18 years after winning her first title. Her last singles victory in 1908 at 37 years and 282 days of age is still a record for the women's singles most senior champion and the same year she took the mixed doubles title with Xenophon Casdagli.[48] This was the last of Sterry's seven All-England mixed doubles titles, which she won five times with Harold Mahoney and once with Laurence Doherty. Along with major Irish, German and Swiss titles, this was a remarkable career spanning over two decades at the highest levels of amateur tennis. Charlotte Cooper was a pioneer who served overhead, played an attacking game and was intensely competitive.

> Miss Cooper's game is a combination of all round excellences. She is good both on the base line and at the net; her service is severe, while her activity and powers of endurance are remarkable. Her back-hand stroke is made with a lot of twist, which, while it somewhat diminishes the pace of the return, often proves puzzling to her opponent. She is clever in luring her antagonist up to the net with a return dropped short, then lobbing her next stroke into the back of the opposite court, to the discomfiture of the player therein. Many is the ace which this little maneuver has gained for her, more especially on a soft court. She

is an adept at cross-volleying fore or backhanded and possesses a very clean 'smash'.[49]

As Cooper outlined in a chapter of a book edited by future Wimbledon star, Dorothea Douglass (married name Lambert Chambers) called *Lawn Tennis for Ladies* (1910), an amateur ethos was mainly motivated by her own enjoyment, but winning ultimately the key drive. Cooper offered many tips in her writing, from fitness and psychological preparation, to nutrition: she enjoyed iced soda water to drink during a match. Clearly a social personality, she also had a fondness for billiards and hockey.

> Of course, it goes without saying that my most memorable and exciting matches will all be those in which I have excelled or been the most distinguished person at the immediate moment. I began to play at thirteen years of age at the back of the court but the first time I played with Mr Mahoney – it was at Bournemouth in 1892 – he made me go up to the net. And very comfortable I felt there at first I can assure you. But from that time I have always taken up that position. Indeed I now find it easier to volley than to play off the ground, and the easiest volley to me is one made overhand on the forehand side… Winning my first championship of Ealing Lawn Tennis Club at age of fourteen was an important moment in my life.[50]

Cooper also became part of the amateur sporting establishment through marriage. In 1901 she married solicitor Alfred Sterry (1876–1955), who would become a future president of the International Lawn Tennis Federation (founded in 1913). The couple had a son, Rex (1903), who was to later serve for many years as Vice Chair of the All England Lawn Tennis Club and a daughter, Gwen (1905), who would also become an international tennis player. The name Sterry still holds a particular gloss at Wimbledon Lawn Tennis Club; such is the family legacy. The twin themes of voluntarism and amateurism are highlighted by this example, even though the discussion here has focused on Chattie's competitive career.

Charlotte Sterry also pioneered another aspect of women's sporting history by becoming the second woman to win the ladies' singles titles at Wimbledon after becoming a mother. Six-times Wimbledon winner Blanche Bingley (married name Hillyard) had become the first in 1897 and Dorothea Lambert Chambers would follow, after the birth of her first son, by winning the title easily in 1910 and retaining it in 1911. This contravened some medical warnings that maternal physical over-exertion could be damaging for the unborn child. As very respectable women nevertheless, Hillyard, Sterry and Chambers combined motherhood with sustained elite athletic careers to relatively advanced ages. Victorian and Edwardian women were neither as hampered by their clothing, or by social convention as many commentators have suggested, and, for reasons of space, this introductory case study can do no more than highlight that more detailed specific research will reinterpret this period, and tennis as particularly important in this regard. Much research then, still remains. Middlesex seems to have had the biggest concentration of female tennis talent, however, the 1902 Wimbledon women's singles winner Muriel Robb (1878–1907), who came from Jesmond, Newcastle Upon Tyne reminds us that elite Edwardian women's tennis was by no means just a London-based or Southern phenomenon.[51]

In conclusion, though well-remembered as a female British 'first' Olympic winner, Chattie Sterry's keenness for Wimbledon surpassed her interest in IOC competition and in this she was typical of the English amateurs of the time. Her doubles partner in Paris 1900, Reginald Doherty, became one of a long line of male multiple medallists spanning more than one Olympics, with a total of three golds and one bronze from the 1900 and 1908 Games. Having chosen not to take part in the London 1908 Olympic tennis competition, Sterry beat the gold medallist Dorothea Lambert Chambers in the third round that year at Wimbledon. She also beat the Olympic silver medal holder Dora Boothby in the quarter-finals in 1908. A winning mentality was undoubtedly part of Sterry's amateur ethos: 'Other characteristic features are her keenness and unvarying good humour. She never allows herself to become slack or to present an anxious countenance. Indeed judging by appearances, her mood is always a winning one'.[52]

There was undoubtedly a competitive national infrastructure within the game of tennis, and maintaining Sterry's position at the top of the women's game for over 20 years cannot have been easy. Although deaf from the age of 26, she was nevertheless able to maintain a high degree of physical fitness well past middle-age. Like other middle class amateurs Charlotte Sterry maintained a range of interests and her enthusiasms became part of family life, which, in turn became part of the British tennis establishment. She continued to cycle to compete at Wimbledon Ladies' Finals until 1919, aged almost 50.

From Paris 1900 to London 1908 and Lottie Dod, 'The Little Wonder'

Croquet, golf and ballooning were to disappear from future Olympic games after 1900. Tennis remained significant in the other early Olympic Games, though it was not to appear in 1904 in St Louis.[53] The 1904 Louisiana Purchase Exposition World's Fair, which President Theodore Roosevelt tapped a telegraph key to open from his office in Washington, DC, marginalised the Olympic sports between May and November, compared to the trade shows, even though one 'athletic' event a day took place. St Louis had negotiated with Chicago to host the Olympic Games, and as the fourth largest city in the USA at the time, was delighted when their diplomacy paid off.

However, St Louis is often remembered as an embarrassment rather than an Olympic success.

Sporting modernity mixed with the politics of ethnicity, gender and race; Alphonse Mucha developed posters in Art Nouveau style, representing the French presence as a white woman holding the hand of a native American chief.[54] This reflected the centenary of the US purchase of the Louisiana Territory from France in 1803, and provided a quasi-scientific rationale for the notorious 'anthropological' sports, in which the athletic talents of various ethnic groups, listed in the official report as 'savages' were tested during the St Louis Olympic Games.

The franchise in the USA was not extended to female voters until 1920. Women's boxing was a 'demonstration' activity and archery a full event but not an international competition.[55] Founder of the Amateur Athletic Union, James E. Sullivan, who oversaw the physical culture section of the Louisiana Purchase Exposition and Directed the operations of the Olympic Games, would become defensive about the criticisms of his show and this would spill over to anti-English feeling four years later at the London Olympics of 1908.

All of the six female contestants in Louisiana (Matilda 'Lida' Scott Howell; Emma Cooke; Jessie Pollock; Laura Woodruff; Mabel Taylor and Louise Taylor) were United States' archers, who competed across three disciplines; the team, the Double Columbia and the Double National rounds.[56] Cincinnati Archery Club's Lida Scott Howell became a triple gold medallist, which was not that surprising since she would ultimately win 17 National Women's Archery titles in the USA from 1883 to 1907.[57] Another Cincinnati resident, Jessie Pollock, took second place in the Double National individual contest with Washington's Emma Cooke third. Unsurprisingly, Cincinnati Archery Club comprising Scott Howell, Pollock, Woodruff, Mabel and Louise Taylor won the team championship. Perhaps Emma Cooke was sanguine about this. Mabel Taylor of the USA was the victor of an unofficial women's shooting competition. Also peripheral to the trade show, the St Louis Olympic Games therefore had a very limited international female resonance.

The Greek Olympic Committee tried to 'reclaim' the Olympic Games and become permanent hosts in what became known as the Intercalated Games of 1906 in Athens. King George I of Greece and his wife Queen Olga, accompanied by his sister, Queen Alexandra, wife of King Edward VII of England, attended along with many other titled dignitaries.[58] Five of the six women competitors were Greek tennis players; Esmee Simiriotis taking the victory from Sophia Marinou and Euphrosine Paspati, Aspasia Matsa and Ioanna Tissamenou. Recently married Marie Décugis of France was knocked out in the early rounds of the women's singles by Aspasia Matsa but won the gold medal in the mixed doubles with her husband Max.

Women's artistic gymnastics was a demonstration sport with a team from Denmark, and Turnen, the military gymnastics regime that spread from Germany to other nations, was also much in evidence. Mallon gives a particularly entertaining account of how Lord Desborough, who was competing in the 1906 fencing competitions, came to persuade his fellow BOA colleagues and Edward VII that London should host the games.[59] Desborough wanted a degree of respectable popularity for the London games. He wrote to Pierre de Coubertin, the head of the International Olympic Committee: 'I should be very sorry to have them there unless they were a *great* success, and were taken up by all the best people from the King downwards'.[60] At relatively short notice, the planned Rome Olympic Games were relocated to London.

Led by Lord Desborough, along with his wife Ettie, the BOA turned the London Olympic Games into a society occasion with many lavish entertainments.[61] These featured a reception by the Lord Mayor at Mansion House; dinners at the Worshipful Company of Fishmongers, the Lyceum Club and at Henley; banquets, balls, receptions, luncheons, and a Garden Party at Coombe Park, where the officials, competitors and special guests were treated to unique highlights all overseen by the Housing and Entertainment Committee.[62] As well as access to The Polytechnic, Regent Street, for all competitors, a large number of theatres and music halls offered reduced price admission.

The scale of the undertaking was so large that Laffan required an assistant to be entitled Honorary Secretary, and Captain F. Whitworth Jones was appointed. Laffan and Jones obtained temporary offices at 108 Victoria Street for £110 per annum, before appointing a lady typist and an office boy.[63] The lack of a suitable main stadium was however, a problem, since it had already been made clear that no government funds would be made available to host the Olympic Games.

However, the Franco-British Exhibition of 1908 had been planned for over three years, as an elaborate affair across a 140-acre site in Shepherd's Bush, West London, and here a dedicated stadium could be built for £44,002.[64] Laid out in a cross pattern, with several white buildings, 'The White City' became the object of a successful agreement with Imre Kiralfy, one of the Franco-British Exhibition organisers, for running and cycling tracks, lawn tennis grounds, swimming pond, changing rooms and conveniences, plus all advertising and printing costs in exchange for giving the BOA £2,000 in working expenses up front.[65] The Franco-British Exhibition would keep three-quarters of the gate; in addition to programme sales; covered stand revenue and programme advertisement receipts and the remaining one-fourth share, minus the £2,000 working capital, would go to the BOA.[66]

With an ambitious potential estimate of 75,000 people per working hour attending White City, this made moving to another ground, like the Crystal Palace less attractive, although the Amateur Athletic Association (AAA) complained that a new track would result in slow times. It was an incredibly shrewd move by the BOA, given their lack of financial security on which to base such a large undertaking but by 12 May 1908 an emergency Finance Committee meeting reported that no tickets had been sold, and in order to oversee the urgent task of distribution to as many registered agents as possible, appointed Richard Streggles, a retired Superintendent from the Metropolitan Police Force, on £5 a week.[67] Lord Northcliffe, owner of *The Daily Mail*, helped a great deal with subscriptions, raising over £12,000 in just over a week and it was on these reserves that the BOA ran until the First World War.

Rebecca Jenkins has convincingly argued that, 'The Franco-British Exhibition of 1908 became the saviour of the Olympic idea' and the Olympics would not have been such a success without the White City stadium built by the exhibition company.[68] Several other 'firsts' were established in 1908, including the introduction of a women's skating event; the adoption of an Olympic Charter and the Marathon distance was changed from being measured in kilometres to 26 miles 385 yards (42 km 195 m) to suit the whims of the Royal family.[69] The race began from the East terrace of Windsor Castle and ended in the stadium at Shepherd's Bush, where Mr Toastmaster Knightsmith oversaw proceedings in a full dress-suit and top hat, relaying announcements to the crowd by the largest available loudhailer.[70]

The arena was particularly widely mediated in 1908, not least because of what the illustrated weekly newspaper *The Graphic*, called 'The Tragedy of the Marathon Race: Dorando, Utterly Exhausted, Entering the Stadium First, Only to Lose'.[71] A reported 100,000 spectators, including Queen Alexandra and other members of the Royal family watched a dramatic end to the marathon race when, in great heat on 24 July, 22 year old Italian, Dorando Pietri, entered the stadium in the lead but fell several times due to exhaustion while completing the final lap.[72] The assistance he received caused his disqualification, when the next runner, Johnny Hayes of America, appealed against his victory.

It remains unclear whether the medical support saved Pietri's life but the fame he received, and public recognition led by Queen Alexandra who presented him with a specially commissioned trophy, translated to a successful short professional athletic career, after which he became a hotelier. If the marathon was run mainly on the public roads, its denouement in full view public of a mass audience, mediated to millions more, caused many to reference the Hellenic origins of the race.

There were approximations of 1,971 male competitors in London, compared with at least 45 female athletes taking part, though at least 10 more tennis players had registered prior to the Games themselves.[73] The British team comprised 641 in all, by far the largest squad, and most of the female athletes, with a few significant exceptions, were from the home nations. Women took part in five sports in 1908: archery, ice-skating, lawn tennis, motor-boat racing, and yachting. This was supplemented by a women's team gymnastics demonstration about which it has been difficult to obtain information.

Women's swimming almost made the schedule at the suggestion of Denmark and Norway, but ultimately did not because the BOA considered that 'the programme was already of a fully representative character'.[74] On 19 July 1908, the Fédération Internationale de Natation (FINA) was formed and the ASA welcomed Olympic and other regular international amateur competition, in large part because it increased the prestige of British swimmers.[75] Even though women made up only a small percentage of the athletes in London, a prominent narrative around the Olympic Games included the political radicalism of the suffragettes and threatened disruption as a result.

At the 1908 London Games, archers William and Lottie Dod became the first brother and sister medallists, he with the gold in the York round, and she with the silver in the National round. Joining Welford Park Archers recently after moving to Newbury, Lottie had beaten 99 competitors to take the Royal Toxophilite Society Ladies' Day Gold Medal in 1906.[76] Brother Anthony used the various practices as compositional exercises for his photograph album, evident in the Dod collection at the Wimbledon Lawn Tennis Museum.[77] This is a particularly valuable collection, including some first names of the archery club members, because part of the amateurism that Lottie Dod pursued included avoiding 'prize-hunting' and giving interviews about her career.[78] This makes accessing her own views, and those of her close circle, particularly challenging. Women's archery competitions often had a larger field than men's and on this occasion, the Olympics was an exception, with 32 in the two male contests and 25 in the single female event.[79]

Therefore, with the largest female field, archery was in many ways the main female sport at the London Olympics in 1908. Dod shot to target number four, representing Welford Park, shared by four co-competitors: Miss Wadsworth of Hereford Bowmen; Miss Vance of Hove Fox; Mrs Wilson of Hampshire and Mrs Rushton of Barnacre. There were strong winds both days and this, along with concentration and experience caused a dramatic contest. Lottie Dod finished day one on 348 points with 68 arrows ahead of Sybil 'Queenie' Newall's total of 338 for 66 flights.[80] On day two, Newall was able to get a score of 688 for 132 hits, compared with Dod's tally of just 642 from 126 shots.[81] After Dod faltered on the second and final day of competition, Queenie Newall of Cheltenham Archers took the gold, with Dod in second place and Beatrice Hill-Lowe of Archers of the Teme taking the bronze.[82]

This established an Olympic record, aside from the archery and the achievements of the Dod siblings. At 53 years and 275 days, Newall is still the oldest woman to win an Olympic gold medal and was described by a contemporary publication as 'The sister of the Honorary Secretary of the Toxophilite Society'.[83] Born in County Louth, and from a well-known family, Hill-Lowe also became Ireland's first female Olympic medallist.

Although she was internationally famous by 1908, Dod had already rejected a higher public profile in favour of pursuing her own enthusiasms. She was a tennis prodigy, and, while also excelling at golf, hockey, Winter Sports and

British Olympic pioneers 1900–1912   31

Figure 1.2 Lottie Dod at home with her brothers, Willy and Tony, with whom she played mixed matches and against rivals.

Source: The Dod Collection, Wimbledon Lawn Tennis Museum.

Figure 1.3 Lottie Dod with Welford Park Archery Club.
Source: The Dod Collection, Wimbledon Lawn Tennis Museum.

archery, her temperament and occasional lack of concentration could impair her performance. A contemporary report was nevertheless disappointed that sibling British gold medallists were lost to history because of Lottie Dod's lack of concentration:

> No one is so worthy to be empanelled as heroes and heroines as the Dod siblings. On this account we cannot but be sorry. But it will prove no inconsiderable consolation to her to know that her brother succeeded, and yet at the same time this is bound to accentuate her own disappointment... Miss Newall's success will be very welcome to her and her friends, and all the more so because her form has been less consistent this year. So Miss Newall, Miss Dod and Mrs Hill-Lowe must be added to that small but honourable company of ladies who will treasure amongst their most prized possessions their Olympic medals, the emblems of their skill.[84]

Like Chattie Sterry, Lottie Dod was not *just* an Olympian. Her tennis prowess had earned her the nickname 'The Little Wonder' as a teenage star. Dod was born in 1871 at Lower Bebington Cheshire and came to prominence in 1883. Together with her sister Annie, who was eight years older, Dod entered the 1883 Northern Lawn Tennis Championships in Manchester. They lost in the second round of the women's doubles to Hannah Keith and Amber McCord, but won the consolation tournament.[85] Julian Marshall, the editor of *Lawn Tennis*, was perhaps the only person to be slightly underwhelmed by the young Lottie Dod in 1886.

> The discovery of a very young girl is amusing. It reads as though the discovery had been the result of one of Mr Farini's world exploring searches rather than the appearance of a young English lady in one or two provincial lawn tennis meetings. I sincerely hope that the young lady, whose play is very remarkable, may be able to come to Wimbledon and take part, with some other excellent lady players whom I could name, in the struggle for supremacy. But the defeat of Miss Watson is not the absolute certainty it is thought to by the country paper to be. Anyhow it is evident that there is not so much difference between the lady champion and her challengers as there is between Mr Renshaw and the players who come next to him in the scale; and there will be more interest about the ladies matches this year than has ever hitherto existed.[86]

Lottie Dod took the Wimbledon women's singles title in 1887 and 1888, missed 1889 and 1890, and won consecutively three times between 1891 and 1893. Four of her five title wins were against Blanche Bingley-Hillyard, who herself later went on to win six Wimbledon singles titles (in 1886, 1889, 1894, 1897, 1899 and 1900). The formidable all round sportswoman and journalist, Toupie Lowther, assessed Hillyard's game in 1903:

> Mrs Hillyard has played and won more matches than any other lady. The number of trophies she possesses in the shape of cups is nearly incredible. She is a most determined player; however nearly she may seem to be losing a match she will never lose heart but will play on with the same pluck and energy to the last stroke. Mrs Hillyard's personal and distinctive stroke is a powerful and wonderfully accurate forehand drive of a perfect length. She is very active and covers the court better than most ladies.[87]

Still the youngest singles winner at Wimbledon, Dod retired from tennis aged 21, mainly to avoid being accused of 'pot-hunting'. Entertaining spectators was considered a vulgarism, with overtones of professionalism, although Dod spent many, many hours specialising in honing her sporting techniques. Lottie Dod's father, Joseph, had made sufficient money that she and her siblings had no need to work. Her second brother, Anthony, or Tony, also excelled in sports and he accompanied Lottie on her winter sports, climbing and cycling tours.

Lottie and her brothers also played mixed doubles with some of the leading male and female players of the time at their home, so the degree of specialised preparation was considerable.[88] She often competed against her brothers and, on occasion, was the only woman in tennis singles or doubles matches with some of the leading male athletes of the day. In 1888, for instance, she played a singles exhibition match with Ernest Renshaw and was partnered by her brother Tony in another friendly tie against the holders of the 1893 Wimbledon men's doubles championships, the Baddeley brothers.

The epitome of amateurism in the sense of loving sport, Dod gave her own philosophy in an interview for *Lawn Tennis, Rackets and Fives* (1891), part of the prestigious Badminton Library series.

> We are fond of games of all sorts at home and when we began lawn tennis a friend taught us to play hard and to practice hard and to play with a proper net and proper balls and to keep our courts in good order. Also we have been every year to see the best players, so that a good standard has been before us. Taking pains I believe is the whole secret. Don't play too much; but whenever you do play, endeavor to play with the head as well as the limbs, so making the pastime worthy of both sexes and, as such, not subject to disparagement from worthies of the old school who do not know how scientific the game of lawn tennis has now become. Finally, let us find encouragement in Burn's lines: 'Wha' does the utmost that he can, will whiles do mair'.[89]

After retiring from top-level tennis, Dod climbed and cycled on extensive international tours with Elizabeth Le Blond, the noted Alpinist (also known by other married names Main and Burnaby). The first President of the Ladies Alpine Club, Le Blond, Tony and Lottie together climbed Zwei Schwestern on 13 February 1896; Piz Zupo (13,101 feet) on 19 February 1896 and Drei Blumen on 23 February 1896.[90] Lottie also passed the St Moritz Ladies' Skating Test in 1896 and then returned for two months the following year to be tutored by Harold Topham for at least two hours a day to become the second woman to pass the more rigorous men's examination.[91] In 1897, she and Tony climbed again with Main in Norway, and Lottie is said to have completed the Cresta Run, although it is difficult to confirm under what circumstances.

Back in England, she went on to play international hockey in 1899 to 1900 and was an important administrator for the All England Women's Hockey Association (AEWHA) and twice played against Ireland in 1899 and 1900, scoring important goals.[92] She rapidly rose to become captain of the Spital club team from 1897 onwards, before also leading the Cheshire county side and was appointed President of the Northern Association.[93] In 1901 her mother died and the family took almost a year's break from sport as part of the process of mourning.[94] Otherwise, we can see Lottie Dod, along with her siblings, embracing aspects of sporting popular culture relatively early in the evolution of national and international networks.[95]

Lottie Dod was a good, if inconsistent, golfer from 1894 onwards, mainly playing at Hoylake, and won the Ladies' Golf Union (LGU) Championship in 1904, to popular acclaim. Again there are many photographs of this in the Dod collection at Wimbledon, including still life compositions that show off her set of clubs.[96] Her opponent in the 1904 final was May Hezlet, the champion of 1899 and 1902. The match was very close: the two were tied after 17 holes and large crowds gathered around as the events of 1904 unfolded on the links.[97] For someone who eschewed collecting titles, Dod looks pretty smug in possession of the fine trophy with which her victory was rewarded. She is also dressed in luxurious style, with a flair for fashion.

Into middle age, Lottie Dod was considered tall and rather muscular, as might be expected from an all-rounder. However, as she aged, her clothing became more mature than the original short skirt and cricket cap that she had first worn to play Wimbledon.[98] Rowing, skating and cricket remained enthusiasms and there are engaging photographs, including action shots and group names, of the Brightwalton Rectory annual cricket match played as men versus women between 1906 and 1910 in the collection.[99] In 1906, the women's team won by a single run scoring 106, to the men's 105. These were clearly huge social as well as sporting occasions with family, friends and neighbours.

Dod's success in elite competitive sport was increasingly marred by long spells of sciatica from 1900 onwards. Subsequent invitations to play golf in the USA produced disappointing performances but cemented her international reputation.[100] A long retirement included club-level tennis at Roehampton; Dod sang contralto and served as honorary secretary for the London Oriana Madrigal Society.[101] We even have a portrait of a very fine looking pet cat, called Alladdin, thanks to Anthony's enthusiasm for photography. Lottie was reputed in her later years to play a good hand of bridge.

At 88 years old, Lottie Dod died listening to Wimbledon on the radio in June 1960. Though sister Annie and elder brother Tony both married and had children, Lottie and younger brother William remained single, living in one another's company until his death in 1954. She maintained her antipathy to trophy-hunters, disliking interviews, although she made an exception for *World Sports* in 1957 as the oldest surviving singles champion and agreed to an 'exclusive' photographic portrait.[102] Importantly, Dod was distinguished during her lifetime, though not perhaps to the extent that we would expect now.

In conclusion, although her Olympic medal was for archery, this was not was one of Dod's strongest sports or the one for which she was most well

The Old Lady Of The Courts

A PROUD, stately old lady ... older, even, than Wimbledon itself. We found her living in a rest home for elderly people in Hampshire. The name: Charlotte (Lottie) Dod ... the girl, who, beginning as a 15-year-old in 1887, won five Wimbledon singles titles; who combined tennis skill with outstanding proficiency at hockey, archery, skating and other sports; who won the women's British open golf championship.

The teen-age "Little Wonder" is now an affable 85; Wimbledon's oldest surviving singles champion; an old lady with time and tranquillity in which to ponder golden memories. As we took this exclusive picture of her in the quiet of her room, it was like walking away from the roar of the modern crowd into the hushed hall of history.

Figure 1.4 Lottie Dod at 85 years of age. 'The Old Lady Of The Courts'.
Source: *World Sports*, June 1957, author's collection.

known. However, in order to focus specifically on Lottie Dod, this case study identified just some of the 25 British female archers present in 1908. It would be good to extend the research to understand the wider context of their participation in this under-researched sport. Having featured in 1904 and 1908, archery was not scheduled in 1912 and disappeared from Olympic competition in 1920 until the Munich Games of 1972.

Other than the archers, the next largest female contingent at the 1908 Olympics were the tennis players.[103] Both indoor and outdoor tennis were played in May, at the Queens Club, West Kensington, London. In the indoor event, Gwendoline 'Gladys' Eastlake-Smith won the gold and Alice Greene the silver medal for Britain, while Märtha Adlerstråhle, even at 40 years of age, perhaps the leading Swedish player of the time, took home bronze. Dorothy Lambert Chambers had withdrawn early on, having previously enjoyed success in covered and open courts. Eastlake-Smith celebrated victory by marrying another tennis player, Dr Wharram Henry Lamplough two days later, and cemented the relationship by competing in 'married-doubles' from then on.[104] The remaining contenders were Violet Pinkney, Penelope 'Dora' Boothby and Mildred Coles of Great Britain, along with Elsa Wallenberg of Sweden.[105]

The women's outdoor singles was an all-British medal board won by Dorothy Lambert Chambers, over Penelope Boothby, with Ruth Winch automatically taking bronze, as the French competitor, Madamoiselle Fenwick, withdrew. About 10 of the players in the lower half of the draw 'scratched', or retired, in the terms of the time. Alice Greene and Agatha Morton were the other two British rivals. Boothby would go on to win Wimbledon in 1909 and Winch was also a very good player, but the towering presence in terms of reputation was Lambert Chambers.

It is intriguing to note that Charlotte Sterry was listed by *Lawn Tennis* as a competitor for the Olympics but scheduled to play in the first round against Madam Mararaz of Hungary.[106] Other first round matches were Madame Czery (Hungary) vs Fraulein Pietrzikowski (Austria) and Madame Fenwick (France) vs Frau M. Amende (Austria), while Byes were offered to Mrs Lambert Chambers, Mrs Hillyard and Miss Boothby. As was the custom at the time, leading players did not play in the first round but faced those who progressed later on.[107] Perhaps if Sterry had been given the same courtesy as Lambert Chambers, Hillyard and Boothby, she may have not have withdrawn.

Nautical contestants at the London Olympics in 1908 included Sylvia Marshall Gorham, who co-crewed *Quicksilver* in the motor-boat racing event with her husband. Frances Rivett-Carnac (née Greenstock) cruised *Heroine* in the 7-metre yachting class with her husband, who was listed as the owner, but their progress was uncontested as there were no other entrants.[108] Constance Edwina Grosvenor (formerly Lewes), better known as The Duchess of Westminster, owned the 8-metre class yacht *Sorais* who came second with five points from three races to *Cobweb* (owned by B. O. Cochrane of Great Britain) with a score of six and ahead of *Fram* (owned by C. Wisbech representing Norway) who was awarded a total of four and *Vinga* (the Royal Gothenburg Yacht Club, Sweden) on three.

After the main events in July, the 'Winter Games' began in October 1908, including Association Football, Lacrosse, Hockey, Boxing and Figure Skating. At the Prince's Skating Club, Knightsbridge, the women's individual skating gold medal went to Florence 'Madge' Syers who had previously retired from a world-class career through ill-health and had come back specifically to try for an Olympic medal.[109] Else Rendschmidt won the silver medal for Germany. Dorothy Greenhough-Smith, who was the reigning British champion in Madge Syers' absence in 1908, took third place for Britain. Gwendolyn Lycett of Britain and Elna Montgomery of Sweden were the remainder of the field.

Madge Syers also won an Olympic bronze in the mixed pairs with her husband, Edgar in 1908. The gold medal went to the German pairing Anna Hübler and Heinrich Burger, ahead of another married British couple Phyllis and James Johnson. Madge's mixed pairs medal was a fitting testament to Edgar's support, as he had coached her to more advanced levels. Having entered the World Figure Skating Championships in 1902, as there were no rules to prevent women from competing, Madge came second to Ulrich Salchow. She won the 'men's' world championships in 1903 and 1904, defeating Edgar. She therefore forced the International Skating Union (ISU) to accept women's competitions as part of their responsibility and her husband had fully supported this. A heart condition forced Syers to cease competition soon after the 1908 Olympic Games. She died, aged just 35, in 1917.

On 31 December 1908, a surplus of about £6,662 enabled the BOA to plan for the future, with an income of about £200 per annum and this required only 150 subscribing members to make the organisation financially sound.[110] However, relations between the British, perhaps more accurately the English, and the American team were bitterly fractious. The degree of animosity occasioned Theodore Cook, a stalwart of the BOA and representative of the Amateur Fencing Council, to write a 60-page booklet specifically refuting claims of unfair and ungracious treatment by officials in London.[111] Cook joined the IOC as a BOA representative in 1908 and so maintained the considerable British influence.

Both the British and French had stayed away from St Louis, so there was already animosity. It was clear that the British team was large, around 614 competitors all told, so there were definitely attempts to obtain as many medals as possible on home soil. Here, British women medallists helped the national tally (as they also did for Germany and Sweden,) and this was an important lesson for other ambitious countries, since there was no division between male and female victories in the summaries.

The bitter tone of intense Anglo-American rivalry can be evidenced by Thomas Rugby Burford's self-published pamphlet, *American Hatred and British Folly* costing a shilling.[112] Burford outlined a series of examples of how American influence had undermined British interests across the world, and specifically reserved a section for the Olympic conflicts that had arisen.

There seems little doubt that with the elaborate festivities, matched only by the number of sub-committees, each with their own rules and regulations, that the British were both welcoming and high-handed: 'The British Olympic Council reserve to themselves the right to refuse the entry of any competitor without being bound to give reasons for their decision'.[113]

As we move on to the 1912 Stockholm Games, the last before World War I interrupted the IOC schedule until 1920, it is worth saying that BOA success in London came with a price: the legacy would be a weight of expectation. In preparation for the Games of 1912, the BOA were mindful that, having notionally 'won' the London Olympics in their own minds with a total of 146 medals compared with the USA in second place by means of 47 and Sweden in third with 25, there was a possibility that they could now 'lose' in Stockholm. Accordingly, most of 1910 and 1911 was spent expanding the membership of the association to include the likes of the Irish Cyclists Association; Irish Amateur Swimming Association; the Marylebone Cricket Club; The Scottish Amateur Athletics Association; University of Oxford and Cambridge representatives; the Directors of the Military Gymnasia and Naval Gymnasia; the National Physical Recreation Society; the Incorporated British College of Physical Education and the Motor Yacht Club.[114]

There was limited debate about the moral obligation of the BOA to send a team to the Greek Olympic Games in 1910 and much more conflict about whether the Amateur Football Association should be invited to join the council, along with the Football Association. The problem of describing a universal definition of amateurism occupied many council hours, as did delineating a minimum schedule for all future Olympic programmes. Barney has suggested that the Stockholm Games of 1912: 'Signalled the arrival of the Olympic Games as the world's premier international sporting event' due to control of the programme by officials of the international sports federations, rather than by individual organising committees.[115]

In moving now from upper class amateurs, who could volunteer to afford to attend in their own right, to the first female working class Olympics representatives, it is worth asking how was their participation funded and by whom? How did British representation at the Olympic Games become an issue of wider national prestige?

'Well done England': Jennie Fletcher and the Stockholm Olympic Games 1912

In 1909, 25 influential supporters were granted life membership of the BOA, including celebrity author and journalist, Sir Arthur Conan Doyle; body builder and entrepreneur, Eugen Sandow; and sporting goods manufacturer, Albert Slazenger, plus eight 'Ordinary' members. By 1911, this had grown to 52 Life Members and 34 Ordinary Members, motivated by the exigencies of sending as large a team to Sweden as possible but without the need for a public appeal. Conan Doyle would prove an adept fundraiser and become co-opted to the British Olympic Council in August 1912.

A largely working class-led administrative body, the ASA had consistently declared that it had insufficient funds to help British entrants to attend the Olympic Games and it was initially sceptical about sending contestants to a planned 100-metres freestyle race for women in 1912. This was somewhat disingenuous. British men had competed in aquatic events with considerable success since the 1896 Athens Games, often winning multiple medals and this may have been what motivated the ASA to send a women's team in 1912, heavily subsidised by the BOA. Olympic swimmers' bodies became more widely mediated with the increased popularity of the Olympic Games.[116]

The logistics of taking a team of 160 fully-funded and 120 subsidised athletes, plus 20 officials concerned the BOA a great deal. The Hull (Wilson Line) and Harwich (Thule Line) sea crossings were thought to offer the best value at £1,475 and 15 shillings, compared with overland travel requiring two nights on a sleeper train.[117] Over 200 British entrants would be entitled to travel on board ship first class, and the remainder second. Charting a special steamer proved prohibitively expensive. As to the accommodation, the offer of the Swedish Olympic Committee to house opponents in local schools was considered 'defective' and there was no hotel large enough to take all of the British team. Paying for individual rooms in houses for a stay of 15 nights was therefore estimated to be the most economical solution, at £1,872.

With grants to sports associations costing £650 and with officials also added, the team eventually approximated 300 people, so the BOA steeled itself to spend between £4,000 and £4,500, potentially leaving just £900 in the bank to sustain activities up until 1916.[118] After this time, a public appeal would have to be made. Under these circumstances, an Opening Ceremony parade uniform, even a basic straw hat and coat, was beyond what the BOA considered it could afford.

At the Stockholm Olympic Games in 1912, the three women's events were tennis and the newly introduced swimming and diving contests.[119] There were also gymnastic displays by Danish, Finnish, Norwegian and Swedish female teams in early July. Of the expanded programme for 54 female athletes, the aquatic competitions involved 40 swimmers and divers from eight countries.[120] Working class swimmers therefore became more evident in British female Olympic amateur tradition than tennis players, in part, because of their larger numbers. Irene Steer of Cardiff Ladies Premier Swimming Club; Isabelle 'Belle' Moore of Glasgow; Annie Speirs of Derby and Jennie Fletcher of Leicester made up the gold-winning team in the 4 × 100-metres freestyle relay event.[121] Steer therefore became Wales' first female Olympic title holder and Moore remains Scotland's only female gold Olympic swimming medallist.[122] Win Hayes is therefore not quite correct in saying that Lucy Morton became the first British female swimming gold medallist in 1924.[123]

Figure 1.5 Jennie Fletcher in 1912.
Source: Steve Humphries Collection, Leicester.

After the relay race, Jennie said: 'The crowning moment of my career was when King Gustav of Sweden placed the classic laurel wreath on my head, put the gold medal around my neck and said, 'Well done England'.[124] We have no record of what Steer and Moore thought of this comment. As well as swimming the final leg of the relay, Fletcher also took third place to become Britain's first individual female swimming medallist in the 100-metres freestyle, behind two Australians: Sarah 'Fanny' Durack and Mina Wylie.[125] Jennie fought hard against Grete Rosenborg of Germany for the bronze medal, while Annie Speirs came in fifth.[126]

Durack and Wylie had not been sponsored to travel by their national association but travelled by public support. The amateur British tradition meant that Jennie Fletcher and her team-mates swam side-stroke to victory in the 4 × 100-metres relay. In the minds of the ASA, who thought crawl was a fast but inelegant and exhausting stroke, it made aesthetic, if not athletic, sense. While Durack and Wylie were leading the freestyle events swimming the crawl, the Australians did not send four women to make up a relay team.[127] Germany and Austria won the silver and bronze medal behind Britain,

Figure 1.6 Jennie Fletcher far right, with gold and silver medallists in the individual 100-metres freestyle Fanny Durack and Mina Wylie of Australia.

with Sweden in fourth place. In fact, only four teams entered the women's 4 × 100-metres relay and so only a final was held, as there was no need for elimination heats. It made for a predictable result, with Britain winning by eight seconds. For Germany, the swimmers were Wally Dressel, Louise Otto, Grete Rosenberg and Hermine Stindtente; and the Austrian team was Margaret Adler, Klara Milch, Jospehine Sticker and Bertha Zahourek. Had there been four Australians, the result would undoubtedly have been different, but the lack of support for female Olympic athletes was not limited to Britain.

Jennie Fletcher came to her moment of fame as one of many working-class female amateur athletes in 1912. She was born 19 March 1890 in Checketts Road, Belgrave, Leicester to John Frederick Fletcher and the former Emily Wilkinson, the seventh child of a family of 11.[128] According to the 1911 census, Jennie's father headed a house of three men and four women.[129] This included John himself, a fish and fruit salesman aged 53, and his sons Ben, who at 14 was an apprentice in a boot factory, and Tom, a schoolboy aged 11.

At 51, his wife, Leicester-born Emily Fletcher, had been married to John for 31 years and had given birth to 11 children, of whom nine survived. Minnie, aged 24, helped in the family business; Jennie, 21, worked as a cutter and machinist in a hosiery warehouse and Violetta, 19, was a stock-room hand in a boot factory. All were single. The eldest of the Fletcher children had moved out, leaving the younger five listed here. Originally listed in the census as 'Jane', she disliked her given name and adopted first 'Jenny', then consistently spelt it as Jennie. Checketts Road, in the Belgrave area of Leicester, was a poor part of the city but this made for entrepreneurialism. The Fletchers ran a fruit and vegetable market, a fish and chip shop and a grocery shop. The adolescent Fletchers also helped out at a stall on Leicester's fish market before going to school or work, bringing fish back to the chip shop, which was the most lucrative of their businesses.

In her own words, Jennie described the joy of learning to swim:

> I attended Mellor Street Board School participating as often as possible in the swimming competitions and exercises. Swimming to me was my greatest pleasure and no encouragement was needed for me to compete in polo, diving or swimming. There was no mixed swimming in those days but with special permission my brother Ben was allowed to pace me. Most of the early swimming was single arm and trudgen with the scissors kick going into the crawl in the later stages. My training was not regimented but consisted of long walks, skipping and deep breathing exercises. Because of our large family there were numerous little chores to be carried out so I was always kept busy.[130]

Jennie won a medal for local schoolgirls in 1903 while a pupil at Mellor Street School. Mellor Street girls' team then won the Leicester Schools Swimming Association Championship in 1903 and there is a photograph of this in the scrapbook that she compiled of her swimming career.[131] By 1905 Fletcher had placed fourth at the national English 100 yards race.[132] Jennie was a regular at Vestry Street Baths as a member of Leicester Ladies Swimming Club, affiliated to the ASA, with Lady Faire as its president. Here she was coached by Jack Jarvis, a previous Olympic medallist, and chaperoned by his wife when attending events.

Jack Jarvis had won both the 1,000-metres and 4,000-metres freestyle gold in the 1900 Olympics, swimming in the River Seine. He also won the 100 metres (unlisted in the official record). Jarvis encouraged Jennie to replicate his own 'racing' style. Photographs show Jennie with at least six large trophies, badges, pendants and shields for more than 150 prizes and a gold brooch presented by the Ravensbourne Swimming Club for breaking the world record in London in 1907.[133] Most notable of all was the Roseback shield awarded by Sir Thomas Dewar, the distiller who sponsored many sporting prizes in his name.

There is little doubt that Jennie Fletcher's stroke evolved without ever becoming a full crawl action. Jack Jarvis' friend Joey Nuttall, previously an amateur champion, became a professional in 1888, and Alf Farrand (or Ferrand) became his manager. Farrand was a French strongman who had become famous at the London Aquarium and he invited Jennie to train in

Southport with him ahead of the national championships in 1906. This must have been acceptable to the Amateur Swimming Association but there was a fine line. Fletcher almost turned professional in 1907, at the request of Annette Kellerman. She was obviously tempted by the offer: 'My main inconvenience was paying all personal expenses and because of the costs many invitations were refused. My parents objected to the acceptance of lucrative offers from America because of my youth and their values of Christian principles'.[134]

On 20 September 1906, 2,000 people crowded into Cossington Street Baths to see Jennie beat Jessie Speirs (sister of Annie) to become the new English 100 yards champion.[135] She was to retain her championship for two years and won again in 1911 and 1912. She improved her time by over 10 seconds over a three-year period between 1906 and 1909, to just under 1 minute 14 seconds. However, in 1910, she lost the 100-yards freestyle championship to Welsh title holder Irene Steer, who swam the crawl and matched Jennie's existing record for the distance in 1 minute 13.6 seconds (Fletcher recalled she had an accident with her foot just before the race).[136] While Jennie adapted her stroke in 1911 and 1912, her times for those years in which she won ASA races went up to 1.15.6 and 1.15.2, respectively.[137]

The memory that Jennie had of leading the individual freestyle final race in Stockholm, before being narrowly beaten by the Australians, does not seem to be borne out by the official report.[138] In her first heat of the 1912 Games on 8 July, Fletcher was said to have got away first but was then easily beaten in a time of 1.23.6, by British swimmer Daisy Curwen of the Ladies Prima Dolphin Club. Curwen then underwent an operation for appendicitis immediately after swimming to second place behind Durack in her semifinal heat at lunchtime on Thursday 11 July. She was 'unable to start' for the final at 7.30 p.m. the next day. Curwen was given medals for both the 220 and 300 yards after her recovery in 1912, raising the possibility that she was a more versatile swimmer than Fletcher. Chances of Olympic glory were evidently precarious, even when an individual made it to the Games themselves.

Jennie was obliged to retire in 1913 from ASA competition, having taken an appointment under the Leicester Baths Committee at Vestry Street. Perhaps it was more attractive than working in a factory but it is unclear whether she was teaching or coaching swimming, generally working as an attendant or a mix of duties. She had corresponded with Henry Hyslop before he enlisted, met again during the First World War, married, and moved to Ontario to raise six children. *The Daily Express* from March 1917 has a brief sentence to the effect that 'Miss Jennie Fletcher, a world's champion swimmer, was married at Leicester, on Saturday to Sergeant Henry Hyslop, a Canadian'. Henry seems to have been quite badly injured in the war and advised to return to Canada for his health. Migration relocated Jennie Hyslop to a farm where she was little known other than as a housewife and mother.

Figure 1.7 Image from Jennie Fletcher's scrapbook, showing a photographic portrait alongside her gold medal.
Source: Graham Budd Auctions, London.

The family gravestone lists 'In Memory of Henry Hill Hyslop, born Annan Scotland, 1888–1964' and 'His Wife Jennie Fletcher, born Leicester England, 1890–1968. First Great Woman Swimmer: Gold Medal Olympics 1912'.[139]

Having taught swimming until she was 60 years of age to local children, Jennie was inducted into the Swimming Hall of Fame in Fort Lauderdale, Florida in 1971, in recognition of which the family donated her Olympic laurel wreath to the collection. She is therefore one of several Olympians whose achievements have been recorded on their headstone; a defining statement. But, having passed down her gold medal to her son, Henry Irving (born in 1920, died 2000) he in turn passed it down to his daughter, Jennifer Heather Patenaude who sold it at Graham Budd auctions in 2012 for £12,000.[140] Perhaps, as a Canadian citizen, its value as a family heirloom was less important than a pressing financial issue.

In Stockholm, the times of the two Australians were significantly faster than Fletcher's bronze medal of 1.27.0 (though she did press Mina Wylie hard in their semi-final battle). The official report described Durack's ease, 'swimming a distinctively Australian Crawl, she won as she liked'.[141] She had previously set an Olympic record in one of the heats, of 1.19.8. The angle of the action photograph in the official report of this final makes it difficult to assess both the stroke action and the margin of Durack's lead. It is nevertheless a significant image for showing women's sport as the subject of interest by the IOC, the officials and spectators present, plus the obvious encouragement of the male swimmers along the side of the pool.

The rest of the British 4 × 100-metres freestyle relay team had similar backgrounds to Jennie Fletcher. Isabella McAlpine Moore was born at 95 McLean Street, Govan, Lanarkshire, on 23 October 1894, the eighth of nine children of Duncan Moore, journeyman iron turner, and his wife, Mary (née Cleland).[142] Belle or Bella, as she was more familiarly known, learned to swim at school, where swimming lessons had been made compulsory in local authority schools, using the public baths provided by the Glasgow Corporation. Moore often walked two to three miles to the pool to train. Moore initially did well in the individual 100-metres race in Stockholm, winning her heat easily. She came fourth in the semi-final heat behind Fanny Durack, Daisy Curwen and Annie Speirs and was eliminated along with fifth placed, Mary Langford.[143]

After winning a gold medal in the 4 × 100-metres freestyle relay in the 1912 Stockholm Olympic Games, Bella Moore became a swimming instructor, which effectively ended her amateur career. 'Swimming teacher' was listed as Bella's occupation at the time of her marriage, in Govan on 1 August 1919, to George Cameron, assistant manager in a shipyard; he was the son of Frederick Cameron, a joiner. They emigrated to Maryland in the United States, where Bella taught swimming to an advanced age. She died there on 7 March 1975. In 2012, she was inducted into the Scottish Sports Hall of Fame.

Irene Steer was slightly better off than the others, having been born at 290 Bute Street, St Mary, Cardiff, on 10 August 1889, the daughter of George Steer, master draper, and his wife, Annie Charlotte (née Lewis).[144] Steer began to compete as a breaststroke specialist, but changed to freestyle, training mainly in Roath Park Lake. She was Welsh champion from 1907 onwards, and did well in the individual 100-metres Olympic heats before being disqualified in the semi-finals. She retired from competitive swimming in 1913. On 28 July 1915, Irene married William Nicholson, dentist, son of Thomas Nicholson, schoolmaster. He was also a director and Chairman of Cardiff City. They had three daughters and a son. She died at 101 Station Road, Llanishen, Cardiff, on 18 April 1977.[145]

Annie Coupe Speirs was born at 120 Leta Street, Walton, Liverpool, on 14 July 1889, the fourth daughter in a family of at least five sons and four daughters of James Speirs, coppersmith, and his wife, Eliza (née Spencer).[146] She worked as an upholsterer from before the First World War until her marriage, at Breeze Hill Presbyterian Church, Walton, on 3 June 1922, to Charles Hillman Coombe, ship's cooper, son of Thomas Coombe, watchmaker and jeweller. Annie died at 107 Rice Lane, Walton, on 26 October 1926, of infective endocarditis

Isabella Mary White came in third behind Sweden's Greta Johansson and Lisa Regnell in the women's plain diving competition.[147] While commended for her speed, White was considered to have over extended her action, or 'back-swanked', and so was inelegant compared with the Scandinavians. Elsa Regnell, Ella Eklund, Elsa Andersson, Selma Andersson and Tora Larsson of Sweden were the other finalists in a predominantly domestic field. White's memorabilia is held at the British Swimming offices in Loughborough.[148] Of all the British female aquatic competitors in Stockholm, London-born White maintained the most impressive Olympic record, though she was unable to claim a medal in either the 1920 Antwerp Games, the 1924 Paris Games or the 1928 Amsterdam Games. She did however, take a gold in the 1927 European Championships; a long-standing career that requires further analysis.

The remaining 14 female entrants in 1912 were tennis players but two German players withdrew before play commenced. The indoor medals went to Britain's Edith Hannam and Mabel Parton who took gold and bronze medals, respectively, split by silver-medallist Thora Castenschiold of Denmark.[149] Helen Aitchison was the third British female representative in

Figure 1.8 The plaque of the winning medallists at the Olympic Stadium, Stockholm, listing Great Britain's victory in the 4 × 100-metres freestyle relay, alongside other international swimming greats.

Source: Author's collection.

the covered courts event, which had four Swedish representatives (Sigfrid Fick, Edith Arnheim, Annie Holmström and Margareta Cederschiöld).

The outdoor singles had no British women in the top three for the first time: leaving Marguerite Broquedis of France, Dora Köring of Germany and Anne Margarethe Bjurstedt (later better known as a nationalised American, 'Molla' Mallory) of Norway to take the honours. Outdoors, the same four Swedish women took part, with the addition of Holmström's sister Ellen Brusewitz. Hannam also won a covered courts mixed doubles gold medal with Charles Dixon. Helen Aitchison and Roper Barrett took silver place ahead of Sigfrid Fick and Gunnar Setterwall of Sweden. The outdoor mixed doubles was an all-Swedish affair. Märtha Adlerstråhle was on the organising committee for the Lawn Tennis, along with her compatriot Ebba Hay.

Like London, the Stockholm Games of 1912 were a model of hospitality and efficiency. In the context of 'declinist' narratives in Britain, it was said by sections of the press that Britain had 'lost' the Games, and with it considerable international sporting prestige. Sweden won a total of 65 medals, The United States of American 64 and Britain just 41. With a planned IOC gathering in Paris in 1914 that would seek to define the Olympic schedule for future Games and the 1916 Olympics due for Berlin, the BOA came under increasing pressure not just to fund teams to future Olympic Games, but to prepare them in advance.[150] Coinciding with an urgent need to raise funds, this would spark debate as to what the purpose of the BOA was, and if the British should participate in future Olympic Games at all.

Conclusion

The Olympic Games began as a relatively small festival of sport and culture that nevertheless set a pattern later copied by organisers in other sports.[151] The standard of lawn tennis at the 1900 Olympic Games was, however, very high because the Wimbledon Championship, inaugurated for men in 1877 and for women in 1884, had established itself as the leading international competition of its kind. Four Wimbledon Singles Champions travelled to Paris, Harold Mahony, Laurence Doherty, Reginald Doherty and Charlotte Cooper, all from the British Isles.[152] By the time that the Olympic Games returned to Paris in 1924, the travelling sporting mega-event had begun to evolve and the presence of female athletes would become more pronounced.[153] As the case study of Chattie Sterry has shown, the amateur ideal for women has arguably been much more enduring than for male athletes of a variety of sports. Sterry was not just an important tennis player amidst several exceptional talents, but also left a considerable legacy in international competition and administration.

There is a rather wonderful photograph taken in 1929, at the Roehampton Club, of Charlotte Sterry, 'A Five Times Wimbledon Champion' on the second left and Lottie Dod, 'A Five Times Wimbledon Champion' on the right.[154] By this time, Sterry would have been almost 60 years old but she evidently still played tennis. She lived to a good age and, being physically fit obviously helped, died at 96 years old, in 1966. Her influence, through family members active in tennis was still evident when I visited the archives at Wimbledon to conduct this research and there remains a longer family history to uncover and analyse. More local history research could also reveal why specifically Ealing, and Middlesex generally, was such a centre for female tennis talent at this time: six of the first ten Wimbledon female singles champions were born there or lived nearby.

Had Lottie Dod not been such an extraordinary talent, the case study of 1908 could just as easily have focused on Dorothy Lambert Chambers (née Douglass) who was also famous by the time she won her gold medal in 1908. Lambert Chambers first won Wimbledon as a single woman in 1903.[155] This was an especially good year because she also won the mixed doubles and a Badminton singles championship, which was her other main specialism. Douglass was also based at the Ealing Common tennis club, taking a handicap singles first prize at the age of 11. After her marriage in 1907 to a local merchant, Dorothy competed as Mrs Lambert Chambers and went on to a longer string of Wimbledon victories than Lottie Dod, Blanche Bingley Hilliard or Charlotte Cooper Sterry, taking the Wimbledon singles title seven times (1903–1904, 1906, 1910–1911, 1913–1914) and appearing in 11 finals.[156]

Lambert Chambers competed at a time when Wimbledon was becoming more significant as an international tournament. She was a beaten finalist in 1905 to May Sutton of the United States, who became the first female Wimbledon singles champion from overseas. Born in Plymouth, Sutton's family had been based at Acton before emigrating to California. Sutton returned to repeat her singles success over Lambert Chambers in 1907, the year when Norman Brookes of Australia also became the men's singles champion. Dora Boothby won the women's Wimbledon singles competition in 1909 when Lambert Chambers was expecting her first child and Ethel Larcombe took the title in 1912, when her second was due.[157] This also partly explains why Lambert Chambers did not appear in the 1912 Stockholm Games.

Dorothy Lambert Chambers attributed her improvement as a player, in part due, to practising against the best male players of her time. She first visited France in 1905 to play in Cannes, an experience she evidently enjoyed, declaring: 'Touring abroad is both an education and a delight'.[158] She also competed at Dinan, Monte Carlo, Nice, Homburg and Baden-Baden. Lambert Chambers might have won more at Wimbledon and more Olympic medals if the war had not intervened. In 1919, when the Wimbledon championship resumed, she was losing finalist to Suzanne Lenglen of France.[159] She was therefore part of a growing internationalism in tennis, quite apart from her Olympic success.

In many respects, Dod exemplified the upper middle class woman who lived all her life from a private income and so could indulge her many and varied interests without stint. Richard Holt has characterised the woman whom contemporary publications had once christened 'The Little Wonder' when she first won Wimbledon at the age of 15 in 1887, as 'The female sporting equivalent of C. B. Fry'.[160] While a given discipline did hold her attention, she displayed a rigorous approach to specialised training, honed her technique and rehearsed mental preparation. So the links between amateurism and professionalism could be seen, even in the most ardent recreationalist. There is little doubt that Lottie Dod was fiercely competitive, both in relation to her own limitations and against other people.[161] The blustery conditions at the archery contest in 1908 must therefore have been frustrating.

Lottie Dod's sporting life was a social round of summer and winter activities. She was probably introduced to archery at the home of the much more proficient Alice Blanche Legh when both families lived in Cheshire. The parents of Canadian-born Alice and her siblings helped renew the fashionable status of archery for a suburban Victorian elite.[162] After her first victory in 1881, Alice Legh lost the national title to her mother for four consecutive years, she then retained it for seven years from 1886 to 1892 and held it for another successive eight-year period between 1902 and 1909. Her record of 23 archery championship titles between 1881 and 1922 remains unbeaten.

Alice Legh considered herself to be an amateur because she paid to enter contests, although she often went home with cash prizes and valuable trinkets.[163] However, Legh did not compete at the 1908 Games, preferring to defend her national title a week later. In this, she and Charlotte Cooper were perhaps making a point about how they saw Olympic competition relative to their respective domestic titles. Legh had coached protégé Queenie Newall and would beat her by over 150 points to win the 1908 national competition.[164]

Newall outdid her mentor to take the title in both 1911 and 1912. At the age of 53 years and 275 days, Newall remains the oldest woman to have won an Olympic gold medal. Although the war interrupted her athletic career, Newall was still competing up to a year before she died in 1929. We have lists of other archers such as Mrs Armitage; Mrs Priestly Foster; Mrs Honneywill; Miss L Newall; Albertine Thackwell (aged 45); Jessie Wadworth (aged 43); Margaret Weedon (aged 53); Mrs Wadsworth; Lillian Wilson (who shared a date of birth with Wadworth) but there remains more to be found.[165] Not least, the age profile of female Olympic amateurs requires more nuanced analysis.

Similarly, we have glimpses of Florence Sandell of Selhurst Road, the leader of The Polytechnic Ladies Gymnasium display team, because Olympic memorabilia became increasingly collectible in the context of the third London Olympic Games in 2012. As well as providing fresh evidence on the career of Jennie Fletcher at the same auction, there were entrance tickets to the White City on 17 July for Florence Sandell on sale, as well as typed instructions of how the squad was to drill and perform when in the stadium itself, along with hand written diagrams.[166] Sandell evidently led the female gymnasts with some confidence. An accompanying press cutting suggests that a gymnastic rehearsal also took place on 13 July but the accompanying letters suggest that the gymnasts were part of more than one procession.[167] John Edward Kynaston Studd wrote on behalf of The Polytechnic on 15 May, to congratulate Sandell and her team-mates on the quality of the display, in spite of feeling 'the deepest sympathy and pity for you having to stand so long in the cold and wet'.[168]

Studd, the President of The Polytechnic, a former cricketer and the flag bearer at the 1908 Olympic opening ceremony, wrote again on 27 May to congratulate Sandell on their display in front of the President of the French Republic. The women were clearly the stars of this occasion, which *Sporting Life* also called 'a triumph' when hoop drills gave way to a routine in which individual flag-bearers coordinated to produce a large combined tricolour while the band played the Marseillaise.[169]

Along with photographs signed by Florence Sandell of the team marching past the King and Queen, this suggests that the gymnastic team had a significant presence and one that was widely mediated. The Polytechnic's men vs women cricket match that followed the gymnastic display was thought sufficiently noteworthy for a photograph and brief report.[170] Studd would later play a very active part in fundraising after the 1912 Stockholm Games and was influential at the BOA, so the success of The Polytechnic Ladies team in 1908 helped future gymnasts, more especially in the inter-war period.

The 1912 swimming Olympic competition indicates a radical change in female racing costumes and this was to change both how women took part in the sporting spectacle and how their bodies were mediated to a wider audience. The women's silk suit was essentially based upon a masculine silhouette and was a considerable concession to androgyny. This was to have major repercussions for the presentation of female athletes at the Olympic Games. Nevertheless, there was considerable debate at the ASA about whether they should also wear skirts and pantaloons for the sake of modesty.

British amateur swimmers had access to some of the finest coaches of their day and used the latest technology available to them in the form of silk racing swimsuits adapted from male costumes. Leicester's Jack Jarvis appears to have been influential in this regard.[171] The silk racing suits (and woollen diving costumes) remained the standard British style until the 1936 Berlin Olympic Games. The official report contains several photographs of women swimmers in costume without a cloak, which Jennie later said she 'Hated. We were told bathing suits were shocking and indecent and even when entering a competition, we were covered with a floor length cloak until we entered the water'.[172] In spite of her reservations, this was an important gain for women's sport to be organised on competitive lines rather than those of modesty. Fletcher had been wearing a sleeveless costume with legs cut above the knee for quite some time, so the ASA guidelines were not always rigidly adhered to:

> At meeting where both sexes are admitted, and in all ASA Championships, competitors must wear costume in accordance with the following regulations.
>
> a. The colours shall be black or dark blue.
> b. Trimmings may be used ad lib.
> c. The shoulder straps shall not be less than two inches wide.
> d. It shall be buttoned at the shoulder, and the armhole cut no lower than three inches from the armpit. Note: For Ladies a shaped arm, at least three inches long shall be inserted.
> e. In the front the costume shall reach not lower than two inches below the pit of the neck. Note: For ladies the costume shall be cut straight round the neck.
> f. At the back it shall be cut straight from the top of the shoulder to top of shoulder.
> g. In the leg portion the costume shall extend to within three inches of the knee, and shall be cut in a straight line round the circumference of each leg.
> h. Drawers must be worn underneath the costume. They must be of triangular pattern, with a minimum width of 2/1/2 inches at the fork; they must meet on each hip, and be of not less width than 3 inches on each side when fastened.
> i. On leaving the dressing room, lady competitors over 14 years of age must wear a long coat or bath gown before entering and also immediately after leaving the water.[173]

While this uniform had gendered aspects, the majority of the regulations remained the same for women and men, although by the end of the 1920s, swimming trunks became more acceptable male clothing than full costumes.

Without the medals of the women tennis players, swimmers and divers in 1912, the overall situation for Britain would have been worse and so gradually the increase in more events would mean more opportunities for working class women like Jennie Fletcher and her team-mates. However, class would remain a significant factor in who could volunteer to represent Britain as an amateur at the Olympic Games. But racing techniques and technology developed quickly.

Olympic rivalry with the United States was not to be so bitter after they became an ally of Britain during World War I, and, as American women also swam crawl rather than sidestroke, their swimmers soon eclipsed the British who would tend to rely on breaststroke and backstroke for their future medals. As the chapter has indicated, working class amateurs often had little time for preparation and relatively short sporting careers, mainly because they needed to support themselves and their families. An Olympic reputation could translate into a teaching role, which was more pleasant than the alternatives on offer, and several of the winning 4 × 100-metres relay team took this route.

After the Stockholm Games, Lord Northcliffe, who had raised so much through public subscriptions via the *Daily Mail* to financially assist the London Olympic Games in 1908, looked to raise more in the light of what he viewed as a dismal national failure. By 1913, he had persuaded Sir Arthur Conan Doyle to become a member of an Olympic financial committee.[174] By February 1914, The Duke of Westminster's Olympic Games Fund (1916) stood at just £5,254 and Conan Doyle was challenging the critics who argued that Britain should stand down from the Games when it had been 'defeated' in 1912. Moreover, Conan Doyle argued, the chief nations had already announced their intention to compete in 1916. In order to prepare the team better for the upcoming Berlin Games, the BOA sent representation to Lausanne for an inaugural Psychology and Physiology of Sport Conference in May 1913.[175]

Lord Desborough offered his resignation soon after the BOA returned from Stockholm, more from illness and exhaustion than disappointment at what had been achieved. He had been a skilled figurehead and, in respect of his diplomacy on behalf of the IOC in Britain and in representing British interests at the IOC, the BOA commissioned a bronze bust of the Greek Olympian Hermes of Praxiteles costing £32, as a thank you gift.[176] Desborough deplored the fact that there was no government funding for the BOA but was otherwise optimistic: His Grace, the Duke of Somerset filled Desborough's place as Chair.

The remainder of 1913 and 1914, up to the outbreak of war, was spent trying to finalise talent identification and systematic training schemes, funded by public subscription to the tune of £100,000. Sections of the British press accused the BOA of veiled professionalisation. In the quest to improve upon the Stockholm result, questions of a British Empire team were also debated in order to increase the potential number of representatives, before being rejected as impractical. Instead, the BOA funded approximately 20 Amateur Athletic Association Olympic Novice Competitions in 1913 and 1914 at a cost of £3,000 to seek out new talent, and the events were set over metric distances, rather than measured by imperial units. The Amateur Swimming Association asked for £600 for its own talent identification system.

Meanwhile a general scheme for the award of Olympic standard medals and badges was launched in athletics, boxing, cycling, fencing, gymnastics, shooting, swimming and wrestling.[177] If Olympic results were to be judged as equating to national efficiency, the British sought urgently to modernise. Particularly in track and field athletics and swimming, the use of professional trainers was thought to be indispensable and if the team did well, a bonus scheme for coaches was agreed upon. Had the planned Berlin Games gone ahead, this would have been the best-prepared British team to date. As it was, the money raised for the sixth Olympiad would be invested in a war loan, and the members of the BOA met annually in order to keep a semblance of the organisation during the conflict.

As the Olympic movement was effectively suspended during the First World War, the need for stamina, courage and determination would become highlighted in women's daily lives; at home and abroad. As Dorothy Lambert Chambers saw it, perhaps sportswomen were better prepared in this regard than their less athletic sisters:

> Athletic girls have a great pull over their sisters. If you are skilled and well drilled in discipline and sportsmanship, you are bound to benefit in the strife of the world. You are the better able to face disappointments and sorrows. For what do these strenuous games mean? Exercise in the open air, and exercise of a thorough and engrossing character, carried out with cheerful and stimulating surroundings, with scientific methods, rational aims and absorbing chances. Surely that is the foundation of health culture.[178]

Notes

1. Karl Lennartz 'The Story of the Rings' *Journal of Olympic History* 10: 3 2002 pp. 29–61; Karl Lennartz 'The Story of the Rings Part II' *Journal of Olympic History* 11: 2 2003 pp. 33–37.
2. Margaret Timmers *A Century of Olympic Posters* London: V & A Publishing 2012 p. 14.
3. Alberto Aragón Pérez 'Royalty and the Olympic Games: From Ancient Greece to the Present' *Journal of Olympic History* 23: 2 2015 p. 25.
4. Karl Lennartz 'Two Women Ran the Marathon in 1896' *Citius, Altius, Fortius* 2: 1 1994 pp. 11–12.
5. British Olympic Association *Minutes of British Olympic Council Meeting May 1905, Bath Club British Olympic Association Minute Book 1900–1910* British Olympic Association Archives, Wandsworth, London.
6. Lottie Dod 'Foreword' Denis Foster *Improve Your Tennis* London: Findon Publications 1950 p. iv.
7. Claire Parker 'The Rise of Competitive Swimming 1840–1878' *The Sports Historian* 21: 2 2001 pp. 54–67; Christopher Love 'Social Class and the Swimming World: Amateurs and Professionals' *International Journal of the History of Sport* 24: 5 2007 pp. 603–619.
8. British Olympic Council *Olympic Games of 1908: Programme, Rules and Conditions of Competition for Swimming, Diving and Water Polo* London: British Olympic Council, 1909 p. 4 BOA Archive, London.
9. Lincoln Allison review of D. Porter and S. Wagg (eds.) *Amateurism in British Sport: It Matters Not Who Won or Lost?* (review no. 678) www.history.ac.uk/reviews/paper/porterwagg.html accessed 22 July 2015.
10. British Olympic Association *Minutes of British Olympic Council Meeting 20 December 1906, Bath Club British Olympic Association Minute Book 1900–1910* BOA Archive, London.
11. Lottie Dod 'Foreword' p. iv.

12 Joyce Kay 'It Wasn't Just Emily Davidson! Sport, Suffrage and Society in Edwardian Britain' *The International Journal of the History of Sport* 25: 10 2008 pp. 1338–1354.
13 Lincoln Allison *Amateurism in Sport: An Analysis and Defence* London: Routledge 2001 pp. 165–171.
14 Steve Bailey 'A Noble Ally and Olympic Disciple: The Reverend Robert S. de Courcy Laffan, Coubertin's 'Man' in England *Olympika Volume VI* 1997 pp. 51–64.
15 The British Olympic Association *The British Olympic Association and the Olympic Games* Surrey: G. Donald and Co. Ltd, 1987 pp. 7–11.
16 British Olympic Association *Chasing Gold: Centenary of the British Olympic Association* London: British Olympic Association, 2005 pp. 12–15.
17 The British Olympic Association *The British Olympic Association* p. 8.
18 Maurice Roche *Mega-Events and Modernity: Olympics and Expos in the Growth of Global Culture* London: Routledge, 2000 p. 101.
19 Linda Nead *The Haunted Gallery: Painting, Photography and Film c1900* New Haven and London: Yale University Press, 2007 pp. 34–35.
20 Tony Bijerk, Volker Kluge, Lennart Volker, Karl Lennartz 'The Controversial Questions! The Games of the Second Olympiad in Paris 1900' *Journal of Olympic History: Special Issue* 16: 1 2008 pp. 3–89.
21 Jeffrey A. Auerbach *The Great Exhibition of 1851: a Nation on Display* New Haven and London: Yale University Press, 1999.
22 David Miller *Official History of the Olympic Games and the IOC* London: Mainstream Publishing, 2012.
23 Brian Braithwaite *Women's Magazines: The First 300 years* London: P. Owen, 1995 p. 10.
24 Margaret Timmers *A Century of Olympic Posters* pp. 3–4.
25 Jill Liddington *Vanishing For the Vote: Suffrage, Citizenship and The Battle for The Census* Manchester: Manchester University Press, 2014 p. 36.
26 M. D. Mérillon (ed.) 'Concours D' Exercises Physiques Et De Sports' *Expostition Universelle Internationale de 1900 À Paris: Concours Internationaux D'Exercises Physiques et de Sports* Part One Paris: Ministére Du Commerce, De L'Industrie Des Postes et Des Télégraphes, 1901 pp. 41–47.
27 Stephanie Daniels and Anita Tedder *A Proper Spectacle': Women Olympians 1900–1936* Bedford: Zee Na Na Press, 2000 pp. 3–5.
28 Bill Mallon 'The First Two Women Olympians' *Citius, Altius, Fortius* 3: 3 1995 p. 38.
29 M. D. Mérillon (ed.) 'Sport Hippique' *Expostition Universelle Internationale de 1900 À Paris: Concours Internationaux D'Exercises Physiques et de Sports* Part Two Paris: Ministére Du Commerce, De L'Industrie Des Postes et Des Télégraphes, 1901 pp. 283–289.
30 Bill Mallon 'The First Two Women Olympians' p. 38.
31 Georges Jeanneau (translated by Kate Huang) *Golf and the Olympic Games* Paris: Fédération Française de Golf, 2003 pp. 3–4.
32 M. D. Mérillon (ed.) 'Jeux de Golf' *Expostition Universelle Internationale de 1900 À Paris* Part One pp. 77–78.
33 Paula Welch *The First Woman Olympic Champion of the United States* Gainesville: University of Florida 1982 Women and Sport File: IOC Archive.
34 M. D. Mérillon (ed.) 'Lawn Tennis' *Expostition Universelle Internationale de 1900 À Paris* Part One pp. 70–71.
35 Paula Welch 'Search for Margaret Abbott' *Olympic Review 1982* p. 753 http://library.la84.org/OlympicInformationCenter/OlympicReview/1982/ore182/ORE182s.pdf accessed 30 July 2019.
36 Paula Welch 'Search for Margaret Abbott'.

37 M. D. Mérillon (ed.) 'Jeux de Golf' *Expostition Universelle Internationale de 1900 À Paris* Part One p. 80.
38 Alberto Aragón Pérez 'Royalty and the Olympic Games' p. 25.
39 Anon. 'French Exhibition Tournament' *Lawn Tennis The Official Organ of the Lawn Tennis Association and Croquet (including Badminton)* 5: 25 April 1900 to 3 April 1901 inclusive London: Lawn Tennis and Croquet, 1901 p. 5.
40 Anon 'The Paris International Exhibition Tournament' *Lawn Tennis The Official Organ of the Lawn Tennis Association and Croquet (including Badminton)* 5: 25 April 1900 to 3 April 1901 inclusive London 1901, p. 12.
41 C. A. Voight 'Letter concerning The Paris International Exhibition Tournament dated 27 April 1900' *Lawn Tennis The Official Organ of the Lawn Tennis Association and Croquet (including Badminton)* 5: 25 April 1900 to 3 April 1901 inclusive London 1901, p. 27.
42 C. A. Voight 'Letter concerning The Paris International Exhibition Tournament dated 27 April 1900' p. 12.
43 Heiner Gillmeister *Olympisches Tennis: Die Geschichte der Olympischen Tennisturniere (1896–1992)* Berlin: Sankt Augustin 1993, p. 4.
44 International Olympic Committee *Official Website of the Olympic Movement* www.olympic.org/medallists accessed 23 April 2012.
45 M. D. Mérillon (ed.) 'Lawn Tennis' *Expostition Universelle Internationale de 1900 À Paris* Part One pp. 70–1.
46 Dr Whitcombe Brown 'A Chat with a Lady Champion' *Lawn Tennis The Official Organ of the Lawn Tennis Association and Croquet* Vol. 3 27 April to 5 October 1898 inclusive London: Lawn Tennis, 1898 pp. 229–230.
47 John Barrett and Alan Little *Wimbledon Ladies' Singles Championships 1884–2011* London: Wimbledon Lawn Tennis Museum 2012, pp. 11–13.
48 J. G. Smyth 'Charlotte Renaigle Sterry (née Cooper) 1870–1966' *Oxford Dictionary of National Biography* Oxford University Press www.oxforddnb.com accessed 30 July 2019.
49 Dr Whitcombe Brown 'A Chat with a Lady Champion' p. 230.
50 Mrs Sterry 'My Most Memorable Match' Mrs Lambert Chambers *Lawn Tennis for Ladies* New York: Outing Publishing Company, 1910, pp. 113.
51 Mark Ryan 'Muriel Robb (1878–1907): A Little-Known Wimbledon Singles Champion' *Tennis Forum* www.tennisforum.com accessed 24 April 2019.
52 Dr Whitcombe Brown 'A Chat with a Lady Champion' p. 230.
53 Charles P. Lucas (ed.) *The Olympic Games 1904* St Louis: Woodward and Tiernan Printing Co. 1905.
54 Margaret Timmers *A Century of Olympic Posters* pp. 7–8.
55 James E. Sullivan (ed.) *Spalding's Official Athletic Almanac for 1905 Special Olympic Number Containing The Official Report of the Olympic Games of 1904* New York: The American Publishing Company 1905 pp. 241–243.
56 Bill Mallon, *The 1904 Olympic Games: Results for All Competitors in All Events*, Jefferson: McFarland & Company, 1999 pp. 47–8.
57 Jim Greensfelder, Jim Lally, Bob Christianson and Max Storm *1904 Olympic Games St Louis Missouri: Official Medals and Badges* Cincinnati: GVL Enterprises, 2001 p. 5.
58 Karl Lennartz 'The Second International Olympic Games in Athens 1906' *Journal of Olympic History* Vol. 10 2002 pp. 10–27.
59 Bill Mallon & Ian Buchanan *The 1908 Olympic Games: Results for All Competitors in All Events, with Commentary* Jefferson: McFarland & Company, 2000 p. 3.
60 Lord Desborough of Taplow, letter to De Coubertin, May 14, 1906 Correspondence of the NOC of Great Britain 1892–1927 file: IOC Archive, Lausanne (emphasis in the original).

61 Jane Ridley and Claire Percy 'Ethel Anne Priscilla Grenfell, Lady Desborough (1867–1952)' *Oxford Dictionary of National Biography* Oxford University Press www.oxforddnb.com/view/article/40733 accessed 4 January 2019.
62 British Olympic Association '*Council Meeting: Minutes 108 Victoria Street 14 April 1908*' p. 3 BOA Archive, London.
63 British Olympic Association '*Council Meeting: Minutes The Bath Club, Dover Street 11 March 1907*' p. 2 BOA Archive, London.
64 British Olympic Association '*Council Meeting: Minutes The Bath Club, Dover Street 18 February 1907*' p. 2 BOA Archive, London.
65 British Olympic Association *Plan of Stadium For International Sports Exhibition and The Olympic Games London 1908 IV International Olympiad 18 February 1907* BOA Archive, London.
66 British Olympic Council '*Council Meeting: Minutes The Bath Club, Dover Street 20 December 1906*' p. 3 BOA Archive, London.
67 British Olympic Association '*Council Meeting: Minutes of the Finance Committee Emergency Meeting 108 Victoria Street 12 May 1908*' p. 2 BOA Archive, London.
68 Rebecca Jenkins *The First London Olympics 1908* London: Piaktus, 2008 p. xv.
69 British Olympic Association *Yearbook 1914: Containing information with regard to The International Olympic Committee, the British Olympic Council and Record of the International Olympic Games* BOA Archive, London pp. 58–59.
70 *The Sporting Life* 'Olympic Games of London 1908: A Complete Record with Photographs of Winners of the Olympic Games held at the Stadium, Shepherd's Bush London July 13–25' London: *The Sporting Life*, 1908 pp. 181 BOA Archive .
71 Anon. *The Graphic: An Illustrated Weekly Newspaper* 1 August 1908 Front Page.
72 British Olympic Association *Olympic Games of 1908: Programme of the Marathon Race Windsor Castle to the Great Stadium Shepherd's Bush 24 July 1908* London: Vail and Co., 1908.
73 Bill Mallon & Ian Buchanan *The 1908 Olympic Games* p. 12.
74 British Olympic Council *Council Meeting: Minutes 21 October 1907 108 Victoria Street* BOA Archive, London.
75 *The Sporting Life* 'Olympic Games of London 1908' pp. 124–145.
76 Anthony Dod *Rectory From Church Gate: Welford Park Archery Club* Lottie Dod Collection Wimbledon Lawn Tennis Museum and Archive (hereafter Lottie Dod Collection).
77 Anthony Dod *Brightwalton Church Porch: Welford Park Archery Club* Lottie Dod Collection.
78 Alan Little *Lottie Dod Wimbledon Champion and All Rounder Extraordinary* London: Wimbledon, 1993 p. 15.
79 British Olympic Council *Olympic Games of 1908: Programme, Rules and Conditions of Competition for Swimming, Diving and Water Polo* London: British Olympic Council, 1909 p. 4 BOA Archive, London.
80 British Olympic Association *Olympic Games of 1908: Archery Programme Rules and Conditions of Competition 1908* London: Vail and Co., 1908 p. 3. BOA Archive, London.
81 *The Sporting Life* 'Olympic Games of London 1908' pp. 211–212.
82 James Bancroft 'Sybil Fenton 'Queenie' Newall 1854–1929' *Oxford Dictionary of National Biography* Oxford University Press www.oxforddnb.com accessed 24 July 2019.
83 *The Sporting Life* 'Olympic Games of London 1908' p. 211.
84 *The Sporting Life* 'Olympic Games of London 1908' p. 141.
85 Lottie Dod *Commemorative Clock: NLTS Ladies Doubles Consolation Prize won by Annie and Lottie Dod June 1883* Lottie Dod Collection.

86 Julian Marshall (ed.) 'Lottie Dod' *The Annals of Lawn-Tennis 12 May 1886* London: Lawn Tennis, 1886 p. 23.
87 Toupie Lowther 'Ladies Play' R. F. and H. L. Doherty (eds.) *Lawn Tennis* London: Lawn Tennis, 1903 p. 66.
88 Anthony Dod 'Edgeworth: Lottie, Tony and William on the Tennis Court' Lottie Dod Collection.
89 J. M. Heathcote *Tennis Lawn Tennis Rackets and Fives The Badminton Library* London: Longman's and Co., 1891 p. 307.
90 Sally-Anne Dod *Lottie Dod's Climbing Expeditions undated* Lottie Dod Collection.
91 Jeffrey Pearson *Lottie Dod: Champion of Champions, The Story of an Athlete* Wirral: Countyvise, 1988 p. 16.
92 Anthony Dod 'England and Ireland Rematch 1900' Lottie Dod Collection.
93 Anthony Dod 'Spital Ladies Hockey Club' undated Lottie Dod Collection.
94 Jeffrey Pearson *Lottie Dod: Champion of Champions* pp. 53–55.
95 James Huntingdon-Whitely and Richard Holt *The Book of British Sporting Heroes* London: National Portrait Gallery, 1999 p. 88.
96 Anthony Dod 'Crowds on the Links at the Ladies Golf Championship 1904' and 'Golf Clubs' Lottie Dod Collection.
97 Anthony Dod 'Champion and Medallists at the Ladies Golf Championship 1904' and 'Golf Clubs' Lottie Dod Collection.
98 Anon. 'Our Portraits: Lady Lawn Tennis Players' *The Queen: The Lady's Newspaper* 29 July 1892 p. 108 Lottie Dod Collection.
99 Anthony Dod 'Brightwalton Rectory Cricket Match 1906'; 'Brightwalton Rectory Cricket Match 1907'; 'Brightwalton Rectory Cricket Match 1908'; 'Brightwalton Rectory Cricket Match 1909' and 'Brightwalton Rectory Cricket Match 1910' Lottie Dod Collection.
100 Jerome D. Travers 'The Fifteenth National Women's Championship' *The American Golfer* 3: 1 November 1909 p. 1; Innis Brown 'Women Crusaders Lined Up' *The American Golfer* 24: 7 July 1921 p. 15.
101 Jeffrey Pearson *Lottie Dod: Champion of Champions* p. 18.
102 Cecil Bear 'The Old Lady Of The Courts' *World Sports* June 1957 London: Country and Sporting Publications, 1957 p. 11.
103 Bill Mallon & Ian Buchanan *The 1908 Olympic Games* p. 43.
104 Rebecca Jenkins *The First London Olympics 1908* p. 65.
105 *The Sporting Life* 'Olympic Games of London 1908' p. 205.
106 Anon. 'Olympic Games Draw' *Lawn Tennis and Badminton The Official Organ of the Lawn Tennis Association 20 February to 1 October 1908 inclusive* London: Lawn Tennis and Croquet, 1908 p. 879.
107 *The Sporting Life* 'Olympic Games of London' 1908 p. 202.
108 *The Sporting Life* 'Yachting' Olympic Games of London 1908 pp. 195–196.
109 Judith Wilson 'Florence Madeline 'Madge' Syers [née Cave] 1881–1917' *Oxford Dictionary of National Biography* Oxford University Press www.oxforddnb.com accessed 24 July 2015.
110 British Olympic Association *Council Meeting: Minutes of the Finance Committee Emergency Meeting 108 Victoria Street 31 December 1908* p. 6 BOA Archive, London.
111 Theodore Cook *The Olympic Games of 1908 in London: A Reply to Certain Criticisms* London: Amateur Athletic Association, 1908.
112 Thomas Rugby Burlford *American Hatred and British Folly* London: Thomas Rugby Burlford 1910.
113 British Olympic Association *Olympic Games of London 1908: Programme and General Regulations* IV International Olympiad London: Vail and Co., 1908 p. 4.

114 British Olympic Association *Council Meeting: Minutes of the Finance Committee Emergency Meeting 108 Victoria Street 2 December 1908* p. 5 British Olympic Association Archive.
115 Robert K. Barney 'The Olympic Games in Modern Times: An Overview' in Gerald P. Schaus and Stephen R. Wenn (eds) *Onward to the Olympics: Historical Perspectives on The Olympic Games* Waterloo, Ontario: Wilfred Laurier University Press, 2007 p. 221.
116 Patricia Campbell Warner *When the Girls Came Out to Play* Amerhurst and Boston: University of Massachusetts Press, 2006 p. 90.
117 British Olympic Association *Council Meeting Room 18 Caxton Hall 28 November 1911* p. 1 BOA Archive, London.
118 British Olympic Association *Council Meeting Room 18 Caxton Hall 16 January 1912* p. 2 BOA Archive, London.
119 British Olympic Association *Council Meeting Room 1 Caxton Hall 30 June 1910* p. 4 BOA Archive, London.
120 Erik Bergvall (translated Edward Adams-Ray) *The Fifth Olympiad: The Official Report Of The Olympic Games of Stockholm 1912* pp. 66–72.
121 Jean Williams, 'Jane 'Jennie' Fletcher (1890–1968)' *Oxford Dictionary of National Biography* Oxford University Press www.oxforddnb.com/view/article/102443 accessed 8 July 2015.
122 Sport Scotland 'Isabella 'Belle' Mary Moore (1894–1975)' *Scottish Sports Hall of Fame* Sport Scotland www.sportscotland.org.uk/sshf/Isabella_Mary_Moore accessed 8 July 2015.
123 Win Hayes 'Lucy Morton (1898–1980)' *Oxford Dictionary of National Biography* www.oxforddnb.com accessed 14 July 2015.
124 Jean Williams 'The Most Important Photograph in the History of Women's Olympic Participation: Jennie Fletcher and the British 4 × 100 Freestyle relay team at the Stockholm 1912 Games' in Martin Polley (ed.) *Sport in History, Special Issue: Britain, Britons and the Olympic Games* 32: 2 pp. 204–230.
125 Jean Williams 'Aquadynamics and the Athletocracy: Jennie Fletcher and the British Women's 4 × 100 metre Freestyle Relay Team at the 1912 Stockholm Olympic Games' *Costume* 46: 2 Summer 2012 pp. 145–164.
126 Erik Bergvall 'Plate 36 Winners in the Fifth Olympiad Fanny Durack 100 m Free style [sic] Ladies and Great Britain's team in 400m Team Race for Ladies' [sic] *The Fifth Olympiad: The Official Report Of The Olympic Games of Stockholm 1912* Part Two p. 851.
127 Dave Day *Professionals, Amateurs and Performance: Sports Coaching in England, 1789–1914* Bern: Peter Lang, 2012 p. 84.
128 I am grateful to Steve Humphries of Leicester City Council for his collection of paperwork on this issue, including personal communication with Betty Smith, Jennie's only daughter of her six children. Much of the personal information that follows relies on this family history and the scrapbook of Jennie's career that accompanied the sale of her gold medal at Graham Budd auctions, London in July 2012.
129 'John Frederick Fletcher: 1 & 3 & 5 Checkett's Road Belgrave Leicester', *Schedule 35 Census of England and Wales 1911*, National Archives, London, www.nationalarchives.gov.uk. I am grateful to Margaret Roberts for this reference and subsequent genealogical details about the Fletcher and Hyslop families.
130 Jennie Hyslop *Letter to Dr George Feledi Teeswater Ontario 11 May 1965* London: Graham Budd Auctions, 2012.
131 Jennie Hyslop *Scrapbook of Swimming Career* Graham Budd Auctions, 2012.
132 Anon, *ASA Handbook 1903 Containing List of English Swimming Clubs, Laws of Swimming and Rules of Water Polo, Past and Present Champions, Programme for the*

Year London: J. Littlewood, 1904; Anon, *ASA Handbook 1905 Containing List of English Swimming Clubs, Laws of Swimming and Rules of Water Polo, Past and Present Champions, Programme for the Year* London: J. Littlewood, 1906.
133 Jennie Hyslop *Scrapbook of Swimming Career* Graham Budd Auctions, 2012.
134 Jennie Hyslop *Letter to Dr George Feledi Teeswater Ontario 11 May 1965* London: Graham Budd Auctions, 2012.
135 Anon. '100 Yards Ladies' Swimming Championship' *The Times* 4 September 1908 p. 7.
136 Jennie Hyslop *Letter to Dr George Feledi Teeswater Ontario 11 May 1965* London: Graham Budd Auctions, 2012.
137 Betty Smith *Letter to Steve Humphries 15 December 2004* Leicester: Steve Humphries Collection.
138 Jennie Hyslop *Letter to Dr George Feledi Teeswater Ontario 11 May 1965* London: Graham Budd Auctions, 2012.
139 Jennie Hyslop *Scrapbook of Swimming Career* Graham Budd Auctions, 2012.
140 Henry Irving Hyslop *Last Will and Testament* 17 November 1993 Ontario, Canada; Turner and Porter Funeral Directors *Proof of Death Certificate: Henry Irving Hyslop* 21 March 2000 London: Graham Budd Auctions, 2012.
141 Erik Bergvall 'Plate 263 100 m Free style Ladies Final' *Official Report Stockholm 1912* Part Two p. 700.
142 Jean Williams and Mark Curthoys 'Isabella McAlpine [Bella, Belle] Moore (1894–1975)' *Oxford Dictionary of National Biography*: Oxford University Press, 2014 www.oxforddnb.com/view/article/102443 accessed 3 August 2019.
143 Erik Bergvall 'Plate 263 100 m Free style Ladies Final' *Official Report Stockholm 1912* Part Two p. 726.
144 Jo Manning 'First champ "would be thrilled"' *BBC News* 11 August 2008 http://news.bbc.co.uk/1/hi/wales/7554196.stm accessed 8 December 2019.
145 Jean Williams and Mark Curthoys 'Irene Steer (1889–1977)' *Oxford Dictionary of National Biography*: Oxford University Press, 2014 www.oxforddnb.com/view/article/102443 accessed 3 August 2019.
146 Jean Williams and Mark Curthoys 'Annie Coupe Speirs (1889–1926)' *Oxford Dictionary of National Biography*: Oxford University Press, www.oxforddnb.com/view/article/102443 accessed 3 August 2019.
147 Erik Bergvall *The Fifth Olympiad: The Official Report of the Olympic Games of Stockholm 1912* p. 749.
148 International Olympic Committee 'Searchable Database of Olympic Medallists' www.olympic.org/medallists accessed 16 July 2015.
149 Erik Bergvall *The Fifth Olympiad: The Official Report of the Olympic Games of Stockholm 1912* Part Two pp. 620–625.
150 British Olympic Association *Council Meeting: Minutes Room 13 Caxton Hall 2 April 1913* p. 2 BOA Archive, London.
151 Alan Tomlinson 'Olympic survivals: The Olympic Games as a global phenomenon' in Lincoln Allison (ed.) *The Global Politics of Sport: The Role of Global Institutions in Sport* Oxon: Routledge, 2005.
152 Alan Little *Tennis and the Olympic Games* London: Wimbledon Lawn Tennis Museum, 2009 p. 3.
153 Karl Lennartz, Stephen Wassong, Thomas Zawadzki (eds.), *New Aspects of Sport History: The Olympic Lectures, Proceedings of the 9th ISHPES Congress* Cologne: Academia Verlag 2007 p. 10.
154 Anthony Dod 'Charlotte Sterry (Five Times Wimbledon Champion) on second left and Lottie Dod (Five Times Wimbledon Champion) on the right. The Roehampton Club 1929' Lottie Dod Collection.

155 Mark Pottle 'Dorothea Katharine Lambert Chambers [née Douglass] (1878–1960)' *Oxford Dictionary of National Biography* Oxford University Press www.oxforddnb.com/view/article/32353 accessed 23 April 2019.
156 John Barrett and Alan Little *Wimbledon: Ladies' Singles Champions* p. 12.
157 Wimbledon Lawn Tennis Museum *Roll of Honour* http://aeltc2011.wimbledon.com/players/rolls-of-honour/ladies-singles accessed 14 July 2019.
158 Mrs Lambert Chambers *Lawn Tennis for Ladies* London: Methuen & Co. Ltd, 1910 p. 25.
159 Alan Little *Suzanne Lenglen: Tennis Idol of the Twenties* London: Wimbledon Lawn Tennis Museum, 2005.
160 James Huntingdon-Whitely and Richard Holt *British Sporting Heroes* p. 88.
161 Jeremy Malies 'Charlotte 'Lottie' Dod (1871–1960)' *Oxford Dictionary of National Biography* Oxford University Press www.oxforddnb.com/view/article/37363 accessed 7 January 2019.
162 Hugh D. Hewitt Soar 'Alice Blanche Legh (1856–1948)' *Oxford Dictionary of National Biography* Oxford University Press www.oxforddnb.com accessed 24 May 2019.
163 Miss Alice Legh 'Ladies' Archery' in C. J. Longman and H. Walrond (eds.) *Archery: The Badminton Library of Sports and Pastimes* London: Longmans, Green and Company, 1894 pp. 380–392.
164 James Bancroft 'Sybil Fenton 'Queenie' Newall 1854–1929'.
165 *The Sporting Life* 'Archery: Olympic Games of London 1908 pp. 211–212.
166 BOA *Gymnastic Display Pass: Olympic Games of London 1908* London: Graham Budd Auctions, 2012.
167 Anon. 'Last Meeting in the Stadium Before Opening of Olympic Games' *The Daily Mirror* 13 July 1908.
168 J. E. K. Studd *Letter of Congratulations to Florence Sandell, The Polytechnic 15 May 1908* London: Graham Budd Auctions, 2012.
169 J. E. K. Studd *Letter of Congratulations to Florence Sandell, The Polytechnic 27 May 1908*; Anon. 'The Olympic Games Displays' *The Sporting Life* 27 May 1908 unpaginated London: Graham Budd Auctions, 2012.
170 Anon. 'Cricket Match: Ladies v Gents' *The Sporting Life* 27 May 1908 unpaginated London: Graham Budd Auctions, 2012.
171 Peter Bilsborough, 'Jarvis, John Arthur (1872–1933)' *Oxford Dictionary of National Biography* www.oxforddnb.com/view/article/65070 accessed 15 October 2011; International Swimming Hall of Fame 'John Arthur Jarvis: Honor Swimmer, 1968' www.ishof.org/honorees/68/68jajarvis accessed 15 July 2015.
172 Jennie Hyslop *Scrapbook of Swimming Career* Graham Budd Auctions, 2012.
173 Anon. *ASA Handbook 1902 Containing List of English Swimming Clubs, Laws of Swimming and Rules of Water Polo, Past and Present Champions, Programme for the Year* Gainsborough: J. Littlewood, 1903; British Swimming Archive, Loughborough.
174 Peter Lovesey 'Conan Doyle and The Olympics' *Journal of Olympic History* 10 December 2001 pp. 6–9.
175 British Olympic Association *Council Meeting Room 13 Caxton Hall 2 April 1913* p. 5 British Olympic Association Archive.
176 British Olympic Association *Council Meeting Room 1 Caxton Hall 18 December 1912* p. 4 BOA Archive, London.
177 British Olympic Association *Council Meeting Room 13 Caxton Hall 22 July 1913* p. 5 BOA Archive, London.
178 Mrs Lambert Chambers *Lawn Tennis for Ladies* p. 5.

Chapter 2

The Olympic inter-war revival and the British Olympic Association

Gladys Carson and the 1924 Paris Games

Introduction: from Antwerp in 1920 to Paris 1924

When Gladys Hewitt (née Carson 1903–1987) was interviewed for *Radio Leicester* in 1976 along with her son, David, and daughter, Josie, she was asked to describe the general reaction to women taking part in competitive sports when she was young. Gladys replied: 'A good many people have said to me: "Oh well, in those days of ladies taking part in sports it must have been easy to train and swim, with very little competition". But that is where they were wrong. It was *very* difficult' (Gladys Carson interview).[1]

This disapproval did not prevent her from continuing to compete. As a 21-year-old, Gladys claimed the bronze medal in the women's 200-metres breaststroke race at the 1924 Paris Olympic Games, in the same race that Blackpool's Lucy Morton (aged 26 years old) won the gold.[2] Even in 1924, the difference between winning an Olympic gold and a bronze medal could be considerable, in terms of a national profile. Unlike Lucy Morton, Gladys Carson would remain a local heroine of the Olympic Games with few people outside of her home county of Leicestershire and the East Midlands aware of her accomplishments. But her connections to sporting networks were transnational.

The British Olympic Association were by no means sure that the Olympic Games would be continued after the Great War. However, the relationship between the British Olympic Association and the International Olympic Committee became increasingly close during this period. There was no female presence on either board, in spite of the considerable expertise of women sports administrators in cricket, golf, football, hockey, swimming, tennis and track and field athletics, to name but a few.[3] The BOA and IOC minutes mention the occasional typist or secretary, so the organisations were not entirely without female staff, but these rare exceptions prove the general rule that both were all-male clubs. It was also clear that the committee members were not primarily interested in providing competitive opportunities for women. The BOA required considerable resources if its athletes were to compete on a world stage with distinction. The problem was how best to fund that aspiration.

Understandably, during the Great War, the international Olympic movement was effectively moribund. The official act, which sealed the establishment of the IOC at Lausanne, Switzerland 10 April 1915, at least gave a permanent base in a neutral country.[4] The British Olympic Association Revenue Account for the year ending 31 December 1918, reported an operating cost of £35.11.00 and an overall balance of £603.09.09, including £550 invested in a War Loan with interest at 5 per cent.[5] The Chair, the Reverend de Courcy Laffan, reported that the work of the IOC had been practically suspended for the duration of the war since the Paris Congress of June 1914. However, the BOA was in an optimistic mood regarding a forthcoming Lausanne meeting to celebrate the 25th anniversary of the revival of the modern Olympic Games. Board members of the BOA discussed a possible 1920 Olympic Games in Paris (Germany and Austria would be excluded). This chapter briefly covers the revival of competition in Antwerp in 1920 before moving onto the Paris Games of 1924 and the case study of Gladys Carson.

In Antwerp there was little infrastructure and few concessions were made to spectators. Nevertheless, the symbolic importance of honouring the people of Belgium and their suffering during the Great War was significant internationally. Some 29 nations made the trip, represented by approximately 2,626 athletes of whom just 65 were female. These are estimates. The number of entries for Olympic events often exceeded those who actually competed and so it can be difficult to be precise, even when using the official reports. Substitutes and squad members confuse the issue, as do a range of ancillary roles (such as chaperones) connected with participation. This said, it is clear that increasing numbers of British working class athletes achieved public acclaim as a result of their Olympic victories during the inter-war period. Examples included 31-year-old railway guard Albert Hill from Tooting, who received national honours after taking the 800-metres and 1500-metres gold medals.[6]

Popular misconceptions about the Paris Olympic Games are evident in the fictionalised Hugh Hudson film *Chariots of Fire* released in 1981.[7] There are elements of truth, in that Harold Abrahams won the 100-metres sprint and Eric Liddell the 400-metres gold medal and the 200-metres bronze at the Paris 1924 Olympic Games. Unlike the film, in which Eric Liddell's religious convictions clashed with his wish to race in the 100-metres final, both he and the BOA knew in January 1924 that a preliminary round of the race fell on a Sunday. As well as Abrahams receiving coaching support from Sam Mussabini, the BOA awarded £2,250 to the Amateur Athletic Association, a further £500 for the Scottish Amateur Athletic Association and £1,190 to refurbish both the White City and Crystal Palace before the 1924 Games.[8] Thus, the story of what constitutes British Olympic tradition requires re-examination.

The Paris 1924 Olympic Games would be the most cosmopolitan to date, involving 44 National Olympic Committees (NOCs) represented by something like 3,089 athletes, of whom roughly 135 were women.[9] Of the total number of female entrants in Paris, 51 were swimming and 26 diving competitors. Significantly, there was an expansion in the number and variety of women's swimming events in a purpose-built facility, with improved accuracy in timing and clean water. The 200-metres breaststroke and 100-metres backstroke were added to the programme along with the inaugural 400-metres freestyle race, the longest for individual female competitors at that point (and replacing the 300-metres race in 1920).

This chapter seeks to fill a lacunae in the academic literature on Olympism, which has been influenced by wider *Chariots of Fire*-style sentimentality in largely neglecting the working class amateur, and women's experiences. Gladys trained as a domestic science teacher and could therefore be seen as part of a growing professional class, there is plenty of evidence that going to Paris was a life-changing experience, and not just in sporting terms.

Carson was quite elderly and unwell when the *Radio Leicester* interview was conducted and the sound quality was not very good. Most of the information about her in what follows comes from family interviews and Gladys' extant papers, most of which were collected into a scrapbook. I met with Gladys' son David Hewitt at his home on 7 July 2011 and we corresponded for over three years regarding his family history. Archival evidence from the British Olympic Association and International Olympic Committee also contextualises Gladys' achievements. These documents show the wider social networks that sport enabled her to access. There are also several contemporary texts showing how increasingly mediated the Olympic Games would become. Even relatively short amateur Olympic careers, such as Gladys Carson's, demonstrate growing consumerist and commercial trends in swimming particularly and women's sport more generally during the 1920s and 1930s.[10]

Readers may well be surprised that I have focused on another swimmer for the case study in this chapter. But this reflects the gendered nature of British Olympic participation. Track and field athletics was evidently the jewel in the BOA crown and the Olympic events in which the British sporting establishment thought most worthy of investment during the inter-war period. Both the National Cyclists Union (£1,000) and the National Amateur Wrestling Association (£800) also benefitted from enhanced BOA funding in 1924, but no Olympic women's events would exist in these sports until 1984 and 2004, respectively. In comparison, it cost a further £700 to send the men and women swimmers and divers to Paris in 1924. The support of the BOA was therefore vital. Swimming and diving also provided the widest range of competitive opportunities for women Olympians, well before Britain sent a team of women's track and field athletics specialists for the first time to the Olympic Games in Los Angeles in 1932.

Antwerp 1920 and the British Olympic Association

With the announcement of the Antwerp Olympic Games between 20 April and 12 September 1920, the BOA was galvanised to try and raise £30,000 to promote sports participation more generally and to widen the search for talent. Lord Downham accepted the role of Chair, upon the Duke of Somerset's resignation, although he was to become ill and die on 2 July 1920. The fund would only realise a little over £6,000 and so the BOA's aims were modified accordingly:[11]

> The ultimate and most important object of the British Olympic Council must not be forgotten. The experience of the Army during the war has shown that there are multitudes of men who have hitherto been only spectators of sport, but who take to it with keenness and success when the opportunity is given them of doing so. Our object is to bring such opportunities within the reach of all; not only that we provide them with healthy recreation, and make them physically fit, but that in the practice of sport they may learn those lessons of discipline, comradeship, cooperation and even of leadership, which are the foundations of good citizenship.[12]

The Municipality of Antwerp asked for help from the Belgian government to refurbish the city. Antwerp's local politicians emphasised the strategic importance of the national harbour and the symbolic impact of Belgium being able to host an international event so soon after a major conflict.[13] A Palace of Ice was among the technologically advanced venues. Although Antwerp would have preferred to host the Games in 1921, it was decided that 1920 was preferable and so luxuries were dispensable. A lottery scheme sought to raise funding. Although Germany and Austria were not invited, the Games were laden with emblems of universality at the Opening Ceremony. These included the Olympic flag with five interlocking rings and an Olympic oath taken on behalf of competitors. Other representations of peace included the release of doves.

Count Clary, President of the French Olympic Committee, reminded his colleagues at the IOC of the need to abide by resolutions voted at the 1914 Congress in Paris, including a case for more female events:

> There is no doubt that we must begin at once to give great attention to the physical education and sporting education of women. A considerable evolution has taken place since 1914, and we should at once face the question of the place which should be made in the Olympic Games of 1924 for Women's Athletics (sic) in all its forms. By the side of the Men's Olympiad, should doubtless be held simultaneously a Women's Olympiad.[14]

The British Amateur Fencing Association also made a request that a women's Foil event be added, and it was included in the Paris 1924 Olympic programme.[15]

The BOA preparations for Antwerp included liaising with the Foreign Office and the government in order to formally accept the invitation to compete; securing the services of keen sportsmen of independent means to Chair sub-committees (housing, transport, competitors); selling the Invested Funds (which realised £522) and employing a shorthand typist on a salary of £50 per year.[16] Even so, office space was in such short supply that many of the BOA meetings were held at the Football Association in Russell Square or one of the other sporting bodies, most frequently the Adelphi headquarters of the Amateur Athletic Association (AAA).

Lack of funds did not prevent the BOA from being snobbish. When the clothing firm Messrs T. H. Downing & Co. Ltd of Leicester offered to donate the British team's ceremonial and sporting uniforms at no cost, the Equipment Committee was careful to draft a letter to appear in the trade journals avoiding the statement that it had 'selected' the supplier. Although the BOA accepted the free Downing and Co. clothes, its officials had insisted upon seeing samples of better quality flannel and other materials to ensure that they met the standard required.[17]

In January 1920, the King headed up a public appeal with a gift of £100 and the message:

> His Majesty recognises that the appeal now being made is not only on behalf of the Olympic Games, but is intended to provide for playing fields throughout the country, and for the encouragement of Sport [sic], outdoor exercises and recreations, which are indispensable to the physical and moral welfare of the people.[18]

The BOA felt a moral imperative, but were limited in funds. The appeal seems never to have reached above £6,000 in firm donations, even by the time that the competitors had returned from Antwerp. By 23 July 1920 plans had to be modified further still to house the British competitors in a refurbished local Antwerp school in the Longue Rue d'Argile at a cost of £1,500.

A further sum of £1,670 was estimated for three square meals, provided by British catering contractors Messing and Co. At a fixed cost of 28 Francs a day, Messing and Co. would provide each British participant with the following robust menu:

> Breakfast – eggs & bacon, boiled eggs, fish when practicable [sic], tea, coffee, chocolate, stale bread, toast, marmalade and butter.
>
> Lunch – one egg dish, cold joints, salads, vegetables, chops or steaks, milk pudding and compote of fruit. Steaks or chops and cold joints will not be provided on the same day [sic].
>
> Dinner – soup, hot roast beef or mutton, vegetables, milk puddings, blancmange, custard, stewed fruits.
>
> (At luncheon and dinner lager beer or minerals will also be provided.)[19]

Given that there had been food shortages and rationing during the war, British contestants could expect to be eating well, if not from a particularly inspiring menu.

The female star of the 1920 Antwerp Games, was French tennis player Suzanne Lenglen, *La Divine*, as she was called by the French press.[20] She had already achieved international recognition, having lost in the final of the French Championship in 1914, aged 14 and was forced to suspend her tennis career during the war. Lenglen returned to win Wimbledon in 1919 as an amateur, retaining the women's singles title every year until 1924 and winning it again in 1925. Lenglen gave up only four games in the Olympic women's singles in Antwerp, three of them in the final against Britain's Edith Dorothy Holman. Lenglen took a second Olympic gold in the mixed doubles with Max Décugis and a bronze in the women's doubles partnered by Élisabeth d'Ayen. She would go on to a well publicised rivalry with Californian Helen Wills Moody and a lucrative touring professional career, in addition to coaching and diversification into fashion lines at Selfridges and other big stores.[21] For the International Tennis Hall of Fame, she remains: 'The greatest woman tennis player in the first half of the twentieth century'.[22]

In Antwerp, British tennis stars were also much in evidence. Kathleen 'Kitty' McKane took the women's singles bronze medal for Britain in a match against Sigrid Fick of Sweden.[23] McKane and Winifred McNair took the gold in the women's doubles, after which McKane also partnered one of Britain's finest all-round sportsmen, Maxwell Woosnam, to take the silver medal in the mixed doubles.[24] Edith Dorothy Holman also won a silver medal in the ladies' doubles with Winifred Geraldine Ramsey Beamish, whose husband Alfred also competed. The four British female tennis players more than made up for their BOA places with their returns in medals.

Though not as famous as Lenglen, Kitty McKane was also able to celebrate a degree of transnational recognition. In January 1926, McKane married Leslie Godfree while on a tennis tour in South Africa and, on their return, won the mixed doubles at Wimbledon: the only married couple to complete the task. She won her second Wimbledon singles title the same year, and came runner-up in the women's doubles. Also a gifted badminton champion and winner of four All England singles titles, Kitty came from a sporting family and her sister Margaret was just as well known.

Antwerp was also the first Olympic Games where the United States Olympic Association (USOA) had sent a team of women swimmers. Although the BOA and the USA sent six female entrants to the swimming events, they were not equal in competitive terms. Specialist preparation and technocratic coaching expertise helped the American women take home nearly all of the medals. Of the three women's swimming events in 1920 (100-metres individual freestyle, 300-metres individual freestyle and the 4 × 100-metres freestyle relay), the only two medals not won by Americans were the British team relay silver, won by Hilda James, Constance Jeans,

Grace McKenzie and Charlotte Radcliffe; and the bronze taken by Sweden. This was more or less a given, as only three national teams had entered the women's relay race. James, McKenzie and Radcliffe were all members of the Garston swimming club in Merseyside. A fourth Garston swimmer, Lillian Birkenhead, was the youngest member of the entire British squad, travelling to Belgium at the age of 15 years 217 days. Florence Sancroft, aged 17, completed the women's team and was eliminated in the 300-metres heats.

Of the three men and two women in the British diving team at Antwerp, Eileen Armstrong of Hendon won a silver medal, aged 26. London-born Belle White was an even more impressive athlete. White had won a bronze medal in the 1912 Stockholm Olympic Games in the 10-metre platform dive event.[25] Though not among the medals in the 1920, 1924 or 1928 Olympic Games, White went on to win the gold in the 1927 European Championships, thereby sustaining a diving career of 16 years at the highest competitive level.

This was all the more remarkable because some commentators considered diving harmful for the supposedly delicate constitutions of women and girls. That said, competitors in Antwerp had to risk diving into a

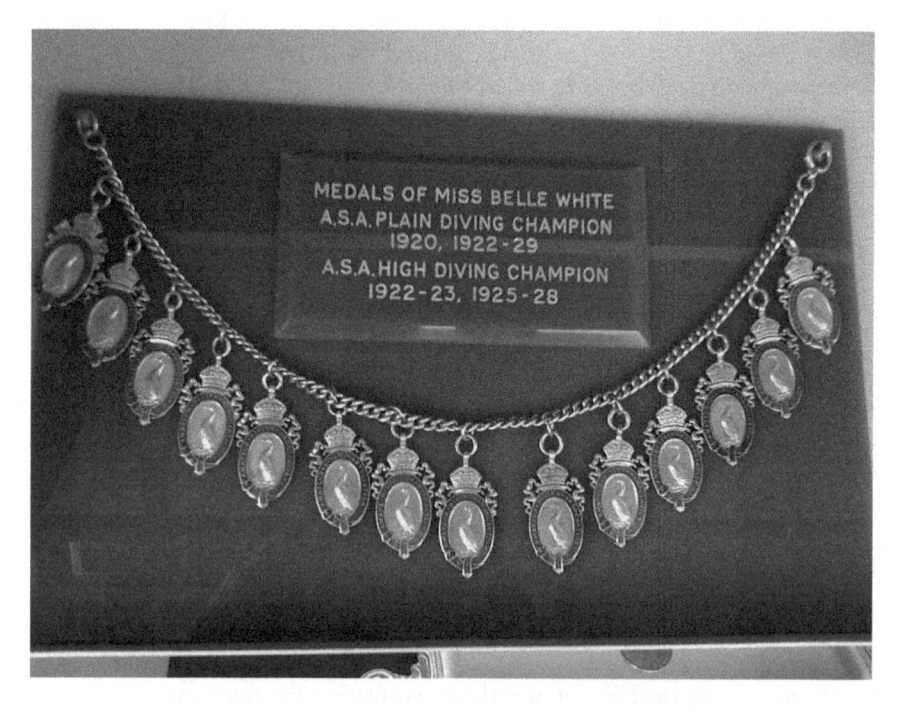

Figure 2.1 A.S.A. Championship Diving medals of Belle White, an Olympian of four games, the last in 1928, and a bronze medallist of 1912.
Source: British Swimming Collection, Loughborough.

canal-basin where the water was silted with mud. This made calculating the exact point of entry into water challenging. Although many female and male divers used gymnastic routines to develop their balance and coordination on dry land, the hazards when diving into open water were not to be underestimated.

As well as the lawn tennis players, swimmers and divers, Britain's Dorothy Wright took gold in the 7-metre class sailing event in 1920 along with her husband Cyril, and co-competitors Robert Coleman and Robert Madison. Phyllis Johnson, who had become a silver medallist in 1908 in the mixed pairs skating event with James H. Johnson, won bronze in 1920 with Basil Williams, and also finished fourth in the singles event, at the age of 33. This still makes her one of the eldest Olympic skating female medallists today. Johnson would go on to become British champion in 1921. By 1924 the skating programme had become part of the Winter Olympics, rather than on the Summer schedule.

Although a pragmatic response to an urgent situation, housing and feeding all the athletes and administrators together was later considered by BOA officials to have contributed to a good *espirit de corps* among the British team. A total of £900 was spent on travel fares, £105 for food en route to Belgium, £500 fees for passports and £900 split between office accommodation in London and Antwerp. This left just over £100 for incidentals. Additionally, most associations with a majority of working class participants (swimming, boxing, wrestling, gymnastics and so on) were awarded around £100 to help competitors to get to London. By 12 November 1920, the BOA realised that it had a deficit of £1,000, although after adjustments this was reduced to £650 and the arguments over who was entitled to what rumbled on for several months. Even with such a tight budget, the Antwerp Olympics were considered to be a success by the BOA in terms of the overall number of medals won by the British team.

Gladys Carson and the Paris Olympics of 1924

In the approach to the 1924 Paris Games, the BOA again fundraised towards a goal of £30,000. This time obtaining almost the full amount. Those leading the appeal for donations included the Earl of Birkenhead, the Earl of Rocksavage, Viscount Curzon, the Honourable Lionel Tennyson, Sir Arthur Oppsfields and Sir Phillip Sassoon.[26] The BOA also focused on a wider role, exploring the establishment of a British Sports Association more systematically from 1922 onwards.[27] In addition, the BOA campaigned against the continuing use of the Entertainment Tax, which had been introduced in 1916, affecting the cinema, music hall and sporting industries.

The inauguration of a separate International Week of Winter Sport in Chamonix in January 1924 (later designated as the Winter Olympics), overseen by the French Olympic Committee, initially added little variety to the events available to female competitors. Overall, six sports and 16 disciplines were included, with individual and mixed pairs figure skating events providing opportunities for just 11 female athletes in total.

Having previously finished fifth in the skating pairs at the 1920 Summer Antwerp Olympic Games with partner Sydney Wallwork, Britain's Ethel Muckelt took bronze in the Chamonix 1924 Winter Games in the women's singles figure skating. She finished behind Herma Planck-Szabi of Hungary and Beatrix Loughran of the USA.[28] Muckelt therefore became the first British athlete to win a Winter Games Olympic medal and narrowly missed out on another victory in the mixed pairs with partner Jack Page. Muckelt's bronze would be Britain's only medal in Chamonix and result in a 10th place finish overall for the team.

Born in 1885, Ethel Muckelt's family made their fortune manufacturing textile dyes. She had learned to skate at the Manchester Ice Rink; the only permanent facility in Britain outside of London at the time. Regional differences could be as important as other factors, like class and gender, in developing Olympic hopefuls. Phyllis Johnson, silver medallist in the 1908 London Olympics and bronze medallist in 1920, could not sustain her place in the squad for Chamonix. Nor could her Antwerp team-mate Madelon St John. Muckelt's fellow Mancunian, Gertrude Kathleen Shaw, came seventh in the individual competition in 1924, before competing again four years later in St Moritz. For Mildred Richardson of London, in eighth place, it would be her only Olympic Games.

Although the numbers were relatively slight, figure skating was to have tremendous popular appeal and spectator interest in Olympic competitions was intense. Though she came last in the 1924 women's figure skating, Norway's Sonja Henie aged 11, would redefine the sport. From 1927 to 1937 Henie won 10 consecutive world titles and three individual gold medals at the St Moritz Olympic Games in 1928, in Lake Placid, 1932 and at Garmisch-Partenkirchen in Germany 1936.[29] Turning professional in 1937, Henie became one of the highest paid actresses in Hollywood with the release of motion pictures *Thin Ice* (1937) *One in A Million* (1939) and *Sun Valley Road* (1941).[30]

In preparation for the Paris Summer Olympic Games of 1924, in January 1923 the BOA inaugurated aristocratic and wealthy gentlemen as Vice Presidents, with a view to raising further donations. These became known as the 30-year anniversary Olympic Games, since the IOC had formed in the city at the Sorbonne in 1894. Earl Cadogan hosted a luncheon for the Press and letters were sent to Lord Mayors, Lord Provosts, the heads of District Councils, Universities, Public Schools, 2,700 social clubs and to all 'Sports Business Houses'.[31] This was shrewd, as A. & W. Gamage Ltd, Bradford Textile Company, Hope Brothers, Selfridges Ltd and the London Woollen Company had all bid to supply the uniforms for the Summer Olympics of 1924. Gamage's won the contract but were required to provide generally better quality clothing than their samples, with most sports opting for silk vests and shorts (or silk swimsuits for the aquatics) as their technology of choice.[32]

Unlike 1920, when costs had been so tight that the Finance and General Purposes Committee had debated whether it could afford to spend £70 on hat bands, the overall costs of clothing in 1924 exceeded £1,000. The cost of transport and accommodation for the BOA party was £13,000. In Paris, competitors and administrators stayed for a guinea a day at the Hotel Moderne, and for a pound a day at the Hotel Terminus and or Hotel du Louvre, on an English breakfast, lunch and dinner basis. A writer, F. Fairlie, was appointed to complete the official BOA publication with Gale and Polden publishers.

The BOA also decided that it would enhance the prestige of the 267-strong British team, of whom 28 were women, if it sent the swimming and diving competitors in advance of their events to parade at the Opening Ceremony. This effectively allowed Gladys Carson and her colleagues to lengthen their stay to a month in Paris rather than two weeks. Of the 1924 competitors, the British women's fencing team included Gladys Davis (aged 31), Alice Walker (no age given), Gladys Daniell (aged 40) and Muriel Freeman (aged 27).[33] Nine nations sent 26 female fencing contestants, with Denmark taking the gold and bronze medal. Britain's Gladys Davis was to win the individual foil silver medal, with Muriel Freeman in fourth place.[34]

But swimming had a larger public popularity and Britain sent a team of 11 women. Lucy Morton remains the most widely recognised of the British female swimmers in 1924 and has an entry in the *Oxford Dictionary of National Biography*. This is not least because her victory was Britain's only swimming gold medal in Paris. Consequently, Morton's story is far more well-known than Carson's today. Irene Gilbert (also aged 21) came in fifth in the breaststroke and was almost lost to history, were it not for the silver medal she helped to win with the British women's 4 × 100-metres freestyle relay team along with Florence Barker (aged 16), Constance Jeans (aged 25) and Grace McKenzie (aged 21). Londoner, Phyllis May Harding, later known under her married name Phyllis Turner, won a silver medal in the 100-metres backstroke event. In fact, the entire British swimming medal haul (one gold, two silver and one bronze) in 1924 was brought home by women.

However, as one of the relatively few inter-war female British Olympic medallists, Carson has been almost entirely overlooked. Paris would be Gladys Carson's first experience of foreign travel, and her transnational sporting success was then mediated by the local and national press. Carson's Olympic experiences were far beyond the opportunities available to most young women from Leicester at the time. Biographical detail can therefore reveal some aspects of the otherwise 'hidden histories' of female Olympic participation.

Gladys Helena Carson and her elder two sisters, May Constance or 'Connie' (born 1891) and Olive (born 1893) were the daughters of Cornelius Daniel Horace Carson who was born in 1866 in Auckland, New Zealand.[35]

Cornelius had come to Leicester in August 1888 to join the police force, rising to the rank of Chief Superintendent in 1914 and retiring with a distinguished 31 years of service in 1919.[36] An enthusiastic athlete, he won a five-mile walking race in full police uniform in 1909, helped establish the Leicester Police Swimming Club and won a plunge diving event for the Hincks Cup the same year.

Cornelius also had five sons: Reginald, born in 1889, who died sometime just before the First World War in India; Cecil, born 1894, who was a capped schoolboy football international, who died in February 1917; John or 'Jack', born 1899, who was severely injured during the Great War but who survived and lived in Leicester until the late 1950s; Cornelius junior, born in 1906, who became Chief Superintendent of the Hackney Police Force during World War II and Daniel, born 1908, who died suddenly of heart failure in 1940.[37]

Perhaps unsurprisingly, Gladys' swimming career began at the instigation of her father. She maintained that she was proficient by the age of five and involved in exhibition swimming from the age of six onwards. Soon after, Gladys joined Leicester Ladies Swimming Club, which had been founded in 1902 as one of the earlier female organisations in the sport with Lady Faire as President.[38] Leicester County Amateur Swimming Association & Humane Society had formed with over 20 affiliated clubs in 1891. Several of these organisations were much older, as is illustrated by the career of John Jarvis (1872–1933), the Leicester Olympian who began competitive swimming at the age 11, representing Leicester Swimming Club.[39] Jarvis' wife was secretary of the Leicester Ladies Swimming Club and entered Gladys Carson for her first ASA national competition in 1921.

Although the ASA oversaw swimming as a proletarian and somewhat piecemeal national governing body, the international successes of British swimmers like Gladys Carson derived from wider opportunities for organised tuition and competition, made possible at increasingly young ages by a growing number of local clubs. Leicester also established a Schools' Swimming Association, which held annual galas involving individual and team races for those under 13 years of age from 1897 onwards, with £10 worth of prizes available.[40] This provided a focal point for popular regional interest, uniting Leicestershire's schools and increasingly allied swimming with physical education, rather than being an ad hoc extracurricular past-time.

With easy access to major cities, in the midlands of England, Leicester had five swimming baths and two outdoor stations. This meant that its venues were frequently chosen for both indoor championships and outdoor international matches. Partly because of its own straightened financial circumstances, the ASA usually awarded national championship races to the swimming baths that offered the highest bid as hosts. The cost of countrywide travel was borne by individuals and the swimming clubs to whom they paid modest affiliation fees, although concessionary third class rail fares were also negotiated nationally by the ASA.[41] Not prone to modesty, John Jarvis bragged of his home town:

> The baths in Cossington Street, although not the largest, are, from a gala point of view, the finest in the world. The bath, which is enclosed in a kind of amphitheatre, is 33/1/3 yards long, so as the make the exact hundred yards for three lengths, and 45 feet wide. All round are tiers of seats rising to a small promenade at the top and seating accommodation is provided for nearly 2,000 people, while a larger number can comfortably witness a gala.[42]

Local children were taught to swim at several of these facilities in batches of 25. Most lessons took place between 4:15 and 5:30 in the afternoon, taught by 20 swimming teachers, of whom six were women. So, swimming was an extracurricular activity not within the remit of the Board of Education. Although this appears an unpromising regime from which to develop Olympic champions, the Leicester Schools' Swimming Association had begun to offer an additional £210 for the girls' prizes from 1901. Although children from very poor schools were taken to one of Leicester's two open-air baths with no entrance fee charged, Jarvis reported that by 1902 'the variableness of the climate interfered with the continuity of the lessons so that afterwards even the most underprivileged could find a halfpenny, granting them half price entry to the penny baths'.[43]

By 1902, 641 boys and 154 girls under the age of 13 had been taught to swim under the scheme, with 300 boys and 48 girls competing at the annual Schools Gala that year. In addition, there were several Life Saving clubs and a vibrant water polo culture within the town, and beyond in the county of Leicestershire, facilities in Hinckley, Loughborough, Market Harborough, Meltown Mowbray and Oadby. For those lucky enough to be able to travel to nearby Lincolnshire, Anderley, Boston, Cleethorpes, Gainsborough, Grimsby, Skegness, Spalding and Stamford all had facilities, while coastal resorts also offered opportunities for sea bathing.[44] Gladys Carson's scrapbook reflects this kind of sociable leisure activity as well as competitive swimming in her youth, with photographs of packed bathing huts labelled 'Diving in at Mablethrope' 'Sutton on Sea' and family snapshots marked 'At Looe'.[45]

In addition, the scrapbook contains studio and indoor portraits of Cornelius in swimwear, with Gladys on his knee at about the age of six, marked 'My Father and Me'. Being photographed in swimwear became an increasingly common part of a family album. The collection is particularly valuable given the lack of material in the public domain on what it was like to learn sports as a child and the choices that individuals made to specialise or to drop a particular activity when young. Historians of childhood and adolescence sometimes do not have access to primary material and rely on secondary sources or the commentaries of adults.

Scrapbooks help us see compilations of mixed media that were valuable either at a given point in a person's career or across a life span. The fact that Gladys is photographed in her Olympic swimming robe and wearing her medal as a 70-year-old in the same scrapbook, provides evidence of how significant the experience of going to an Olympic Games in Paris was for her and her family, lifelong. After looking at the swimming careers of the three sisters, we will return to this theme.

In many ways, the local and regional interests of the Carson sisters reflected internationally diverse swimming-related activity. The eldest of the three, Connie, was a strong sprint swimmer in her youth and a goalkeeper for the Leicester Ladies Water Polo Team.[46] However, her active career was increasingly curtailed by a curvature of the spine, which became more severe as she became an adult. Originally, swimming was considered to be therapeutic for the condition but Connie was obliged to give up all together as her disability grew worse. However, she remained a swimming coach at the Vestry Street Baths for over 40 years, in addition to her professional work as a teacher at the Newarke Girls School.

In some ways, Connie Carson epitomised the dilemma facing swimming instructors of the inter-war period. She could either keep teaching swimming as an unpaid hobby alongside her professional occupation in education or accept whatever small financial incentives were on offer and lose her status as an amateur.[47] As we saw with Jennie Fletcher, ASA rules automatically disbarred from competitive swimming anyone taking employment as a baths attendant, coach or teacher.[48]

The middle daughter, Olive Carson, was a long distance swimmer. This meant that she engaged with a much wider transnational competitive network and in this, she was world class. In 1909, at the age of 17, she came second overall in a five-mile race in the River Thames. In 1911, Olive came sixth overall to become the 'Long Distance Amateur Lady Champion' over 15 miles in London. Her time beat 61 male competitors, many of whom were obliged to retire.[49] As this was an international event, Olive could claim to be a world champion, at a time when distance swimming was becoming more competitive globally.[50] Future silver and bronze medallist in the 1924 Olympic Games, Frank Beaurepaire of Australia, was one of the male competitors who failed to complete the 1910 15-mile race in London, having trained in impoverished circumstances mainly on bread, cheese and ginger beer.[51]

A postcard from 1911 in the scrapbook shows Olive's swimsuit adorned with at least 20 gold and silver medals and she stands next to a gold cup awarded by *The Daily Mail*, who sponsored the 15-mile events.[52] Olive's career took her to Norway, Sweden and Monaco, and she also competed against male and female internationals in the UK.[53] We will probably never know the extent of the ephemera related to these kind of sporting contests (amateur or professional) since tokens of various kinds could mark specific events.⁵⁴ These might include silver shields, gold cups, jewellery, medals, tea-sets, bronze figurines, certificates and so forth. Combined with the visual and family material, this degree of civic recognition requires further consideration. Although amateurs like Olive could not earn money directly from swimming or teaching others to swim, there were subtle ways of supplementing an income within the strict amateur rules. Trinkets and items that might be used in the home were part of the benefits usually ignored by sporting administrators.

In addition to these activities all three Carson sisters took part in 'ornamental' swimming displays, gala socials and 'fancy-swimming Christmas pantomimes' at the Leicester swimming club. Like her sisters, it perhaps helped Gladys' access to leisure and sport that her family was of some standing in the community. In a local history of the Leicestershire police force, *Peelers to Pandas*, there is a picture of Cornelius along with the caption 'The presence and identity of the small child seated between Carson's legs is unexplained'.⁵⁵

Figure 2.2 Gladys Carson's head and shoulders photograph portrait taken at the 1924 Olympic Games; from Gladys Carson's scrapbook.

Source: David Hewitt Collection.

Gladys claimed that this was her at about the age of nine. There is also a white teddy bear in the photograph, almost the same size as the child. Gladys reported that the bear was a gift for a life-saving exhibition at a gala where she demonstrated rescue techniques, including bringing a policeman who weighed 15 stones to the side of the swimming baths. According to David Hewitt, the white bear, presented to his mother by the Mayoress of Leicester, stayed in the family for many years.

Gladys won the 220 yards Breaststroke Championship of All England at Beckenham, Kent on 29 September 1921 in a time of 3 minutes 12.4 seconds, beating Doris Hart of the Mermaid Club and Lucy Morton of Blackpool.[56] She recalled in a letter:

> I won this championship at 17¾ years and still at teacher training college. I slipped out of college and caught the London train, went to Beckenham and came back again on the midnight train. I was there for the first session at college the next morning. I dare not tell the head at the college because she had said to me a fortnight before, 'If you gave up your swimming and gave more time to your work here, you would do better. Swimming will never get you a job'.[57]

Gladys retained the title in 1922 at Leamington Spa, along with the Midland Championship. Still coached by her father, the national attention she received as a possible Olympic contender entitled her to certain local training privileges. Awarded the status of a city in 1919 in recognition of its contribution to the Great War, Leicester's local politicians began to use sport more regularly as part of attempts at civic 'boosterism'. Successful amateur swimmers were issued with a free pass to use any city facility during opening hours. However, since Gladys lived in a Police house in Laurel Road, winter training mostly took place at the Vestry Street facility and the larger Spence Street Bath House, since Cossington was on the other side of the city.

Gladys' training regime included swimming twice a day, in the winter at lunchtime and in the evening. After shouting to the facility manager at Vestry or Spence Street to signal her arrival at lunchtime and quickly changing, the baths would be cleared for Gladys to do her training and the public allowed to re-enter the water as she left. This was supplemented by calisthenics and dumb-bell work. From September 1923 onwards, training was mostly conducted outdoors because the public baths did not open until 9am, by which time Gladys had to be at teacher training college. Rising at 6am, she cycled to the Blue Bank Lock of the canal at Old Aylestone, changed in a small hut, and dived into the canal from the lock gate. She would swim 220 yards to match the Paris Olympic 200-metres distance and then cycle back to a breakfast of porridge with cream and two boiled eggs.

While maintaining a competitive profile, Gladys also began her first job as a secondary state school domestic science teacher in Stratford Upon Avon.

> I was appointed to my first teaching job at Stratford Upon Avon and there were 62 applicants for the position. But they wanted a teacher who could swim because one of the children had drowned in the Avon the year before, so I was lucky. Soon after this I heard from the Amateur Swimming Association that I had been chosen to go to swim in the 200 metres breast stroke in the 1924 Paris Olympics.[58]

This was an important distinction. Had she been paid to teach swimming, she would have lost her amateur status. As a domestic science teacher, she was not technically breaking the ASA rules. Gladys did however teach swimming at the school as part of her role. Amateur rules were tightly monitored even so. When a Leicester rubber company whose swimming hats she usually wore asked her to advertise their products, this was forbidden by the ASA, as it would have meant earning money directly from swimming.

Two years of training were rewarded by a formal letter to confirm selection in June 1924, announcing that the British Olympic swimming party would leave London on 4 July.[59] The swimming events took place in the week of 13–20 July. As a matter of urgency, Gladys was instructed to send dimensions for a skirt, blazer, hat, silk swimsuit and bathing gown to Miss Verrall Newman of Finchley Road, London who would relay the details to Gamages. By this time, Gamages of Holborn, London had become the largest sporting goods retailer in Britain and a key supplier to the British Olympic Association.[60]

Gladys Carson went to the Paris 1924 Olympic Games as a 21-year-old single woman, funded by the BOA with strict guidance on everything from how to behave on the journey, to how to get into the Folies Bergère.[61] The tone of the advice is indicated by the rather grand set of instructions on what to do 'Previous to Entraining' as a second class railway passenger in London. Similarly precise conditions about the clothing standards meant that only competitors and reserves could have the words Olympic Games 1924 around the Union Jack on their uniforms, officials were not extended this distinction. Having never stayed in a hotel before, let alone travelled to a foreign country, this must have been some experience. Gladys noted that the British female swimming and diving team comprised 16 women but there are at least 19 in swimsuits featured in official postcards, and almost 30 male competitors.[62] It is quite likely that P. Gant and J. E. Hatch, mentioned in the official report as reserves for the women's relay team, were included in these general team photographs.

Before looking at the swimming races themselves, menus, maps and autographed photographs tell us about the less easily definable ways that Gladys

Figure 2.3 Team Photograph Postcard of Britain's Olympic swimmers in 1924; from Gladys Carson's scrapbook.
Source: David Hewitt Collection.

experienced Paris as an honoured guest of the Olympic festival. It would be a large and challenging project to compile the entire month's social activities but in a longer interview, Gladys indicated that she had free entry to the museums, theatres and shops of Paris while she was there, as well as attending at least 13 formal dinners arranged by the BOA, the ASA and the hosts. Athletes were told what to wear, how to travel, how to address dignitaries and so on at these official functions.[63] Photo-identity cards (in Gladys' case number 6264) gave Olympians a range of benefits, acting as a 'passport' to free transport on the Metro, and as an entrance pass.[64] Within these general guidelines, it was clearly indicated that competitors should enjoy Paris, and large department stores, such as the Magasins Du Louvre, circulated their own maps.[65]

Gladys and her team-mates travelled by train from London to the coast, then across the English Channel by boat, followed by another train to Paris where British Olympians were housed in one of four hotels (rooms at the Continental were held in reserve).[66] Gladys stayed at the Hotel du Louvre. The French Olympic Committee hosted a religious service on 5 July and a visit to the Tomb of the Unknown Soldier at the Arc de Triomphe. A garden party at the Elysée Palace followed the next day. The BOA were not to be outdone. After a reception banquet for the Teams of the Dominions on

6 July, the first official gala given by the BOA for the International Olympic Committee and the French Olympic Committee took place the next day.

Menus were often in a French style of eating, with a separate fish, meat and salad course. Breakfasts in the Olympic village were costed in the 'continental style' in the official report, as comprising coffee (or tea), croissant, meat and cheese. As a student of domestic science, this new approach to food intrigued Gladys, as she later reported in interviews. Home economics teacher, Ginette Mathiot would later publish *La Cuisine Pour Tous*, which contained over 1,400 traditional French recipes for family cooks in 1932.[67] Reprinted many times as *Je Sais Cuisiner* (I know how to cook) this went on to sell over six million copies and made many standard French dishes part of the repertoire of home-makers.

On 9 July, the British team attended a BOA reception at the Hotel Continental and were introduced to the Prince of Wales and Prince Henry.[68] Gladys' menu card was autographed by other athletes, and the signature of Lucy Morton, Belle White, Gladys Luscombe and others remain evident today. The menu itself included fillet of Brill, chicken or roast beef, Haricot beans 'a l'anglaise', desserts, fruit, Champagne, coffee and liqueurs. The following day, the British athletes attended the Paris Opera as the guests of the French Olympic Committee. On 13 July, a second official banquet was given by the BOA for the teams of the other countries involved. This round of social functions continued throughout the festival of sport and culminated in a Grand Fête to celebrate the closing of the Olympiad on 27 July.

The Magasins Du Louvre also issued a full list of the sporting competitions. The same booklets featured a series of advertisements for sports clothing and equipment, stocked by the store.[69] As well as tailored casual sports suits to be worn by spectators, the store stocked hosiery, sleeveless cricket sweaters and footwear. Men's accessories included gloves, cameras, braces, cravats and caps. Women's spectator-wear included a range of dresses, skirt suits and overcoats. These could be accessorised by scarves featuring Olympic sports like tennis, boxing and running. Other additions included hats, parasols, hosiery, perfume (Les Fleurs du Louvre) and jewellery. Commercial elements sat alongside several art exhibitions and cultural expositions across the city, blending what was athletic, glamorous and fashionable.[70] Not all entertainment was so highbrow and live shows also featured on the schedule. As the religious and memorial functions also indicated, there were serious elements to the functions too, so soon after the Great War.

During the opening ceremony to the Olympic Games themselves, the British team were led around by Scottish pipers and Gladys Carson was on the far right of the front row, clearly visible to photographers.[71] The Paris Games of 1924 had the first 50-metre pool to be used, Le Stade Nautique Des Tourelles, which measured 18 metres across and had plenty of room for spectators.[72] The pool was laned by means of coloured tiles in the floor and by ropes in the water.[73] This was the most technically advanced Olympic Games to date, with electronic announcements, telephone systems to convey information and facilitate communication, timing devices, photography and film. As can be evidenced from the number of judges, spectators and reporters in the photographs and films of the official report, this was a sophisticated and highly organised swimming tournament.

This media interest magnified the spectacle of relatively unclothed young women swimming in competitive events. In the *Radio Leicester* interview, Gladys was very clear that the leg length of the women's costumes was required to be five and half inches long, so that it covered the thighs. This was to remain an issue until the more high cut costumes became standard wear in the late 1930s and 1940s. Since 1912, Olympic male and female swimmers had worn silk racing costumes and divers knitted swimsuits. This would continue until 1948, when Rayon and other synthetics such as Nylon replaced the expensive silk fabric.

The ASA had defined its own regulation swimming costumes in 1902 and this remained the standard style for until 1948. From the photographic evidence, the men are wearing very similar costumes to the women with the exception of being lower cut at the chest, with thinner shoulder straps and slightly more high cut on the leg.

However, although there are photographs in the scrapbook of the heats and final, Gladys' account of how her races went differs from the Official Report. Maybe this is not that unusual? Gladys qualified first in the third heat of the 200-metres breaststroke on 16 July in a time of 3 minutes 30 seconds.[74] Both Lucy Morton (3 minutes 29.4 seconds) and 17-year-old Agnes Geraghty of the USA (3 minutes 27.6 seconds) won their previous heats in slightly better times. The final of the women's breaststroke was held at 4pm on 18 July in front of at least 4,000 spectators. Gladys remembered that she had led the race but had caught a mouth-full of water when turning for the final time and this had slowed her to third place. The official report indicated that Lucy Morton led from the front, achieving a relatively slow winning time of 3 minutes 33.2 seconds and with 3 minutes 35.4 seconds for Carson in third.

The favourite to win the race before it took place was the American Agnes Geraghty. At the time of the Paris Olympic Games, Britain's Irene Gilbert was the current world record holder, having set a time over 220 yards of 3 minutes 20.4 seconds in Rotherham in 1922. The official report does commend Gilbert as a favourite of the crowd, and she became one of the Olympic Games' 'nearly' women. Having been bed-ridden with illness for several days, Gilbert had nevertheless qualified for the 200-metres backstroke final and finished fifth. We might well have expected a healthy Irene Gilbert to have won the gold rather than Lucy Morton or at least to have taken the bronze rather than Gladys Carson. If chance played an important role in whether an individual got to the Olympic Games in the first place, it also had a major part to play in the outcomes of the tournament itself.

Figure 2.4 This somewhat controversial photograph of Gladys Carson and an annoyed male opponent was widely mediated; from Gladys Carson's scrapbook.

Source: David Hewitt Collection.

The 11 British female swimmers outperformed their male team-mates at the Paris Olympic Games in winning medals. Unsurprisingly, the largest field for a female swimming event in 1924 was the 100-metres freestyle race. The British duo of Constance Jeans and Iris Tanner (aged 18) finished behind an American top three (Ethel Lackie, Mariechen Wehselau and Gertrude Ederle), and did not make the medals in the 400-metres event either. A third British competitor, Florence Barker, was eliminated in the semi-finals. In the 100-metres backstroke, Britain's Phyllis Harding (17 years of age) took the silver medal sandwiched between Sybil Bauer and Aileen Riggins of the United States. Harding's team-mates Helen Boyle (16 years of age) and Ellen King (aged just 15) were eliminated in the backstroke semi-finals. Ethel Lackie, Mariechen Wehselau, Gertrude Ederle and Euphraisa Donnelly won the 4 × 100-metres freestyle relay for the USA in a new world record of just under 5 minutes. The British team led by Irene Gilbert was nearly 18 seconds slower, and the Swedish team in third almost half a minute behind the Americans. Doris Molesworth had the best showing, to come fourth in the 400-metres freestyle.

Britain also sent a team of six female and five male divers but only one, Harold Clarke, would return with a medal (a bronze). Most of the female divers were older than the women swimmers in 1924: Beatrice 'Eileen' Armstrong, was aged 30; Belle White, 29; Verrall Newman, 27; Catherine O'Bryen, 25; Amelia Hudson, 22 and Gladys Luscombe was just 16 years of age.

All the 1924 Paris Olympic aquatic events were dominated by superior technicians from the USA; Peter John 'Johnny' Weissmuller won three gold medals in the men's 100-metres freestyle, 400-metres freestyle and 4 × 200-metres freestyle relay. America's Duke Kahanamoku and Sam Kahanamoku were also stars of the men's swimming, taking second and third place in the 100-metres freestyle. This was a return to form after World War I, as both Duke and Sam Kahanamoku had established themselves at the 1912 Stockholm Olympics and subsequently promoted the popularity of surfing. There were also many female US stars. The 18-year-old Aileen Riggin of Newport, Rhode Island became the first person to earn medals for both diving (a silver in the women's springboard event) and swimming (bronze in the women's 100-metres backstroke).[75]

As Mark Dyreson has indicated, dominance in swimming and diving events was part of a wider process of Amercanisation through Olympic sport on a global stage after 1918.[76] The veneer of Californian references included an expanding consumerism, of which Hollywood glamour was a significant element. The private lives and personalities of some sports stars would become commodified well beyond their athletic prowess. Weissmuller would go professional shortly after the Paris Olympic Games to advertise BVD Swimwear in Los Angeles and was appearing in Hollywood films such as *Tarzan* by 1932. Like Weissmuller, Duke Khanamoku and Aileen Riggin would go on to lucrative acting careers in major motion pictures.[77] Best known for coaching films edited by Grantland Rice, and Hollywood films *Girls and Records* (1923), *Building Winners* (1924), and *Olympic Mermaids* (1924), Riggin also had a tandem career as a sports journalist. She supplemented this income by appearing live in touring Aquacades and was generally entrepreneurial in promoting her own public image.

Although the degree of fame achieved by individual athletes was an uneven general trend, even those who would remain out of the spotlight for most of their lives, like Gladys Carson, came into contact with stars who would go on to sustain high profile careers. The sale of souvenir merchandise included posters, postcards, badges, limited edition stamps, medals and other trinkets. Over 1,000 journalists reported the Paris Olympic Games across various media platforms and so the profile of female winners was magnified beyond their relatively small numbers.[78] In spite of these much larger changes in connectivity, Gladys Carson seemed immune to the Californian charm of Johnny Weissmuller and his co-competitors. In the *Radio Leicester* interview, she recalled that her main impression was that Weissmuller seemed 'a bit full of himself' when they met. Of course, Weissmuller had not made his name in the movies by then, but Carson's indifference is quite amusing.

At 22 years of age, Doris Molesworth would come fourth in the new Olympic event, the individual 400-metres freestyle behind 17-year-old Gertrude Ederle of the United States, and ahead of Hedevig Rasmussen of Denmark.[79] As well as being a multi-medal winning Olympic athlete, Ederle would later become a global star when she became the first woman to swim the English Channel on her second attempt in 1926, with backing from the *New York News* and *Chicago Tribune*. This made Ederle international front page news in what was reported as: 'The Greatest Sports Story of the World'.[80] What were the experiences of Carson, Molesworth and their contemporaries when selected to compete against the leading international competitors of the time, on behalf of Britain? This chapter has begun to address a much wider research agenda.

Swimming, because of its class base, often meant a short amateur career. Gladys continued to compete until 1927, became something of a local hero and well-known on the ASA swimming circuit. She also continued to beat her own previous records. At the Midland Counties Championship, hosted by the Leamington Spa Amateur Swimming Club, in 1925 she knocked five seconds off her previous best for 200 yards, to 3 minutes 10 seconds.[81] Both Lucy Morton and Gladys Carson had retired from competitive swimming by the 1928 Amsterdam Olympic Games, having married.[82] Collected in Glady's scrapbook, *The Leicester Mercury* published several photographs of the wedding of the 'champion swimmer' Miss Carson to Mr George Davies Hewitt of East Park Road. Gladys and George had two children. David Hewitt was born in 1928 and his sister Josie two years later.

After marrying and retiring from competitive swimming Gladys taught at Tugby in Leicestershire before moving to Lincolnshire. It is probably difficult to assess exactly how many now, but Gladys estimated that she had taught over 500 pupils to swim and her sister Connie over 1,000 children. Gladys also taught at a local Primary school for many years, so her interests in French food and culture were passed on to children in more subtle ways. What was it like to be taught to swim by an Olympian and did Gladys make much of her experience in Paris during her teaching career in general? How did it affect what she cooked at home and how she marked special occasions?

Looking at the scrapbook of Gladys Carson as she aged, we can see her teaching successive generations of her family and friends to swim, wearing bathing suits very different from those she wore as a young woman. Many of these are 'seaside' scenes. In the changing design of 1920s swimsuits, and embodied consumption of material goods and experiences, the history of Olympic sport intersects with a wider business and technology context, as well as media history. For instance, by 1930, a young English textiles entrepreneur, Percy Adamson had begun to collaborate with the United States Rubber Company to produce elasticated fabrics and in so doing, revolutionised the mass market for close fitting swimsuits worn on beaches and in the water.[83] Although sheet rubber had been used for women's corsets, weaving elastic thread with two way stretch gave a more forgiving silhouette. Swimming or poolside scenes became a Hollywood set-piece and the accessory market in relation to bathing caps, sunglasses, shoes, beach bags, suntan lotions and so on multiplied under the broad category of 'resort-wear'. Personal transport also increased opportunities for tourism and Gladys moved to live nearer

Figure 2.5 Gladys Carson Hewitt's headstone showing the Olympic rings, which is not so unusual for proud British women Olympians and their families.

Source: Author's collection.

to the sea with her family. By 1935, Latex-satin mix suits gleamed on British beaches, for a wealthy and fashion conscious minority. The idea of freedom, leisure and modernity and going on holiday was however, more democratically available.

Gladys Hewitt also had lifelong friends in the Leicester Ladies Swimming Club and there are photos of the water polo team reunion in 1960. Swimming lends itself to the maintenance of fitness in later life. Looking at these women when older, still enjoying sociable sporting ties, prompted me to think about generations of athletes, trainers and coaches and how knowledge has been passed down through such networks, especially by women. What were the friendships and rivalries here? How do Olympic experiences become part of wider sporting culture?

Gladys predeceased her husband George on 17 November 1987 at the age of 84. At the request of the family, at the top of the headstone in the village church of Hogsthorpe in Lincolnshire, the Olympic rings are depicted in colour. The Olympic experience was something that the family thought defined Gladys Carson Hewitt's life. It is not uncommon to see either the Olympic rings or the maiden name used by the athlete when she competed at the Olympic Games, on a gravestone. Jennie Fletcher, another Leicester swimmer, had a similar design on her memorial in Canada. This convention troubled Gladys' son David when I talked to him because his mother was known by her married name. The Olympic experience was relatively short and the marriage a long one, so we can perhaps understand his equivocation. George Davies Hewitt died on 9 December 1997 and the inscription on the stone includes the phrase, 'To that brightest and blessed of all meetings bring us Jesus Christ at last'.

Conclusion

The 1924 Olympics would be the last time that lawn tennis was contested at the Summer Olympic games until the 'open' era of professional players in 1984, though swimming and fencing were to remain on the schedule. Some 31 women from 14 nations entered the tennis competitions held at the three courts at Colombes in the Paris Olympics in 1924.[84] Women's singles, doubles and mixed double events were available. The British women's Olympic tennis team again included Kitty McKane who established herself as Britain's number one player, taking over from Dorothea Lambert Chambers.

In addition to beating the American Helen Wills in the Wightman Cup, McKane had also won Wimbledon, beating Wills in the only singles final she would lose there in nine appearances. However, McKane was defeated by French Champion Julie 'Diddie' Vlasto in the semi-final, before Wills, then only 18 years of age, won the gold medal.[85] McKane's bronze for the singles was complimented by a silver in the women's doubles with Phyllis Covell. This brought McKane's total to five Olympic medals in all (one gold, two silver and two bronze). Dorothy Shepherd-Barron and Evelyn Colyer took the bronze in the women's doubles. Phyllis Satterthwaite was eliminated early on.

This chapter has concentrated mainly on the sporting career of Gladys Carson but it is widely accepted that the spectacle of the Paris Olympic Games was considerably enhanced by the exhibitions, artistic competitions (architecture, literature, music, painting and sculpture) and other cultural events.[86] Dorothy Margaret Stuart, who won a silver medal in the literature competitions for *Fencer's Song*, also studied fencing and was taught by Alfred Hutton, founder of the British Amateur Fencing Association. Sculptor Katherine Maltwood was unplaced. The art competitions in 1920 were somewhat underwhelming, with several categories failing to award gold medals due to unsatisfactory submissions. For the second time, Paris had welcomed Olympic visitors in 1924 to one of the most vibrant cities in the world. The BOA fundraising campaign was so successful that an eventual operating profit saw the team return from Paris and begin to prepare for the 1928 St Moritz Winter Games in Switzerland and the Amsterdam Summer Games in the Netherlands, with £1,800 already in the bank.[87]

The financial concerns of the BOA continued however. Sandy Duncan, a long time administrator at the BOA, attempted in 1976, to write an historical summary of how much it cost to send each person in the British Olympic team to a Games. In 1924, an estimated 224-strong British delegation (including athletes and administrators) cost the BOA in the region of £6,500.[88] Surprisingly, over a quarter of people who the BOA funded to attend the Paris Games did not compete. The Paris Olympics of 1924 provided an extensive array of hospitality including,

> at the Piccadilly Hotel, through the instrumentality of the British Olympic Association, the greatest gathering of Sportsmen of the Motherland gathered together to honour the members of the New Zealand Rugby XV, on the eve of their return to their homes. The occasion has rightly been termed historic.[89]

The benefits of being a sporting bureaucrat require an in-depth study in themselves, perhaps. However, those who would have to work all their lives until retirement age, like Gladys Carson, could also benefit from such generous hospitality.

Certainly by the Amsterdam Games of 1928, food and beverage manufacturers like Coca-Cola saw the Olympic Games as opportunities to promote their products to an international audience of tourists, administrators and competitors. This is a research agenda in itself and, in the context of restrictive legislation within Olympic stadia covering even basic items like which water can be consumed, one with considerable contemporary resonance. Many of the personal collections left by various Olympians contain these fragments. What happened on the pitch, the track, or in the pool is of course important. However, the social arrangements are equally fascinating. How can we use items of ephemera such as menus, seating plans, snapshots and scrapbooks as part of our research?

The evidence in the scrapbook shows that the Paris Olympic Games in 1924 changed Gladys Carson's life in ways that are still memorialised by her children, grandchildren and local community. Personal memorabilia indicates what the individual thought significant to keep and preserve and the scrapbooks are a kind of life-writing; half diary, half travelogue. In this sense, this chapter worked out from a single case study to look at wider processes and networks.

The chapter also looked at the expansion of the Olympic programme for women in this context. The sailing events were not formally mixed or gender-segregated and much depended on circumstance. Swiss sailor Ella Maillart took part in the Olympic monotype yachting competition at 21 years of age, in 1924.[90] A skier, explorer and photographer, Maillart was also captain of the national women's hockey team in Switzerland. Two further notable aspects of the official report were the presence of a female administrator, Madamoiselle Simonses, photographed among Les Délégués au Congre`s de la Fédération Internationale d'Escrime and the level of detail with which the women's competitions were reported.[91]

In terms of source material, family history provides evidence of how sporting careers were initiated, maintained and ended. In some ways, Olive Carson was as much part of the zeitgeist as Gladys, but women's distance swimming was not then an Olympic event. When Gertrude Ederle first decided to swim the English Channel in 1925, she held 29 amateur and world records from 50 yards to 1.5 miles.[92] Ederle crossed the Channel at the second attempt from Cap Griz-Nez in France on 6 August 1926, with backing from the *New York News* and the *Chicago Tribune*.[93] The record time was just under 15 hours.

Successive British women took on long-distance swimming, including the Channel crossing in the 1920s. Brighton-born Mercedes Gleitze became the first to cross in 1927 and thereafter swimming the Channel became feminised for a time.[94] There was high commercial value in such activity. Known as 'The Jazz Swimmer' Gleitze became the first person to swim the Straits of Gibraltar in 1928, and Rolex approached her to wear their newly designed Oyster case watch to prove that it was indestructible. Gleitze wore the timepiece on a chain around her neck and, although the swim was unsuccessful, the watch kept time. This made the durability and glamour of a female swimmer synonymous with an item of high-end jewellery, mainly a male product, promoted as 'the best waterproof watch in the world'. The endorsement reinscribes Gleitze's reputation even today in contemporary promotions, long after she retired from swimming in 1932.[95] In a spectacle that could appeal to voyeurs and those who admired her determination and stamina, Gleitze wore costumes that were very similar to those used by the amateur Olympic swimmers.[96]

In turn, Ederle and Gleitze inspired other endurance athletes, such as the marathon runner Violet Piercy who was frequently in the public eye between 1926 and 1938 running marathon distances and longer road races.[97] Tolerated, though not actively encouraged, Piercy organised the first women's road race over three miles in Mitcham, in which 13 competitors took part, in 1934. However, women's road running was less glamourous than swimming, and the women's marathon did not feature as an Olympic discipline until 1984.

Finally, the chapter explored how a rapidly expanding connectivity between sport and the media enhanced the worldwide profile of a few Olympic competitors.[98] Rather than seeing this as a process of Americanisation, heralded by the Lake Placid Winter Olympic Games or Summer Olympic Games in Los Angeles in 1932, this chapter has suggested that the 1924 Paris celebrations had considerable resonance.[99] It showcased new leisure opportunities for many women, at the same time as technocratic forms of entertainment increasingly enabled a few to work in the industry.

In this, the radio was as influential in the twentieth century as television. In 1922, the British Broadcasting Company (BBC) began to send out short 'sponsored' programmes to 8,000 owners of a radio constructors' licence, which cost 15 shillings.[100] The Writtle independent experimental Marconi radio station 2MT broadcast Norah Scott as the first woman's voice from its prefabricated headquarters, in 1922.[101] Although independent radio ceased to broadcast in 1923 in Britain until the 1960s, listening to publicly funded radio, especially local radio stations, became increasingly popular, especially among women.[102] During the inter-war period in the USA, national wireless networks emerged, like the National Broadcasting Company (NBC), the Columbia Broadcasting System (CBS) and the American Broadcasting Company (ABC).[103] As both a public and domestic medium that could be listened to while doing other activities, radio was fundamentally different from leisure activities requiring specific commitments.[104]

For a few pence, British audiences could also go to the cinema to watch the newsreels, like Pathé. Short films often featured international sports stars such as Suzanne Lenglen, Kitty McKane, Aileen Riggin and Lucy Morton.[105] Newsreels were a hybrid of news and entertainment within a cinema exhibition format.[106] The surviving newsreel clippings are far from the complete range of coverage, because these films were meant to give topical news and were not stored particularly carefully.[107]

Gladys Carson was only just well-known enough to briefly be part of these wider processes, but her sporting excellence enabled her to meet in person those who would use sport to become famous. From the early 1920s onwards, more newspapers used photographs rather than illustrated cartoons. Photographers therefore increased the visibility of female athletes even among those who were unwilling or unable to read reports in full.[108]

A wider audience who had not attended in person could have an opinion, through reading about matches or listening on the radio or watching excerpts on screen.

The bureaucratisation and international expansion of the Olympic Games also created more work from women in administrative, sports technician, public relations and media roles. More than 38 women (compared with nine men) were employed centrally by The Netherlands Olympic Committee in facilitating the 1928 Amsterdam Games, for instance.[109] Wilhelmina, the Queen of the Netherlands, was Patron of the event and her presence much in evidence in the official report. By the 1928 Amsterdam Olympic Games, general portrayals of athletic women and personally-endorsed products of a few stars were being used in advertisements for everything from cars and wristwatches to food and medicine.[110] While it might have shocked some commentators when Gladys Carson was young, that she swam competitions that revealed her legs, consumerist modernity meant that she would no longer be considered an exception by the time of the 1928 Amsterdam and 1932 Los Angeles Olympic Games.

Notes

1. Gladys Hewitt 'Speak for Yourself' Personal Communication to *Speak For Yourself*, Nationwide, *BBC Radio Lincolnshire* David Hewitt Collection: Sutton on Sea, Lincolnshire undated p. 1.
2. Win Hayes 'Lucy Morton (1898–1980)' *Oxford Dictionary of National Biography* www.oxforddnb.com accessed 14 July 2019.
3. Jean Williams *A Contemporary History of Women's Sport, Part One Sporting Women, 1850–1960* London and New York: Routledge, 2014 pp. 25–26.
4. Monique Berlioux 'Managing a Gentleman's Club' *Journal of Olympic History* 23: 1 2015 p. 13.
5. British Olympic Association *Minutes of the BOA Council, The Football Association Russell Square 31 January 1919* BOA Archive, London p. 2.
6. Nick Yapp (ed.) *Chasing Gold: Centenary if the British Olympic Association* London: British Olympic Association, 2005 pp. 42–43.
7. Hugh Hudson *Chariots of Fire* (Allied Stars/Enigma Productions, 1981); Mark Ryan *Running with Fire: The True Story of 'Chariots of Fire' hero Harold Abrahams* London: JR Books, 2011.
8. British Olympic Association *Minutes of the BOA Finance Committee 166 Piccadilly W1 8 September 1924* BOA Archive, London p. 1.
9. International Olympic Committee 'Paris 1924 04 May – 27 Jul' www.olympic.org/paris-1924-summer-olympics accessed 15 July 2019.
10. Jean Williams 'Aquadynamics and the Athletocracy: Jennie Fletcher and the British Women's 4 × 100 metre Freestyle Relay Team at the 1912 Stockholm Olympic Games' *Costume* 46: 2 June 2012 pp. 145–164.
11. British Olympic Association *Report to the Annual General Meeting: Confidential Minutes 24 Abingdon Street Westminster 21 January 1921* BOA Archive, London p. 1.
12. British Olympic Association *Report on Estimates of Expenditure for the Period 29 September 1919 to 31 December 1920 Aldershot 6 March 1919* BOA Archive, London pp. 2–3.

13 Comite Belge De La VIIme Olympiade *Sous le Haut Patronage de D. M. le Roi Presidence D' Honneur de S. A. R. Prince Leopold Brussels 19 May 1919* IOC Museum and Archive, Lausanne pp. 1–2.
14 Count Clary President of the French Olympic Committee *Report of the Secretary General of the French Olympic Committee RE: The Olympiad of Antwerp* IOC Museum and Archive, Lausanne pp. 2–3.
15 British Olympic Council *Confidential Minutes, The Football Association Russell Square 20 November 1919* BOA Archive, London p. 4.
16 British Olympic Council *Memorandum on Organisation The Football Association Russell Square 23 October 1919* BOA Archive, London pp. 1–3.
17 British Olympic Council *Confidential Minutes The Football Association Russell Square 8 January 1920* BOA Archive, London p. 2.
18 Lord Downham *The King's Message and Gift 10 January 1920* BOA Archive, London p. 1.
19 British Olympic Association *Finance and General Purposes Committee Confidential Minutes 24 Abingdon Street Westminster 5 August 1920* BOA Archive, London p. 3.
20 Suzanne Lenglen and Eustance E. White (eds.) *Lawn Tennis for Girls* New York: American Sports Publishing Co., 1920.
21 Martin Smith (ed.) *The Daily Telegraph of Sports Obituaries* London: Pan Books, 2001 p. 16.
22 International Tennis Hall of Fame 'Suzanne Lenglen' International Tennis Hall of Fame www.tennisfame.com/hall-of-famers/suzanne-lenglen accessed 29 July 2019.
23 Ian Buchanan *British Olympians: A Hundred Years of Gold Medallists* Enfield Middlesex: Guinness Publishing, 1991 p. 50.
24 International Olympic Committee *Olympic Games Medals, Results, Sports, Athletes: Antwerp 1920* International Olympic Committee www.olympic.org/content/results-and-medallists/gamesandsportsummary/ accessed 10 April 2019.
25 International Olympic Committee 'Searchable Database of Olympic Medallists' www.olympic.org/medallists accessed 16 December 2019.
26 British Olympic Association *Finance and General Purposes Committee Minutes 10 John Street Adelphi* (by kind permission of the Amateur Athletic Association) 23 November 1922 BOA Archive, London p. 1.
27 British Olympic Association *Minutes 10 John Street Adelphi 12 July 1922* BOA Archive, London p. 1.
28 Nick Yapp (ed.) *Chasing Gold* pp. 48–49.
29 George M Lattimer (ed.) *III Olympic Winter Games: Official Report Lake Placid 1932* Lake Placid and New York: III Olympic Winter Games Committee, 1932 pp. 220–221.
30 Mary H. Leigh 'The Enigma of Avery Brundage and Women Athletes' *Arena Review* 4: 2 May 1980 pp. 11–21.
31 British Olympic Association *Finance and General Purposes Committee Minutes 24 Abingdon Street Westminster* (by kind permission of the British Commonwealth Union) 10 January 1923 BOA Archive, London p. 1.
32 British Olympic Association *Minutes of the Housing Committee Meeting 6 Piccadilly W1 15 May 1924* BOA Archive, London p. 1.
33 Dan Heckscher 'Jeux Olympiques de 1924-Fleuret, Les Finalists du Championnat' Paris: Dan Heckscher, 1924 www.olympic.org/photos/paris-1924/fencing accessed 4 February 2019.
34 Albert Avé, Charles Denis and Georges Bourdon (eds.) *Les Jeux de La VIIIE Olympiade Paris 1924* pp. 274–276.
35 David Hewitt 'Leicester Swimming Sisters' *Personal Communication*, 1 May 2011 pp. 4–5.

36 Ben Beazley *Peelers to Pandas: An Illustrated History of the Leicester City Police* Leicester: Breedon Books, 2001 p. 54.
37 David Hewitt 'Carson Family History' Personal Communication to the Author 10 June 2012 pp. 3–4.
38 Jean Williams 'The Most Important Photograph in the History of Women's Olympic Participation: Jennie Fletcher and the British 4 × 100 Freestyle relay team at the Stockholm 1912 Games' in Martin Polley (ed.) *Sport in History: Special Issue: Britain, Britons and the Olympic Games* 32: 2 2012 p. 209.
39 Peter Bilsborough 'Jarvis, John Arthur (1872–1933)' *Oxford Dictionary of National Biography* Oxford: Oxford University Press, 2004 www.oxforddnb.com/view/article/65070 accessed 15 October 2019.
40 John Jarvis *The Art of Swimming with Notes on Water Polo and Aids to Life-Saving* Leicester: W. H. Clarke, 1902 pp. 70–71.
41 T. M. Yeaden (ed.) *ASA Handbook 1913 Containing a List of English Swimming Clubs; Laws of Swimming and Rules of Water Polo; Past and Present Champions and Programme for the Year* London: Hanbury, Tomsett & Co., 1913 pp. 262–263. The annual yearbooks were printed early in the following year, so this summarizes developments in 1912.
42 John Jarvis *The Art of Swimming* p. 70.
43 John Jarvis *The Art of Swimming* pp. 71–72.
44 Amateur Swimming Association *Amateur Swimming Association Yearbook 1902* Nottingham: J. Littlewood, 1903 British Swimming Archive, Loughborough p. 200.
45 Anon. 'Family Snapshots' *Gladys Hewitt's Scrapbook* David Hewitt Collection, unpaginated.
46 David Hewitt 'Leicester Swimming Sisters' David Hewitt Collection pp. 4–5.
47 Jean Williams 'The Most Important Photograph in the History of Women's Olympic Participation...' p. 211.
48 British Olympic Council *Olympic Games of 1908: Programme, Rules and Conditions of Competition for Swimming, Diving and Water Polo* London: British Olympic Council, 1909 p. 4 BOA Archive, London.
49 P. H. Adams 'Miss Olive Carson Postcard circa 1910' in *Gladys Hewitt's Scrapbook* David Hewitt Collection unpaginated.
50 Lisa Bier, *Fighting the Current: The Rise of American Women's Swimming 1870–1926* Jefferson, NC: McFarland and Company, 2011 p. 15.
51 Sport Australia 'Frank Beaurepaire' *Sport Australia Hall of Fame* www.sahof.org.au/hall-of-fame/ accessed 14 July 2019.
52 Anon. 'Miss Olive Carson Postcard circa 1911' *Gladys Hewitt Scrapbook* David Hewitt Collection unpaginated.
53 Anon. 'Olive Carson, Former World Champion Swimmer Dies' *The Leicester Mercury* 4 July 1971 *Gladys Hewitt's Scrapbook* David Hewitt Collection unpaginated.
54 Frank Trentmann, 'Materiality in the Future of History: Things, Practices, and Politics' *Journal of British Studies* 48: 2 April 2009 pp. 283–307.
55 Ben Beazley *Peelers to Pandas* p. 57.
56 Austin Rawlinson MBE *Letter to David Hewitt regarding the career of Gladys Carson* Brodie Avenue Liverpool 10 April 1987 David Hewitt Collection.
57 Gladys Hewitt 'Speak for Yourself' pp. 3–4.
58 Gladys Hewitt 'Speak for Yourself' pp. 4–5.
59 George W. Hearn 'British Olympic Swimming Paris 1924 Selection Letter to Gladys Carson 4 June 1924' *Gladys Hewitt's Scrapbook* David Hewitt Collection.
60 Geraldine Biddle-Perry 'The Rise of 'The World's Largest Sport and Athletic Outfitter': A Study of Gamage's of Holborn, 1878–1913' *Sport in History: Special*

Issue: Sport's Relationship with Other Leisure Industries. Part I: Sites of Interaction 34: 2 2014 pp. 295–317.
61 British Olympic Association *Instructions for Governing Bodies in Connection with the Assembling, Transportation, Housing of British Representatives Selected to Represent Great Britain in Paris 1924* London: The British Olympic Association, 1924 David Hewitt Collection.
62 A. N. Paris 'Jeux Olmpiques de 1924-Natation Èquipe De Grande Bretagne' *Gladys Hewitt's Scrapbook* David Hewitt Collection.
63 The British Olympic Association *The British Olympic Association British Team Handbook* London: The British Olympic Association, 1924 David Hewitt Collection.
64 Le Président du Comité Olympique *VIII Olympiade Paris 1924* Gladys Carson No. 6264 (Paris, 1924) David Hewitt Collection.
65 Magasins Du Louvre *Métropolitan Nord, Sud, Boulevard Voltaire* Magasins Du Louvre: Paris, 1924 David Hewitt Collection.
66 British Olympic Association *Instructions for Governing Bodies* pp. 15–17.
67 Ginette Mathiot *La Cuisine Pour Tous* Paris: Albert Michel, 1932.
68 Hotel Continental *Menu Given by The Duke of Sutherland to the British Athletes On The Occasion of the VIII Olympiad* 9 July 1924 David Hewitt Collection.
69 Magasins Du Louvre *Guide Pour Les Jeux Olympiques De 1924* Paris: Magasins Du Louvre, 1924 David Hewitt Collection.
70 Elizabeth Wilson *Fashion and Modernity* I. B. Tauris and Co. Ltd 2003; first published by Virago 1985 p. 49.
71 A. N. Paris *Jeux Olympiques De 1924 L'Èquipe de Grande Bretagne Postcard* in *Gladys Hewitt's Scrapbook* David Hewitt Collection.
72 Albert Avé, Charles Denis and Georges Bourdon (eds.) *Comité Olympique Français Les Jeux de La VIIIE Olympiade Paris 1924: Rapport Official Titre III* Paris; La Librairie de France, 1924 pp. 437–440.
73 David Hewitt 'Leicester Swimming Sisters' pp. 4–5.
74 Albert Avé, Charles Denis and Georges Bourdon (eds.) *Les Jeux de La VIIIE Olympiade Paris 1924: Rapport Official Titre III* pp. 475–477.
75 Frank Litsky 'Aileen Riggin Soule, Olympic Diver and Swimmer, Dies at 96' *The New York Times* 21 October 2002 www.nytimes.com/2002/10/21/sports/aileen-riggin-soule-olympic-diver-and-swimmer-dies-at-96.html accessed 28 July 2019.
76 Mark Dyreson 'The Republic of Consumption at the Olympic Games: Globalization, Americanization, and Californization' *Journal of Global History* 8 2 2013 pp. 256–278.
77 Jeffrey Richards *Cinema and Radio in Britain and America 1920–1960* Manchester: Manchester University Press, 2010 p. 239.
78 International Olympic Committee 'Highlights of the 1924 Paris Games' www.olympic.org/paris-1924-summer-olympics accessed 24 July 2019.
79 Albert Avé, Charles Denis and Georges Bourdon (eds.) *Les Jeux de La VIIIE Olympiade Paris 1924* pp. 477–9.
80 Patricia Vertinsky and Christiane Job 'Celebrating Gertrudes: Women of Influence' in Annette R. Hofmann and Else Trangbaek (eds.) *International Perspectives on Sporting Women in Past and Present* Denmark: Institute of Exercise and Social Sciences University of Copenhagen, 2005 p. 252.
81 Leamington Spa Amateur Swimming Club *Programme of Championship Galas Royal Pump Room Baths* 28 July 1925 p. 3 David Hewitt Collection.
82 Win Hayes, 'Lucy Morton (1898–1980)' *Oxford Dictionary of National Biography* Oxford: Oxford University Press.

83 Hannah Andrassy 'Spinning a Golden Thread: The Introduction of Elastic into Swimwear' *Things* 5 Winter 1996–1997 pp. 59–85.
84 Albert Avé, Charles Denis and Georges Bourdon (eds.) *Les Jeux de La VIIIE Olympiade Paris 1924 Titre II* p. 377.
85 Alan Little *Tennis and the Olympic Games* London: Wimbledon, 2009 pp. 54–55.
86 Albrt Avé, Charles Denis and Georges Bourdon (eds.) *Comité Olympique Français Les Jeux de La VIIIE Olympiade Paris 1924: Rapport Official Titre IV* Paris; La Librairie de France, 1924 pp. 602–615.
87 British Olympic Association *Minutes of the Finance Committee Meeting 166 Piccadilly W1 20 October 1924* p. 2 BOA Archive, London.
88 K. S. Duncan 'British Olympic Association spend per Games 1896–1968 6 March 1972' *Correspondence File 1964–1978* unpaginated BOA Archive, London.
89 Lord Cadogan 'The Chairman's Annual Statement 1924' *British Olympic Association Minutes 26 February 1925 166 Piccadilly W1* p. 2 BOA Archive, London.
90 Albert Avé, Charles Denis and Georges Bourdon (eds.) *Les Jeux de La VIIIE Olympiade Paris 1924* pp. 589–591.
91 Albert Avé, Charles Denis and Georges Bourdon (eds.) *Les Jeux de La VIIIE Olympiade Paris 1924* p. 263; 274–276.
92 Lisa Bier *Fighting The Current* p. 135.
93 Patricia Vertinsky and Christiane Job 'Celebrating Gertrudes' p. 252.
94 Doloranda Pember *Mercedes Gleitze: A Sea Career* unpublished manuscript, 2014 personal communication 2 May 2014.
95 Ciara Chambers 'An Advertiser's Dream: The Construction of the "Consumptionist" Cinematic Persona of Mercedes Gleitze' *Alphaville Journal of Film and Screen Media* 6: 2 Winter 2013 pp. 10–11 www.alphavillejournal.com/Issue6.html accessed 31 July 2019.
96 Underwood & Underwood *Mercedes Gleitz Postcard* 26 June 1928 National Portrait Gallery NPGx136729 www.npg.org.uk/collections/search/person/mp58662/mercedes-gleitze accessed 3 July 2019.
97 Peter Lovesey 'Violet Piercy (b. 1889?)' *Oxford Dictionary of National Biography* Oxford: Oxford University Press www.oxforddnb.com/view/article/103698 accessed 17 August 2019.
98 Lynne Robinson *Tripping Daintily Into the Arena: A Social History of English Women's Athletics 1921–1960* unpublished PhD thesis, Warwick University Warwickshire, 1997.
99 Maurice Roche *Mega-Events and Modernity: Olympics and Expos in the Growth of Global Culture* London and New York: Routledge, 2000 p. 101.
100 The Daily Express 'These Tremendous Years 1919–1938: A History in Photographs of Life and Events, Big and Little, in Britain and The World Since The War' London: Daily Express Publications, 1938 p. 48.
101 Associated Newspapers Ltd. *The Royal Jubilee Book 1910–1935: Telling in Pictures the Story of 25 Momentous Years in the Reign of Their Majesties King George V and Queen Mary* London: Associated Newspapers Ltd, 1935 p. 124.
102 Stephen G. Jones 'The Leisure Industry in Britain 1918–1939' *Service Industries Journal* 5: 1 1985 pp. 90–106.
103 Jeffrey Richards *Cinema and Radio in Britain and America 1920–1960* p. 1.
104 Jeffrey Hill *Sport, Leisure and Culture in Twentieth-Century Britain* London: Palgrave Macmillan, 2002 pp. 24–26.
105 British Pathé 'Tennis Film 1920–1929' British Pathé Archives FILM ID: 2448.08 www.britishpathe.com/video/tennis-film/ accessed 21 July 2019.
106 Jean Williams *A Beautiful Game: International Perspectives on Women's Football* London: Berg, 2007 pp. 120–2.

107 Ciara Chambers 'An Advertiser's Dream' pp. 1–15.
108 Sue Macy *Winning Ways: A Photohistory of American Women in Sports* New York: Henry Holt and Company, 1996 p. 61.
109 G. Van Rossem (ed.) on behalf of The Netherlands Olympic Committee *The Ninth Olympiad Being the Official Report of the Olympic Games of 1928 Celebrated at Amsterdam Part One* Amsterdam: J. H De Bussy Ltd, 1928 p. 54.
110 Erik Jensen *Body By Weimar: Athletes, Gender, and German Modernity* New York: OUP USA, 2010.

Chapter 3

The first all-female British Olympic team at Lake Placid, USA in 1932

Mollie, Joan, Cecilia and Megan

Introduction

This chapter analyses the status of the British Olympic Association (BOA), and its representative women's teams, between the 1928 Winter Olympics in St Moritz and the Winter Games of Garmisch-Partenkirchen in 1936. The broad themes here continue to be amateur and voluntary participation, nuanced by social class and by the BOA's consciousness of international rivalry on a world stage, as the Olympics themselves became increasingly consumerist and technocratic in their staging, and distinctly more hostile as the Berlin Summer Games of 1936 approached. There were many firsts established in these years, from lighting the Olympic flame in the stadium, to Hollywood intervening in the staging of the Lake Placid Winter Olympics of 1932. At Lake Placid, Britain had its first all-female team; four figure skaters whose attendance also nuances our understanding of how amateur sport could benefit from techniques honed in professional environments, such as specialising in a discipline at an early age, and practicing year-round with top level coaching to compete at the highest level. Also becomes notable across this period are the range and variety of Olympic female competitors, which expanded considerably in both additional sports and disciplines, although this process was contested and uneven.

St Moritz and Amsterdam 1928

Of the 32-strong British team at the St Moritz Winter Olympic Games in February 1928, the three women who took part, Kathleen Lovett, Ethel Muckelt and Kathleen Shaw, were all skaters from Manchester. Lovett finished last in the Pairs competition with Proctor Burman, while Muckelt and Jack Page took seventh overall.[1] Ethel Muckelt was 42 years of age and although she continued to compete into her 50s, this would be her final Olympic Games. Kathleen Shaw finished 14th in the women's singles. Led by Sonja Henie, 'The Girl With the Golden Skates', 'Pavlova of the Ice' and 'Queen of the Ice, the women's competitions had moved on considerably, as had the technical proficiency in the Pairs.[2] A single bronze medal overall for the British team, won by David, Earl of Northesk in the skeleton bob event, saw them finish last equal, with Czechoslovakia, Belgium, Switzerland and Germany. Winter Olympics were still very small affairs; there had been 464 competitors in all, comprised of 438 men and 26 women and so the damage to national prestige was nowhere near as large as coming last in a Summer Games would have been.

The two most repeated concerns of both the BOA and the British Press, in the approach to the Summer Games in Amsterdam in July and August 1928, were the relative weaknesses of preparation of the British and Empire teams, compared with the effects of the specialist intensive training of US athletes.[3] A narrative of American excess was widely reported by the British media, extending even to reports of US competitors eating four ice creams a day; two steaks at lunch and 12-course dinners, including many luxuries from 'from soup to nuts'.[4] There would be almost 3,000 athletes in Amsterdam, and women would number just over 10 per cent of those competing.

There were also several very strong European national teams. This was evident at the first Olympic female gymnastics display in 1928, which included a team of 12 British women who took the bronze medal behind teams of the same size from the Netherlands and Italy.[5] The team was: Alice Broadbent; Lucy Desmond; Margaret Hartley; Amy Jagger; Isobel 'Queenie' Judd; Jessie Kite; Marjorie 'Midge' Moreman; Edith 'Carrie' Pickles; Ethel Seymour; Ada Smith; Hilda Smith and Doris Woods. There are particularly engaging photographs of the British and Italian women's teams in the official report.[6] Additional mixed gymnastic displays of 16 men and/or women were not classified as worthy of medals and Britain did not enter. A potential line of research would be a collective biography, to find out how each of the British women came to be selected; presumably Ada and Hilda Smith were related.

Two women were involved in the mixed yachting events in Amsterdam and both also suggest fascinating lines of enquiry for researchers. The star of the gold medal-winning 8-metre yachting class was captain of the French vessel *L'Aile VI*, Virginie Hériot. Hériot was heiress of the Grands Magasins du Louvre retail empire in Paris and sailed with five male colleagues. Born in 1890, and enjoying the title Viscountess of Haincque de Saint-Sénoch, Hériot was dedicated to sailing to such a degree that she was called 'Madam de la Mer'. After her Olympic success, Hériot had a distinguished international career before injury at sea caused her premature death in 1932. The annual Coupe Virginie Hériot still memorialises her achievements, as does a plaque outside what used to be her Parisian apartment.

The female British representative in the 8-metre yachting class was Margaret Roney, aged 28, of Lambeth in London. Roney sailed aboard the yacht *Yeo* with her younger brothers Ernest, aged 27, and Esmond, aged 20. Since Ernest had already won a silver medal at the Paris Olympic Games with an all-male crew, it would be particularly worthwhile to know how Margaret came to join him and her other brother in 1928, along with team-mates Philip Faile, Thomas Riggs and Thomas Skinner. However, unlike the three wins led by Hériot, the British had a relatively undistinguished competition and finished seventh overall.

Women's track and field athletics had been introduced at the Amsterdam Olympic Games in 1928, with just five disciplines available (100 metres; 800 metres; 4 × 100-metres relay, high jump and discus).[7] The Women's Amateur Athletic Association (WAAA), formed in 1922, boycotted the Amsterdam Olympic Games in protest at the limited range of competition, although 95 women did compete in the track and field events. Published poet, Halina Konopacka of Poland won the discus competition with the other medals going to Lillian Copeland of the USA and Ruth Svedberg of Sweden.[8] Konopacka thereby became the first track and field female gold medallist in Olympic history: she was suitably nicknamed 'Miss Olympia'.[9] Elizabeth 'Betty' Robinson of the USA won the 100-metres race, with Canadians Bobby Rosenfeld and Elizabeth 'Betty' Smith in second and third place.[10] The Canadian team won the 4 × 100-metres relay ahead of the Americans, with Germany taking the bronze.[11]

However, it was the 800-metres race that distilled anxieties about women's athletics on behalf of track and field's world governing body, the International Amateur Athletics Federation (IAAF), even though there were successes such as a world record time by first place athlete Linda Radke of Germany in 2 minutes 16.4 seconds, who knocked seven seconds off her previous best time.[12] There were also personal bests for silver medallist Kinuye Hitomi of Japan and third placed Inga Gentzel of Sweden.[13] In spite of these good performances however, and those of North American athletes, the 800 metres was not contested again by women in the Olympic Games until 1960.[14] This left the longest Olympic track and field distance for women after 1928 to be the 200-metres race.

Allegations that competitors were physically distressed and fell onto the tracks at the end of the race were much exaggerated in the British Press with *The Daily Sketch* warning of enlarged hearts, premature ageing and unspecified 'racial evils'.[15] The International Amateur Athletics Federation used the controversy to limit female track events to short sprints.[16] In spite of appeals by Dr Bergmann of Germany and Britain's Lady Heath, the Federation used the occasion to vote to retain women's track and field athletics on the Olympic programme (by 16 votes to 6) but to reject (by 14 votes to 8) proposals for future 800-metres races, a long jump contest, and a shot-put event.[17] Florence A. Somers, Associate Director of the Sargent School of Physical Education of Boston University, was prompted to write on the need for careful medical supervision and scientific methods in coaching women's sport.[18]

Since this was the first time Germany had joined Olympic competition since World War I, Radke's success marked an international resurgence for their female athletes. She was also the first international success for the Sportschuhfabrik Gebrüder Dassler specialist spiked running shoe manufacturer formed in 1924 by brothers Rudolph and Adi Dassler, later developers of the Puma and Adidas brands.[19] Anti-German feeling may have been why the British press were so keen to undermine Radke's success. In the absence of British women, some newspapers instead chose to promote the 'Empire Success' of athletes like Ethel Catherwood 'The Saskatoon Lily' who, competing for Canada, set a world record in the high jump 'with curls and a smile'.[20] Behind Catherwood, came Carolina 'Lien' Gisolf of the Netherlands to win the silver medal and America's Mildred Wiley in bronze position.[21]

At the Amsterdam Olympic Games in 1928, Muriel Freeman would again take the silver medal in the women's foil competition, a feat matched four years later by Heather Seymour Guinness in 1932.[22] Gladys Daniell concluded her Olympic career in 1928 with a fifth place overall. Her brother, Cyrus 'Leaf' Daniell had won a silver medal in the Men's Épée Team event at the 1908 London Olympics Games. Peggy Butler finished in sixth place overall in 1928 and would come tenth in 1932. Again, the official reports have wonderful photographs of the competitors.

Scottish swimmer Ellen King would return to her second Olympic Games in 1928, to take a silver medal in the 100-metres backstroke, behind Marie Braun of the Netherlands and ahead of her team-mate Joyce Cooper.[23] Cooper also took a bronze in the 100-metres freestyle on a vote by judges ahead of Jean McDowell in fourth place.[24] Cooper and Ellen King would combine with Sarah 'Cissie' Stewart and Iris Tanner to take the silver medal in the 4 × 100-metres freestyle relay and this was widely reported back in Britain.[25] Like King, Stewart was a Scottish swimmer, perhaps as well known for her two bronze Empire Games medals in 1930 as her Olympic feats, having come fourth in the 400-metres freestyle event in Amsterdam behind Martha Norelius (USA); Marie Braun (the Netherlands) and Josephine McKim (USA).[26] Jean McDowell's presence also illustrates that Scottish women's swimming made a significant contribution to the squad.[27]

Ceylon-born Joyce Cooper's father was a tea planter and she would become a stalwart of British swimming for the Mermaid club and at international level. Cooper won one gold, four silver and a bronze medal at the 1927 and 1931 European championships and, while representing England, four gold medals at the 1930 British Empire Games, and another Freestyle relay bronze in the Los Angeles Olympics in 1932. Cooper married rower John Badcock, who won a silver in the rowing eights at Amsterdam and would later take a gold in the coxless fours in Los Angeles. Their elder son Felix later went on to row in the 1958 Commonwealth Games, with his younger brother David a substitute for the squad. How many British 'Olympic couples' and 'sporting families' have existed? Their individual and joint experiences of successive Games remain to be unpicked as yet.

Remembering her career in the 1928, and the 1932 Olympic Games as a 90-year-old, Joyce Badcock had clearly lost none of her drive:

> I have to say I feel I got there largely in spite of the ASA rather than because of them! Naughty, I know! What speed I had was due to the fact in school holidays I saw Vera Tanner who was in our 1924 team doing the crawl stroke. To that point my legs and back had given me trouble. We were swimming self-taught in the sea and if I tried to raise alternate arms out of the water my legs froze. Was the crawl the solution to my troubles? Yes! I had some lessons summer 1925 – outwith whooping cough – having joined Eastbourne SC. I came from a school girl with weak legs etc to a national standard in about eighteen months... In my later racing days when I was pretty well tee-total, those looking after me, as I often collapsed, would give me literally about 2 teaspoonfuls of whiskey and I would be fine in a matter of minutes, whereas in ordinary life if I had whiskey I used to get 'giggly'.[28]

Not all of the women swimmers in Amsterdam were young. Hammersmith's Dora Gibb, who was eliminated in the first rounds of the 200-metres backstroke, was 40 years old at the time of her only Olympic appearance. At 23, Croydon's Mabel Hamblen was also eliminated early on, as was Manchester's Marjory Hinton, aged just 12.[29] Hinton was the youngest competitor at the Games, a source of pride in the regional press, as well as the nationals.[30] Torquay's Edith Mayne represented Britain briefly in the women's 400-metres freestyle. Doris Grimes also left the High Diving competition in its early stages, whereas Kathleen Le Rossignol of the Jersey Swimming Club, Saint Helier came seventh overall and Belle White, in her fourth and final Olympics, eighth. Like the Fancy Diving competition, in which there were no British contenders, the High Diving was dominated by the US women, with just one Swedish bronze medal breaking up the American monopoly.

In 1928, British painter Laura Knight began her Olympic career at the age of 50, by submitting two works (Boxers and Repos) to the painting section of the Arts competition.[31] Boxers took the silver medal amid some exceptional work, including her British contemporaries Anna Airy, Alfred Munnings, Kathleen Bridle, Lilian Davidson and Lizzy Ansingh.[32] Born in Long Eaton, Derbyshire, Laura Knight's husband, Harold, also entered the competition.

Laura Knight was honoured Dame Commander of the British Empire in 1929 and became the third woman elected as a Full Academician to the Royal Academy of Arts in 1936.[33] The previous two female Academicians had been founder members Mary Moser and Angelica Kauffman in 1768. Known for her depictions of active entertainment figures (dancers, circus performers and actors), Knight was also an official war artist in both World Wars; including at the Nuremberg trials on the leadership of the Third Reich. Laura

Knight also entered the 1932 Los Angeles and 1948 London Olympic art competitions; in the latter case with Boxing II, which received an honourable mention at fourth place.

Direct costs associated with the 1928 Amsterdam Olympic Games can be difficult to determine, since they were paid over a protracted period of time, in different amounts, but they were certainly in excess of £8,750, excluding office rent and administrative expenses.[34] Participating in the St Moritz Winter Games had cost just £556 in comparison.[35] Perhaps unsurprisingly, roughly half of each budget was spent on housing and feeding the competitors.[36] The public appeal had brought in over £18,000 (along with £7,000 pledged but as yet uncollected by the end of 1928) and the surplus was placed in a deposit account at Lloyds bank.

Interestingly, over one-third of this money had come from individual donations. The role of *The Daily Mail* in supporting the appeal was considerable. On 15 February 1928, the funds had reached £5,000. After Lord Rothermere had committed *The Daily Mail* to the BOA cause, £12,000 was secured by the end of the month, with considerably more promised. It is also clear that sports clubs and associations accounted for less than £1,000 of the money raised overall.

Lake Placid and Los Angeles 1932

The lease on the BOA's Piccadilly offices was not renewed after Christmas 1928 and some of the support staff were dismissed, including typist Miss Colby, who enjoyed a £5 honorarium for her hard work. After the British Olympic Council met in the Board Room of the British Chemical Manufacturers Ltd on 19 December 1928, a more permanent office was obtained for £100 per annum with the National Playing Fields Association in 1929, with a view to constituting a new committee for the Winter and Summer Olympics of 1932.[37] This rental seemed good value, as it included rates and taxes, lighting, heating, cleaning and the use of the Board Room.

It also provided a good base for the broader ambitions of the BOA to improve Britain's sporting culture and by January 1929, the BOA could afford to invest a £7,000 surplus with the National Discount Company at 4.5 per cent interest.[38] Very gradually, women became more evident in the BOA infrastructure. Mrs Cambridge, the editor of the *British Olympic Journal*, was joined at Council meetings by Verrall Newman, who had been a competitor in the women's plain high dive in the Paris 1924 Olympic Games.

Women also became more prominent as competitors. At the Winter Games in 1932, held at Lake Placid in the USA over 11 days from 4 February, figure skating singles and pairs competitions remained the only full medal events open to women. In spite of unsettled, and therefore challenging, weather conditions and the economic consequences of the Depression, 364 athletes from 17 nations attended. Invitations had, however been sent to 65 national teams. The Lake Placid Winter Games of 1932 introduced women's speed skating as a demonstration event over 500 metres, 1,000 metres and 1,500 metres for the first time.[39] Contested by five competitors from North America, the gold medals went, respectively, to Canadians Jean Wilson and Elizabeth Dubois, with Kit Klein of the USA taking the bronze.[40]

Lake Placid therefore saw the first all-female British Olympic team of just four figure skaters, who could only participate in the individual competitions.[41] The figure skating as a whole was contested by 13 nations; more than any other sport. However, the women singles was restricted to seven national representatives (including Austria, Belgium, Canada, Great Britain, Norway, Sweden and the USA) with the mixed pairs contested by just four teams (Canada, France, Hungary and the USA). However, social class was an important part of the story of how, and why, the four British women came to comprise the entire team at Lake Placid.

The reasons for a small team were mainly financial, so far as the BOA said it was concerned, but also because the Winter Olympics still had much less prestige than the Summer Games. A letter from the Skating Association was considered in November 1931, that forecast no British representative would be in the medals and, in view of cost, one man and one woman should be sent as a token gesture with the hope of a top six placing.[42]

Similarly, the British Ice Hockey Association sought to identify male British-born players in Canada and the USA, both to enlarge the search for talent and to save on travel costs. Bobsleigh was not considered a national sport, so any male competitors had to fund their own way. As late as December 1931, the BOA decided that only one skating competitor was proficient enough to fund at Lake Placid, presumably Mollie Phillips although she was not named, and allocated £75, 14 shillings and 3 pence for the purpose.

For the first time in Olympic history, Great Britain's flag bearer at Lake Placid was a woman. Mollie Phillips was by far the senior member of the team at the age of 24, when compared with Joan Dix at 13 years of age; Cecilia Colledge and Megan Taylor were both just 11 years old.[43] Colledge was 11 years and 83 days, making her slightly younger than Taylor, at 11 years and 102 days, and she remains the youngest ever Olympian.[44] Dix's father Fred was originally from Norfolk and he had been a speed skater, competing at the 1924 and 1928 Olympic Games.

Megan Taylor was the highest-placed British athlete in seventh position, just ahead of Cecilia Colledge, Mollie Philips and Joan Dix. There are many press cuttings in the IOC archive files relating to these games, although many are unfortunately unattributable, which illustrates how the British women, particularly Taylor and Colledge, were mediated to an international audience, with their photographs accompanying reports in Czechoslovakian, English, French, German, Hungarian, Norwegian and Swedish.

Born in Wimbledon, Megan Taylor was coached from infancy by her father, Philip, who had been a speed skater. She would be a long-time rival to

Cecilia Colledge and, by extension, Sonja Henie. Colledge, was the daughter of a surgeon and was coached by Jacques Gerschwiler, and had trained at the exclusive Ice Club, Westminster from 1928. In each case therefore, the young women of the team (Colledge, Dix and Taylor) had a considerable amount of financial support and family interest in their chosen sport. It was this, and some private appeals by the Skating Association, rather than the BOA, that got one woman and three girls to Lake Placid.

The stageing of the Lake Placid and Los Angeles Olympics of 1932 caused the BOA once again to debate the relationship between amateur values and specialist preparation. Given the hours that Colledge and Taylor in particular spent training each day, with specialist coaching and a huge parental financial commitment, this was a little disingenuous. Even the timings, using a chronometer rather than a stopwatch, evidenced this increased technocracy. This was primarily described as an American 'problem' but correspondence between the BOA with the IOC over 'broken time' payments and implied professionalism had been sustained since 1920; especially regarding Olympic football tournaments.[45]

Somewhat redundantly, given the constitution of committee members, a rule issued at the end of 1929 stipulated that anyone joining the British Olympic Association or Council should sign a form including the words: 'I declare myself an amateur'.[46] By 1931, Lord Rothermere had stood down as Chairman of the BOA, in favour of Sir Harold Bowden and the committee eventually decided it could send a team to Los Angeles for around £150 per individual.[47]

With the Los Angeles Games approaching, each innovation, from the housing of athletes at the Olympic village, to the competition to find an Olympic Hymn was cautiously and judiciously weighed by the BOA.[48] A typist who had worked for the first Empire Games administration, Miss Shale, was employed on a salary of £12 per month; she undoubtedly earned every penny, and by 1932, this had risen to £15 with an assistant, Miss Fox, also employed on £11 a month.[49]

Logistically, the scale of the BOA tour to Los Angeles was larger than anything it had attempted before, including attending St Louis in 1904 and hosting the Olympic Games themselves in 1908. The Los Angeles Games were also very expensive after Britain had fallen off the Gold Standard in 1931.[50] Although there were outstanding performances, the BOA sent the lowest number of competitors since 1904; almost half the size of the team in 1928. A long running rivalry with a close ally meant that the BOA were keenly aware of the public relations significance of competing in America.

Even so, most competitors were to arrive in Los Angeles, via ship to New York and then by train through Chicago, just a day or so before they competed.[51] Gymnastic tunics were among the most expensive items of clothing equipment at 39 shillings each; while a formal dress for the Opening and Closing Ceremony cost 24 shillings and 6 pence and swimsuits were priced at 21 shillings.

The bungalow village scheme enabled the administrators and competitors to be housed together, with a dedicated kitchen and dining room, for $2 per person per day 'all in'. The BOA were to find and fund their own cooks and other staff in the USA. The railway timetables were analysed for opportunities for the British team to 'work-out' en route, and it was estimated that the trip from Chicago to Los Angeles would take 63 hours 10 minutes if this was decided upon, with a saving of four hours if no chance for exercise was given.

At the 1932 Summer Olympic Games, the women's track and field athletics events involved 54 participants from 11 countries. The United States of America had the largest team, with a 15-strong team; Japan 11; Canada 7; Germany 5; Great Britain 5; the Netherlands 5; Poland 3 and Australia, Mexico, New Zealand and South Africa had one single entrant. Each woman could take part in up to three events. Initially the WAAA requested a team of four sprinters to make up a relay team; the Amateur Swimming Association planned to send seven female competitors, and the Amateur Fencing Association just two.[52]

The decision to fund a five-strong women's track and field team was taken as late as 20 June 1932.[53] By then the appeal fund stood at just over £7,200, with some of the invested funds to be used to make up the remainder of an estimated £10,500 to send a team, with officials, coaches and masseurs, of 103 individuals, although again it can be difficult to say since the Football Association usually paid for its own expenses, as did individuals who took part in the more well-off sports such as yachting.[54]

Captain F. A. M. Webster became the official editor of the *Olympic Journal* and was a strong supporter of the BOA in wider sporting circles. To magnify their appeal, the BOA again resorted to the support of Lord Rothermere at *The Daily Mail* to improve matters but he declined to attempt to raise £10,000 in the dire economic circumstances. Grudgingly, Leicester greyhound track was authorised to use BOA letter-headed paper for a special meeting to raise funds. Both the makers of *Horlicks* and *Ovaltine* offered to provide malted milk to British Olympians free of charge.

British women's track and field athletics five-strong Olympic team in 1932 did not reflect the vibrant mix of international competition between the wars. In Britain, this included business house competitions, educational tournaments and friendly networks with international rivals. Both the financial constraints and some antipathy to women's athletics explain why no British female contestants were sent for the high jump, the javelin and the discus.[55] The team comprised sprinters Gwendoline Porter, Eileen Hiscock and Ethel Johnson (100 metres) and Violet Webb (80-metres hurdles) and Nellie Halstead. Webb obtained a fifth place in the hurdles final and Hiscock matched this in the 100 metres. Nellie Halstead was the fourth leg of the 4 × 100-metres relay team, along with Webb, Porter and Hiscock, to take the bronze medal behind the United States and Canada, and ahead of the Netherlands, Japan and Germany. Ethel Johnson was injured during her 100-metres heats, enabling either Halstead or Webb to substitute, depending on source material, and win her place in Olympic history.

The US track and field team was led by the brilliant all-rounder Mildred Ella Didrikson, who dominated media headlines as Fanny Blankers Koen would again in 1948. However, Didrikson was on home soil and, having been inspired by reports of the 1928 Amsterdam Olympics, she appeared to embody the American Dream coming from 'a financially poor but richly happy family' to win her medals after a lot of hard work.[56] Born in 1911 as the sixth of seven children to a family of Norwegian heritage, 'Babe' was small, at just over 1.53 metres and weighing 48 kilos.[57]

There were some concerns about her amateur status, as she had reportedly earned £25 a week as an entertainer before taking up sport seriously and had been employed as a clerk at the Employers' Casualty Insurance Company, based in Dallas, on $75 dollars a month, entitling her to play basketball for the work's team, The Golden Cyclones. Although governed by the Amateur Athletic Union, the competition led to a lot of shamateurism as firms employed women more for their athletic skills than their administrative ability. In typical style, Babe declared that she had exceeded at both.

By the time of the 1932 Olympic selection trials, her ability was already clear therefore, and it was track and field athletics that really made her name. Babe Didrikson won the 80-metres hurdle race and the javelin, breaking the world record in each to establish new Olympic standards. In the 80-metres hurdles. Evelyne Hall of the USA and South Africa's Marjorie Clark, who had previously held the world record, took the silver and bronze. Didrikson narrowly missed out on winning a third gold medal, when tied for the high jump, but her attempt in the jump-off, using a Western roll technique was ruled as illegal and disqualified her, although her previous efforts won second place. She concluded that 'I have lost but I was not beaten' by the judges' decision.[58] Babe had a subsequent career as an entertainer and was America's leading professional female golf celebrity in the 40s and 50s, before her untimely death from cancer, aged just 45 years.

Along with Tilly Fleischer of Germany (who came third in the javelin, fourth in the discus and sixth with the German relay team), the Los Angeles track and field events showcased a number of all-rounders. Stanislawa Walasiewicz of Poland was the other most high-profile athlete, winning the 100 metres and coming sixth in the discus. She held records over three sprint distances in the 1930s (60, 100 and 200 metres) representing the Pologne club, a nationalist organisation in Poland and overseas.[59] Walasiewicz could legitimately have expected to win more gold medals in 1936. However, this was not to be.

In fencing, Britain's Heather Seymour Guinness, the daughter of the engineer, banker and politician Henry Seymour Guinness from the Irish brewing family, beat Helen Meyer of Germany to get to the final.[60] Meyer was just

17 years old at the time and was well known to British competitors, having recently won the Alfred Hutton Memorial Cup for the first time. The British champion Maude 'Peggy' Butler had previously been eliminated, coming in fourth place overall.[61]

Guinness went into the final against Ellen Preis of Austria, tied for the overall number of bouts won (eight each) but with fewer points against her, which suggested a competitive advantage. A judge twice gave Guinness the gold medal before she raised the two hits that had not been counted, and the match went to rival Helen Preis, giving her the gold by five bouts to three. An outstanding athlete, Preis was to go on to compete for a 24-year period at the Games, from 1932–1956, which, even with the suspension due to the Second World War is an incredible record. Erna Bogen of Hungary won the bronze medal in 1932. British foilists who came to prominence after 1945, such as Gillian Sheen (1956 Olympic gold medallist and 10 times British foil champion); Betty Arbuthnot and Mary Glen Haig (both twice British foil champions) can be seen to have benefitted from this longer tradition.[62]

The swimming races cost spectators one dollar to attend in the morning and two dollars in the afternoon. With 17 events on offer, the swimming stadium had space for 10,000 onlookers, drawing some the largest crowds and revenues of the Los Angeles Games.[63] There were no British female diving competitors in 1932, and Americans won four of the five women's swimming events, with Clare Dennis of Australia capturing the only other gold medal. The British swimmers were versatile; perhaps of necessity.[64] Elizabeth Davies took home the bronze medal in the 100-metres backstroke, while her team-mates Phyllis Harding and Joyce Cooper came in fourth and sixth, respectively. In spite of little medal success in the 100-metre freestyle individual race from Edna Hughes, Elizabeth Davies and Joyce Cooper, another bronze followed in the team 4 × 100-metres freestyle relay, with the addition of Helen Varcoe.

Phyllis Harding in particular had reason to be disappointed with her individual time, having set a world record previously that year of 1 minute 18.6 seconds, bettered only by 0.3 of a second in 1932 by the gold medallist Eleanor Holmes. Cooper would go on to come fourth overall in the individual 400-metres freestyle competition, after winning her heat. In the 200-metres breaststroke, Marjorie Hinton came in fourth place but Cecilia 'Cee Cee' Wolstenhome was eliminated in the heats by a margin of almost 10 seconds. She had previously won a gold medal in the first British Empire Games in 1930, over 200 yards. Both she and her sister Beatrice were members of Moss Side Swim Club and trained under Northern Counties Coach Jack Laverty and his daughter Nellie. Given the schedule, it perhaps comes as no surprise that seven of the British swimmers were treated in the on-site hospital; mostly for muscle aches and strains but, intriguingly, in one unnamed case, for acute appendicitis.

Women were notable for their presence in the staging of the Los Angeles Games, as the official report indicates. From increased public relations leadership, to ticket sales and logistics, communications technology and so forth, the extent of female employment at such a mega event demonstrated the increased role of women in the workforce. This remains an under-researched area, quite apart from the competitors in the various arenas and their mediation to international audiences. Not only were women increasingly the focus of sporting spectacle but also part of the expanded mechanics of how an Olympic Games actually worked.

Garmisch-Partenkirchen 1936

Following Los Angeles, the British Olympic Association was able to invest an additional £2,000 of Western Australian Stock and deposit £500 with the National Discount Committee.[65] It concluded in 1933 with £3,751 with the National Building Society and £1,000 with the Woolwich Building Society, a sign of how investing the fundraising from 1928 continued to pay dividends.[66] More than preparing for Garmisch-Partenkirchen and Berlin in 1936 however, their immediate concern was fundraising and assisting the English committee of The British Empire Games of 1934. To this end, Lord Burghley became Vice Chair of the BOA, and several influential Vice Presidents were installed, including Lord Aberdare, Lord Moynihan, Lord Rochdale, Sir Horace Rumbold, Sir John Simon and Philip Noel Baker. Due to other commitments, Lord Rochdale and Brigadier Kentish had resigned from the IOC. Lord Burghley and Noel Curtis-Bennett were elected as replacements. Due to a slightly cheaper rent, the BOA moved offices from 71 to 77 Ecclestone Terrace at the end of 1933.

By this time, the BOA were keenly aware of potential problems around the participation of Jewish athletes in the Berlin Olympic Games and although F. A. M. Webster had written an article on the subject, approved by Lord Aberdare, a decision was taken not to publish this 'in the official organ of the Association'.[67]

A carefully worded resolution was eventually passed in October 1934:

> That this Association, having taken note of the undertakings given to the International Olympic Committee on behalf of the German Government and relying upon their faithful observance and the removal and/or absence of any discrimination against Jewish athletes desiring or eligible to represent Germany in the forthcoming Olympic Games, accepts the invitation extended by the German Olympic Committee to participate in those Games at Berlin and Garmisch-Partenkirchen in 1936.[68]

Otherwise, perhaps because of the London Empire Games of 1934, where 500 athletes competed, it was a slow year, in terms of BOA business.

Accordingly, in May, typist Miss Shale was dismissed with six weeks' notice and Muriel Cornell joined the British Olympic Council as the Women's Amateur Athletic Association (WAAA) representative.[69] Miss Shale was re-hired in January 1935 on a salary of £14 a month and in 1936, she was again provided with an assistant. Miss Shale would also provide secretarial support in Berlin at the Games themselves.

The main BOA business of 1935 related to the media and accreditation rights for Berlin, which were strictly controlled. No Press photographers of individual newspapers would be permitted into arenas, the BOA was advised, and only a small fixed number of reporters would be allowed.[70] Even private 16 mm films of the athletes when competing for governing body instructional and coaching purposes were refused. In view of the costs, it was deemed impossible for the BOA to support the expanded Arts competitions for 1936, with those who wished to do so funding their own costs.[71] Like the French, British artists were notably absent. Even so, the British sent a team of 208 competitors to Berlin, perhaps conscious of at least some of the propaganda related to national virility. At the same time, in view of the scale of the conflict and human cost that was to follow the Olympics, there was a serious degree of naivety in insisting upon going to Berlin.

Compared with the small competition in 1932, women's figure skating was intensely competitive by the time of the 1936 Garmisch-Partenkirchen Winter Olympics, with 43 women and 41 men involved in the events. Cecilia Colledge was to take home a silver medal, the only female to do so of the 17 won by British competitors, the majority being a dozen Ice Hockey team golds and four bronzes for the men's bobsleigh crew.[72] Sending the bobsleigh crew cost around £330 alone. Helen Blane, Birnie Duthie, Jeanette Kessler and Eve Pinching also represented Great Britain in the women's Alpine Skiing event. The uniform costs were kept to an absolute minimum of a tie and a Union Jack badge with the words 'Olympic Winter Games 1936' embroidered in red.

Violet Cliff, Mollie Phillips, Belita Jepson-Turner (aged 12), and Gweneth Butler made up the rest of the women's singles skating team at Garmisch-Partenkirchen, Megan Taylor having suffered an accident just before the Olympic trials. Violet Cliff would skate with husband Leslie to finish seventh overall in the Pairs competition and Rosemarie Stewart would partner Ernest Yates for tenth place.

Although finishing 11th in the singles at the Garmisch-Partenkirchen Olympic Games, Germany in 1936, Mollie Phillips was a pioneer of women's skating and an accomplished sporting administrator. A trained lawyer, Phillips had notable dual roles in administration and as a skating judge. She was elected to the Council of the National Ice Skating Associations in 1939, becoming the first woman to have such a role. She went on to become a high-profile figure skating judge and, at the 1948 World Figure Skating Championships, the first woman to referee at that level. Holding several public offices, including a Justice of the Peace, Phillips later briefly also became a dairy farmer before a well-earned retirement.

Ahead of Colledge, Sonja Henie would win gold in her final Olympics. Henie had won all World and European Championships in the years between 1932 and 1936. Megan Taylor had finished second behind Henie at the World Championships in 1934 and 1936. Shortly after winning her third gold medal and tenth successive world championship, Henie turned professional. She was to become one of the wealthiest and most famous Olympians ever. The ice spectacular, 'Ice Capades', became part of the Sonja Henie portfolio, as were clothing and equipment endorsements that increased the popularity of figure skating worldwide. The child star had amassed an international property portfolio worth over 10 million dollars by the time she was 42, and this shrewd investment, in addition to her ice spectaculars made her one of the wealthiest women of her time.[73] The examples of Sonja Henie, like earlier athletes Suzanne Lenglen and US swimmer Aileen Riggin, indicate that Olympic sporting success could increasingly transition to an entertainment industry career, and back again. Appearance, display and consumerism became an increasingly significant element of Olympic competition and some women were world-leading in pioneering broader developments in this regard.

After Henie's retirement, Cecilia Colledge and Megan Taylor became 'one of figure skating's great rivalries'[74] Colledge won the World, European and British Championships in 1937, while Taylor won the World Championships in 1938 and 1939. Taylor came second to Colledge in three successive European Championships (1937, 1938 and 1939). After her retirement from amateur competition, Taylor joined the 'Ice Capades' before World War II broke out and she emigrated to the USA. Colledge drove an ambulance during World War II and the family were greatly affected by the death of her brother, Maule, who went missing in action. She did however, return to compete as an amateur for one year in 1946. Upon turning professional, she won the Open championship in 1947 and 1948 before moving to Boston in 1951 and coaching for 43 years.

Conclusion

In March 1936, the lack of sophistication of the BOA was perhaps reflected in its serious consideration of a proposal from the Blackpool Corporation to host a future Olympic Games.[75] A sub-committee, including IOC members, was duly dispatched from London at the beginning of April. Given how politicised the Berlin Olympic Games were to be, the idea that a famous funfair location and pleasure beach could host an impending Olympics innocent of world events, was clearly not realistic.

The BOA mood was much more sombre; both in response to its own situation and to sporting international relations. Whereas it had previously decided not to respond to criticism from those who had agitated against the Berlin Olympics, including from the British Non-Sectarian Anti-Nazi Council, the use of propaganda was evident for all to see.[76] The abstention from intervention made the BOA look complicit in some minds, while in others, it complied with a larger sympathy for appeasement. Collections at The National Archives show that opposition to Britain's participation came through formal channels, like the appeal to the BOA from the Archbishop of York against discrimination in Germany, to informal lobbying, like the complaints to the Home Office Swimming Club. However, the BOA was also determinedly optimistic. Restrictions on finance, uniforms, press and so on in Berlin barely registered on the Minute Books. The permanent Secretary to the BOA, Evan Hunter, was more concerned to prepare for the Empire Games in Sydney in 1938 and the Tokyo Olympic Games of 1940, by securing funding and receive a number of international visitors, such as the Secretary of the Mayor of Tokyo.[77]

Notes

1 International Olympic Committee 'Women Figure Skaters St Moritz 1928: Photograph 5185925710' Olympic.org Official Website of the Olympic Movement www.olympic.org/multimedia-player/all-photos/1928/02/01/51859257-10 accessed 30 July 2010.
2 Dr Willy Meisl 'Sonja-Pavlova of the Ice' *World Sports: Official Magazine of the British Olympic Association* February 1954 London: Country and Sporting Publications, 1954 pp. 24–25.
3 Marathon 'Olympiad After-Thoughts: Our Indifferent Finish' *Swindon Advertiser* 9 August 1928 p. 3 BOA Archive, London.
4 Anon 'Ice Cream Four Times a Day: 350 athletes share 580 Steaks' *Daily Chronicle* 2 August 1928 *Women and Sport File* International Olympic Committee Museum and Archives, Lausanne.
5 G. Van Rossem (ed.) on behalf of The Netherlands Olympic Committee *The Ninth Olympiad Being the Official Report of the Olympic Games of 1928 Celebrated at Amsterdam Part Two* Amsterdam: J. H. De Bussy Ltd, 1928 p. 670.
6 G. Van Rossem (ed.) *Official Report of the Olympic Games of 1928 Celebrated at Amsterdam* pp. 648–649.
7 British Olympic Association *Finance and General Purposes Committee Minutes 10 John Street Adelphi (by kind permission of the Amateur Athletic Association) 23 May 1921* BOA Archive, London pp. 1–2.
8 G. Van Rossem (ed.) *Official Report of the Olympic Games of 1928 Celebrated at Amsterdam* pp. 477–479.
9 Anon 'Miss Olympia' *Daily Sketch* 3 August 1928 p. 3 *Women and Sport File* International Olympic Committee Museum and Archives, Lausanne.
10 G. Van Rossem (ed.) *Official Report of the Olympic Games of 1928 Celebrated at Amsterdam* pp. 467–470.
11 G. Van Rossem (ed.) *Official Report of the Olympic Games of 1928 Celebrated at Amsterdam* pp. 479–480.
12 Anon 'Start of the Women's 800 metre race' *The Morning Post* 4 August 1928 p. 12 *Women and Sport File* International Olympic Committee Museum and Archives, Lausanne.
13 G. Van Rossem (ed.) *Official Report of the Olympic Games of 1928 Celebrated at Amsterdam* pp. 471–473.

14 Lynne Emery 'An Examination of the 1928 Olympic 800m Race for Women' *NASSH Prooceedings 1985* p. 30 www.la84foundation.org accessed 10 July 2012.
15 Anon 'Women's Perils as Athletes' *Daily Sketch* 5 August 1928 p. 9 *Women and Sport File* International Olympic Committee Museum and Archives, Lausanne.
16 From Our Geneva Correspondent 'Olympic Games and Women: Ban Likely' *Manchester Guardian* 12 April 1929 p. 5 *Women and Sport File* International Olympic Committee Museum and Archives, Lausanne.
17 Anon. 'Athletics for Women: Ban on 4 Olympic Events' *The Daily Mail* 8 August 1928 p. 17 *Women and Sport File* International Olympic Committee Museum and Archives, Lausanne.
18 Florence A. Somers *Principles of Women's Athletics* New York: A. S. Barnes and Company, 1930.
19 Jean Williams 'Given the Boot: Reading the Ambiguities of British and Continental Football Boot Design' in Jean Williams (ed.) *Sport in History Special Issue Kit: Fashioning the Sporting Body* 25 1 pp. 89–90.
20 Anon. 'Empire Beauty Wins' *Daily Mail* 6 August 1928 p. 28 *Women and Sport File* International Olympic Committee Museum and Archives, Lausanne.
21 G. Van Rossem (ed.) *Official Report of the Olympic Games of 1928 Celebrated at Amsterdam* pp. 473–476.
22 G. Van Rossem (ed.) *Official Report of the Olympic Games of 1928 Celebrated at Amsterdam* pp. 640–643.
23 G. Herbert Spencer 'Not What Was Expected: Miss King's Narrow Defeat' *Daily News* 26 July 1928 *Women and Sport File* International Olympic Committee Museum and Archives, Lausanne.
24 B. Bennison '100 Metres Freestyle Women' *Daily Telegraph* 13 August 1928 *Women and Sport File* International Olympic Committee Museum and Archives, Lausanne.
25 Anon. 'Final Scenes at Amsterdam: British Lady Swimmers Do Well' *Sporting Life* 13 August 1928 *Women and Sport File* International Olympic Committee Museum and Archives, Lausanne.
26 Percy Rudd 'English Girl Fourth in Great Race' *The Daily Chronicle* 6 August 1928 p. 10 *Women and Sport File* International Olympic Committee Museum and Archives, Lausanne.
27 G. Van Rossem (ed.) *Official Report of the Olympic Games of 1928 Celebrated at Amsterdam* pp. 790–799.
28 Joyce Badcock 'Letter to the British Olympic Association undated' *Women and Sport File* International Olympic Committee Museum and Archives, Lausanne.
29 Anon. 'Plucky Swim by 12 year old English Girl' *The Daily Express* 8 August 1928 p. 12 *Women and Sport File* International Olympic Committee Museum and Archives, Lausanne.
30 Anon. 'Marjorie Hinton, the 12 Year old Manchester Girl Swimmer' *Stockport Express* 9 August 1928 p. 18 *Women and Sport File* International Olympic Committee Museum and Archives, Lausanne.
31 Anon. 'Women Athletes: Art at the Olympic Games' *Evening Standard* 5 August 1928 p. 4 *Women and Sport File* International Olympic Committee Museum and Archives, Lausanne.
32 Anon. 'Woman ARA's Win at Olympiad' *Daily Chronicle* 3 August 1928 p. 7 *Women and Sport File* International Olympic Committee Museum and Archives, Lausanne.
33 The Royal Academy of Arts 'Our story: Women at the Royal Academy' *The Royal Academy of Arts* www.royalacademy.org.uk/about-the-ra#our-story accessed 11 May 2019.

34 British Olympic Association *Agenda for Finance Committee Meeting 166 Piccadilly W1 16 October 1928* BOA Archive, London p. 1.
35 British Olympic Association *Minutes of Council Meeting 166 Piccadilly W1 19 December 1928* BOA Archive, London p. 1.
36 British Olympic Association *Minutes of Council Meeting 166 Piccadilly W1 19 December 1928* BOA Archive, London p. 1.
37 British Olympic Association *Minutes of Finance Committee Meeting 166 Piccadilly W1 13 December 1928* BOA Archive, London p. 1.
38 British Olympic Association *Minutes of Finance Committee Meeting 71 Ecclestone Square SW1 10 January 1929* p. 2 BOA Archive, London.
39 George M Lattimer (ed.) *III Olympic Winter Games: Official Report Lake Placid 1932* Lake Placid and New York: III Olympic Winter Games Committee, 1932 p. 258.
40 George M Lattimer (ed.) *III Olympic Winter Games* pp. 259–262.
41 George M Lattimer (ed.) *III Olympic Winter Games* p. 216.
42 British Olympic Association *Finance Committee Minutes 71 Ecclestone Square SW1 12 November 1931* p. 1 BOA Archive, London.
43 George M Lattimer (ed.) *III Olympic Winter Games* p. 175.
44 Obituaries 'Cecilia Colledge: Champion figure skater' *The Independent* 21 April 2008 www.independent.co.uk/news/obituaries/cecilia-colledge-champion-figure-skater-812673.html accessed 14 May 2015.
45 British Olympic Association *Finance and General Purposes Committee Minutes 71 Ecclestone Square SW1 12 December 1929* p. 1 BOA Archive, London.
46 British Olympic Association *Finance and General Purposes Committee Minutes 71 Ecclestone Square SW1 12 December 1929* p. 1 BOA Archive, London.
47 British Olympic Association *Finance and General Purposes Committee Minutes 71 Ecclestone Square SW1 12 February 1931* p. 1 BOA Archive, London.
48 British Olympic Association *Housing and Transport Committee Minutes 71 Ecclestone Square SW1 19 November 1931* pp. 2–5 BOA Archive, London.
49 British Olympic Association *Finance Committee Minutes 71 Ecclestone Square SW1 11 February 1932* p. 1 BOA Archive, London.
50 Juliet Gardiner *The Thirties: An Intimate History* London: Harper Press, 2010 p. 116.
51 British Olympic Association *Finance and General Purposes Committee Minutes 71 Ecclestone Square SW1 9 July 1931* p. 1 BOA Archive, London.
52 British Olympic Association *Finance Committee Minutes 71 Ecclestone Square SW1 14 April 1932* p. 1 BOA Archive, London.
53 British Olympic Association *Finance Committee Minutes 71 Ecclestone Square SW1 20 June 1932* p. 1 BOA Archive, London.
54 British Olympic Association *Finance Committee Minutes 77 Ecclestone Square SW1 20 June 1936* p. 1 BOA Archive, London.
55 Tenth Olympiade Committee (eds.) *Official Report: The Tenth Olympiad 'Los Angeles 1932'* Los Angeles: Tenth Olympiade Committee Official 'Los Angeles 1932' Ltd Part One pp. 462–475.
56 Willy Meisl 'The Babe: A Genius With An Infinite Capacity for Taking Pains' *World Sports The Official Magazine of the British Olympic Association* November 1956 London: Country and Sporting Publications, 1956 pp. 34–35.
57 'Babe' Didrickson Zaharias *This Life I've Led* London: Robert Hale Ltd, 1956.
58 Willy Meisl 'The Babe' p. 35.
59 Fédération Sportive Féminine Internationale *Jeux Féminins Mondiaux Londres 1934: Fourth Womens World Games Official Programme Thursday-Saturday 9–11 August 1934* White City Stadium, London p. 7 London: Fleetway, 1934 WAAA files, Box 2 Birmingham University.

60 Tenth Olympiade Committee *Official Report: The Tenth Olympiad 'Los Angeles 1932'* pp. 520–522.
61 Agnes Mackenzie 'Fencing at the Olympic Games' *The Daily Mirror* 3 August 1928 p. 4 *Women and Sport File* International Olympic Committee Museum and Archives, Lausanne.
62 International Olympic Committee Medallists www.olympic.org accessed 2 February 2020.
63 Tenth Olympiade Committee (eds.) *Official Report: The Tenth Olympiad 'Los Angeles 1932'* Part One pp. 110–112.
64 Tenth Olympiade Committee (eds.) *Official Report: The Tenth Olympiad 'Los Angeles 1932'* Los Angeles: Tenth Olympiade Committee Official 'Los Angeles 1932' Ltd Part Four pp. 639–640.
65 British Olympic Association *Finance Committee Minutes 71 Ecclestone Square SW1 16 March 1933* p. 1 BOA Archive, London.
66 British Olympic Association *Finance Committee Minutes 77 Ecclestone Square SW1 14 December 1933* p. 1 BOA Archive, London.
67 British Olympic Association *Finance Committee Minutes 77 Ecclestone Square SW1 14 December 1933* p. 1 BOA Archive, London.
68 British Olympic Association *Finance Committee Minutes 77 Ecclestone Square SW1 11 October 1934* p. 2 BOA Archive, London.
69 British Olympic Association *Finance Committee Minutes 77 Ecclestone Square SW1 10 May 1934* p. 2 BOA Archive, London.
70 British Olympic Association *Finance Committee Minutes 77 Ecclestone Square SW1 16 April 1935* p. 2 BOA Archive, London.
71 British Olympic Association *Finance Committee Minutes 77 Ecclestone Square SW1 10 October 1935* p. 3 BOA Archive, London.
72 Anon. 'Olympische Ehrentafel' undated circa 1936 *Women and Sport File* International Olympic Committee Museum and Archives, Lausanne.
73 Dr Willy Meisl 'Sonja-Pavolova of the Ice' p. 25.
74 James R. Hines 'Cecilia (Magdalena) Colledge 1920–2008' in Lawrence Goldman (ed.) *The Oxford Dictionary of National Biography* Oxford: Oxford University Press, 2008 p. 234.
75 British Olympic Association *Finance Committee Minutes 77 Ecclestone Square SW1 12 March 1936* p. 1 BOA Archive, London.
76 British Non-Sectarian Anti-Nazi Council *Agitation against holding the Olympic Games in Germany in 1936; suggestion from British Non-Sectarian Anti-Nazi Council* FO 371/19940/306 The National Archives www.nationalarchives.gov.uk/olympics/1936.htm accessed 19 May 2019.
77 British Olympic Association *Finance Committee Minutes 77 Ecclestone Square SW1 10 December 1936* pp. 1–2 BOA Archive, London.

Chapter 4

The 1936 Berlin Olympic Games

How gender and politics shaped the career of athlete Audrey Brown

Introduction

Adolf Hitler opened the Berlin Olympic Games of 1936 with messages of friendship and peace:

> Sporting and chivalrous competition awakens the best human qualities. It does not sever, but on the contrary, unites the opponents in mutual understanding and reciprocal respect. It also helps to strengthen the bonds of peace between the nations. May the Olympic Flame therefore never be extinguished
>
> Adolf Hitler[1]

Jesse Owens, the African-American who would go on to outrage Hitler by winning four gold medals as star of the Games, in turn commented on the relative lack of preparation by the British athletes in the approach to the 1936 Olympic Games:

> You people only seem to go in for training just before an event and work up for all you are worth. You cannot get the best out of a man in that way. Systematic training all the time to a definite schedule, that is our method and I am convinced that it is the proper one. Americans have demonstrated the value of it everywhere in athletics.[2]

Adding that he had specialised in track and field athletics from the age of 14 and had adopted regular and methodical training since that age, Owens also promoted milk as his preferred drink of choice. A week previously, Joe Binks, the ex-holder of the British mile record, had deplored the sorry showing of the British team, compared with overall advances in the United States, Germany and Finland.[3]

This chapter is based on the experiences of track and field athlete Audrey Brown (later Court) at the Berlin Olympic Games in 1936 when these tensions in British amateurism were politicised to an unprecedented degree. Audrey

Brown attended Birmingham University from 1932 and took up running there. This makes her case particularly compelling. As Carol Dyehouse has shown, the number of women entering English universities by the late 1930s had risen to almost 8,000, compared with over 28,000 men.[4] Compared with the figures in 1900, the number of women taking higher education had trebled, even though they were still a significant minority. This placed Brown at the centre of developments in women's athletics, since British institutions of higher and further education were crucial in developing international ties.

Before the case study of Audrey Brown's life is examined, a brief introductory section of the chapter looks at the early foundations of the Women's Amateur Athletic Association (WAAA) that were to benefit Audrey Brown and her colleagues. The argument moves on to consider Audrey's early life in India, and living with to her maternal grandparents near Sutton Coldfield, Birmingham, before going to Boarding School, as a day girl from the age of nine and a boarder at 13. The example demonstrates that Brown was from quite a different class to Gladys Carson and her interest in sport engaged her in radically different networks. Education and public service was, however, central to the lives of both women, though Brown was to go on to have a much wider influence.

Audrey Brown's impressions of the Olympic Games in 1936 follow in the final section of the chapter, focusing on her subsequent working and family life. So much has been written about the 1936 'Nazi' Olympics that the literature is already well-advanced.[5] However, little has been written of how the women who represented Britain in Berlin interpreted the Games at different times in their lives.

The first generation of Women's Amateur Athletic Association pioneers

The structures of women's track and field athletics in Britain grew mainly in institutions of further and higher education, and were explicitly linked to women's increased role in public life. Elaine Burton epitomised this, winning a Northern Counties Ladies' 100 yards championship at the age of 16, wearing spikes, at a Salford Harriers meeting in 1919.[6] Later Baroness Burton, after being a long-time Socialist Party MP for South Coventry from 1950 onwards, Elaine remained a supporter of physically active leisure for women all her life and promoted the message far and wide, including at the House of Commons.[7] Elaine's upper class father was a hurdles finalist at the 1908 Olympic Games, finishing fourth, and he inspired her lifelong enthusiasm. A good hockey player and swimmer, with aspirations to make the Channel crossing, why did Burton choose politics over sport?

> I was only earning £3 a week, and that did not allow enough margin to concentrate on a sport for world-championship purposes. For four years

from the age of twenty I was teaching at an elementary school in Leeds and I would swim for an hour and a half after work in the town bath. But I found that, for one who must work for a living, it was impossible, with such little time and money to develop further in that direction.[8]

In 1921, a women's section was formed at London's Kensington Athletic Club. Sophie Eliott-Lynn and Vera Palmer (later Searle), helped to found Middlesex Ladies' Athletic Club in 1923 after being important members at Kensington.[9] However, the number of working class female athletes was also growing. Business houses hosted athletics meetings for women (including the Dunlop corporation, Lillywhites clothing, Lyons' Tea Houses, the Post Office, the Police and Selfridges Department Store), as did universities like Manchester in 1921 and Birmingham from 1922. The presence of female athletes also became more pronounced in art, literature and culture, as increasing numbers of women participated in track and field athletics. For instance, the controversial ballet *The Bolt* by Dmitri Shostakovich, which would be performed once in 1931, referencing industrial and collective action, including sport and particularly athlete Olga, costumed in shorts and a running vest.[10]

There was strength in depth 10 years later therefore when Audrey joined the networks of women's athletics. Where women worked or studied together, they often played together.[11] War-work, often done alongside men, could be both strenuous and dangerous, either munitions manufacturing on the home front or nursing at the front line. For instance, Eliott-Lynn rode a Harley Davidson as a despatch rider for the War Office and served in France in the Women's Army Auxiliary Corps (WAAC) before returning to her agricultural and zoological studies in peacetime.[12]

Oral history material supplements the range of interviews with Audrey already in the public domain. Unlike Gladys Carson, Audrey was a well-known athlete who was often sought out by the media in later life. In part, this was because her brother Godfrey was the star of the British track and field athletics team in Berlin, winning an individual silver medal in the 400-metres final and a gold medal as the anchor leg of the 4 × 400-metres relay against strong American and German teams, with Freddie Wolff, Bill Roberts and Godfrey Rampling. From an affluent sporting family, of the four brothers Godfrey was closest to Audrey growing up, in age and sentiment. However, they were to develop very different post-Olympic views of the world. Like the material gathered from the family of the relatively unknown Gladys Carson, it is possible to see how invaluable oral histories can be for releasing evidence in the private domain, especially for the Olympic Games prior to 1948, given the passage of time. I have supplemented the oral history material with official material from the BOA and IOC archive and the oral history collections at the British Library.[13] The sound files on the British Library site include seven Audrey Court interviews. These, and many others available in the same collection, are easily available to researchers.

Although famous as sibling medallists in 1936, Audrey and Godfrey Brown were by no means the only family members who attended the same Olympic Games and did well. There had also been many British 'sporting couples' who won medals and still others who formed friendships while away at the many social events. As the case of Brown's team-mate, Violet Webb indicates, there were several men and women whose children went on to excel at sport and some also became Olympians. After retiring at the age of 21 to marry and pursue a career in sales, Violet Webb disproved that sport was harmful to women in an emphatic way when her daughter Janet Simpson also won a bronze medal as a member of the 4 × 100-metres relay team at the 1964 Olympics. So this is a whole research agenda with rich potential.

In 1921, female representatives from France, Great Britain, Italy, Norway, Sweden and Switzerland took part in an international athletics meeting inaugurated by Alice Joséphine Marie Million, better known by her married name, Alice Milliat, staged in Monte Carlo. The key figure in regards to increasing the IOC schedule for women, was a French rower who went on to lead an international movement, Alice Milliat. She inaugurated an international congress on women and sport attended by American, Austrian, British, Czechoslovakian, French and Spanish representatives. The purpose of this meeting was to gather support for women's track and field events to be included in the International Olympic Committee's version of the Games. Milliat's main target was to persuade the Swedish administrator Sigfrid Edström that the International Amateur Athletics Federation, of which he was head, should promote women's sport.

Milliat had first visited Britain in 1920 as a non-playing administrator with the Paris-based Femina women's football team. She was much impressed by the local hospitality and public support for the Dick, Kerr Ladies football team in Preston. In her subsequent career as an administrator and activist, Milliat devoted considerable energy to promoting women's sports, not just track and field. With the expansion of the programme of the Olympic Games now overseen by the international federations of sport, rather than local organising committees, Milliat viewed female track and field athletics disciplines as fundamental to the expansion of the programme.

The International Amateur Athletics Federation (IAAF) had been created in August 1913 with Sigfrid Edström elected as its President. The IAAF worked closely with the IOC because of the central role of track and field athletics in the Olympic programme. This enhanced Edström's relationship with de Coubertin and therefore his administrative career. In 1920, Edström was co-opted as a member of the IOC, and one year later he joined the first executive board.

While women's swimming, diving, skating, tennis and a mixed yachting event would feature at the Antwerp Olympic Games in 1920, female track and field athletics were not admitted. As a direct response to the International Olympic Committee's refusal of Milliat's request that these events be included in the 1920 Games, the Monte Carlo Games were followed by a conference where, on 31 October 1921, the Fédération Sportive Féminine Internationale (FSFI) was formed. The inclusion of women's track and field athletics in the Olympic programme became politicised to an unprecedented degree. Milliat became the head of the FSFI lobbying the IOC, until the IAAF took control of the women's programme in 1936.

After the first Women's Olympic Games held in Paris (1922), Milliat gave in to pressure to re-name these meetings as the Women's World Games. Subsequent meetings in Gothenburg (1926), Prague (1930) and London (1934) were held apart from, but in tandem with, the IOC version of the Olympics and effectively merged at the Berlin Games in 1936. Since the British Women's Amateur Athletic Association participated in Milliat's Women's World Games, hosting the 1934 competition, as well as sending teams to the IOC Olympics in 1932 and 1936, access to international competition helped youngsters like Audrey Brown to win her place in history.

Although this was an emerging transnationalism, the parallel Women's World Games and IOC competition provide examples of unmistakable connectivity between different kinds of sport and therefore diverse women from a range of backgrounds. The star of the seven-woman English squad at the Monte Carlo meeting in 1921 was captain Mary Lines (1893–1978), a relatively unknown worker for Schweppes (a carbonated drinks manufacturer in Drury Lane, London) who trained at the Lyons company track nearby and attended physical education classes at both the Regent Street and Woolwich Polytechnic.[14] The Lyons coffee house company directors supported many sports and leisure pursuits for their workers and subsequently gave The Perpetual Cup to a women's athletics meeting from 1924. This featured in the company magazine *Lyons Mail* with Vera Searle the winner for the first three years.

In Monte Carlo, Mary Lines set world records to win both the 60-metres and 250-metres races. She also won the long jump; contributed to victories in both sprint relays and finished second in the 800-metres event.[15] The group formed the first exclusively women's athletic club on the return journey, which came to be known as London Olympiades. Between 1921 and 1924, in her short international career, Lines set a total of 33 world records or best performances in track and field events.[16] This included an IOC-recognised female 100-metres sprint record of 12.8 seconds in 1922, which stood for some time.

In 1922, the first Women's Olympic Games was staged in Paris as a separatist event with 101 competitors taking part in front of crowds of 20,000 spectators. At the seventh Olympiad, held in Antwerp, there had been approximately 80 female participants. Significantly, 38 countries sent representatives to the second parallel congress in 1922, signalling a growing international movement for women's sport.[17]

Most of the English team were drawn from the more middle class Regent Street and Woolwich Polytechnics, however Mary Lines dominated again

Figure 4.1 Mary Lines, Britain's first big female track and field athletics star in the 1920s, a working class clerk for Schweppes, from London.

Source: Author's collection.

in 1922 to lead an England victory by 50 points to the United States' 31. France took third place (29 points); followed by Czechoslovakia (12) and Switzerland (6).[18] Paradoxically, although Mary Lines' record time is recognised by the IOC, she is not considered by them to be an Olympian because this was not an officially endorsed competition. One of the reasons for documenting the careers of women like Lines in this chapter alongside Audrey Brown and other 'recognised' Olympians is to argue that they should retrospectively be acknowledged and their achievements known.

This situation was not unique to British women track and field athletes. In spite of the strength in depth of Czechoslovakian worker's sport, only Marie Mejzlikova won an event by taking the 60-metres sprint in 7.75 seconds. She would later become a world record holder over 100 metres. Unfortunately, Mejzlikova is but one of the leading figures of women's athletics about which little is now known. Quite how points were calculated also remains unclear and there were occasionally tied events: Britain's Hilda Hatt (1903–1975) and Nancy Voorhees (1904–1979) of the USA came equal-first in the high jump, though subsequently the record was awarded to the American woman for fewer failed attempts.[19] Hatt was an impressive athlete and subsequently made the hurdles her main event, but had ceased to compete by the time Britain sent women to the 80-metres hurdles in Berlin.

Much remains to be known about Mary Lines, Vera Searle and more famous British athletes like Sophie Eliott-Lynn. It would seem that Ethel

Figure 4.2 Mary Lines practices the relay, a multiple world record holder, often overlooked in the record books, although her times are often referenced.
Source: Author's collection.

Edburga Clementina Scott, a member of the 4 × 100-metres relay team, which came second in Prague, might be the first woman of Caribbean descent to represent Britain internationally in athletics.[20] Her father was a Jamaican merchant seaman, and Ethel was born in London where she later worked as a medical secretary. Along with Ivy Walker, Eileen Hiscock and Daisy Ridgley, Ethel took a second place to Germany, and rising international standards combined with more participating nations so that the British team won just four medals. Other competitors and administrators involved in the widening scope of international women's sport have yet to find their place in history and more transnational research is needed to address this agenda. Muriel Cornell for instance, went on to join the British Amateur Athletic Board in 1934 and, the following year, became the WAAA representative on the BOA Council. The British team manager in Berlin, Muriel also officiated in 1948 and helped to set up a national coaching scheme.

However, financial weakness meant that the FSFI had to curtail its activities, underlined during the third congress on 31 July 1924 when the situation was so acute that an annual meeting had to be deferred to a biannual assembly. The 1926 Gothenburg Women's World Games would be privately funded and have 81 participants. The captain was Florence Ethel Birchenough, a talented javelin and shot thrower, who held the WAAA discus title from 1924 to 1928.

By 1926, the IAAF had agreed to take control of the women's programme at the 1928 Olympic Games but rather than the 10 events agreed with Milliat, they offered only five. The British Women's Amateur Athletic Association (WAAA) read the inclusion of just five events in 1928 as a de facto attempt by the IAAF and the IOC to dissolve the FSFI and withdrew a team in protest. This remains the only gender-based boycott in Olympic history. However, the British media covered the women's athletics programme so those interested in the topic could read about Kinue Hitomi, Lina Radke and other stars.[21]

The stand-off eventually led Milliat to comply with a delegation from the IAAF, conforming to the technical rules and general conduct outlined by them. Financial difficulties in maintaining an international network of the scope of the FSFI would later dictate further assimilation. More concessions followed.

British women's track and field athletics five-strong Olympic team at the 1932 Los Angeles Olympic Games was not representative of international competition between the wars therefore. Nellie Halstead, Ethel Johnson, Gwendoline Porter, Eileen Hiscock and Violet Webb sailed from Southampton aboard the Empress of Britain. However, Johnson ruptured a muscle in training and so the bronze medal winning relay team comprised the remaining four Britons, behind the USA and Canada. Bury's Nellie Halstead was the leading female British athlete of her generation.[22] By 1933, Alice Milliat was ill and struggling to coordinate the sporting success for which she had largely been responsible at international level.

She had dropped football from the activities of the FSFI, though Liselott Diem found evidence of a request for soccer by an English Women's Sport Federation.[23] A proposed triathlon competition was probably not as we would know the sport today, but was deemed less interesting as multi-sport competition by 1934 than a pentathlon of athletic events.

Germany's 19 athletes led the medal tally at the 1930 Women's World Games, with England in second place, as they were again in London in 1934. The German 4 × 100-metres relay team had put in a particularly good performance in London and their friendly rivalry against a very good American team promoted expectation for the next time that they would meet at the 1936 Berlin Olympic Games. There is consequently much to research regarding the role of the FSFI competitions in developing national athletics cultures in a range of countries, not just in Britain. However, at the point when Audrey Brown was becoming increasingly interested in developing her skill as a sprinter while a student at Birmingham University, the WAAA prepared to host a Women's World Games in London.

The fourth Women's World Games and the eighth congress of the FSFI in 1934 incorporated athletes and activists from Australia, Argentina, Austria, Belgium, Canada, Czechoslovakia, Estonia, France, Germany, Great Britain, Greece, Hungary, Ireland, Italy, Japan, Latvia, Lithuania, Luxemburg, Palestine, Poland, Norway, New Zealand, Romania, South Africa, Sweden, Switzerland, the Netherlands, the United States of America and Yugoslavia.[24] Muriel Cornell and the WAAA were exceptionally busy preparing events at the White City, and for the Congress on 12 August, for which there was a formal dinner, social activities and souvenir memorabilia.

The WAAA London hosting committee for the Women's World Championships in 1934 was led by John Beresford, Baron Decies, and patrons included the British sporting elite such as Lord Aberdare, Lord Desborough, Lord Hawke and those from London society such as Gordon Selfridge.[25] This was clearly a major event. Eileen Hiscock (1909–1958), who had captained of the British women's athletic team at the 1932 Los Angeles Olympics and was the current English 100-metres record holder, spoke the oath at the opening ceremony: 'We take part in the true spirit of sportsmanship ... for the honour of women's athletics and for the glory of sport'. Lord Desborough released a dove. The programme notes featured Gladys Lunn as the 800-metres race title holder.

Unlike Olympic competition, middle-distance events, including the half-mile and various off-road distances, continued to develop under WAAA rules and here cross-country running was significant. A post woman in Birmingham, Gladys Lunn started running with the Birchfield Harriers and her first international success came in 1930 at the Women's World Games, when she won the 800-metres race. At the WAAA championships in 1932 she broke the world 880 yards record in a time of 2 minutes 18 seconds. At the White City World Games in 1934, she set a world 1,000-metres record, completing the distance in almost 3 minutes flat and registered a mile time of 5 minutes 17 seconds in 1937. Evidently, if there had been a women's 800-metres race at the 1932 Los Angeles or the 1936 Berlin Olympic Games, Lunn would have been a strong medal contender. Unlike her Birchfield Harriers team-mate, it favoured Brown that she was a sprinter and there were 100-metres events in the Olympic Games.

There were ambitious proposals that visiting teams would have free accommodation and full board, so the practical and social arrangements also deserve more attention from researchers. The events were the 60-metres sprint; 80-metres hurdles; 100-metres sprint; 200-metres race; 800-metres race; 4 × 100-metres relay; pentathlon; high jump; discus; javelin; shot put; basketball and Hazena (a Czechoslovakian hand ball game). Countries competing included America, Austria, Belgium, Canada, Czechoslovakia, England, France, Germany, Holland, Hungary, Italy, Japan, Latvia, Palestine, Poland, Rhodesia, South Africa, Sweden and Yugoslavia. A chest infection ruled Audrey Brown out of competition for the 1934–1935 season, but she came back to fitness in her final year at university and earned her Olympic selection with a particularly strong performance in the WAAA national championship at the White City stadium.

By 1936, women's athletics became controlled by the IAAF. In this sense, Milliat had been successful in her long campaign. While the IOC and IAAF did not want to regulate, let alone develop women's sport, by 1936 these organisations could not be seen *not* to control aspects of international competition. The gradual and contested process of FSFI assimilation between 1920 and the 1936 Berlin Olympics reflected a policy tension as to whether women's athletics could, and should, be a separatist movement. The relative proximity of Berlin to London helped the BOA to send a team of women in 1936 twice the size of the team that had gone to Los Angeles. Audrey Brown was among those who benefitted. Each track and field event was limited to three competitors from each national team. So again there was an advantage in being a sprinter, as there was also a 4 × 100-metres relay race, with runners relatively good value to fund, in terms of being eligible to enter several events. The women who had pioneered track and field athletics, road running, and cross country events are comparatively neglected when we consider the Olympians such as Audrey Brown. This section has shown how crucial they were to what followed, and argues that we need to know much more about their individual stories and collective actions.

Audrey Brown and the 1936 Olympic Games

Audrey Brown was born on 24 May 1913 as the third child and only daughter of the Reverend Arthur E. Brown, and his wife, Gertrude Parsons.[26] Her parents met at Cambridge, before embarking on Methodist missionary work in India, as Arthur's father had before him, until 1936. Audrey's father was

Principal of Bankura College, West Bankura, India (affiliated to the University of Calcutta), Mayor of the municipality and medical superintendent of the hospital, although not medically qualified. The main paternal influence was both spiritual and a physical enthusiasm for sports, particularly athletics. Muscular Christianity still had considerable currency in the first half of the twentieth century among the privately educated, although the academic literature on the subject neglects women almost entirely. Audrey's maternal grandparents, based at Four Oaks, Warwickshire, particularly valued education, and ensured she was given the same chances as her brothers. As well as a strong educational ethos, a strong social conscience and an expertise in medicine were notable in the family. For instance, Audrey's uncle, Sir Leonard Parsons, was a renowned paediatrician.

Audrey seems to have been an all-rounder at school, playing hockey and other team games, encouraged by her younger brother, Godfrey. The family expected Audrey to go to university, preferably to Cambridge, so she felt she had let her parents down when she was not accepted. Audrey Brown took up running seriously at Birmingham University, where she studied social and political science, and preferred to train alone and it seems to have been a rather solitary enthusiasm, rather than a sociable experience. She was coached by W. W. Alexander of the Birchfield Harriers, among the most prominent track and field clubs in Britain at the time, and the name came from a strong cross-country tradition. Both Audrey and Godfrey would bestow distinction upon the club by becoming the first Birchfield Harriers to become Olympic medallists. Audrey's first international was the world student games in Turin in 1933. This appears to have ignited a competitive instinct as she realised she was fast over 100 and 200 metres. However, there was to be no 200-metres race in the 1936 Berlin Olympic Games.

Audrey Brown was selected for the individual 100 metres and the 4 × 100-metres relay in 1936, having come third in the WAAA 100-metres championship at the White City stadium that year. She later confessed to being 'amazed at my inclusion' and this may have been genuine, as some deafness meant that she did not always hear the starter's pistol clearly.[27] The Women's Amateur Athletics Association was a very respectable organisation, and it is clear from Brown's interview comments that she was conscious of the pressures of propriety in terms of dress and deportment.

The selection of the team for Berlin was based on the BOA model used at Amsterdam in 1928 and refined for Los Angeles in 1932.

> At Amsterdam the teams numbered 353 and cost £8928. For the Los Angeles Games no competitor who was not up to the standard of the sixth competitor at Amsterdam was taken and the teams, including officials, were kept down to 103 [sic]. It seems reasonable to suppose that Great Britain's team for 1936 will number about 220, of which 30–40 will be women. And that the cost will be between £5000 and £6000 with

an additional £1000 for unforeseen circumstances and expenses, transport of boats etc. This would make the total cost between £6000 and £7000 and, in my opinion, the Appeal should be for £10000.[28]

As well as the large mass gymnastic displays, women comprised 360 of the overall competitors in Berlin, while men numbered 4,433.[29] The 38-strong British female team comprised eight gymnasts; 17 swimmers and divers; two fencers, and a yachtswoman plus the track and field athletes. Eileen Hiscock led the relay team of Audrey Brown, Barbara Burke and Violet Olney to a silver medal in a dramatic race, and memories of this would be contested.[30] As Audrey Court remembered the tactics: 'Knowing we had little chance in the individual races, we trained very hard together to run the best we could' to reach the 4 × 100-metres final.[31] The only other British female track and field medal in 1936 was the silver won by 16-year-old Dorothy Odam for the high jump.

Suffice to say, that the women and men who competed in the Berlin Olympic Games did so in a highly charged atmosphere where every medal counted for national teams. Perhaps unsurprisingly, Germany and the USA sent the largest women's teams. However, as the official report indicates, women were much in evidence both in the organisation and hosting of the Berlin Olympics and as contestants. The representation of the female athlete had never been more prominent.

Ladies' hats for the British team to wear at the Opening Ceremony were sourced from Holdron, costing £13, 2 shillings and 10 pence, whereas the ties, badges and scarves from Hoares for the whole team came in at just over £61.[32] As well as Umbro tracksuits for the athletes priced at £112, the gymnastic tunics for the women's team cost nearly £14. Jaegar-LeCoultre, the Swiss watchmaker, provided timing equipment and shooting pistols, worth nearly £20 and what could not be sourced elsewhere was provided by Lillywhites and Harrods.

The basic provision of ceremonial attire therefore left quite a bit of room for individual interpretation, since women were required to provide a spare white dress and shoes to attend the many functions, and sportswear, such as individual running shoes, shorts and other basic items.[33] Female athletes were provided with a Jaeger blazer, dress and hat for the ceremonial 'parading uniform' by the British Olympic Association, but also had to sew British insignia on their running vests and fund their own running equipment. The sartorial uniformity of the British team in Berlin is therefore open to question. This was not the only home-made aspect of the trip.

On the outward journey, the couchettes were not attached to the train and the women arrived sleepless in Berlin, some having tried to use luggage racks as makeshift beds. Housing the women competitors was described in the official report as a 'problem' in need of a solution:

After long and intense training, women are very high strung immediately before difficult contests. We wished the quarters to be separate from those of the men and also outside the radius of the metropolitan traffic. We were fortunate enough to possess an entirely new, large students' dormitory, the 'Frisian House', in a part of the Reich Sport Field far away from traffic This seemed to us an especially happy solution of the problem of quarters.[34]

The Directions for the Opening Ceremony itself were meticulous and choreographed to the minute and, unlike Los Angeles where some British participants considered attendance optional, it was stipulated that 'The active participants of all nations will take part, led by their officials'.[35] Athletes were transported into the stadium by the National Army Transportation Division from the Frisian House and other dormitories, overseen by Baroness Johanna von Wangenheim, also active in Red Cross work.

Following the ringing of the Olympic Bell, the parade started by Greece and followed according to German spelling in alphabetical order, with salutes made to officials 'according to the custom of the country'. These further direct links between Athens and Berlin were reinforced by the invented tradition of Spyridon Louis, the postal worker who won the first Olympic marathon in 1894, handing an olive branch to Hitler.[36] Many other symbolic physical features included the Olympic bell, the torch relay from Athens and the infrastructure to house national teams and host competitions. Cultural and aesthetic innovations were no less important with music, literature, film and artistic interpretations of Olympism much in evidence.

An Opening Ceremony banquet of Oxtail Soup, Baked Sole, Roast Chicken and Vanilla Parfait concluded the days' events.[37] There were many such receptions, fetes, entertainments and so on for the British team, which arrived in Berlin on 27 July. The British were considered to be 'moderate eaters' favouring: 'grilled meat, medium done; three to four eggs, oatmeal, tea, milk, fruit and toast for breakfast; Horlick's malted milk and plainly cooked vegetables'.[38] Both the makers of Horlicks and Ovaltine offered again to nourish the British Olympians for free with their malted drinks. The BOA also funded an assembly for WAAA officials at the Wilton Hotel, to the tune of nearly £4, with further travel expenses of £2 and 5 shillings.

With the athletics events scheduled from 2 to 9 August, there was some spare time before and after the games to see the sights and meet other athletes. Audrey remembered that she had to be very careful and stay with chaperones at the banquets, particularly the farewell event in the Deutschland Hall where she was bored by 'lots of speeches'. Audrey also confessed to being 'irked by the German aim to prove themselves as a superior nation'. There were also outings to West Berlin, providing many photo opportunities as a tourist, since the city was decorated extensively for the Olympic Games. Brown was also impressed by the scale of the Reich Sport Field with the

Olympic Stadium, but found Leni Riefenstahl, who directed *Olympia* the official film of the games, to be something of 'a nuisance' and intrusive in her commitment to obtain as much footage as possible.

As to the events themselves, track and field athletics dominated the schedule with 44 events involving a total 880 competitors, with just under 750,000 spectators in the Olympic stadium over the eight days of competition. Both Germany and America funded larger track and field athletic teams than Britain, with 17 and 16 women, respectively.

American Helen Stephens easily won the individual 100-metres final race in 11.5 seconds, ahead of rival Stella Walasiewiczowna (representing Poland), and Käthe Krauss (Germany) in third overall. Brown came fifth in the third heat and was eliminated, as were Eileen Hiscock and Barbara Burke. Hiscock had held the British 100-metres record at 11.9 from 1935, and this would remain unbeaten for 21 years. Consequently, no British women made it to the 100-metres final, which took place on 3 August. In contrast three Germans did (Käthe Krauss, Marie Dollinger and Emmy Albus) along with Helen Stephens and Annette Rogers for the USA. In addition, the USA had Harriet Bland on the first leg of the relay team, followed by Rogers and the 1928 100-metres gold medallist, Betty Robinson on the third leg, with Stephens completing the race. The German women's relay team had broken the world record in 46.4 seconds in the semi-final heat and were expected to win. Eileen Hiscock and the team came second behind Germany in their heat with a British record of 47.5, and this would stand until 1950.

In the final itself on Sunday 9 August, the German women's relay team established an 8-metre lead over the American women, after Emmy Albus and Käthe Krauss had run. Germany's third runner, Marie Dollinger, should have passed the baton to Ilse Dörffeldt on the final handover but she failed to secure it and it was dropped on the track.[39] Dörffeldt was inconsolable, although Stephens ran such a good final leg for the US team, she could possibly have made up the time anyway. As a consequence, Eileen Hiscock would lead the 4 × 100-metres relay team of Audrey Brown, Barbara Burke and Violet Olney to a silver medal at the Berlin Olympics, ahead of Canada.[40]

Audrey recalled that the team was very surprised with their second place and excited because the British men also won the 4 × 400-metres relay final race that day.[41] Both Audrey and Godfrey's decision to run on Sunday, had been vindicated. Audrey remembered that she had tried to help up Dörffeldt, who had fallen on the track in her distress, and considered that Hitler had refused to present the medals. This did not tie with Godfrey's memory of the medal ceremony: he maintained in several public comments that Hitler had already left the stadium for the day, rather than snubbing anyone. Audrey remembered that the German women's team was under terrific pressure throughout the Olympics, and found it difficult to fraternise with other teams. She was also keenly aware that the USA, Canada, German and Polish teams were very well prepared, including specific training camps. Amateur

British success in comparison evidenced a wider lack of structural support for women's track and field athletics among several national associations. Although the case of the Netherlands, Poland and Hungary, suggests this general trend requires nuance.

Eileen Hiscock, Audrey Brown and her colleagues were not the only British female track and field stars in 1936. As a 16-year-old, Dorothy Odam cleared 1.60 metres in an exciting high jump contest watched by 80,000, also on Sunday 9 August. She came second, in a jump-off against the Hungarian Ibolya Csáktook to win Britain's first individual female track and field silver medal, ahead of Elfriede Kaun of Germany. Dorothy's athletics career began when she was 10 years old and she obtained two successive Mitcham Athletics Club scholarships for promising youngsters, which entitled her four years' worth of free membership and some basic training. Eleanor 'Nellie' Carrington came ninth in the same event. It perhaps speaks to the amateur values of time that Odam used a 'scissors kick' technique and would not receive individual coaching until she prepared for her third Olympic competition by changing to a 'western roll' method in 1951.[42] She also declared herself against specialist or intensive preparation for large events throughout her 20-year athletics career.

Kathleen Connall, who trained at the University of Leeds, came 14th in the javelin throw which was won by Tilly Fleischer, with her compatriot Luise Krüger second and Poland's Maria Kwasniewska in third place. Kathleen Tiffen was eliminated in the heats of the 80-metres hurdles, as was Grethe Whitehead and Violet Webb. The hurdles' gold medal was won by Ondina Valla of Italy, with Anni Steur of Germany taking silver place and Elizabeth Taylor of Canada the bronze. The new technology of a timing camera was used to separate the three who all recorded 11.7 seconds but, due to the additional measurement, by hundreds of a second, Valla took victory.

In all, 11 British women were entered in the track and field competitions in 1936, of whom 10 actually competed.[43] The BOA funded £378 of the costs. For most women, it would be their only Olympic appearance. Dorothy Odam was to be more fortunate because of her young age and brilliant athleticism. She later regretted that she had no formal coaching until the age of 28 and her own antipathy to specialised training was of its time. Winning a second silver medal 12 years later at the 1948 London Olympics behind Alice Coachman, Dorothy Tyler went on to hold a world record height of 1.66 before becoming an innovative coach.[44]

One of the things that particularly made Audrey Brown famous was that her brother Godfrey won a gold and silver medal in Berlin. Audrey's older brother Ralph (1909–2003) and her younger brother Godfrey Brown (1915–1995) were equally talented athletes. Ralph would become the Amateur Athletic Association 440-yards hurdles champion in 1934. But for injury, Ralph would have joined Godfrey and Audrey in Berlin for the 1936 Olympic Games and he remained interested in athletics, as a member of the elite

Achilles club. According to one biographer, not making the 1936 Olympic Games was Ralph's 'greatest disappointment'.[45] He was later knighted Sir Ralph Kilner Brown and became a high court judge.[46]

Godfrey was a versatile athlete and ran all distances from 100 to 880 yards. Going up to Peterhouse, Cambridge, to read history in 1935, he won a blue for athletics in his first year and made his first international appearance. He was still something of an unknown when he travelled to Berlin with the British Olympic team. As the final leg of the 4 × 400-metres relay team, Britain's only track and field gold medal, along with his individual silver 400-metres medal, Godfrey received considerable public attention. Although he retired from athletics in 1939, Godfrey coached summer schemes, acted as an official at meetings and built a cinder running track at Cheltenham College, where he taught from 1943 to 1950. From 1950 until 1978, he was headmaster of Worcester Royal Grammar School. So the broader family history was inflected by the Olympic success of two siblings and the missed chance of Ralph. Audrey Brown's parents witnessed her Olympic success and that of her brother. She described this as 'a great joy' to her parents, who 'never saw any difference between my taking up athletics and my brothers doing so'.

Of the total 39 British women who went to Berlin to compete, 38 did so. The swimming and diving contingent was still the largest, with 17 representatives, funded at a cost of £497. In the 100-metres freestyle competition, Zilpha Grant, Margery Hinton and Olive Wadham were eliminated in the heats. Lorna Frampton, a Polytechnic athlete who later worked at Lloyds in the city, finished sixth in the 100-metres backstroke and Phyllis Harding seventh, with Audrey Hancock unplaced. Doris Story also came sixth in the 200-metres breaststroke, whereas Margaret Gomm and Vera Kingston did not qualify from the heats. In the 400-metres freestyle, Margaret Jeffrey and Gladys Morcom also left the competition after the first round. The 4 × 100-metres freestyle relay team (Zilpha Grant, Edna Hughes, Margaret Jeffrey and Olive Wadham) came sixth behind the Netherlands, Germany, USA, Canada and Hungary. Jean Gilbert, who trained in St Helier, Jersey, achieved seventh in the women's platform dive, 11 places in front of Madge Moulton. Britain's youngest competitor at the age of 15, Betty Slade, finished ninth, ahead of her compatriot Kathinka Larsen in the women's springboard dive. It did not seem to strike anyone as odd that women could swim a 400-metres freestyle Olympic race, but the longest running race on the track and field schedule was 100 metres. Evidently, the international swimming governing body and the IAAF had different ideas about the limits of female stamina.

A team of eight female gymnasts made the journey to Berlin (Doris Blake, Brenda Crowe, Edna Gross, Clarice Hanson, Mary Heaton, Mary Kelly, Lilian Ridgewell and Marion Wharton), although the BOA had initially refused to fund the £500 participation costs of both a men's and women's team.[47] In the end, no men's team was entered and the women offered to go at their own expense, although the BOA did subsidise them to the tune of £222. In the meantime, smaller-sized all-male teams for events like weight-lifting were being funded wholly by the BOA; in this case for five competitors and two officials.[48]

In fencing, Betty Arbuthnot was accompanied by Judy Guinness Penn-Hughes and both were eliminated in the heats of an intensively political individual foil competition. It cost the BOA £50 to send them to Berlin. Guinness had married the racing driver and entrepreneur Clifton Penn-Hughes in 1934. The three medallists were all Jewish. Ilona Elek-Schacherer of Hungary; Helene Mayer (the daughter of a Jewish father and a Protestant mother) for Germany and Ellen Preis for Austria. Mayer was a resident in California at the time of her selection, and, as well as her obvious ability, her selection was intended to allay criticisms over the selection of Jewish athletes for Germany. Finally, Beryl Preston sailed with her husband Kenneth and his brother Francis aboard the British vessel 'Saskia' to take sixth place in the 8-metre class with colleagues Joseph Compton, John Eddy and Robert Steele.[49] Britain would not have a female yachting representative again until 1960, when Jean Mitchell took part in the Star class.

Much of the vast Olympic public relations campaign in Berlin focused on women and they were perhaps over-represented given their numerical minority. The first baton change of the successful American women's 4 × 100-metres relay team made the cover of *Berliner Illustrirte Zeitung* on 13 August 1936.[50] A special collectible edition of this magazine was published exclusively in Germany to mark the 1936 Games. There were also photo stories of Tilly Fleischer's gold and that of Gisela Mauermayer, along with an in-depth feature on women's track and field athletics at the Olympic Games under the title 'Deutsche Mädel im Olympischen Kampf' equating success with the 'The League of German Girls' or 'Band of German Maidens', the female wing of the Nazi Party youth movement, the Hitler Youth.

As well as explicitly politicising the victories of female German athletes, magazines like *Berliner Illustrirte Zeitung* and the official report was fascinated by the US women and girls, especially those who were fair-skinned or had blonde hair. These included photographs of 13-year-old diver, Marjorie Gestring, the youngest person to win an Olympic gold medal.[51] Other photographs included Eleanor Holm-Jarret the 1932 100-metres backstroke gold medallist and world record holder in both the 100 and 200-metres backstroke. Holm-Jarret had been deselected by the American Olympic Committee because she enjoyed what they considered to be too much champagne on board the liner 'Manhattan' taking the team to Germany and the wave of indignation made her more famous worldwide than winning another gold medal could ever have done.

This coverage confirmed the judgement of the British Diplomatic observers prior to the 1936 Berlin Games, that an American boycott was the thing that the organisers most feared, and thus the inclusion of Californian fencer Helen Mayer, was intended as a strategic attempt to broker accord.[52] Diminutive blonde Dorothy Poynton-Hill was also featured in several photographs wearing a gingham bathing suit, blowing a horn and sporting a jaunty cap.[53] Poynton-Hill had first become a silver medallist in the 3-metre springboard competition at the 1928 Amsterdam Olympics before taking the gold medal in the 10-metre platform event in Los Angeles in 1932. In 1936, she was to go on to improve this, winning both the gold medal in the 10-metre platform dive as well as the bronze medal in the 3-metre springboard competition.[54]

Conclusion

Like many young women of her time, Audrey Brown enjoyed sport as part of her Higher Education studies, but also used the status she obtained as an Olympian to contest the wider place of women in public life. This would be an emerging trend among both male and female Olympians in 1936, the growth of which would accelerate after the Games returned in 1948, in London. However, Brown had a very short career as an amateur, and was not fully fit on the day of the 1937 WAAA Championships, as a consequence of which she missed selection for the 1938 Empire Games. Godfrey also missed the Empire Games due to his finals year at University.

Audrey Brown was well enough to attend the 1937 World Student Games in Paris, and then the highly charged European Championships for women in 1938 in Vienna, where she was captain. Her father did not want her to go and this view seemed vindicated, given the escalation of hostilities. Athletes were told, 'You go on your own responsibility'. Thrower Kathleen Connal, who had competed reluctantly at the 1936 Berlin Olympics, did not go to Vienna because she was Jewish, and made a public protest at the time.[55]

In Vienna, Betty Lock (Mitcham AC), ran the anchor leg of the 4 × 100-metres relay, as the 1938 WAAA 100-metres champion, preceded by Dorothy Saunders (Spartan Ladies' AC). Lillian Chalmers (Portsmouth Atalanta AC), ran the lead-off stage in the relay with Audrey Brown second. However, the team was controversially eliminated for going outside their lane and awarded sixth place as a consolation. Brown found this to be very unprofessional, and the German team took victory, with Poland in second place.

European competition again offered more events than an Olympic programme and the British team comprised Kathleen 'Kitty' Tilley (Mitcham AC), in the discus; Bevis Reid (Mitcham AC), in both the shot and the discus; Ethel Raby (Middlesex Ladies' AC), who came fourth in the long jump and was also third in her 80-metres hurdles heat in 13.2; Vedder Schenk (Mitcham AC), in the long jump; Dorothy Cosnett (Birchfield Harriers) and Dora Gardner in the high jump; Evelyn Matthews and Kate Robertson in the 80-metres hurdles. In all, the 12-strong team represented Britain across several track and field disciplines without particular distinction. The increasingly politicised atmosphere seems to have hampered any enjoyment of such an event and soon after, Audrey lost much of her enthusiasm for active competition.

After initially moving to York to become a personnel officer with Rowntrees, Audrey married William 'Harry' Court in March 1940, whom she had met when he was a lecturer at Birmingham University. Her husband was not athletic and their three daughters (Sarah, Bridget and Alison) followed their father's interests, although Audrey remained President of the Women's Amateur Athletic Association for the Midlands. From 1947, Harry became a Professor of Economic History at the University of Birmingham until shortly before his death. After a career break from 1943 to 1949, the rest of Audrey Court's working life was dedicated to the Family Planning Association (FPA), first as a volunteer and then Chair of the Birmingham branch from 1961 onwards. Birmingham was the first place outside London to do trials of the Contraceptive Pill, extending availability to young women, ethnic minority groups and the unmarried. In 1968, Court contacted Helen Brook in London who gave financial and moral support for a Brooks Advisory Centre in Birmingham, to which there was great opposition. The FPA handed over responsibility for unmarried women to the newly formed Brooks Advisory Centre that year. In 1991, Audrey Court was appointed MBE for her services to family planning. At the time of the British Library oral history interview, Court was still Vice President of Brooks Advisory Clinic in London and President of Brooks Advisory Clinic in Birmingham.[56]

Audrey Court was proud of her involvement in Family Planning history and documented this in a historical work.[57] Voluntary work helped her to focus after the unexpected death of Harry in 1971. She maintained an interest in Community Health, passing on this professional enthusiasm to her children and grandchildren. Compared with this body of voluntary work, public service and committee expertise, Audrey considered her Olympic success 'a passing moment', saying sport and athletics 'were not really her world'.[58] She moved closer to Cheshire to be with her family in 2003 and died in 2005. It seems appropriate to be writing in 2020, coinciding with the 90th Anniversary of the Family Planning Association that, by making contraception available, Audrey Court and her colleagues made such a difference to so many women's lives. However, her athletic success was both part of a wider move for equality in women's lives and a great personal achievement, given the odds facing sportswomen at the time.

Although progressive in regards to the role of women, Audrey Court's concerns about 'manly' athletes in women's track and field events chimed with wider moral panics in the Olympic movement. Avery Brundage, who was head of the US delegation and a key player in the large American team going to Berlin, claimed to have received a letter from a 'concerned citizen' who had met a female athlete with a deep voice and large feet, in Germany. Brundage used this as evidence in support of his opinion that women competitors should have gender tests to protect those who were 'truly' female.[59] This heralded a series of insensitive commitments to keep women's track and field athletics free of male competitors from which the IAAF and the IOC have not relented, even today. Gender verification and testing was to border on the inhumane, throughout its history in the name of 'protecting' women's sport.

In the 1920s, the case of Mary Weston had shown how early examples of inter-sex and transitioned gender did not accord with the binary of 'men's' and 'women's' athletics. Weston was the daughter of a leading stoker on 'HMS Vivid', and his wife, Susan Ann (née Snow). Weston took the WAAA title in the shot in 1925 and 1928, before achieving victories in the shot, discus and javelin at the WAAA championships in 1929. Weston's gender was identified as female at birth, and she was brought up as a girl. Following surgery, Weston's birth was re-registered in 1936 as male. Mark Edward Louis Weston was quite open about the change, later married and had three children, earning a living as a physiotherapist. Czech runner, Zdenka Koubkova had changed sex in 1934. Although no competitive advantage was proven, future IOC narratives on gender-testing held that any detectable male attributes might constitute a competitive advantage over female rivals.

This symbolic value of female athletes as fundamentally different to, and lesser than, male athletes was also enshrined in administrative terms. Until the formation of the British Athletic Federation in 1990, the Women's Amateur Athletic Association took sole charge of female track and field in England after its formation in 1922, merging with the Amateur Athletic Association (AAA).[60] The WAAA was not wholly administered by women, like Vera Searle and Muriel Cornell, but it was largely so. It had a cordial, if patronised, relationship with the AAA, as is evidenced by the Harold Abrahams Collection at the University of Birmingham, which has an extensive collection of material up until his death in 1978. Abrahams was to gradually change his attitude to women's athletics and this slow thaw reflected the broader AAA attitude. Searle and Cornell were known too, for their own conservatism in preferring shorter sprint distances for women, rather than middle- and long-distance running.

In one of her interviews Audrey Brown overstated the extent of athletes with male characteristics competing in women's track and field, saying 'The biggest problem for women was women themselves. "Was a woman a woman?" Four or five big names in the 100 and 200 metres may have been men'.[61] This was an interesting, if challenging, comment on many levels. First, the Olympic Games were still undoubtedly a patriarchy in 1936 and have remained so since. Second, we can see that women were encouraged not just to control and contain their own behaviour within stated norms, but to conduct surveillance of their co-competitors for evidence of male characteristics. The assumed advantage, combined with the intensely nationalistic environment, made this an issue away from sport itself. Finally, it may also indicate that women athletes internalised the norms of female participation being in itself a 'problem' at the end of the protracted period of negotiations led by Milliat.

There is little doubt that these were invented myths but that does not mean that they were not influential. Notably in 1936, Dora Ratjen of Germany was also raised as a woman, before being identified as a man in 1938 and living the rest of his life as Heinrich. Ratjen returned his gold medal for the 1938 European Athletics Championship, having set a world record in the high jump. There has been some speculation that the German national team knew of her male characteristics and thought this might give Ratjen an advantage in the high jump.[62] As the examples indicate, there was conflicting evidence that male characteristics, however defined, actually constituted a competitive advantage. Ratjen finished fourth in 1936 and, given that he returned his European medal, Hilton's assessment seems harsh, preferring conspiracy over compassion. Edith Halstead, sister of Nellie, later became known as Eddie so there were well known British examples, as well as European athletes.

However, medicalised narratives of 'protecting' sport for women were complex and deliberately based on a lack of scientific evidence. Gender identity is itself multiple and shifting, without a binary logic. The IOC continue today to be confused by this. Stanisława Walasiewiczówna (also known as Stefania Walasiewicz) was also an FSFI record holder from 1930 in three sprint distances (60, 100 and 200 metres) representing the Pologne club, a nationalist organisation in Poland and overseas.[63] As well as being an Olympic gold medal winner in 1932, Walasiewicz was listed in the 1934 Women's World Games programme as holding world records over the same three distances. Having accused Helen Stephens of being a man, Walasiewicz came second to her in the 100 metres. As Stella Walsh, she eventually took US citizenship in 1947 and had a short-lived marriage to boxer Neil Olsen, working as an inspector in a toy-making factory and competing in sport well into her late 40s in regional Southern Pacific meetings.[64]

Although the rules had been changed in time for the 1956 Olympic Games in Melbourne to allow athletes who had competed previously for one country to appear for their adopted nationality, Stella's time was marginally slow in the selection trials and instead she had to accept ancillary roles, such as travelling with the American track and field team to a meeting with their Russian counterparts at the Lenin Stadium, Moscow in 1959.[65] At her untimely death in 1980, unspecified male characteristics were identified at the autopsy, though Walsh's records stand, as do her medals.

We can see many shifting identities across one lifetime, as we might expect. The notion that gender can be easily identified and verified continues to have contemporary resonance.[66] There remains no gender testing in men's sport. So-called 'gender verification' remains one of the most invidious affronts to personal freedom in an age today of increasing equality and contested human rights.

Audrey Brown also identified a further issue that would affect the representation of gendered sporting bodies in her comments about 1936, saying that: 'The overall organisation and administration was more sympathetic to men. The Press were also more interested in the men's events'.[67] This suggests the extent to which the media already had a gendered perspective when the Berlin Olympic Games were covered. Certainly, it is possible to see women working in the newspaper, radio and telephone-communication systems from the official report.

However, just the presence of female workers does not preclude them from considering male sports and victories more significant. For one thing, the sheer number of male athletes in relation to female competitors meant that there were many more stories to tell. Perhaps too, those who attended were more accustomed to covering the key events in the male sporting calendar, rather than the emerging transnationalism that this chapter has described. The forthcoming conflict would further politicise the bodies of men and women, at the same time as providing new kinds of work and innovative communication technologies. The first edition of *World Sports*, the official publication of the British Olympic Association, however, considered that sport could avoid such conflict:

World concord through sport

If it is not within the wit of politicians to bring about World concord and amity, can sport do it? Are people likely to extinguish national passions on the playing fields any more than in the Forum or the schools for national propaganda? Can sport stifle racial and political emotions? Is brotherhood likely through the athletic champions of every country matching prowess? We think it reasonable to answer affirmatively. Most of the world's troubles are not the will of the people. Usually ill-will is created by propagandists. More are playing games; every nation had difficulty in securing enough playing areas; if we can have millions of players, abiding by the rules of sportsmanship, there will be less international friction, especially if players more frequently meet on each others playing fields. Nationalistic ebullitions are better worked off on a playing field than round a parish pump.[68]

This now looks hopelessly naïve but there remains a tantalising research agenda to explore how the changes of 1936 would prepare for the 1948 Olympic Games when festivities were revived after such colossal social upheaval. Not only had Berlin hosted the largest women's Olympic programme to date, but it had mediated female athletes to a worldwide audience, using ground-breaking techniques on an unprecedented scale. Women's track and field athletics had been established as an Olympic staple, and it would remain so, by growing along with other sports on the schedule. Along with the Olympic Games, the Paralympic movement would also expand in the second half of the twentieth century.

Overall, the BOA team in Berlin had done well enough and Harold Abrahams said as much in the official BOA report, while also conveying some of his own ambivalence. The cost was estimated to have been approximately £7,419. This left £3,000 in the balance of the appeal fund to be invested along with the £2,000 deposited with the Woolwich Building Society and just under £800 with the National Building Society.[69] By the end of 1937, plans were in place for the trip to Tokyo and, financially, even before the BOA had set a range of fund-raising activities in action, there was considerable stability.

Lending the offices to the British Empire Games Federation and Council for England showed how comfortable the association was, at the same time as talking much less about its wider mission to develop British sport. Tokyo did not give up its intention to host the 1940 Olympic Games until 1938, by which time the 1938 Empire Games in Sydney had taken place as part of the 150th anniversary celebrations of the establishment of the city (which also heralded the foundation of British settlement in Australia).[70]

Japan had won the right to host the 1940 Games through the strength of its athletes in both the 1932 and 1936 Olympics, winning widespread admiration. When the next Olympics were staged in 1948, they would be held in London, with much of the symbolism reacting to how Los Angeles and Berlin had been delivered as a commercial and propaganda sporting spectacle.

As such, the British sought to defend the Olympic ideals, as they interpreted them, in 1948 but could not help but be influenced by the impressive aspects of both 1932 and 1936. The considerable influence the British already had increased within the International Olympic Committee after 1945. The changing nature of international relations that followed a major conflict meant that the importance of sporting national prestige was amplified. Both the BOA and the Olympic games themselves would grow ever larger and become more important as the twentieth century progressed.

Notes

1. Adolf Hitler in Organisationskomitee Für Die XI Olympiade Berlin 1936 E. V. *The XITH Olympic Games Berlin, 1936 Official Report Volume 1* Berlin: Wilhelm Limpert, 1937 p. 6.
2. Jesse Owens (as told to Frank Dudley) 'World's Wonder Man Tells His Secrets' *Sunday Graphic and Sunday News* 16 August 1936 p. 7 BOA Archive Press Files, London.
3. Joe Binks 'Coloured Sprinters Superiority in the Olympic Games: Berlin Lessons for British Athletes' *News of the World* 9 August 1936 p. 19 BOA Archive Press Files, London.
4. Carol Dyehouse *Students: A Gendered History* London: Routledge, 2006 p. 4.

5 Arnd Krüger 'What's The Difference Between Propaganda For Tourism or For A Political Regime?: Was The 1936 Olympics The First Postmodern Spectacle?' in John Bale and Mette Krogh Christensen *Post-Olympism? Questioning Sport in the Twenty-First Century* Oxford and New York: Berg, 2004 pp. 33–49.
6 Susan Noel 'Women in Sport' *World Sports: The International Sports Magazine July 1949* London: Country and Sporting Publications, 1949 p. 26.
7 Duncan Sutherland 'Frances Elaine Burton, Baroness Burton of Coventry (1904–1991)' *Oxford Dictionary of National Biography* Oxford: Oxford University Press www.oxforddnb.com/view/article/49597 accessed 18 December 2019.
8 Susan Noel 'Women in Sport' *World Sports July 1949* p. 26.
9 Mel Watman 'Women Athletes Between The World Wars (1919–1939)' *Oxford Dictionary of National Biography*, Oxford: Oxford University Press www.oxforddnb.com/view/article/103699 accessed 18 December 2019.
10 Muriel Zagha 'Ban the Bolt!' *World of Interiors* 9 January 2015 London: Condé Nast Publications pp. 116–120.
11 Patricia Vertinsky *The Eternally Wounded Woman: Women, Doctors and Exercise in the Late Nineteenth Century* Manchester: Manchester University Press, 1990 p. 132.
12 Mark Pottle '*Sophie Catherine Theresa Mary Heath, Lady Heath (1896–1939)*' *Oxford Dictionary of National Biography* Oxford: Oxford University Press www.oxforddnb.com/view/article/67141 accessed 10 August 2010.
13 Rachel Cutler 'Audrey Court (Brown) 1913–2005' *Oral History of British Athletics* catalogue no: C790/02–4 London: The British Library 1996 http://sounds.bl.uk/Oralhistory/Sport/021M-C0790X0002XX-0100V0 accessed 19 May 2019.
14 J. Lyons & Company online archive www.kzwp.com/lyons/index.htm accessed 10 August 2015.
15 Mel Watman 'Women Athletes Between The World Wars 1919–1939' www.oxforddnb.com/view/article/103699 accessed 18 December 2019.
16 Fédération Sportive Féminine Internationale *Jeux Féminins Mondiaux Londres 1934*, Paris: Fédération Sportive Féminine Internationale 1934 Author's collection p. 8.
17 Florence Carpentier and Pierre Lefèvre 'The Modern Olympic Movement, Women's Sport and the Social Order During the Inter-war Period' *The International Journal of the History of Sport* 23: 7 2006 pp. 1112–1127.
18 Chris Rowell 'Our Ludy' Comes Home' *The Winthrop College News* 20 October 1922 cover Women and Sport File reference DGI 204964 IOC Archive, Lausanne.
19 Anon. 'The American Girls At The First Women's Olympiad' *New York World* 10 September 1922 unpaginated press cutting Women and Sport File reference DGI 204964 IOC Archive, Lausanne.
20 Mel Watman 'Women Athletes Between The World Wars' www.oxforddnb.com/view/article/103699 accessed 18 December 2019.
21 Anon. 'Women in The Olympic Games' *The Daily Mail* 1 August 1928; Anon. 'Miss L Radke (Germany) defeating Miss Hitomi (Japan)' *The Daily Mirror* 3 August 1928 unpaginated press cuttings Women and Sport File reference DGI 204964 IOC Archive, Lausanne.
22 Mel Watman *The Official History of the Women's Amateur Athletic Association (WAAA) 1922–2012* Cheltenham: Sports Books Ltd, 2012 pp. 38–39.
23 Liselott Diem 'Woman [sic] and Olympism: Retrospection on Former Publications of the Olympic Academy' *The Olympic Academy Conference 1978* pp. 7–8. Women and Sport File reference DGI 204964 IOC Archive, Lausanne.
24 Fédération Sportive Féminine Internationale *Jeux Féminins Mondiaux et Congrés Londres 1934: Fourth Womens World Games Congress, Records and Modifications of*

Rules January 1934 3 Rue de Varenne, Paris p. 2 WAAA files, Box 2 Birmingham University.
25 Fédération Sportive Féminine Internationale *Jeux Féminins Mondiaux Londres 1934* p. 8.
26 Rachel Cutler 'Audrey Court 1913–2005' *British Library Oral History*.
27 Richard Holt 'Audrey Kathleen Court (1913–2005)', *Oxford Dictionary of National Biography*, Oxford University Press, 2009 www.oxforddnb.com/view/article/96973 accessed 17 August 2019.
28 Evan Hunter BOA *Finance Committee Minutes 77 Ecclestone Square SW1 8 January 1936* p. 1 BOA Archive, London.
29 Organisationskomitee Für Die XI Olympiade Berlin 1936 E. V. *The XITH Olympic Games Berlin, 1936 Official Report* Part 1 Berlin: Wilhelm Limpert 1937 p. 268.
30 Richard Holt 'Audrey Kathleen Court [née Brown] (1913–2005)' *Oxford Dictionary of National Biography*.
31 Richard Holt 'Audrey Court interview' 7 February 2001 tape Author's collection.
32 British Olympic Association BOA *Finance Committee Minutes 77 Ecclestone Square SW1 8 October 1936* p. 1 BOA Archive, London.
33 Evan Hunter *Germany Circulars: BOA Transport Arrangements 4 July 1936* p. 2 BOA Archive, London.
34 Organisationskomitee Für Die XI Olympiade Berlin 1936 *Official Report* Part 1 p. 225.
35 Major Feuchtinger *Directions for the Opening Ceremony of the XIth Olympiad Berlin 1936 1 August 1936 in the Stadium at the Reich Sports Field* p. 2 1936 File IOC Archive, Lausanne.
36 Major Feuchtinger *Directions for the Opening Ceremony of the XIth Olympiad Berlin 1936* p. 8.
37 Major Feuchtinger *Directions for the Opening Ceremony of the XIth Olympiad Berlin 1936* p. 11.
38 Organisationskomitee Für Die XI Olympiade Berlin 1936 *Official Report Volume 1* p. 241.
39 Beilage zur Sammel-Dokumentation Das III Reich *Ich Rufe die Jugend der Welt: Olympia 1936* Berlin: Olympia Zeitung, 1936 p. 4 IOC Archive, Lausanne.
40 Richard Holt 'Audrey Kathleen Court [née Brown] (1913–2005)' *Oxford Dictionary of National Biography*.
41 Rachel Cutler 'Audrey Court 1913–2005' *British Library Oral History*.
42 Susan Noel 'Women in Sport: Let's Jump Back 20 Years' *World Sports Official Magazine of the British Olympic Association March 1955* London: Country and Sporting Publications, 1955 p. 38.
43 International Olympic Committee 'Berlin 1936: Searchable Database Of Medallists' International Olympic Committee www.olympic.org/content/results-and-medallists/gamesandsportsummary/ accessed 7 May 2010.
44 Brian Oliver 'Dorothy Tyler Obituary' *The Guardian* 28 September 2014 www.theguardian.com/sport/2014/sep/28/dorothy-tyler accessed 20 July 2019.
45 Brian Oliver 'Sir Ralph Kilner Brown Obituary' *The Telegraph* 20 June 2003 www.telegraph.co.uk/news/obituaries/1433497/Sir-Ralph-Kilner-Brown.html accessed 20 July 2019.
46 Richard Holt '(Arthur) Godfrey Kilner Brown (1915–1995)' *Oxford Dictionary of National Biography*, Oxford University Press, 2004 www.oxforddnb.com/view/article/59785 accessed 20 July 2019.
47 British Olympic Association BOA *Finance Committee Minutes 77 Ecclestone Square SW1 12 December 1935* p. 3 BOA Archive, London.
48 British Olympic Association BOA *Finance Committee Minutes 77 Ecclestone Square SW1 9 July 1936* p. 4 BOA Archive, London.

49 Organisationskomitee Für Die XI Olympiade Berlin 1936 E. V. *The XITH Olympic Games Berlin, 1936 Official Report Volume 2* Berlin: Wilhelm Limpert 1937 p. 1045.
50 Baatz 'Der Erste Wechiel der Fiegreichen Americanischen 400 metre Frauencstaffel: Rechts, Bland, Lints und Rogers' *Berliner Illustrirte Zeitung* 13 August 1936 cover 1936 File IOC Archive, Lausanne.
51 Beilage zur Sammel-Dokumentation Das III Reich *Ich Rufe die Jugend der Welt: Olympia 1936* Berlin: Olympia Zeitung, 1936 p. 3 1936 File IOC Archive, Lausanne.
52 Sir E. Phipps 'Olympic Games to be held in Germany 1936; German Chancellor's interest, fears of Germany that United States would withdraw, inclusion of Jewish woman in fencing team' FO 371/18884/7552 *The National Archives* www.nationalarchives.gov.uk/olympics/1936.htm accessed 19 May 2019.
53 Organisationskomitee Für Die XI Olympiade Berlin 1936 *Official Report Volume 2* p. 977.
54 Organisationskomitee Für Die XI Olympiade Berlin 1936 *Official Report Volume 2* p. 983.
55 Wilf Morgan 'Track Stats – Audrey Brown How Britain was deprived of a European Championships relay medal in 1938' *National Union of Track Statisticians Bulletin* November 2006 www.nuts.org.uk/trackstats/index.htm accessed 22 July 2019.
56 Rachel Cutler 'Audrey Court 1913–2005' *British Library Oral History* Tape 4 Side A C790/02 accessed 22 July 2019.
57 Audrey Court and Cynthia Walton *Birmingham Made a Difference: The Birmingham Women's Welfare Centre and the Family Planning Association 1926–1991* Birmingham: Barn Books, 2001.
58 Rachel Cutler 'Audrey Court 1913–2005' *British Library Oral History* Tape 4 Side B C790/02 accessed 22 July 2019.
59 Avery Brundage *American Olympic Committee Letter to Count Henri Baillet-Latour 23 June 1936* p. 1 Women and Sport File IOC Archive, Lausanne.
60 At the WAAA AGM in March 1983 a working party was established that suggested a single governing body for UK athletics and this was reported in the minutes of 25th October 1983 as motion carried. Out of a possible 493 votes, 151 were for and 79 against the proposal *WAAA Report of the Honorary Secretary 1985/6* p. 5 Special Collections WAAA Box 1 Birmingham University.
61 Rachel Cutler 'Audrey Court 1913–2005' *British Library Oral History* Tape 2 Side B.
62 Christopher Hilton 'Amazing tale of man called Hermann who finished fourth in women's high jump' *The Independent* 20 July 2008 www.independent.co.uk/sport/general/athletics/amazing-tale-of-man-called-hermann-who-finished-fourth-in-womens-high-jump-872322.html accessed 22 July 2019.
63 Fédération Sportive Féminine Internationale *Jeux Féminins Mondiaux Londres 1934: Fourth Womens World Games Official Programme Thursday-Saturday 9–11 August 1934* White City Stadium London p. 7 London: Fleetway, 1934 WAAA files, Box 2 Birmingham University.
64 Cecil Bear 'Off the Beaten Track' *World Sports Official Magazine of the British Olympic Association April 1956* London: Country and Sporting Publications, 1956 p. 36.
65 Jeane Hoffman 'Stella Walsh 47 – And She Won 100 Events Last Year' *World Sports: The International Sports Magazine June 1959* London: Country and Sporting Publications, 1959 pp. 24–9.
66 Vanessa Heggie *A History of British Sports Medicine* Manchester: Manchester University Press, 2011 pp. 110–111.
67 Rachel Cutler 'Audrey Court 1913–2005' *British Library Oral History* Tape 2 Side B.

68 F. A. M. Webster (ed.) *World Sports: the Official Organ of the British Olympic Association* London: British Olympic Association 1:1 1936 p. 3.
69 British Olympic Association *Finance Committee Minutes 77 Ecclestone Square SW1 8 October 1936* p. 1 BOA Archive, London.
70 Sandra Collins *The 1940 Tokyo Games: The Missing Olympics: Japan, the Asian Olympics and the Olympic Movement* London: Routledge, 2007 p. 10.

Chapter 5

Austerity and the second London Olympic Games in 1948

How Margaret Wellington swam to fame as 'The Peppy Kid'

Introduction

The second London Olympic Games, in 1948, hosted approximately 390 women athletes, and roughly 3,714 male contestants, plus the necessary judges, coaches and other related officials.[1] Though statistically small, the number of women competitors was a 10-fold increase on female representation at the previous London Olympics in 1908. However, the British medal tally at the first London Olympic Games (a total of 141 in all, divided into 56 gold, 48 silver and 37 bronze awards) would not be matched 40 years later. The British Olympic Association (BOA) funded a team of 324 men and 51 women in 1948, for a return of just 23 medals (3 gold, 14 silver and 6 bronze titles). Nevertheless, the perceived British 'failure' to excel in Olympic competition that had persisted from 1912 to 1936 was a weaker narrative during the domestic media coverage of the Olympic Games 1948, because post-war reconstruction and austere conditions created a sense of moral victory for the British in being able to stage festivities at all.

Robert Edelman has argued that 1948 should be seen as, 'The last of the pre-war Games' before Cold War rivalries changed the intensity of nationalism from the 1952 Helsinki Olympics onwards.[2] In the assessment of Bob Phillips, London 'rescued' the Olympic Games, from the highly politicised atmosphere in Berlin.[3] This goes a little far, as the degree of pomp and ceremonial British nationalism made them a political statement in their own right.[4] Even so, David Kynaston has questioned if most people cared about the Olympic Games in 1948, given the everyday priorities of post-war reconstruction.[5] Similarly, Peter Beck has argued that the cricket Test matches, for which the Australians would visit Britain, were more intensely followed by the public and the Press.[6]

This chapter considers the 1948 Olympic Games, in context of the British Olympic Association increasing its formal contacts with both the government and Royalty, particularly Elizabeth Windsor. The Atlee government assured the BOA that the 1948 Olympic Games would have the full support of the government, and King George VI acted as patron. Princess Elizabeth and her younger sister Margaret were frequently featured in the Royal Box at Wembley during the events themselves. The editors of *World Sports* thought that the Olympics had returned to 'the Motherland of Sports'.[7] As well as riding to hunt from a young age, both Princesses were keen field sports exponents; including shooting, salmon fishing and deer stalking. Elizabeth and Margaret had been taught to swim and dive at the Bath Club at the age of ten and eight, respectively. Many pioneering firsts that were celebrated by a new form of monarchy began when the princesses were young. Elizabeth had become the first person to be awarded the Royal Life Saving Society's Junior Resuscitation Badge, at the age of 12. While young, she became Patron of many sporting bodies, including the Amateur Swimming Association. Both Elizabeth and Philip were also accomplished sailors; the Cowes Island Sailing Club had given the Royal couple *Bluebottle*, a Dragon-class yacht as a wedding present, for instance.

This chapter focuses in particular on the career of swimmer, Margaret Wellington. What did the second London Olympic Games tell the British about themselves when Margaret and her co-competitors were performing? Where did women fit into that narrative and how did young athletes like Margaret Wellington articulate individual identities within the wider British team? How had women, as a substantial minority within the Olympic movement as a whole, changed the public face of the Games and the IOC? With the resumption of competition after a devastating world conflict, could the British help to re-imagine the Olympic Games anew?

Sporting appeasement had provided the main background of the 1936 Berlin Games, but London was able to host the 1948 Olympics due to having well-developed plans well before war had broken out. There was a particularly strong continuity because the BOA had begun to prepare for a very large London Olympic Games of up to 7,000 contestants in 1940 costing £50,000, going so far as to raise contracts with Arthur Elvin at Wembley stadium in 1936.[8] When Tokyo appeared to become the favoured choice for the 1940 Olympic Games, the British modified their ambitions, postponing plans to host the contest to 1944.[9] Similarly, Helsinki had begun work on an Olympic stadium in 1938 in preparation for the 1940 Games and this development would become the basis of their successful staging in 1952.

On 5 November 1945, the BOA decided to bid for 1948, using their existing plans and proposals.[10] Wembley stadium was partly a pragmatic solution as a host venue. The symbolic importance of Wembley also reflected that 'legacy' in 1948 meant establishing a peace movement for youthful sporting cooperation, rather than brand-building and infrastructure projects.

An expanded Olympic movement also reflected changes to women's lives in the public domain after World War II. Long serving secretary to the IOC, Lydie Zanchi, became formally recognised as full-time head of the secretariat in 1946, serving in that role until 1966.[11] A feminist who campaigned for women's enfranchisement in Switzerland, Zanchi had begun to work in this role as a friend of Marie-Louise Fauvannat, personal secretary to the Mayor of Lausanne, whose services were extended to the IOC's chief administrator, Lieutenant Colonel Berdez, on an ad hoc basis. When Berdez died in 1940, Zanchi was appointed acting secretary for the remainder of the Second World War and Sigfrid Edström appointed her permanently at the first IOC meeting after the conflict.

From being a part-time, volunteer go-between from the Mayor of Lausanne's office to the IOC, Lydie Zanchi would become central to the business of the Olympic movement and worked with four Presidents: Count Baillet-Latour, Sigfrid Edström, Avery Brundage and Lord Killanin, often appearing as the only woman noted by name in the Minutes of meetings. Her role was pivotal. The bureaucratic workload of the IOC would increase dramatically once the Games became more stable again after World War II. Whereas previously, the Executive board had completed clerical tasks somewhat erratically, Zanchi's appointment correlated with an increasingly managerial culture in world sport. There would be almost 40 secretarial staff under her direction by the time she retired. The expansion of sporting bureaucracy therefore gave women a new way into positions of significant importance during this period, and with a worldwide reach. In 1956, for instance, Otto Mayer, Chancellor of the IOC from 1946 to 1964, and therefore one of the key architects of a more systematised ruling code across the organisation as its unpaid Secretary General, acknowledged the debt of the organisation to Zanchi's oversight during this period.[12] During Mayer's illnesses, as his health deteriorated in the later 1950s, Zanchi often represented the Chancellerie in his stead.

The British aristocracy also became more significant to the IOC during this time. David Cecil, the sixth Marques of Exeter, and better known as Lord Burghley, took an increasing role in global sport, as President of the International Amateur Athletic Federation from 1946 until 1976. So there was much continuity in the gradual change from an all-male Olympic oligarchy. From 1946 onwards, Lord Burghley acted as President of the Organising Committee for the London Olympics, becoming also the Vice President of the International Olympic Committee. A cautious moderniser, Burghley's multiple appointments symbolised how transformation in sporting administration could be incredibly slow, partly because the IOC was such a conservative organisation. The IOC was not the only traditionalist entity shaping the 1948 Olympic Games. Artist G. T. Knipe submitted a design for a commemorative stamp depicting a hurdler, based on a photograph of Burghley, to the selection committee, only for it to be considered improper that the King's image should be represented as smaller than one of his subjects. The design was not selected.

More women were permitted to enter more Olympic sports and disciplines as time progressed and the movement expanded, but this was a slow and incremental process. The 1948 London Games saw women's canoeing introduced to the already crowded Summer schedule. The 500-metres K1 (Kayak Singles) race for women had 10 participants from 10 nations. Karen Hoff was victorious for Denmark, leading Lida van der Anker-Doedens representing the Netherlands and Fritzi Schwingl of Austria. Britain's Joyce Richards was eliminated in the heats.

The development of the women's Olympic schedule was uneven, to say the least. Winifred Pritchard, who had already won four races in the Royal Yacht Association trials was prevented from an Olympic debut in 1948, since mixed sailing events would be 'introduced' in 1952.[13] The next British female representative would be Jean Mitchell, who would sail *Twinkle* at the Rome Olympics of 1960, with her husband Roy in the mixed two-person keelboat class, to come 24th overall. Jean would be the only female sailor of the 11-strong British team.

Opening on 29 July and closing on 14 August, the second London Olympic Games staged technological innovation, allied to ritual and pageantry. The March of the Guards' Band during the Opening Ceremony, in scarlet tunics with brass buttons and bearskin hats, typified the use of heritage displays, as impractical as it was in the heat, which was so considerable that some of the volunteer boy scouts fainted while on parade. Mediated widely by BBC outside broadcasts and a J. Arthur Rank feature film of the Games, the Olympics was one of the first big post-war opportunities for national communion, across the UK and its remaining Empire.[14]

Although most of the half a million TV viewers lived within 80 miles of London, many more could access newsreels and features in the cinema.[15] While less than 5 per cent of the adult population had a television in their homes, around 70,000 sets, Olympic outside broadcasts provided one of the milestones of post-war TV transmission, following the Victory Parade in 1946 and the Royal Wedding of Princess Elizabeth and Prince Philip in 1947. Given different national identities, regional variation and personal inclination, it remains difficult to assess how many people experienced either close association with Olympic ideals or any kind of unity with the British team. The extent of volunteering nevertheless suggests that many British people who would never become Olympians themselves helped to stage a contest that would have been impossible to host without them.

In 1948, London was short of accommodation, building materials, food, fuel and transport. Many of the women competitors were housed at Southlands College in Wimbledon, and for some, training took place at the Butlin's Holiday Camp, Clacton-on-Sea. In spite of austerity, or perhaps because of the financial circumstances, a strong commercialisation was evident in the way that the Olympic Games were sponsored, used to sell related merchandise and funded.[16] One advertisement in *World Sports* boasted, 'At the London Olympic Games in 1948 over 25,000 cups of Ovaltine were served to the athletes'.[17] It also chimed with a growing consumerism in society as 'it dawned upon the businessmen of the country that the Little Woman was now Big Business'.[18] The special edition of *Picture Post* that accompanied the Olympic Games contained over 40 advertisements across 30 pages, the vast majority aimed at, or featuring, women and selling everything from bile beans to National Savings Bonds.[19]

Margaret Wellington: 'swim and see the world'

Although not a medallist in 1948, the swimmer Margaret Olive Wellington was to achieve a degree of transnational fame as a result of becoming an Olympic and Commonwealth competitor. Swimming would take Margaret places that she otherwise would not have seen, and to meet people outside her immediate circle of friends as a celebrated athlete. The following biographical information is based on an interview with Margaret's daughter, Lesley, in December 2015 and private source material from Margaret's 10 scrapbooks, compiled over a lifetime of love for swimming. Born in Sydenham in December 1926, Margaret had an elder brother born the previous January, Peter Beresford Wellington. She did not care for her middle name, Olive, but preferred Maggy and this was one of several nicknames she acquired throughout her life.

Margaret's mother, Ivy, was the presiding influence in her upbringing, as her father left the family when the children were young. Both Ivy and the children kept the Wellington surname after his departure. Ivy returned from

Figure 5.1 Margaret Wellington at the 1948 London Olympic Games.
Source: The Lesley 'Zelly' Restorick collection.

the marriage to live with her siblings Doris, Alice and Leslie Joel. The family name had been vol Joel so this may have been an anglicised Jewish name. Ivy and Alice remained at home to do the domestic chores in the house owned by Margaret's paternal grandfather, known as 'Pop', and Leslie and Doris worked to support the others. Margaret first attended Alexandra Junior School, then Beckenham Girls Grammar and was said to have wanted to swim to a high level, specifically 'to be a champion', from the age of seven. The family was supportive of her ambitions and gave her additional portions of food when training from their rations.

The physical signs of a future Olympian were not initially evident if Margaret's own account is to be believed, as she reported having,

> tried almost every other game and had been a miserable failure... If there is one thing I have proved in my life as a sportswoman, it is that a national swimming champion can be fashioned out of the most hopeless-looking material.[20]

Margaret was small, had glasses from an early age and for a while had to wear a patch over one eye, leading to the unkind nickname 'five eyes' at school. Wellington declared that she had little natural talent and 'her weekly visits with the Junior School to the local pool were enough to make most coaches weep'.[21]

Both Margaret and her brother swam, from the evidence of the scrapbooks, in local baths and on family holidays. Lacrosse was Margaret's other main school sporting interest, before she left at the age of 16 to join Lloyds Bank, before later also joining The Bankers Trust. The sibling bond became less strong as Peter went to work at Cable and Wireless from the age of 18, often travelling and living abroad.

At the relatively late age of 15 and a half, Margaret set her mind to swim seriously, seven days a week and train with the Beckenham Ladies Swimming Club. As well as strong school performances in the freestyle, Margaret became Junior Southern champion in 1942. In 1944, she came to national prominence as a potential Olympic hopeful in the freestyle events over both 100 and 400 metres. For the next three years, her friendship and rivalry with the Scottish freestyle competitors Cathie Gibson and Nancy Riach provided a South vs North narrative upon which many newspapers capitalised. The youngest British aquatic competitor of all in 1948 would be a breaststroke specialist; 15 year-old Elenor (also known as Helen) Orr Gordon, from Hamilton, South Lanarkshire. The rivalry between Scottish industrialism, and English metropolitanism was evident in the media coverage of these swimmers, as Wellington worked in London's financial district.

Having emerged as junior talents during the war, Margaret, Cathie, Nancy and Elenor were relatively young compared with established British swimmers like Helen Yate, who was born in 1921. Plymouth-based Yate had been the 1938 national backstroke champion but had not had an auspicious start to her swimming career either:

> When we were about 7 years old, my father took my twin sister, my cousin and me to the local beach. I was the last to learn to swim. We joined the Port of Plymouth Swimming Club and progressed through club races to district, county and Western county championships. There was no indoor pool in Plymouth, so we had season tickets to the outdoor pool from 1 May to 30 September. From about 12 years my mother took us to a 50 yard, open air pool in Devonport, it was filled straight from the sea, the sides were Lime Washed, then chlorine was added to the water, and we did not wear goggles in those days.
>
> When I was about 15 years of age, we heard that there was an indoor pool in the Naval Barracks, nearby HMS Drake, and my father arranged to get me permission to use it during the lunch hour when it was not needed by the Navy. The presiding Physical Training Officer, Mr Ward, was a marvelous coach and I began to train seriously. I had the pool to myself and his sole attention, swimming both lunchtimes and evenings. As you will have gathered, my family were very supportive and, when I was fifteen, took me to London to see Mr Howcroft. He said I would win the ASA women's breaststroke championship within two years and he was right. As I could not use the Navy pool and get a job, my parents supported me until war broke out. Then I joined the WRNS as an immobile officer and stayed in Plymouth (my father was away a lot, my sister was due to be called up and so mother would otherwise have been alone).
>
> When I left the WRNS in December 1947, it was decided, in consultation with Mr Howcroft, that I should go to London to try and get selected for the Olympic Games. We had no family or friends in London but I knew some of the Mermaid swimmers, who Mr Howcroft coached, so I joined them. I got a job with the Great Western Railway at Paddington; the perks included good travel facilities for weekends at home, and I lived in a hostel at Marble Arch. I trained with Mr Howcroft's squad. The Mermaids were very good to me and some have become lifelong friends. It is hard to say what I felt at being selected for the team, after I came second at the National Championships in Scarborough in 1948. I was 27 years old. It was a lifetime's ambition that had come rather late, but, all the same, it was a wonderful feeling.[22]

As the excerpt shows, geography could be a deciding factor as Yate was able to continue to train during the war in her home-town of Plymouth due to a Women's Royal Navy Service posting and quickly returned to intensive training after being de-mobbed.

The difference between the training regimes of Riach, Gibson, Wellington and Yate illustrated how approaches to junior and senior amateur swimming

Austerity in the 1948 London Olympic Games 147

Figure 5.2 A training photograph taken of Margaret Wellington, to refine her technique prior to the 1948 London Olympic Games.
Source: The Lesley 'Zelly' Restorick collection.

could vary, with distinct regional and local practices across the British Isles. As the superintendent of the corporation baths, David Crabb a member of the Communist Party, persuaded the Motherwell and Wishaw Council to keep the facility open in wartime, as part of his wider belief in working class mutual support.[23] Crabb trained children as young as eight, intensively for competition. By the age of 12, Riach had shown ability in crawl, backstroke and breaststroke before breaking the British 100-yard freestyle record of 61 seconds, then one and one-fifth of a second outside the women's world record.[24]

Margaret Wellington's other main rivalry was much more local, as Patricia Nielsen of Bromley, who had been born in 1930, was also a promising young freestyle specialist. This sharpened Margaret's appetite for increased training, with dramatic effect, as she would finish second in the 100-yards freestyle final, third in the 220-yards race and fourth over 440 yards, at the National Championships in 1946 in New Brighton. A close third to Riach and Gibson then followed at the 1947 national finals, held at Hastings. This led Pathé News to dub Wellington the 'Mermaid in the City'.[25] Often described as 'the personality girl' of the English or British team, Wellington was also frequently referenced as 'tawny-haired' in the newspapers.

In Hastings, Margaret Wellington also improved on her performances with two second places in the 220-yards and 440-yards races. Wellington was keenly aware of the advantage that intensive training gave the Scottish swimmers, writing a spiky letter in response to a journalist's criticism that she had not achieved her potential, which ended 'I am now the fastest swimmer in England over all distances... No doubt if Beckenham swimmers could train six hours a day like the regime of the Scottish swimmers, they would gain the same honors'.[26]

Margaret then set herself a series of goals and these were 'To win all three freestyle national titles, and to represent Great Britain in the European, Empire and Olympic Games'.[27] She would go on to achieve all of these targets between 1947 and 1950, although she represented England, rather than Great Britain in the Empire Games. Having begun to train more seriously, and swimming three times a day when working at the bank, Wellington then further refined the technical aspects of her stroke during several preparatory Olympic summer schools at Loughborough University, with lead Amateur Swimming Association coach Harry Kowskie. She clearly relished both the sporting and social camaraderie.

Margaret first went overseas to swim in 1946 when she was part of an ASA English national team that flew to Antwerp, along with female teammates Helen Yate, Vera Ellery and Jean Caplin. The ASA had never before funded a team to travel by air and this was also the first time that Margaret Wellington had ever been abroad. The next year, in Monte Carlo at the European championships in 1947, Margaret was ill and bedridden with tonsillitis, which had affected her training but she was nevertheless able to compete. The British team stayed at the Royal Hotel and in some comfort but worse news than Margaret's ill-health would define the memory of these championships.

In Monte Carlo, Nancy Riach died of polio at just 20 years old having already won a bronze medal in the 4×100-metres freestyle relay, with Catherine Gibson, Lillian Preece and Margaret Wellington. Newsreels covered the large sombre crowds at the funeral.[28] At the time, Riach was said to have been 'the finest swimmer that the British Empire has ever produced, and the finest ambassador of sport that Scotland or any other country within the British Empire has ever turned out'.[29]

The age and personality of competitors like Margaret Wellington are partly revealed by social events, including practical jokes, which happened during training camps and 'on tour'. For many young Olympic hopefuls, the focus was not entirely on serious physical preparation. One evening while at Loughborough University, Margaret was a passenger in a car accident. The driver of the red MG in question, was a male track and field athlete, and Margaret had been warned not to fraternise with the other team members at the Summer School. Unhurt, Wellington kept her adventure quiet to avoid any disciplinary sanction.

Later, while staying in the Park Hotel Odense, Denmark as part of an ASA English team, the hotel management sent up a large cake as a welcome gesture. Fellow British swimmer and 1948 Olympian, Pat Kendall threw the cake out of Margaret's top floor hotel room after deciding that it was not to his taste. A motor coach trip through the Danish Riviera to Elsinore and a visit to the Carlsberg Brewery, where the swimmers christened the lager beer 'fizzy lemonade', completed the trip. The phrase would appear from time to time in autograph books as an in-joke that alcohol had been consumed while touring.

So with relatively little international experience, Margaret Wellington would represent Great Britain in the London Olympic Games of 1948. However, she was national 100-yards freestyle champion that year, having taken the title in Scarborough. In 1949, she would go on to take both the 220-yards and 400-yards freestyle national championships in Derby.

Swimming at the Empire Pool during the London Olympic Games in 1948 was really spectacular with crowds of up to 8,000 people. Even so, in the words of Helen Yate:

> The Games were not glamorous. The London swimmers journeyed to Wembley on the Tube, except when we were competing and were transported by coach. I had moved from the hostel at Marble Arch to a hostel at Victoria by then. All the same, I have always felt that we were lucky there were any Games at all. The opening ceremony was very moving with the teams, the flags and the swearing of the Olympic Oath. For me, all that it should be.[30]

Scotland's hopes would rest on eventual bronze medallist Cathie Gibson in the women's 400-metres freestyle race, as she finished behind Ann Curtis of the USA and Karen Harup of Denmark. Curtis had been identified as having Olympic potential, aged 11 by coach Charles Sava and had been swimming two miles a day, six days a week under his instruction for three years, before making her national debut in 1943.[31] This was even more specialised and intensive training than coach David Crabb had used to develop his Motherwell swimmers.

Gibson's was to be the only aquatic medal for Great Britain, with Patricia Nielsen unplaced in the same event. This was not an auspicious return for Britain, having sent a team of 16 men and nine women to the swimming events. Austerity meant that swimmers were often obliged to be all-rounders and an original line-up of 12 female British competitors included some substitutes. Karen Harup also took the 100-metres backstroke gold, followed by America's Susan Zimmerman, closely followed by Australia's Judy Joy Davies (Helen Yate, Cathie Gibson and Vera Ellery of Britain were unplaced). The 200-metres women's backstroke was won by Nel van Vliet of the Netherlands ahead of Nancy Lyons for Australia and Éva Gérard-Novák of Hungary (Jean Caplin and Elenor Gordon were eliminated in the heats). Gordon would also take part in the 1952 Olympics to win the sole individual medal; a bronze in the 200-metres women's breaststroke.[32]

The women's 4 × 100-metres freestyle relay final provided a sensational finish in the final leg from Ann Curtis to win for the USA, ahead of Denmark, Holland and Great Britain, who all broke the Olympic record. Wellington was part of the team that finished fourth with colleagues Cathie Gibson, Patricia Nielsen and Lillian Preece.[33] It remains a matter for speculation whether Riach, rather than Nielsen, might have helped the team to make bronze. Although the British press had decided that Cathie Gibson was the best female medal hope, they liked Wellington and used her shock of auburn curly hair to characterise her as 'The Ball of Fire' and 'The Peppy Kid'. Local newspapers reported that Beckenham had made a unique contribution to the 1948 Olympic Games, with fellow swimmer Ronnie Stedman also selected for Britain.

In perhaps the most intensely competitive women's swimming event, Margaret Wellington, Lillian Preece and Patricia Nielsen were all eliminated in their respective heats in the 100-metres freestyle individual race. The Official Report summarised the significance of female Olympic solidarity as the medals were handed out:

> The most poignant moment came not during the battle for supremacy in the water, but when the three fastest women swimmers in the world mounted the victory rostrum. They were Greta Andersen of Denmark, who had just beaten Ann Curtis (U.S.A.), by a finger touch in the 100 metres free-style, and Marie Vaessen, from Holland who was third [sic]. As the first woman to win an Olympic swimming medal for 12 years, young Greta was not unnaturally thrilled, but, had it not been for a simple gesture by Miss Curtis, she might have failed to appreciate fully one of the greatest moments in her life. As the Danish national anthem was played a hush fell over the arena. Behind the swimmers, the winner's flag, with its white cross on a red background was unfurled and slowly hoisted. Ann noticed it and tapped the Danish girl on the shoulder. She turned, and watching the flag rise, her face filled with happiness and pride at the honour she had brought to her country. Although deprived of a victory she had been considered certain to gain, Ann Curtis captured the true spirit of sportsmanship of the Olympic ideals.[34]

Greta Andersen had created one the most dramatic moments in the Empire pool by collapsing during her 400-metres freestyle heat, and had to be saved by her fellow competitors. However, her stamina was never in doubt. In 1957, she won a cross-Channel race in 13 hours 53 minutes, to take home £500 and a 1,000 guinea trophy.[35]

Margaret Wellington remained well-known following her Olympic appearance. In 1949, the BBC paid her 10 guineas and all travelling expenses to deliver an 8-minute talk as part of a light programme, called 'Hullo Children: Spotlight on Swimming'.[36] It is important to note that often a top six finish was judged to be distinguished at the time.

If national and Olympic representation had so far taken Margaret Wellington to mainland Europe, Commonwealth swimming would offer more exotic travel destinations. Margaret wrote of the opportunities for travel provided by swimming in order to promote the activity to young women and also meticulously documented these journeys in her scrapbooks. She summarised the opportunities with clarity: 'Success was marvellous. So was travelling round the world. I had never looked at swimming in the light that it offered such a wonderful opportunity for meeting people of all nationalities at home and abroad'.[37]

Figure 5.3 Flight and travel tickets. Invitations to overseas international competitions enabled Margaret, 'The Peppy Kid', to see the world and meet some of her heroes, including fellow athletes and movie stars.

Source: The Lesley 'Zelly' Restorick collection.

Along with the rest of the English team, Margaret Wellington and Helen Yate travelled to the British Empire Games in New Zealand in 1950 onboard ship with the Shaw Saville Line. As Helen Yate remembered the voyage:

> The Empire Games in New Zealand was a different experience. We were the last team to go by Sea, five weeks out and five weeks back on a passenger/cargo ship. Across the Pacific with Scottish, Welsh, Nigerian and Celonese swimmers, athletes, boxers, wrestlers and cyclists on the same boat, so it was good fun'.[38]

Margaret Wellington was careful not to over-indulge onboard ship during the 12,600 mile voyage but this was not easy as the breakfast, lunch and dinner menus extended to several courses, supplemented by mid-morning snacks and afternoon tea. Many snapshots show her continuing to train during the journey and socialising with other athletes like Sylvia Cheeseman while aboard the *Tamaroa* in the Caribbean. On arrival, the teams were housed in an ex-army camp. Friendships made through competition could be abiding and the memories of these events could last through life. Helen Yate remembered:

> The Games were a success as far as the swimmers were concerned although I was disappointed with third in the backstroke. The New Zealanders were very generous and we were given a lovely woollen blanket (I still have mine) and shiny stretch satin swimsuits which were unobtainable in England. As we were still rationed, everyone sent food parcels home.[39]

This was the first time for 12 years that the British Empire Games had been held and Wellington's discipline paid off. Representing England, she came second in both the individual women's 110-yards and 440-yards freestyle events. The English team were runners-up to Australia in the 3 × 110-yards medley relay, with Elizabeth Church swimming breaststroke and Helen Yate backstroke. Elenor Gordon led the Scots into third place. In the 4 × 110-yards freestyle relay, the English team of Margaret Wellington, Grace Wood, Helen Yate and Lillian Preece came in third behind Australia and New Zealand.

Arguably, only Elenor Gordon, the individual 220-yard breaststroke gold medallist and 3 × 110-yards medley relay team bronze medallist for Scotland, outshone Wellington's individual achievements for UK teams in Auckland. Being a multiple Empire Games medallist was a considerable accolade, at least in the British Press. The British Empire Games were followed by a tour of both North and South Island in New Zealand, where the hospitality was both elaborate and generous. Returning again on the *SS Tamoroa*, Margaret noted that she arrived in London on 8 April 1950, where she found 'it was snowing'.[40]

An even more exciting trip followed with Qantas Airways for the Christchurch Centenary Celebration Games in 1951; the trip included stop-offs in Rome, Cairo, Karachi, Calcutta, Singapore, Darwin, San Francisco, Hollywood and New York. The whole itinerary comprised two months, incorporating five weeks competing and two more sight-seeing in New Zealand. Wellington and Yate holidayed separately before the return flight to San Francisco via Fiji and Honolulu, where Margaret purchased a Hawaiian shirt; a much prized memento of the trip.

In San Francisco, Wellington and Yate both competed at the Crystal Plunge, the club of Ann Curtis and her coach Charles Sava. Wellington was reportedly shocked by the intensity of training advocated by Sava of at least three kilometres in the pool a day. Helen Yate remembered the occasion slightly differently:

> Charlie Sava, who coached Ann Curtis, coached us for the three weeks at Crystal Plunge. I was swimming faster than I had ever done when I got home. Charlie gave up his flat so Maggie and I could stay longer. We were only going to stay for a week. He slept at the pool.[41]

Sava and Curtis instigated a 'grand gesture' as the two British women were amateurs and only those travelling on business were allowed to exchange pounds Sterling for dollars, at that time. So, in order that Wellington and Yate could fund a short vacation in the USA, and it seems like they lodged at the Plaza Hotel for a few days at least, the Crystal Plunge staged a fundraising gala evening. By the time of their return Margaret and Helen also had the autographs of Test cricketers Denis Compton of England and Ray Lindwall of Australia. The stopover in America allowed Wellington and Yate to meet film stars, such as Dorothy Lamour and Jane Powell, also taking home their autographs as souvenirs. In addition, scrapbook items like menus and entertainments illustrate how sociable amateur sport could be, even if the logistics were somewhat improvised and the means of sustenance somewhat precarious.

In these senses, the scrapbooks are like a first version of history authored by the competitors themselves, providing a view unlike any others in the public domain. Even newspapers, which are often called the first version of history, do not have the intimacy, emotional immediacy or sense of personal significance across a lifetime of private collections of memorabilia.

Wellington and Yate's brief moment of fame shows that amateurism could clearly have its benefits. We can only imagine how exciting it was to be treated as special guests on the other side of the world, as a result of being Olympic and Commonwealth swimmers in their 20s. It is also clear from the personal sources that both Margaret and Helen were proud to remain amateurs and would have declined opportunities to take up professional swimming careers. Margaret married Basil Restorick in 1951 and continued to appear in national events until she announced the end of her competitive swimming career in 1957. However, she continued to swim regularly and frequently for her own enjoyment until the age of 85 and obtained several coaching badges. As daughter Lesley remembers her mother:

> Mum was a swimmer until she was 85 years of age, ideally in a 50 metre pool and with a dedicated lane to herself. Her determination to be a swimmer – apparently originating in her childhood – was an amazingly inspirational journey. Working full-time, she often swam three times a day, postwar, in a time of rationing. A small, slight woman, she demonstrated how dreams can come true, if someone is determined enough and willing to practice and actively put in the effort required. A vivacious, vibrant member of the British team, she ate, drank, dreamt, lived, breathed swimming. Gutsy, committed and determined, she especially loved the time she spent at Loughborough University; every day dedicated to improving her talent. Mum was extremely proud to be an amateur, never wanting to associate money with her skill. She believed that swimming was not only the best exercise for the whole body, but also a sport available to everyone.[42]

This longevity is a subject to which the conclusion returns. First though, who were the other significant female athletes in 1948?

Figure 5.4 Margaret swam into her 80s, ideally in a 50-metre pool, with a lane reserved for her at the local swimming baths. In the 1980s, the mineral water company, Evian, photographed Margaret and some of her fellow swimmers in red sparkly swimsuits to celebrate their vitality and health, as part of a promotional campaign.

Source: The Lesley 'Zelly' Restorick collection.

The Flying Housewife and the 1948 Olympic Games

Although this chapter focuses mainly on Margaret Wellington and the swimmers, the female star of the London Olympic Games was the track and field athletics all-rounder, Fanny Blankers-Koen of the Netherlands. Blankers-Koen took four gold medals in the 100-metres and 200-metres races, the 80-metres hurdles and the 4 × 100-metres team relay race. The official report considered her quadruple victory the most talked about achievement of the Games.[43] Having already competed in 1936, now a mother of two and 30 years old, Blankers-Koen dispelled myths about the straining effects of high-level competition on the female reproductive system. In a very understated way, she summarised the difference between 1936 and 1948, from a personal point of view:

> Being a novice (in 1936), I did not have any worry that my friends *expected* me to win... But what really impressed me was the playing of the national anthem of each winner's country after every final. How proud I would be if the band ever played for me ... But I had to wait twelve years before my dream came true, when sport was only a means of relaxation to forget for a while the sadness of those dark days.[44]

Blankers-Koen held both the long jump and high jump world records but since the schedule placed these competitions on the same day as important track finals, she had to choose which events were priorities. She was however, able to take part in four track and field events compared with the IAAF and IOC restriction of three when Babe Didrikson competed in 1932. Entirely different in personality, modest and humble Blankers-Koen's Olympic achievements would outshine 'The Babe'.

Already pregnant with her third child, the British treatment of Blankers-Koen as 'the Flying Housewife' reflected a media that used references to the family life of female athletes as a way of domesticating their image on a world stage. This was ostensibly admiring, at the same time as making sport marginal to their life stories. This is a typical piece written by Albert Milhado:

> There has never been a better all-round champion in women's athletics than Fanny Blankers-Koen. She is too, a wise and charming woman; wise because she takes the advice of her husband (now sports editor of one of Holland's leading newspapers *De Telegraaf*), charming because she is the perfect mother of two lovely children, the friend to her of all who meet her, and because, to her, her athletics success is just one of those things and not much to talk about.[45]

The 100 metres was the largest single female track and field event with 38 entries from 21 countries. Fanny Blankers-Koen won the 100 metres in

156 Austerity in the 1948 London Olympic Games

WOMEN WIN ATHLETIC FAME
First Games in which women took part were those in Amsterdam in 1928. Out of 5,970 athletes who compete in this Olympiad 330 are women.

Figure 5.5 The star of the 1948 London Olympic Games, Fanny Blankers-Koen, with four gold medals, here beating Britain's Dorothy Manley, a typist from Woodford Green.

11.9 seconds by 'a good three yards' from Britain's Dorothy Manley, with Shirley Strickland of Australia in third place.[46] Originally from Woodford Green, Manley was 21 years old, worked full-time as a typist in the City for the Suez Canal Company, and the London Olympic Games was her first international sprint event: hence the rather unimaginative nickname 'Speed Typist'.[47]

Manley had been interested in athletics from the age of nine, as a member of the Essex Ladies' Athletic Club, had recently changed from the high jump to sprinting disciplines, at the advice of coach Sandy Duncan, a BOA stalwart.[48] Britain's Audrey Williamson was 22 years old and, along with Doris Batter (aged 19), was eliminated in the heats. The wider field of entrants was noticeable, given that after Viola Myers and Pat Jones of Canada came Cynthia Thompson, who ran a personal best of 12.5 to come sixth for Jamaica.

The 200 metres was slightly smaller with 33 entrants, from 17 nations. Blankers-Koen won in 24.4 seconds, ahead of Audrey Williamson for Britain and Audrey 'Mickey' Paterson for the United States. Judges took 45 minutes to award the bronze to Patterson, ahead of Shirley Strickland, and the New Orleans resident therefore became the first African-American woman to win an Olympic track medal on 29 July 1948.[49] Shirley Strickland of Australia, Margaret Walker of Britain and Daphne Robb of South Africa were the other beaten finalists. British contenders Margaret Walker, at the age of 23, and Sylvia Cheeseman, aged 19, were eliminated in the heats. Soon after, Cheeseman had her tonsils removed, and, unsurprisingly, this improved her form in anticipation of the 1950 Empire Games.[50] She went on to become a popular athlete with the public and the media alike, no doubt helped by the fact that Cheeseman worked as an administrator in the *World Sports* office, while training in the evenings and competing most weekends.[51]

The range of opponents against whom British track and field athletes competed continued to diversify and this was very evident during the London Olympic Games in 1948. Jamaican sprinters Kathleen Russell and Vinton Beckett contested the 80-metres hurdles and the long jump. Carmen Phipps competed in the high jump, along with Beckett. More South American women were also in evidence in the sprint events with a noticeable team from Brazil (Melânia Luz, Helena de Menezes, Elisabeth Müller, Benedita de Oliveira, Lucila Pini) and two contestants from Chile (Betty Kretschmer and Annegret Weller-Schneider).

In the 80-metres hurdles, 21 women from 12 nations took part. Britain's Joan Upton and Bertha Crowther were eliminated in the heats. In the most exciting race of all the women's track and field finishes, Blankers-Koen tied for a time of 11.2 seconds ahead of Britain's Maureen Gardner, with Shirley Strickland narrowly third. Yvette Monginou of France, Maria Oberbreyer-Trösch of Austria and Libuše Lomská of Czechoslovakia completed the final field.[52] Gardner appeared to slightly jump the starting pistol and it took Blankers-Koen two hurdles to catch her before going ahead slightly herself.

From Oxford, Gardner was a favourite of the British media, variously referred to as a typist or a ballet dancer and, at 19 years of age, the British press had forecast her youth would be the deciding factor in the hurdles race.[53] In particular, the noted sports journalist, Jack Crump, had said that Blankers-Koen, was too old for Olympic victory against the young British athletes, predicting the victory of domestic youth over foreign experience. Jan Blankers-Koen, who coached his wife, had used the criticism to motivate Fanny when her energy sapped: she would eventually compete 11 times in heats and finals to win every event that she entered in 1948.

There was also much praise for Shirley Strickland's all-round achievements at Wembley and she had a claim to be among the best female athletes in London. Strickland's total achievements included two bronzes in the 100-metres and 80-metres hurdles; a fourth place in the 200 metres and a silver medal as part of the Australian 4 × 100-metres relay team, which finished behind the Dutch and ahead of the Canadians. Under her married name of Shirley de la Hunty, a long and illustrious career was commemorated with a special series of stamps as part of the Australian Legends series in 1998. The British team, which came fourth, comprised of Dorothy Manley; Maureen Gardner; Muriel Pletts (who was aged just 17) and Margaret Walker.[54] Denmark took fifth place and Austria sixth.

Micheline Ostermeyer of France was another versatile contestant, with two gold medals (both Olympic records) for putting the shot (13.75 metres) and throwing the discus (41.92 metres), in addition to her bronze medal in the high jump. A noted pianist, Ostermeyer might also have been considered female athlete of the Games, were it not for Blankers-Koen's dominance.[55] There were 21 women from 11 nations in the discus event, where Edera Cordiale-Gentile won second place for Italy and Jacqueline Mazéas placed third for France. Pong Sik Pak, in the discus, would be the only woman in the Korean team.[56] The shot was a slightly smaller field with 19 participants from 12 countries. Amelia Piccinini won silver for Italy and Ine Schäffer bronze for Austria. Margaret Birtwhistle, Bevis Reid and Elspeth Whyte finished some way down the field for Britain in both of these throwing events. In the javelin, the medal winners were Herma Bauma of Austria, Kaisa Parviainen of Finland and Lily Carlstedt-Kelsby of Denmark. Kay Long and Gladys Clarke took penultimate and last place, respectively for Britain.

The high jump produced one of the most exciting duels, with people sitting in their seats for an hour longer than expected to see the outcome. Both the winner, Alice Coachman, and Dorothy Tyler of Great Britain, cleared 1.68 metres, to set a new Olympic record.[57] The fact that Coachman cleared this height at her first attempt, while Tyler required a second jump, decided the tie in the American's favour. Britain's Margaret Birtwhistle and Dora Gardner came in sixth and eighth place, respectively. As has been noted, Coachman's specialist preparation before the London Games evidenced a new era of African-American educational institutions identifying and developing talent, especially among women at the Tuskee Institute (now Tuskee University) and Tennessee Agricultural and Industrial State College. Many more African-American female athletes would become Olympians through these pioneering programmes and others that replicated their success.[58]

Having worked as a physical training instructor and then as a driver in the Air Force during the war, Tyler was posted to different stations and at one time served with the Dam Busters. She married and had her first son, David, in 1946 and the second, Barry, in 1947. A widely circulated photograph featured Dorothy Tyler holding a washing up bowl and 'training' for the Olympic Games by leaping over a line of nappies, while David played in the garden.[59] In this sense, the virtue of British amateur sport as essentially spontaneous, rather than the result of careful preparation, could tend towards pastiche and caricature.

Britain's Margaret Erskine, Lorna Lee and Joan Shepherd were all unplaced in the Long Jump. In the absence of Blankers-Koen and leading

Japanese and Soviet contenders, Olga Gyarmati of Hungary took the gold medal; Noemí Simonetto de Portela of Argentina the silver; Ann-Britt Leyman of Sweden the bronze; with the other places going to Gerda van der Kade-Koudijs, Nel Karelsen of the Netherlands and Kathleen Russell of Jamaica. De Portela thereby became the first South American woman to win an Olympic medal.

The patchy results of the female track and field athletics team did not occasion much soul searching. Jack Crump was not alone in his opinion that female hopefuls suffered from neglect by the sporting establishment, but this improved only very slowly after Lilleshall Hall became designated by the Central Council of Physical Recreation as a national home for sporting education in 1949.[60] British women continued to improvise ad hoc training regimes between themselves and their coaches, including Mary Bignal who, (after marriage), as Mary Rand, would win the first British women's Olympic Gold medal in track and field athletics with a new world record in the Long Jump at the 1964 Tokyo Olympics.[61] This was, however, some way off.

There were 42 entries for the women's foil in 1948 where Ilona Elek of Hungary retained the title she had won in the Berlin Games. The first Olympic female foilist to keep her championship, Elek shared the victory rostrum with Karen Lachmann of Denmark and Ellen Müller-Preis for Austria (winner of the Olympic title in 1932). For Britain, Elizabeth Arbuthnot, who had also competed in the 1936 Olympic Games, was joined by Mary Glen Haig and another newcomer, Gytte Minton. Glen Haig did the best of the three British women, going through to the final and finishing in eighth place overall.

Like Scottish swimmer Elenor Gordon, Glen Haig would fare better as a British Empire Games champion than in the Olympic Games, winning in New Zealand in 1950 as reigning British champion.[62] Elek would fail to retain the title again in Helsinki in 1952 and came second in a spectacular barrage against Irene Camber of Italy, who had dropped out of the semi-finals in London.[63] Karen Lachmann took the bronze medal in 1952. Ellen Müller-Preis was eliminated at semi-final stage, along with Britain's Mary Glen Haig, whereas Patricia Bulman and Gillian Sheen did not progress from the heats.

In the 1948 women's team gymnastics competition, Czechoslovakia won, ahead of Hungary and the USA. Czechoslovakia had brought Eliksa and Miloslava Misáková, sisters, as part of the team but Eliska was taken ill and died of polio on the morning the event started.[64] The life of Eliska Misáková was commemorated on a stamp issued in 1998 in the Czech Republic. Finishing ninth of the 11 countries represented, the British team comprised of Cissy Davies, Joan Airey, Pat Hirst, Pat Evans, Dorothy Hey, Audrey Rennard, Irene Hirst and Dorothy Smith.

More diversified representation for Great Britain extended beyond the Summer Olympic Games. Ludwig Guttmann, a German-born Jew who moved to Britain before the Second World War, as head of the National Spinal Injuries Centre at Stoke Mandeville Hospital, set up in 1944 by the

Ministry of Pensions for war casualties. Under Guttmann the unit grew to 125 beds and the mortality rate of quadraplegics treated there dropped to 8 per cent, from being almost 80 per cent in World War I.[65] Guttmann's team effectively reinterpreted physical therapy from a rest cure to re-activating the competitive instincts of patients, and used sport to challenge their sense of their own abilities for the future.

On 28 July 1948, to coincide with the Olympic Opening Ceremony, 14 paralysed ex-servicemen and two ex-servicewomen competed against the Royal Star and Garter Home for Injured War Veterans in an archery competition on the lawns of the Stoke Mandeville hospital in Aylesbury.[66] As Stoke Mandeville patients, Joan 'Bunty' Noon and Robin Imray made their way into history as among the first British Paralympians; both in archery competitions.[67] Noon had been injured during flight in the Women's Royal Air Auxiliary and Imray was hospitalised also as a result of active service.

'Clinical sport' was not new. The earliest recorded wheelchair games in the UK took place as a 'Gymkhana' for staff and patients held at the Royal Star and Garter in Surrey in 1923. The idea of sporting physical therapy spread. In Edinburgh, the Thistle Foundation created accommodation for disabled ex-servicemen and women, funded by Sir Francis and Lady Tudsbery, with a swimming pool and gymnasium.[68]

Expanded in 1949 to an international event with six teams and the introduction of 'wheelchair netball' (later wheelchair basketball), the 'Grand Festival of Paraplegic Sport' then became increasingly large annual International Stoke Mandeville Games. In 1949, Joan 'Bunty' Noon won the highest ladies archery score and Betty Green recorded the highest number of hits. Successive Stoke Mandeville Games added more teams and more sports for men and women. As such, the internationalisation and expansion of the Stoke Mandeville Games began to showcase the competitive abilities of disabled women athletes as integral to the Paralympic spectacle. As more international teams joined the tournament, the range of transnational rivalries grew and multiplied.

Conclusion

Fanny Blankers-Koen was generous about the British, in spite of their criticisms about her age before she won her victories. Later, her daughter, also named Fanny, ran races in Britain after her mother retired:

> My visits to Great Britain have always been the most memorable part of my happiest days as an athlete. I have been very much at home in the United Kingdom, the greatest hospitality and friendship continually showering on me. I first came to Britain in 1936. From these first days in Blackpool I have repeatedly crossed the Channel with the greatest of pleasure. I do not know how many times I have been in your country,

but I can say that my friend Dorothy Tyler Odam and I have seen several generations of English athletes come and go. During the events I was often hard pressed. The result has always been a friendly and sporting contest. I am proud to say that victor and losers have become, and still are, the best of friends.[69]

Blankers-Koen was taken ill in Helsinki at the 1952 Olympic Games and had a miserable time. She reached the 80-metres hurdles final, only to stumble at the third hurdle and retire. In the 100 and 200 metres she was eliminated in the preliminary heats. Nevertheless, it was a distinguished career and Blankers-Koen was awarded with the Taher Pacha Trophy by the IOC in recognition of her achievements.[70] Founded by the Egyptian IOC member H. E. Mohammed Taher Pacha in 1950, the award was first made in 1951 and given annually to the athlete whose career merited a special distinction in the name of Olympism. Later, Blankers-Koen would be voted by the IAAF on her death at 85, the 'female athlete of the twentieth century'.[71] While those who have documented the career of Babe Didrikson might disagree, the four Olympic gold medals at the same Games remains a historically significant achievement. For collectors of Olympic memorabilia, philately and numismatics, Blankers-Koen has the distinction of being one of the most commemorated women worldwide, with stamps issued in the Netherlands, the Dominican Republic, Guyana, Mongolia, the Maldives, Palau, Isle of Man and St Kitts.[72] Maureen Gardner is shown on at least two of these editions. With cigarette cards, postcards, Panini stickers and other likenesses reproduced, Blankers-Koen was, perhaps, the most widely mediated Olympian of 1948, and remains a popular subject with transnational appeal now.

The Olympic revival of 1948 did not end with the Summer Games. At the fifth Winter Games in Saint Moritz in 1948, 34 women from nine countries took part in the figure skating singles and 16 in the mixed doubles.[73] Born in India, Jeanette Altwegg was brought up in Lancashire where her father worked for the Liverpool Cotton Exchange. Both originally Swiss-born, Jeanette's parents became naturalised British citizens but moved back to Switzerland in 1946 when the Cotton Exchange was nationalised. A promising lawn tennis player, who had progressed to the junior finals at Wimbledon in 1947, Jeanette had skated seriously since the age of six years.[74]

Altwegg had long prepared for competition by training for seven hours a day, five days a week, either at Streatham or Richmond Ice Rink or near the family home in Switzerland, depending on her parents' schedule.[75] Though this was nominally an amateur sport, she clearly devoted herself full time to it, apart from a two-month break in the summer for other interests, mainly tennis. This was not unusual in the world of figure skating, as we have seen. Altwegg's rival from Czechoslovakia, Aja Vrzanova the 18-year-old World figure skating champion in 1949, trained extensively in England as there were no artificial ice facilities in her own country.[76]

Altwegg was to win an Olympic bronze medal for the individual figure skating in St Moritz in 1948, behind Barbara Ann Scott of Canada and Eva Pavlik of Austria.[77] Altwegg outscored Pavlick on the compulsory figures but lost points in the free programme. Britain's Bridget Adams, Marion Davies and Jill Hood-Linzee finished further down the field. Altwegg provided half of Britain's two bronze medals; the second was won by John Grammond in the men's skeleton bob. This helped Britain to a reasonable mid-table finish overall;. Winnie and Dennis Silverthorne came fifth in the mixed pairs, with Jennifer and John Nicks in eighth place. The British female skiers in 1948 across the downhill, slalom and a combined event, included Bridget Duke-Wooley, Sheena Mackintosh, Rosemarie Sparrow, Isobel Roe and Xanthe Ryder.[78] All finished near the bottom of the field.

Defending her European title eight days before the Oslo Olympic Games in 1952, Altwegg took the gold medal ahead of Tenley Albright of the USA and Jaqueline du Bief of France. Britain's Barbara Wyatt, Valda Osborn and Patricia Devries were the other singles women's figure skating entrants, with Jennifer and John Nicks narrowly missing out on a bronze medal place in the mixed pairs, well ahead of Peri Horne and Ray Lockwood.

In 1952, a giant slalom event replaced the women's combined Alpine skiing class but, again, none of the British skiers managed to challenge the dominant nations. Sheena Mackintosh and her sister Vora both competed in this event and the downhill along with Fiona Campbell and Hilary Lang.[79] The women's slalom was contested by Lang and Sheena Mackintosh; one of four siblings to have represented Britain in the Olympic ski competitions in the 1950s and 1960s. Women's figure skating attracted some of the largest crowds of the Oslo Games which, in themselves, lifted the sophistication of the Winter Olympics to new heights. An international conference on sport and health, held at the Norwegian Medical Society in Oslo in conjunction with the games on 25 and 26 February, heard over 50 papers from physiological, psychological and humanities disciplines.

Altwegg also appeared at the closing ceremony in 1952 with a free skating display and her gold medal was significant, since it was the only one that the British team took home, having sent 18 competitors. Soon after her victory in Oslo, Altwegg refused large sums of money to turn professional and perform in ice shows. The male skating singles gold Olympic medallist in 1948 and 1952, Dick Button, pioneered athletically daring jumps and spins before going on to a professional career.[80] Altwegg therefore competed at an exciting time in the increasing specialisation in her sport but shunned the links with the entertainment industry, preferring to retire as an amateur.

After Altwegg retired from skating competitively, she moved to Switzerland to work with war orphans for a year at the Pestalozzi Children's village and was awarded a CBE before marrying Marc Wirz and having four children. In 1983, Jeanette's daughter, Christina, became the world curling champion at Moose Jaw, Canada. Altwegg was to be the lone British female figure-skating gold medallist between Madge Syers in 1908 and Jayne Torvill in 1984.[81] As the example indicates, much depended on personal circumstances and choice; amateurism could take many forms.

This chapter has focused on the 1948 London Olympics as the Summer Games were still more significant to national pride, so far as the British were concerned, than the Winter Olympics. However, this was gradually changing and there could be exceptions, as Altwegg's fame indicates. The media environment had yet to reach the lows of tabloid journalism and much of the reportage of Wellington, Altwegg and their compatriots was respectful, as might be expected from national sporting heroes.

Subsequent to her Olympic victories, Margaret Wellington was invited as an expert to provide coaching tips for the *Daily Graphic* and other publications. Although it was often reported that Margaret was coached by her husband Basil Restorick, it seems unlikely that he did more than support her with timing and other practical help. Margaret was the specialist and her style of coaching and swimming was recorded in a series of *Daily Graphic* tutorials in 1950. She was to travel abroad only once more as a competitive swimmer when married, in 1951 to Berlin. Competitive swimming and its related social functions, remains a clear area for future research projects.

It is also noticeable that a local history publication, *A History of Beckenham Swimming Club*, mentions Wellington's Olympic selection in passing, focusing more on Ronnie Steadman as the second man to represent the club at an Olympic Games after Romund Gabrielsen in 1936.[82] Although there are some photographs of Margaret, the club history is as much concerned with the quality of annual galas as the international careers of its women stars. Easy then, to see how Olympians like Margaret Wellington become effectively written out of local history, let alone more academic and popular titles.

Margaret Wellington continued to swim regularly in her specially designated lane, at Crystal Palace swimming baths, until the age of 85 and this suggests a degree of respect for her achievements almost 60 years later. She continued to swim for love of the activity, rather than any particular urge to make money or become recognised for her sporting prowess. Helen Yate made slightly different lifestyle choices:

> I did not try for the 1952 Games, but I still swam for the Mermaid team in ASA championships and local competitions, eventually helping out with the committee and staying with them until I retired. Then I came back to Plymouth, where I did not continue to swim for leisure, except for a dip in the Sea now and then.[83]

This seems to be an area of considerable research in need of attention. Both examples suggest that many women who finished their competitive careers, still contributed to their sport. In Margaret's case, the fact that she retained

Figure 5.6 The actual swimming costumes that Margaret Wellington, Helen Yate and the British team wore in 1948 were the latest technology of the time, in finest silk and with the distinctive Jantzen diver logo. Contestants nevertheless had to sew on their own badges.

Source: Graham Budd auctions.

her own lane at the local pool, indicates that her identity as an Olympian remained important over time. Perhaps the same was not the case for Helen Yate but she, and other senior swimmers like her, had an important role to play as chaperones for young women's teams on international tours. For instance, in 1957, Yate accompanied an 11 strong English team to one of the earliest international matches against China (including Judy Grinham, Christina Barry, Margaret Edwards, Elspeth Ferguson, Christine Gosden and Anne Marshall) competing in Peking, Canton and Shanghai.[84] Important aspects of transnational competition, pioneered as form of sporting diplomacy by female Olympians, has been almost entirely neglected in the academic literature.

Amateur Olympic careers were often short-lived. But this does not necessarily imply that representing a team like Great Britain, or one of the home nations, remained unimportant in the lives of Olympians, even when family life and subsequent careers intervened. There are rich family and community histories here, in need of further examination. Margaret and her female colleagues were photographed in their glamorous red sparkly costumes as for an Evian mineral water commercial and the example suggests that there remains commercial interest in those with a lifelong passion for health and active leisure; another under-explored research topic.

So far as amateurism was concerned, the decision to admit ski teachers to compete from 1952 allowed those who earned a living from their expertise to compete alongside those for whom Winter sport was primarily a recreation.[85] There were many debates around how the Summer Olympic schedule had grown and how to pare down the numbers of competitors, including serious proposals in 1953 to omit all team games and to stage women's Olympic Games as separate tournaments.[86] Avery Brundage was particularly critical of political regimes that sought to reinforce their world-view through Olympic victories, and effectively funded full-time professional athletes. His hypocrisy aside, considering that he had supported the 1936 Olympics as promoting international peace initiatives, this meant that increasingly, the competitions were not about individual success but about national pride.

As the career of Margaret Wellington, Maureen Gardner, Jeanette Altwegg and other Olympians in this chapter has indicated amateurism was a nuanced, shifting and ultimately individual experience. Six weeks after the 1948 London Olympics, Gardner married her coach Geoff Dyson and had two children, Timothy and Judith. They became something of a celebrity story thereafter, aside from their sporting interests, frequently photographed *en famille* with their dog, Flax and later, after his demise, with a bloodhound named rather grandly Simon of Oakhurst.[87] Maureen then hosted many of the athletes Dyson trained at her home and partnered her husband's rise to become the first national coach for the AAA, simultaneously while running a part-time ballet school and endorsing products like Gymphlex tracksuits and windcheaters.[88] Gardner continued to use both her maiden and married surnames for endorsements. Like Pat Smythe, who is the subject of the next chapter, Gardner became part of the 1950s sporting elite, bur her success was sadly to be short-lived.

Geoff Dyson (along with F. A. M. Webster, Lionel Pugh, Jimmy Alford, John Le Masurier, Tony Chapman and Denis Watts) would revolutionise British coaching and pedagogical schemes for track and field athletics, through courses mainly based at Loughborough and Oxford Universities. Existing women's colleges of physical education, such as Bedford and Carnegie, increasingly became co-educational as more men and women trained as human kinetics specialists. The focus on physical fitness education opened up new professional opportunities in teaching and coaching. The great England footballer famed for his health regimes, Stanley Matthews, had a daughter, Jean, typical of the young women who qualified as a 'games mistress' at this time.[89] Geoff Dyson had a vision as Head National Coach to promote a programme of coach education across the country and he fought a long-term battle against the idea that track and field Olympic champions were born to win, rather than needing coaching. Frustrated, the Dyson family moved for a time to Ottawa in 1962 before returning to Britain in 1968. Maureen Dyson continued to promote sport for women, and also became an examiner at the Royal Ballet before her early death from cancer in 1974, aged just 45 years old.

As the 1960s and 1970s progressed, many sporting bodies had tacitly admitted that amateur rules were largely unenforceable and held back British athletes in the face of increasing specialisation. If Britain considered itself 'the land of sport' as marketers suggested in this period, it would have to modernise its attitude or risk increasing chances of embarrassment as the Olympic Games changed and adapted to new challenges.[90] The Rome 1960 Olympic Games were to herald several aspects of future events, with commercial broadcasts, doping scandals and athletes endorsing products at the same time as new nations were entering the festivities, reflecting an altered international relations profile. Amateur values that Margaret Wellington and so many other Olympians held dear would eventually give way to the beginning of full professionalism, as the Olympic Games began to move towards a new Open era of the best athletes performing in the tournament, regardless of their professional status.

Notes

1 Organising Committee for the XIV Olympiad *The Official Report of the Organising Committee for the XIV Olympiad* Part One and Part Two London: Organising Committee for the XIV Olympiad, 1948.
2 Robert Edelman *Serious Fun: A History of Spectator Sport in the USSR* New York: Oxford University Press, 1993 p. 25.
3 Bob Phillips *The 1948 Olympics: How London Rescued the Games* London: Sports Pages, 2007.
4 Janie Hampton *London Olympics, 1908 and 1948* London: Shire, 2011; Janie Hampton *The Austerity Olympics: When the Games Came to London in 1948* London: Aurum Press, 2012.
5 David Kynaston *Austerity Britain 1945–1951* London: Bloomsbury, 2007 pp. 292–293.
6 Peter J. Beck 'Britain and The Olympic Games: London 1908, 1948, 2012' *Journal of Sport and History* 39: 1 2012 p. 37.
7 Tom Hopkinson (ed.) *Picture Post: Olympic Games Special* 40:7 14 August 1948 London: Hulton Press Ltd p. 10.
8 Alderman H. E Fern *Proposed 1940 Olympiad in London: Sub Committee of the British Olympic Association* 8 June 1936 71 St Georges Square London p. 1 BOA Archive, London.
9 Evan Hunter *British Olympic Association Investigation Committee: Olympic Games of 1944* 9 November 1938 71 St Georges Square London p. 1 BOA Archive, London.
10 Evan Hunter *British Olympic Association: Minutes of Meeting* 5 November 1945 Chancery Lane London p. 1 BOA Archive, London.

11 Marie-Hélène Roukhadzè 'The Small Beginnings of the Secretariat: An Interview with Lydie Zanchi' *Olympic Review* 1986 p. 593.
12 Otto Mayer 'Letter to Sandy Duncan 5 May 1956' p. 1 British Olympic National Association File, IOC Archive, Lausanne.
13 Janie Hampton *The Austerity Olympics* p. 144.
14 The Organising Committee for the XIV Olympiad London 1948 and the Olympic Games of 1948 Film Company Limited *Heads of Agreement 9 March 1948 66 Lincoln's Inn Fields, London* p. 1 BOA Archive, London.
15 Tim O' Sullivan 'Television and The Austerity Games: London 1948' in Jeffrey Hill, Kevin Moore and Jason Wood (eds.) *Sport, History and Heritage: Studies in Public Representation* Woodbridge: Boydell and Brewer Ltd, 2012 pp. 79–80.
16 Tim O'Sullivan 'Television and The Austerity Games: London 1948' p. 80.
17 Ovaltine 'Leading Athletes Drink Ovaltine' *World Sports: Official Magazine of the British Olympic Association May 1956* p. 4.
18 Carol Dyhouse *Glamour: Women, History, Feminism* London and New York: Zed Books, 2010 p. 3.
19 Tom Hopkinson (ed.) *Picture Post: Olympic Games Special*.
20 Margaret Wellington 'Swimming to be a Champion-7 Days a Week' in Carolyn Dingle (ed.) *News Chronicle: Sport For Girls* London: News Chronicle Publications Department, 1951 p. 29.
21 Margaret Wellington 'Swimming to be a Champion-7 Days a Week'.
22 Helen Yate *Personal Communication* 5 March 2016 Hooe, Plymouth pp. 1–2.
23 Graham Walker 'Nancy Riach and The Motherwell Swimming Phenomenon' in Grant Jarvie and Graham Walker (eds.) *Scottish Sport In The Making Of The Nation: Ninety-Minute Patriots?* London: Leicester University Press, 1994 pp. 142–153.
24 Angus Calder 'Nancy Anderson Long Riach (1927–1947)' *Oxford Dictionary of National Biography* Oxford University Press www.oxforddnb.com/view/article/65073 accessed 17 November 2019.
25 British Pathé *Margaret Wellington: Mermaid in the City 1946* film number 1388.02 www.britishpathe.com/video/mermaid-in-the-city accessed 29 May 2016.
26 Margaret Wellington 'A Letter From Margaret Wellington' *The Advertiser* 5 May 1946 Lesley 'Zelly' Restorick Collection.
27 Margaret Wellington 'Swimming to be a Champion' p. 31.
28 British Pathé *Nancy Riach Funeral, 1947* film number 2168.10 www.britishpathe.com/video/stills/nancy-riach-funeral accessed 29 May 2016.
29 Graham Walker 'Nancy Riach and The Motherwell Swimming Phenomenon' p. 153.
30 Helen Yate *Personal Communication* p. 2.
31 W. J. Howcraft 'She Ruled the Waves-But Never Waived the Rules' *World Sports: The International Sports Magazine June 1950* London: Country and Sporting Publications, 1950 pp. 21–23.
32 Pat Besford 'Helsinki to Hove' *World Sports: The International Sports Magazine September 1952* London: Country and Sporting Publications, 1952 p. 30.
33 Ian Buchanan *British Olympians* pp. 162–167.
34 Organising Committee for the XIV Olympiad *The Official Report of the Organising Committee for the XIV Olympiad* Part Two p. 443.
35 Cecil Bear 'Greta 1948, Greta 1957' *World Sports: The International Sports Magazine October 1957* London: Country and Sporting Publications, 1957 p. 23.
36 British Broadcasting Corporation *Margaret Wellington: Hullo Children* London: Broadcasting House, 12 December 1949.
37 Margaret Wellington 'Swimming to be a Champion-7 Days a Week' pp. 31–32.
38 Helen Yate *Personal Communication* p. 2.

39 Helen Yate *Personal Communication* p. 2.
40 Margaret Wellington *Scrapbook* 8 April 1950 unpaginated Lesley 'Zelly' Restorick Collection.
41 Helen Yate *Personal Communication* p. 3.
42 Lesley Restorick *Margaret Wellington: Personal Communication* 20 January 2016 London.
43 Organising Committee for the XIV Olympiad *The Official Report of the Organising Committee for the XIV Olympiad* Part Two p. 235.
44 Fanny Blankers-Koen 'It's Fun When You Are An Unknown' *World Sports: Official Magazine of the British Olympic Association* November 1956 London: Country and Sporting Publications, 1956 p. 11.
45 Albert Milhado 'My Friend Fanny' *World Sports: Official Magazine of the British Olympic Association December 1950* London: Country and Sporting Publications, 1950 pp. 26–27.
46 Tom Hopkinson (ed.) 'Women Win Athletic Fame' *Picture Post* p. 19.
47 Anon. 'Speed Typist: Dorothy Manley Strides to Victory' *Sunday Pictorial* 1 August 1948 p. 2.
48 Jack Crump 'Dorothy Manley's Big Day' *World Sports: Official Magazine of the British Olympic Association July 1949* London: Country and Sporting Publications, 1949 pp. 26–27.
49 International Olympic Committee 'Audrey Mickey Patterson 29 July 1948' *London 1948* www.olympic.org/news/audrey-mickey-patterson-athletics/179793 accessed 29 May 2016.
50 Susan Noel 'Women in Sport' *World Sports: Official Magazine of the British Olympic Association* September 1949 London: Country and Sporting Publications, 1949 p. 30.
51 Cecil Bear 'Star Sprinter: Sylvia Cheeseman' *World Sports: The International Sports Magazine July 1950* London: Country and Sporting Publications, 1950 pp. 22–23.
52 Organising Committee for the XIV Olympiad *The Official Report of the Organising Committee for the XIV Olympiad* Part Two p. 279.
53 Maureen Dyson 'Over My Shoulder' *World Sports: Official Magazine of the British Olympic Association August 1952* London: Country and Sporting Publications, 1952 pp. 12–13.
54 Kathleen Green '1948 Olympians: Dorothy Parlett and Dorothy Tyler (Athletics)' *London, Oral History and Publication* www.katherinegreen.co.uk/1948-olympians/ accessed 29 May 2019.
55 Edgar Joubert 'Madame Ostermeyer: Top Notch Athlete: Top Note Pianist' *World Sports: The International Sports Magazine* July 1949 London: Country and Sporting Publications, 1949 p. 35.
56 Anon. 'Pong Sik Pak: The Competitor From Korea' *Picture Post* p. 20.
57 Jack Crump 'Never Say Die Dorothy' *World Sports: The International Sports Magazine September 1951* London: Country and Sporting Publications, 1951 pp. 22–23.
58 Paula Welch and Margaret Costa 'A Century of Olympic Competition' in Margaret Costa and Sharon Guthrie (eds.) *Women and Sport: Interdisciplinary Perspectives* Champaign, Illinois: Human Kinetics, 1994 p. 130.
59 Janie Hampton *The Austerity Olympics* pp. 196–197.
60 Jack Crump 'Women's Athletics' in Carolyn Dingle (ed.) *News Chronicle: Sport for Girls* London: News Chronicle Publications Department, 1951 pp. 137–138.
61 Mary Rand *Mary, Mary: Autobiography of an Olympic Champion* London: Hodder and Stoughton, 1969 pp. 39–44.
62 C. L de Beaumont 'Empire Fencing Champion' *World Sports: Official Magazine of the British Olympic Association October 1950* London: Country and Sporting Publications, 1950 pp. 22–23.

63 Sulo Kolkka (ed.) *The Official Report of The Organising Committee For the Games of the XV Olympiad Helsinki 1952* Helsinki: The Organising Committee 1952 pp. 503–504.
64 Organising Committee for the XIV Olympiad *The Official Report of the Organising Committee for the XIV Olympiad* Part Two p. 391.
65 Ludwig Guttmann 'Olympic Games for the Disabled' *World Sports: Official Magazine of the British Olympic Association October 1952* London: Country and Sporting Publications, 1952 pp. 12–13.
66 The National Spinal Injuries Centre (NSIC) 'Our History' The National Spinal Injuries Centre (NSIC), Stoke Mandeville Hospital www.buckshealthcare.nhs.uk/NSIC%20Home/About%20us/nsic-history.htm accessed 5 August 2015.
67 Ian Brittain *From Stoke Mandeville to Sochi: A History of the Summer and Winter Paralympic Games* Champaign, Illinois: Common Ground Publishing, 2014 p. 5.
68 J. R. Silver *The Role of Sport in the Rehabilitation of Patients with Spinal Injuries* Stoke Mandeville: National Spine Injuries Centre, 2004 pp. 237–243.
69 Mrs Francina Blankers-Koen 'Foreword' George Pallet *Women's Athletics* London: The Normal Press, 1955 p. iv.
70 Comité International Olympique *Général Rapport 47eme Session Helsinki 1952* Lausanne: Comité International Olympique 1952 p. 23 IOC Archive, Lausanne.
71 Obituary 'Fanny Blankers-Koen' *The Times* 26 January 2004.
72 Bob Wilcock *The London 1948 Olympic Games: A Collector's Guide* London: The Society of Olympic Collectors, 2012 pp. 71–72.
73 Comité Olympique Suisse Secrétariat *Général Rapport Général Sur Les Ves Olympiques D'Hiver St-Moritz 1948* Lausanne: Comité Olympique Suisse Secrétariat Général 1948 p. 30.
74 International Olympic Committee *Jeanette Altwegg: Olympic Athlete 1948 St Moritz, Oslo 1952* www.olympic.org/jeannette-altwegg accessed 29 May 2016.
75 Susan Noel 'Women in Sport' p. 22.
76 Susan Noel 'Women in Sport' *World Sports Official Magazine of the British Olympic Association January 1950* London: Country and Sporting Publications, 1950 Cover and p. 34.
77 Cecil Bear 'Jeanette Altwegg: World, European and British Figure Skating Champion' *World Sports Official Magazine of the British Olympic Association February 1952* London: Country and Sporting Publications, 1952 Cover.
78 Comité Olympique Suisse Secrétariat *Général Rapport Général Sur Les Ves Olympiques D'Hiver St-Moritz 1948* p. 45.
79 Rolf Petersen (ed.) (translated by Margaret Wold) *VI Olympiske Vinterleker: The Olympic Winter Games: Oslo 1952* Oslo: Utgitt Av Organisasjonskomiteen, (The Organising Committee) 1952 pp. 227–230.
80 Mary Louise Adams *Artistic Impressions: Figure Skating, Masculinity and The Limits of Sport* Toronto, Buffalo and London: University of Toronto Press, 2011 pp. 158–159.
81 Rolf Petersen (ed.) *VI Olympiske Vinterleker: The Olympic Winter Games: Oslo 1952* unpaginated plates between pp. 221 and 222.
82 Professor J. M Cameron *The History of Beckenham Swimming Club* London: Beckenham, 1993 p. 45 Lesley 'Zelly' Restorick Collection.
83 Helen Yate *Personal Communication* p. 3.
84 Judy Grinham *Water Babe* London: Oldbourne Book Co Ltd, 1960 pp. 115–117.
85 Viscount Montgomery 'Amateurism and the Olympic Games' *World Sports: The International Sports Magazine March 1952* London: Country and Sporting Publications, 1952 p. 5.

86 Avery Brundage 'Should We Prune The Games?' *World Sports Official Magazine of the British Olympic Association January 1953* London: Country and Sporting Publications, 1953 p. 5.
87 Susan Noel 'Women in Sport'*1950*, pp. 10–11.
88 Gymphlex 'Maureen Gardner Looking After Women's Interests' *World Sports Official Magazine of the British Olympic Association January 1952* London: Country and Sporting Publications, 1952 p. 3.
89 Cecil Bear 'Matthews-A Sporting Name Lives On' *World Sports: Official Magazine of the British Olympic Association February 1958* London: Country and Sporting Publications, 1958 p. 25.
90 The British Travel Association 'Britain: Land of Sport' *World Sports Official Magazine of the British Olympic Association March 1952* London: Country and Sporting Publications, 1952 p. 4.

Chapter 6

Elizabeth II, Britain and Olympic Cold War rivalries

Equestrian Pat Smythe and the New Elizabethans 1952–1960

Introduction: the New Elizabethans

Pat Smythe epitomised the increased public role of women in post-war Britain during the 1950s and 1960s.[1] This chapter covers the Olympic Games of 1952, 1956 and 1960, during which time a perceived 'new' Elizabethan era reinterpreted aspects of British history and popular culture. If the Olympic Games were constantly re-imagined to reflect contemporary sporting culture, a correlating new Elizabethan age reinvented selective aspects of British social life. Although Elizabeth II was already married and a mother by the time she came to the throne, unlike Elizabeth I, the British media drew strong links between the two women, and their respective monarchies.

The chapter's theme explores how a 'new' (or second) Elizabethan age correlated with Smythe's equestrian career, and several new female Olympic events. Like backstroke Olympic, European and Commonwealth gold medallist, Judy Grinham, whose autobiography appeared when she was already a retired international swimmer aged just 21, Smythe was among the self-styled new Elizabethans who constructed an imaginary innate British national character comprising heroic individualism, and the resistance of a small but powerful nation to larger international adversaries. Often interpreted in sport as the need for modernisation, inspiration and initiative, new Elizabethanism was as much a critique of continuity as an argument for change.[2]

In an age of increased politicisation of sport, competing against European neighbours and larger international rivals, was thought to reveal something about the character of the individual and of wider British identity. The next section of this chapter briefly considers the 1952 Helsinki Olympic Games, before looking in detail at Pat Smythe's career.

Equestrian Pat Smythe's life story appeared to be in perfect accord with new Elizabethan values. A recurring motif of the underdog, overcoming both personal tragedy and intimidating larger forces, sat alongside Smythe's entrepreneurial activities. In this, Smythe was partly the author of her own myth-making, publishing many autobiographical books to reinforce the image. Like the young Queen Elizabeth II, who favoured equestrian pursuits above all her other sporting commitments, Smythe embodied a particular brand of 'feminine courage' by competing alongside men (and other women) in a challenging, dangerous and aspirational sport.[3]

The young Elizabeth Windsor was often photographed in connection with sport, and horses in particular. Sport was something that the Queen Mother, Elizabeth Bowes-Lyon, encouraged, herself shooting small bore rifles aboard *HMS Vanguard* while en route with the King to tour South Africa in 1947.[4] Princess Elizabeth had been a focal point at the 1948 London Olympic Games, along with her sister, Margaret, and husband, Philip. A few years later, *World Sports: International Sports Magazine*, which was established as the official publication of the British Olympic Association, was prompted by the accession and coronation of a 27-year-old female head of state to issue a commemorative edition, celebrating a new Elizabethan era: 'Of rich inventiveness, achievement and glory-in sport and all things'.[5]

The theme would continue for the rest of the decade as Elizabeth II was a constitutional monarch, and Head of the Commonwealth at the 1954 British Empire and Commonwealth Games in Vancouver; the 1956 Melbourne Olympic Games and the 1958 British Empire and Commonwealth Games in Cardiff. Although the Olympic movement remained ambulatory, hosted at Helsinki in 1952, and Rome in 1960, the role of the British in promoting the Games would continue to be considerable.

It mattered little that, personally, Elizabeth was more interested in the unusual Equestrian Games, held in Stockholm in June of 1956, because Australian quarantine rules regarding horses would have meant that animals would need to spend months in the country before the Olympic events. The British Empire and Commonwealth Games would follow in Cardiff in 1958, presided over by Lord Aberdare and promoted by Ted Glover and former Olympic swimmer Margaret 'Pip' Linton.[6] Sporting events were then fundamental to the way that modern monarchy connected with the wider public. The changing nature of Britain's place in the world was reflected by the way that the British Empire Games changed to become the Commonwealth Games as the 1950s and 1960s progressed.

In the media's coverage of a new Elizabethan age, the young monarch's interest in the outdoor life was represented to have both ancient antecedents and modern expressions. A good horsewoman, Elizabeth II's equestrian skill was as much showcased by the ceremonial aspects of her duties, such as Trooping the Colour, as by her private taste for active leisure. As Stephen Gundle said:

> In February 1952 *Time* magazine selected the 27 year old princess as the world personality who most embodied the hope of the times. She captured on an international scale the magazine asserted the mysterious power of ancient monarchs 'to represent, express and effect the aspirations of the collective subconscious.' In fact, the era had seen the

overthrow of more than one monarchy and, it was the youth and beauty of Elizabeth that appealed most.[7]

There was a global glamour in aristocracy, and the carefully orchestrated sense of lavish ritual that accompanied Elizabeth's monarchy made her the most celebrated of luminaries. In many senses, the more relaxed side to her personality was shown through sport, and active leisure pursuits also characterised the enthusiasms of her growing family. However, this was a highly groomed and polished presentation of the private life of the Royal family, making them icons of style. The young Queen and her consort celebrated the place of the Royal family in relation to the British sporting establishment. In 1949, the Duke of Edinburgh became President of the Marylebone Cricket Club, at that time the leading body for world cricket, and Elizabeth II became the first Queen Regnant to attend a cricket match at Lord's in 1952.

The British Olympic Association had always been keen to have more Establishment support for its activities and it would be Elizabeth Windsor, more than any previous monarch, who would cement ties between the British Royal family and the Olympic movement. However, her presiding personal interest was equestrianism, and in particular horse racing. With the birth of Prince Charles in 1949, many newsreels emphasised that, as well as being a Head of State, Elizabeth was also a young wife and mother, performing a duty to the nation in providing a future heir. The birth of Princess Anne followed soon after in August 1950 and, she would remain Elizabeth's only daughter and the first royal Olympian.

By 1951, the Festival of Britain sought consciously to reinscribe a modern British state upon a longer historical past, rich with heritage. This included the much-recycled myth that Britain was a land of sport, even if some sections of the population were not included as much as others. The Royals were clearly not a family like anyone else. But an invented tradition suggested that they were, away from the ceremonial aspects of monarchy. This illusion was created partly through the considerable resources of the Royal public relations offices and the use of new communications technology, such as Technicolour film and colour photography.

All Olympic equestrian events organised by Fédération Équestre Internationale (FEI, founded in 1921), had been closed to non-commissioned officers from the 1924 Paris Games until Helsinki in 1952. The British Show Jumping Association (BSJA) was formed in 1923 with Lord Lonsdale as its first President. The reinstatement of Open Equestrian events began, firstly with the dressage at Helsinki in 1952, then show jumping in Stockholm 1956 and three-day eventing (combining dressage, show jumping and a cross-country course) in 1964.[8] The militaristic tone of Olympic equestrian events gradually changed to allow women to compete alongside men: in May 1956, Otto Mayer of the IOC wrote to Sandy Duncan advising that, on the matter of women in equestrian events, following the rules of the international federation was the best course of action, since it was 'much better that we don't intervene in a technical matter'.[9] Male or female, the BOA equestrian team were specifically keen to overturn a stereotype in the equine world that the British rode 'beautiful horses, abominably'.[10]

This chapter covers the period between 1952 and 1960 but, after a brief section on the 1952 Helsinki Olympics and East-West tensions, focuses specifically on the career of equestrian Pat Smythe in that wider context. Women had long been knocking on the stable door of the Olympic equine programme. Helen Preece appears to have been the first woman since Elvira Guerra to apply to compete in an equestrian event. Having won a £1,000 Gold Cup at the Madison Horse show in 1912, Preece's application to contest the modern pentathlon (shooting, cross-country, fencing, swimming and horse riding) in Stockholm was declined by the Swedish Olympic Committee at the instigation of Pierre de Coubertin.[11] The question of 'Amazones' entering Olympic equestrian events had also been raised in 1934 and caused much consternation.[12]

Horse racing epitomised Elizabeth II's sporting enthusiasm but was not an Olympic event, although National Hunt Racing (or jump racing) had some links with show jumping and cross-country events. Part of the fascination of racing was the question of breeding and this had a wider aristocratic resonance for those interested in bloodlines. More than any other activity, Smythe's equestrian success as a show jumping specialist reflected a particular brand of upper middle class glamour. She even looked a little like Elizabeth Windsor. Smythe's accomplishments also exemplified the contested amateur tradition as it manifested itself across a range of sports during this period. More women became increasingly visible to the general public in a wider range of sports.[13] Professional female experts, like Smythe, were embedded in British cultural life. While lots of women took part in sport more for their own enjoyment than for financial reward, there were increasing numbers who were able to make a career in sport and its related industries. Before continuing with the autobiographical material on Pat Smythe, it is worth assessing the changing nature of female Olympic representation in 1952 as context for the heightened political atmosphere of later Olympic Games

Helsinki and Cold War rivalry

There was much general continuity in the women's schedule of the Summer Olympic Games, in spite of specific changes such as these new equestrian opportunities. The Helsinki female track and field athletics programme had just nine events; the women's swimming seven classes and fencing a single ladies foil category, the same as in London in 1948. The art competitions were replaced by an exhibition, to which Ireland's Cornelia Egan contributed some short poems and Laetitia Hamilton an oil painting, *Punchestown Races*.

The Olympic Games reflected Britain's changing political relations, with some uneasy new alliances. The USSR was admitted to the IOC in 1951, and Germany re-admitted the same year.[14] The People's Republic of China sent only swimmers to the 1952 Games. Japanese swimmers who had trained in tailored and tapered training schedules returned too. There was also some soft diplomacy in 1952: three British companies donated tea to the British team and Shredded Wheat provided breakfast biscuits.

The addition of new women's sports events was to remain contested from 1952 onwards. Proposals to reintroduce a women's 800-metres track and field event, and to introduce male and female butterfly stroke swimming events were declined without debate in 1954.[15] One year later, with his usual conservatism, Avery Brundage wished to lessen the programme, rather than extend it but was challenged both by sporting federations who wanted to join the Summer Olympic programme (such as volleyball, archery, roller skating and judo) and Russian calls for new women's team events in basketball, volleyball, rowing and, in the Winter Olympics, speed skating).[16] All of these proposals failed to reach the necessary two-thirds majority of 34 votes out of the 50 available, with 26 in favour of volleyball, the most well-supported.

Britain sent a team of 53 women to Helsinki, the USA sent 48, France 42, Finland 41 and Germany 39 female competitors. The United Soviet Socialist Republics sent 145 female contestants.[17] The close geographical proximity of the USSR to Finland highlighted the wider tensions of Cold War politics. Most of the female competitors in 1952 were housed in The Nurses Training College, one mile from the Helsinki stadium. With 64 single rooms and 198 rooms for three people, The Nurses Training College accommodated 658 athletes in all, overseen by Village Commandant Hilja Vikkilä.

Equestrian Lis Hartel of Denmark, made Olympic history in the most inspiring way in 1952. At the age of 23, Hartel had been almost entirely paralysed by polio. Through riding and a regime of clinical exercise, she had gradually regained the use of most of her muscles, although she did not recover the use of her lower legs. Aged 35, Hartel made her Olympic debut by being lifted onto and off her horse, 'Jubilee'. Nevertheless, she took the silver medal with a score of 850, just 10 points behind the gold medallist Henri St-Cyr, who rode Master Rufus for Sweden to victory. André Jousseaume of France on 'Harpagon' took the bronze medal. Hartel was helped by St-Cyr onto the podium to receive her honour, and the medallists received their awards in tears.

Given that dressage required careful control of the horse, Hartel's ability to nuance the performance while paralysed below the knee was especially remarkable. *The Sunday Herald* was keen to point out that Hartel was a 'housewife, and mother of two' and St-Cyr was a major in the Swedish Cavalry.[18] Hartel was not the only woman competing in 1952. Ida von Nagel of Germany came in 10th, riding 'Afrika', Else Christianson rode 'Diva' to take 15th place for Norway and Marjorie Haines represented the USA, to take 17th on 'The Flying Dutchman'.[19]

In a move that would later influence the growing Paralympic schedule, Lis Hartel and her therapist founded Europe's first Therapeutic Riding Centre. The medical community responded to this example of 'clinical sport' for a range of conditions and Therapy Riding Centres spread throughout Europe. Both Pat and Monique Smythe ran sessions for children with physical and mental disabilities at Miserden, for example. This tradition of riding for mental and physical therapy continues today, with one of Britain's most famous sporting charities led by women established in 1969, the Riding for the Disabled Association.

Sending a large female Russian team to Helsinki was to have immediate Olympic medal success, although the shining star of the women's track and field athletics was Marjorie Jackson of Lithgow, Australia, who won both the 100- and the 200-metres races. Having beaten the Soviets added to the kudos of the victory. Known as 'The Blue Streak' in honour of her birthplace in the Blue Mountains of Australia, *World Sports* attempted to domesticate Jackson's achievements by reporting that she cycled to work as a stenographer after kissing her mother goodbye each morning and helped to cook the evening meal on her return.[20] In 1953, Jackson was awarded the MBE for her accomplishments. The 100-metres silver medal went to Daphne Hasentager of South Africa and the bronze to Shirley Strickland (married name de la Hunty), of Australia.

In the 200 metres, Bertha Brouwer of the Netherlands came second and Hnykina Nadezda third for the USSR. Britain's June Foulds, Heather Armitage, Isobel 'Quita' Shivas, Ann Johnson and Patricia Devine were eliminated in the heats of the sprint events. Shivas was a doctor who was born in Aberdeen, but had moved to London to work at Hammersmith Hospital and train at Spartan Athletics Club at the time of her selection.

The best performance came from Sylvia Cheeseman, who won fourth in the 200-metres semi-finals. The hurdle race was won by Shirley de la Hunty ahead of Marija Golubitshnaja of the USSR and Marija Sander of Germany. Both Jean Desforges and Pamela Seaborne made the semi-finals of the 80-metres hurdles, but Pauline Threapleton did not progress. Desforges eventually finished fifth overall, although she had matched the winning time of 10.9 seconds in her semi-final. De la Hunty would later be given the usual domestic treatment by *World Sports* as they found her to be a 'charming, versatile and wonderfully efficient Perth housewife', mentioning only in passing her mathematics degree, and job as lecturer in Physics and Mathematics at Perth Technical College.[21]

The 4 × 100-metres relay was again the most exciting track and field race, in spite of the dominance of Australian sprinters. Winsome Cripps knocked the baton from Marjorie Jackson's hand at the changeover when they were leading after legs by Shirley de la Hunty and Verna Johnson and, although it bounced and was retrieved, the Australians could only finish fifth. This meant that the USA (Mae Faggs, Barbara Jones, Janet Moreau and Cathy Hardy) won, from Germany (Ursula Knab, Maria Sander, Helga Klein and Marga Petersen) and Great Britain (Sylvia Cheeseman, June Foulds, Jean Desforges and Heather Armitage). Foulds, in particular, had a strong preparation for the Olympics by setting a new British 100 yards record of 11 seconds flat in 1950 and had anchored the 4 × 100-metres relay team at the European championships that year to beat a team from the Netherlands that included Fanny Blankers-Koen.[22] Desforges was a great all-round athlete who captained the Women's Amateur Athletic Association team and received many accolades, including the Lord Hawke trophy for best individual performance in a championship, and she was voted WAAA 'Woman athlete of 1953'.[23]

Esther Brand of New Zealand took the high jump gold, ahead of Sheila Lerwill (née Alexander) for Britain and Aleksandra Tshudina (or Chudina, as her name was sometimes spelled in *World Sports*).[24] Lerwill was a talented field event specialist and all-round athlete who also played international netball for England and represented Surrey nationally.[25] Britain's Thelma Hopkins came fourth and Dorothy Tyler finished seventh overall. Having been born in Hull to an English mother and Irish father, Hopkins excelled as a young athlete. A dental student at Queens University Belfast, she was fortunate to be coached in the western roll technique at Cherryvale Athletics ground by Franz Stamfl who was official coach of Northern Ireland Amateur Athletics Association at the time.[26] In the long jump, Britain's Shirley Cawley came third and Constance Willoughby 19th, behind Yvette Williams of New Zealand and Aleksandra Tshudina of the USSR. Williams was another Commonwealth athlete honoured by an MBE for her services to sport.

Although the Helsinki track events had been good for the USSR, it was in the throwing events that they really dominated. There were no British entrants in the shot put, which was won by Galina Zibina and her compatriot from the USSR Klavdija Totshenova in third place, split by Marianne Werner of Germany in silver medal position. Nina Romashkova, Elizabet Bagrjantsev and Nina Dumbadze took a clean sweep for USSR in the discus, where Britain's Suzanne Farmer could only come in 15th. Predictably labelled by the British newspapers as 'Wife, Mother and World Record holder' Dumabdze's powerful control epitomised a wider Eastern European ascendency in the throwing events.[27] Czechoslovakia's Dana Zátopeková, won the javelin event on the day her husband, Emil, won the 5,000 metres, and the couple became celebrities, as much for their ambitious fitness regimes as their marriage.[28] Behind Dana Zátopeková was the 'Russian Wonder Woman' Aleksandra Tshudina and Elena Gortshakova for the USSR.[29] Britain's Diane Coates could only manage to 15th place.

The USSR were less convincing in the women's swimming, with only a sixth place in the 200-metres breaststroke, which was won in a new Olympic record time of 2.51.7 by Hungary's Éva Székely, using the butterfly stroke, while her compatriot Éva Novák swam in orthodox style to register 2.54.4. Elenor Gordon tipped Klára Killerman almost with her last stroke to prevent a Hungarian clean sweep, though both times were recorded as 2.57.6. Having begun to race internationally at the age of 14, at the 1947 Monte Carlo European Championships that had been so tragic for Nancy Riach, Gordon's experience perhaps helped in this regard.[30] In the 100-metres freestyle, Hungary's Katalin Szöke and Judit Temes were split for the medals by Johanna Termeulin of the Netherlands, with the best placed British swimmer, Angela Barnwell, eighth overall. Britain's Jean Botham and Lillian Preece failed to make the semi-finals.

In the women's 400-metres freestyle heats, Daphne Wilkinson of Great Britain tied with Evelyn Kawamoto of the USA to set up a new Olympic record of 5.16.6, but in the semi-finals, the British swimmer came only 11th. In spite of swimming up to two miles a day in winter and more intense summer training, Wilkinson's schedule was light compared with the Americans, the Australians and the Dutch.[31] The other British swimmers, Lillian Preece and Grace Wood, were eliminated in the heats. Valéria Gyenge and Éva Novák of Hungary took the top places followed by Evelyn Kawamoto. In the 100-metres backstroke, Britain's Margaret McDowell came in seventh place overall and Pauline Musgrove failed to make it out of the heats. Joan Harrison took gold for South Africa, ahead of Geertje Wielema of the Netherlands and Jean Stewart of New Zealand. The 4 × 100-metres relay brought a new world record; Hungary led from start to finish, followed by Holland, the USA and, in fourth place, Denmark. Phyllis Linton, Jean Botham, Angela Barnwell and Lillian Preece finished in fifth place for Britain. Preece had intensified her training regime across her career to swim at least 14 miles a week as preparation for Helsinki but this regime failed to match the ambition of the successful women's swimming nations.[32]

In the diving, Patricia McCormick of the USA succeeded in winning both the women's springboard and high diving events, having narrowly missed the US team in London. As the wife of the wrestler Glen McCormick, the British press gendered their reportage of events:

> 'I want to star in the Olympics and then retire', says Pat with an air of finality. 'Holding Five Titles may be a thrill-but I'd be much happier having five children. Medals are nice - but you can't cuddle 'em'.[33]

Mady Moreau of France took silver in the springboard and Zoe Olsen-Jensen the bronze but not without dispute, since the judges were divided. Britain's Charmian Welch came fifth overall, Phyllis Long eighth and Dorothy Drew 11th. The high dive was a clean sweep for the USA in the medals, as Paula Myers and Juno Irvin finished second and third. Phyllis Long was Britain's best-placed high diver in fifth, ahead of Diana Long in seventh and Valerie Lloyd-Chandos in 12th place.

The 1948 London Games had seen women's canoeing introduced and female Soviet athletes began to become important on the world stage as potential medal winners for the State-sponsored regime, often in less obvious Olympic sports and disciplines. At the 1952 Helsinki Games, in the 500-metres K1 (Kayak Singles), Sylvi Saimo of Finland, the 1950 World Champion, won by 0.4 of a second from Austria's Gertrude Liebhart, with Nina Savina (USSR) third, ahead of Alida van de Anker-Doedens (the Netherlands). Savina won her heat in 2.22 to get to the final, with Britain's Shirley Ascot finishing last, over 12 seconds behind.

By 1956, the Soviets were dominant in the kayak singles event, with Yelizaveta Dementyeva winning ahead of Therese Zenz for Germany and Tove Søby of Denmark. Patricia Moody, a Civil Service cartographer from Esher, Surrey came seventh for Britain out of a total of 10 entrants. As the lone British female canoeist, it cost Patricia more than the price of her £41 kayak and considerable self-sacrifice to compete. Government departments allowed annual leave with pay for the duration of their employee's Olympic competition, but only half pay for the remainder of their time away from work, including travel.[34] In 1960, Britain's Marianne Tucker would make the semi-finals, before competing again as the solo representative in Tokyo in 1964. A women's K2 (Kayak Pairs) 500-metres event was introduced in Rome and won by the Soviet duo, ahead of Germany and Hungary.

At Helsinki in 1952, the gymnastics programme was expanded from just a women's team event to six further disciplines (floor, beam, parallel bars, eight exercises combined and a team exercise with portable apparatus, where the previous world champions, Sweden, took the gold medal). Only the USSR and Hungary contested the individual events, with Maria Gorohovskaja and Nina Botsharova the outstanding individual performers, ahead of Hungarian Margit Korondi. The Soviets won the overall team competition, ahead of Hungary and Czechoslovakia.[35]

The British Olympic Association and its constituent sporting bodies were slow to respond to these international rivalries and continued to under-fund women's sport. Britain's Cissie Davies, Mary and Irene Hirst, Gwynedd Lewis, Margaret Morgan, Valerie Mullins, Margaret Thomas and Marjorie Raistrick managed 16th place overall in the gymnastic team competition, a poor performance compared with the Russians, who the official report considered 'physically powerful, agile and well trained'.[36] Probably because of the cost, no British team was sent to the women's gymnastics in Melbourne 1956, but Mary Patricia 'Pat' Hirst of Leeds, a PE teacher and member of Saltaire Gymnastic Club, travelled to be the lone representative at 38 years of age, coming in 60th position in the individual all-round contest. In 1960, a team of six gymnasts travelled to Rome (Gwynedd Lewis, Pat Perks, Margaret Thomas-Neale, Marjorie Raistrick-Carter, Jill Pollard and Dorothy

Summers), including some experienced Olympians, again finishing well down the field, in 17th place.[37]

As Cold War politics became more entrenched between East and West, the British media, and the public, would often characterise their athletes as representatives of a mighty little nation, doing their best against much larger forces.[38] This went just as much for the men as the women. However, as had been noted, Chris Brasher and other stars of the Melbourne Olympics sometimes resisted this characterisation. However, the programme continued to expand and diversify, especially at the Summer Olympic Games. Debates rattled on however, over whether the government should wholly fund, or partly assist, the British Olympic team. Some analysts argued that State-subsidy would effectively end amateurism and others considered that conferring temporary status on British Olympians as sporting civil servants would do no harm to the amateur ideal.[39]

There were also important international competitions, held under the auspices of sporting federations, like track and field athletics and swimming, which focused Anglo-Soviet rivalries into personal battles. Judy Grinham would later represent Britain in an international swimming competition in Moscow, against Hungary, the Netherlands, France and the USSR in 1955, before her Olympic appearance at the Melbourne games, for instance.[40] In a variety of fixtures, new kinds of East-West rivalry became gendered and this made the role of female athletes all the more dramatic to the media. Both male and female State-sponsored Soviet athletes were known as Masters of Sport, giving them a status unmatched by British amateurs.

As well as keenly reporting many Spartakiad athletics meeting in Russia, the Amateur Athletic Association and the Women's Amateur Athletic Association frequently invited Russian teams to London and enjoyed the boost to track and field as a result of this rivalry. Raisa Kuts, a Moscow-based journalist and wife of double Olympic gold medallist in Melbourne, Vladimir Kuts, was invited to contribute to *World Sports*, evidencing that it was not just British writers like Susan Noel and Pat Besford who had established themselves in journalism.[41] The growth in sporting print journalism in this period opened new professions to women, from a range of specialisms.

There were several Great Britain vs USSR athletics matches to cover and, though relations were generally cordial, others were more fractious. One such London-based fixture was cancelled in 1956, when discus star Nina Ponomaryeva was charged for stealing five hats from a London store but failed to appear in court and subsequently disappeared. Russian diplomatic personnel interpreted the arrest as 'a provocation' and withdrew the entire team hours before the scheduled start of the competition.[42] Against this background, Pat Smythe's opportunity to become an Olympian would have to wait until 1956, as the schedule of summer games slowly expanded to include more equestrian events.

The chapter now turns to the case study of Pat Smythe and her career as a professional equestrian in 1950s and 1960s Britain.

Pat Smythe: 'Britain's greatest and best-loved horsewoman'

The dust jacket of the autobiography *Leaping Life's Fences*, written by Pat Smythe in 1992, described the author as 'Britain's greatest and best-loved horsewoman'.[43] In many senses, her career followed on from amateurs like Charlotte Cooper and Lottie Dod, because Smythe did not rely on the Olympic Games for her fame. But, unlike Cooper and Dod, she was a professional equestrian, deriving the largest part of her income from working with horses until her writing, which began with paid journalism and extended to autobiographical works, and children's books, which became her most lucrative income in the mid-1950s. From a well-connected family who fell on hard times while she was young, Smythe would become an adept businesswoman from the relatively young age of 16 years.

Patricia Rosemary Smythe was born 22 November 1928 in East Sheen, London. Elder brother Ronald was three and a half years her senior, and a second brother, Dickie, had died of a heart complaint two years before. Pat's father, Eric Smythe had been to Heidelberg University and qualified as a Civil Engineer working in the military, before becoming the youngest staff officer in the Intelligence Corps. Captain Eric Smythe did not seem overly excited by the arrival of his only daughter, noting in his diary 'Patricia born 10.05 am, Monique splendid! Dull wet morning. To office after lunch. Aunt Isobel died today'.[44]

Pat's mother, Monique Smythe was the daughter of the Reverend Frank Curthoys and was brought up with three brothers at Cromhall Rectory in Gloucestershire, riding farmer's hunters and point to point horses. Educated at St Swithun's Independent Girls Boarding School in Winchester, Monique was captain of the cricket XI and head of house, so perhaps inspired Pat's general love of sport. A precarious kind of upper middle class upbringing followed the marriage, as the family briefly owned a £2,000 property called Beaufort House, by Barnes Common. Stable family life was continually upset by Eric Smythe's ill-health, mainly rheumatoid arthritis, and he was advised to go for a dry cure in North Africa.

When Pat Smythe was growing up, the establishment of riding schools in which young women worked full time was relatively new. Lady Wright, Marjorie Avis Bullows, had previously become the first woman to ride astride at Olympia, winning the show-jumping championship there in 1928. With her husband Robert Wright, she established a prestigious riding school near Edgbaston. Initiating the model of 'working pupils' who lived-in and taught children to ride, well-known female equestrians like 'Pug' Verity and 'Tinka' Taylor could earn a full-time living working with horses. Riding schools proliferated, for a wider range of pupils both in terms of age and social class. The first youth gymkhana was held in 1928, a forerunner to the formation of the Pony Club in 1929, which had 8,350 members in 1934.[45] Recovering from a fractured pelvis in 1936, Wright won the *Daily Mail* Cup at Olympia on her horse, 'Jimmy Brown'.

Monique Smythe was one of several founding figures in the business of equestrian professionalisation. Having good horse sense was an aptitude that Pat inherited from her mother. The Irish-Argentine polo professional, Johnny Traill, would often send Monique Smythe horses to break-in and school. Johnny's father and uncle had emigrated to Argentina in the 1860s, from where they established large ranches and introduced bloodlines of horses imported from England, eventually numbering a stock of 2,000.[46] Born in Penge in 1882, Traill's Irish heritage was also important for links to bloodstock in County Down and he settled in England in the 1920s, becoming known as an outstanding polo player (along with his sons Jim and Jack) until his death in 1958.[47]

As such, the Smythe family were linked with important breeders and traders of horses and ponies, but Monique had a particular gift for bringing on more temperamental and less fortunate animals. 'Pixie' was such a pony, having been given to Pat for her fifth birthday, later kicked and blinded in one eye by one of the horses being trained by Monique Smythe. With 13 as her lucky number, Pat won equal first prize on 'Pixie' at the Richmond Royal Horse Show in June 1939, tying with Dougie Bunn (later to become the owner and promoter of Hickstead Place Equestrian Venue), and Fred Winter (who became a famous jockey and trainer).[48] From the age of 11 onwards, Pat would continue to fund her own entry to horse and pony shows, saving a pound from each of her prize money winnings to continue her career.

During the Second World War, the family had to give up Beaufort House due to Eric's continuing illness. Pat was sent to boarding school at Talbot Heath School, Bournemouth; Ronald was packed off to Newquay and Monique joined the Red Cross in London. Beaufort House was let and 'Pixie' stabled for the duration with the Drummond-Hay family at Ferne in Dorset, where Pat spent the holidays. After moving to Crickley Lodge, the Smythes bought a £40 half share of the horse 'Finality', with Johnny Traill funding the remainder. The horse was a 3-year-old mare, and its mother had been 'honourably retired to stud' after kicking her milk cart to pieces on Tunbridge Wells High Street. 'Finality' inherited this sense of humour.

Although Monique was able to bring Eric back to Britain, he was to die on 19 January 1945, having unsuccessfully tried a range of cures from gold injections to psychic healing. The dislocating experience of being away from her own family was to persuade Pat never to send her own children to boarding school. It was also to affect the basis of her fiction for children. The adventures were not to be school stories but based on travel, comradeship with other equestrians and self-reliance.

In 1947, Pat Smythe's performance at the first International Horse Show at the White City earned her selection to the British team for an international show in Belgium. Unfortunately, this success meant that 'Finality' was now worth nearer £1,500 and Traill wanted to sell. Smythe was also obliged to lend 'Finality' to the British Olympic team in 1948, though he did not take part. Effectively, Pat was left without a means to earn a living while 'Finality' was away, and she was not recompensed for the duration of the loan. This was, however, to be an important Olympic Games for the changing nature of contestants in the horse riding events.

At the equestrian events held during the Berlin Games in 1936, only 29 riders from 11 countries had competed. This meant that there were few preliminary stages in the contest. At the 1948 London Games there were just 46 entrants from 17 counties, with Brazil the most notable newcomer. A 'shadow of a scandal' in the 1948 dressage event, won by the Swedish team, showed how arbitrary amateur rules could be. Lieutenant Gehnäll Persson had been promoted from Sergeant on 20 July 1948, just before the Olympic Games began. He rode his horse, 'Knaust', as part of the winning team. Two and half weeks later, Persson was demoted back to Sergeant. The FEI, with the approval of the IOC, disqualified Persson on 27 April 1949. Sweden was also disqualified from the team event and lost the gold medal. The episode illustrated that defining non-commissioned officers as amateurs and commissioned officers as professionals was clearly class-based nonsense.

Thereafter, the International Olympic Committee gradually admitted women to the three equestrian disciplines at the Games. This saw a rapid increase in equestrian Olympic competition, as from 1952 onwards, the top 25 riders in each discipline contested the final round. However, at its meeting in 1951 the FEI decided that show jumping would not be open to women for 1952, merely the individual and team dressage contests. This opened the way for only the smallest events (a field of 52 in jumping; 27 competing in dressage; and 59 riders in the eventing class).[49] The US team was therefore forced to drop Carol Durand of Kansas City, the sole woman in the Incorporated Equestrian Squad, although she had completed the intensive training approaching the Olympic Games.[50] As the Incorporated Equestrian Squad name indicated, the US team was the first fully private line-up since the previous military side had been disbanded in 1950.

The late ruling also meant that Pat Smythe could not represent Britain at the height of her career. She had been second in the Princess Elizabeth Cup, riding her horse 'Leona', at the International Horse of the Year Show at the White City, also taking the *Country Life* Cup on 'Prince Hal' and coming second overall in the prestigious *Daily Mail* Cup.[51] But things were slowly changing. Whereas the vast majority of the contestants in 1948 had ridden in uniform, almost half of those who went to Helsinki were civilians. Even without Smythe, the British show-jumping team of Lieutenant-Colonel Harry Llewellyn on 'Foxhunter', Dougie Stewart, riding 'Aherlow' and Wilfred White on 'Nizfella', won the team gold medal for the first time.[52] 'Foxhunter' became so famous in his own right that several books and magazine articles were devoted to his life.[53]

In the meantime, the Smythe family had taken a lease on Miserden House and began to teach children to ride. Pat celebrated her 21st birthday in Paris, watching Josephine Baker perform at the Folies Bergère. By now, 'Finality' had been sold but was often loaned back to Pat Smythe to show, and together they won the George VI Cup in 1948. The next year, a Princess Elizabeth Cup for Ladies was introduced to save male rider's egos. Smythe then won the French Ladies Cup on 'Leona' and the Belgian Grand Prix on another loaned horse called 'Nobbler'. This so surprised the International Equestrian Federation that they did not have rules in place to prevent a woman from winning.

Smythe's reputation in Europe helped her domestic fame in Britain. Following Smythe's win at the 1949 Grand Prix in Brussels, she was named leading show jumper of the year in a new initiative launched by Mike and Victoria Ansell. The Ansells wanted to capitalise on the popularity of the 1948 Olympic equestrian event with the public, and reinvented the International Horse Show as an indoor arena exhibition, mainly staged at the White City in July every year. Having begun as an indoor event at Olympia in 1908 it had been held outdoors after World War II. An indoor arena gave an annual focus to the calendar of show jumping and other equestrian disciplines, also including a degree of pageantry, just as people were owning their first television sets and later, the new colour models.

Televised show jumping displayed a simple points 'fault system', making the outcome easy to calculate from an armchair, and more exciting still when rounds were ridden against the clock, which could be displayed simultaneously on screen. These simple devices framed the action for viewers who were not necessarily familiar with the rules of show jumping. Later, the Horse of the Year Show at Harringay Arena would add to the sense of a televised equestrian calendar, since it was scheduled annually in October. This more explicitly raised the profile of show jumping as a media spectacle with all the technological developments available to light and stage the equestrian performance in the Autumn.[54]

In 1950, Smythe bought a bay for £150 at the National Hunt meeting, regarded as a failed steeplechaser, and renamed him 'Prince Hal'. She paid a similar price for 'Tosca'. The television public were again entertained by the Horse of the Year duel in 1950, between Smythe on 'Finality' tying equal first with Llewellyn and 'Foxhunter': this pitched a relatively small pairing against the statuesque 16 hands 3 inches bay hunter and his owner, who had both seen distinguished military service.[55] In this sense, the tie summarised the changes in equestrian sport after 1945. Pat Smythe's dominance in national championships continued until 1963, often helped with issues of transportation and logistics by Harry Llewellyn. Conscious that the point of these shows was to blend public entertainment and sport, Smythe competed with a trademark white carnation in her buttonhole.

As had been indicated, Pat Smythe's horses were each bought from her winnings at national and international shows but this was not a secure income. She was again obliged to loan a horse, in this case 'Prince Hal', to the British Olympic team in 1952 and he was returned in a sorry state. It was therefore fortunate that Smythe had a very successful year, including a win at the Horse of the Year Show in 1952, with 'Tosca'. However, the following January her mother was killed in a road traffic accident and the bank immediately required Monique's £1,500 overdraft to be settled. 'Leona' was sold to pay the debt and Smythe was not to be financially secure until her books for children began to be published.

Meanwhile, back in the equestrian world, Pat Smythe was named *Daily Express* Sportswoman of the Year in 1952 (with Len Hutton as sportsman), celebrated by a gala at the Savoy and the award presented by the Marquis and Marchioness of Exeter. Part of the reason for this popularity was that the Prince of Wales Nations Cup, held at the White City, had opened to women for the first time and Smythe was part of the winning British team with Llewellyn, White and Peter Robeson, riding 'Craven A'. At the end of 1954, Smythe came third in the *Sporting Record* 'Sportsman of the Year' award with just over 10 per cent of the public vote, behind Roger Bannister in first place, with 24 per cent of the ballot, and Chris Chataway in second place.[56] This was the first time that the awards had been televised. It was one of a series of media appearances cementing Smythe as part of the sporting elite in *Fifties Britain*: she also appeared on *Desert Island Discs* and Madame Tussauds made a waxwork of her likeness. Later that year, the seven-foot high bank at the Nice Horse Show would injure Pat, 'Tosca' and 'Prince Hal'. All three were to recover well and 'Tosca' repaid the investment in his training, in particular by winning £1,542 in 1952 and £1,350 in 1953 before a tour of America further supplemented this income.

Pat Smythe endorsed the carbonated drink Lucozade and Harry Hall clothing, in cooperation with the British Equestrian Fund, and won other valuable items such as Rolex watches, as part of her international career.[57] The IOC president Avery Brundage, was troubled by her endorsements for Rolex and for her media work, but was not in a position to disqualify Smythe for selection to the British team, without raising the problematic issue of whether military officers were also 'pseudo-amateurs', to use the terminology of the subsequent inquiry into her case.[58]

At one point the over-zealous Brundage was trying to get potential Olympians to sign a pledge that they intended to remain amateurs life-long in order to be eligible to compete. Critics rightly pointed out that such a scheme was practically un-enforceable. Even so, Smythe chose not to file copy for the duration of Olympic competition once selected for the Equestrian Games in Stockholm. The issue of how free of financial concerns an amateur should be, remained a problematic issue with proposals in 1957 that sporting administrators, among them Harold Abrahams, should also receive no fees at all, including for writing and broadcasting work.[59]

Although she was a sporting icon for a more meritocratic Britain, Smythe was also astute in shaping her own public image as a hardworking woman who had earned her opportunities, and overcome personal tragedy by sheer determination.[60] In using sport as a platform to 'something better' Smythe was not alone; Chris Brasher, who won the Steeplechase gold medal in 1956, had already outlined that he did not run for nationalistic causes but for a chance to improve his opportunities.[61]

Pat Smythe's written output was extensive: *Jump For Joy* (1954); *Pat Smythe's Book of Horses* (1956); *One Jump Ahead* (1958); *Tosca and Lucia* (1959); *Florian's Farmyard* (1960); *Horses and Places* (1961); *Jumping Round the World* (1962); *Leaping Life's Fences* (1992). Her children's books were to include *Jacqueline Rides for a Fall* (Cassel, 1956); *Three Jays Against The Clock* (Cassel, 1958); *Three Jays On Holiday* (Cassel, 1958); *Three Jays Go To Town* (Cassel, 1959); *Three Jays Over The Border* (Cassel, 1960); *Three Jays Go To Rome* (Cassel, 1960); *Three Jays Lend A Hand* (Cassel, 1961). There were also many excerpts, reprints and new editions, such as 'What a Night!' in John Canning (ed.) *Adventure Stories for Girls* (London: Octopus, 1978, reprinted 1979, 1980, 1981 and 1982). This list does not include her journalism, including skiing articles for the *Daily Express*, forewords to numerous books and other paid writing.

After winning the prestigious gold buttons as the victor of the Algiers Championship in 1955, ahead of Pierre Jonquères d'Oriola, Paco Gogoya and Hans Winkler, it was clear that Pat Smythe was one of the world's leading equestrians.[62] She won *Sporting Records* Sportswoman of the Year in 1955 and came 11th in the overall ballot (men and women) that was headed by Gordon Pirie.[63] It perhaps contextualises this achievement that *World Sports* announced that for the 10th time in a row, Stanley Matthews had managed to make the top 12 in the *Sporting Records* list.

Sue Whitehead, Pug Verity's daughter, was also initially selected for the 1956 equestrian Olympic team but broke her collarbone, effectively ruling her out. Just before the team departed for Stockholm in June 1956, Smythe was awarded the OBE in the Queen's Birthday Honours. She described her Olympic training to that point as:

> One of the best times of my life. We were stabled at Ascot in lovely boxes where I could keep Flanagan, Prince Hal and a young horse Brigadoon, and we usually started riding the horses at 6.00 am which meant that the rest of the day was free…I would drive down to Miserdon for an afternoon's work but the evenings and nights were free to explore London life. I seized the chance to see as much theatre and opera together with a social round that I had not experienced

before, going dancing at the '400', the Allegro and some of the other night clubs and getting back to the stables in time to blow away the cobwebs with a good workout.[64]

Britain sent a team of eight equestrians in total to Stockholm, where preparations had included a special lottery to fund refurbishments of the Olympic stadium, as there had been in 1910 to fund its original construction. The lottery supplemented private and Swedish State funds to provide the necessary training grounds, although a fire near one of the stables suggested that preparations did not go entirely smoothly. Fortunately, no horses or riders were harmed.

A State visit aboard the Royal yacht *Britannia* was organised immediately prior to the 1956 Stockholm Games, with the Queen and Prince Philip staying on in a private capacity for one week after to attend festivities along with Lord and Lady Mountbatten, Princess Margaret Rose and the Duke and Duchess of Devonshire. Elizabeth and Philip accompanied the official patrons of the Games, King Gustav VI Adolf and Queen Louise of Sweden, driving in open carriages into the arena to commence the proceedings, flanked by the Swedish Royal Guard, before taking in the remainder of the contests from the Royal Box.[65] There were close personal ties, since Mountbatten was Gustav's brother in law. For the first time, the march past the Royal Box was entirely on horseback and in another innovation, 100 riders in relay had carried the Olympic flame from Malmo to Stockholm and into the stadium.

In all, there were 13 female and 145 male riders from 29 countries in 1956; meaning that most were all-male teams. Dressage entrants Lillian Williams on Pilgrim and Lorna Johnson on Rosie's Dream joined Pat Smythe on Flanagan as the three women of an eight-strong British team. Unlike Smythe, who was 27 when she made her Olympic debut, Williams was 61 years old and Lorna Johnstone was 53, so Stockholm reflected changing age and gender profiles of British equestrian representatives. Lillian Williams would again contest the Dressage in Rome, joined by 26-year-old Johanna Hall, to take 11th and 13th place, respectively.

In the German team, three of the nine riders were female dressage specialists: Liselott Linsenhoff (on her horse 'Adular'); Anneliese Küppers (riding 'Afrika') and Hannelore Weygand (astride 'Perkunos'). Else Christoffersen on her horse 'Diva'; Anne Lise Kielland ('Clary') and Bodil Russ ('Corona') represented Norway. The Danish team had two female riders, Lis Hartel and Inger Lemvigh-Müller (riding 'Bel Ami'), of a team of four. Elaine Shirley Watt of New Jersey, USA also took part in the dressage, coming 30th overall on her horse, 'Connecticut Yankee'. This meant that all of the female contestants took part in the dressage apart from show jumpers Smythe and Brigitte Schockaert of Belgium riding 'Muscadin'. Canada had no female riders but, like Australia, had women grooms. Nina Gromova and Tamara

Koulikovskaia were both reserves for the USSR dressage team, and featured in the official report.

The Queen watched as the British team won bronze in the Grand Prix Jumping competition, behind Germany in gold medal place, with an outstanding individual performance by Hans Winkler, with Italy in second place, mainly thanks to the brothers Raymondo and Piero D'Inzeo. These three riders took the individual medals, whereas Wilf White came fourth overall, Pat Smythe 10th and Peter Robeson 19th.[66] Brigitte Schockaert came 34th overall.

Smythe was more successful in the International Show held immediately after the Games, individually winning the King of Sweden Cup, which also helped the British team to an overall victory in the Nation's Cup, ahead of Italy. Soon after, Smythe's Olympic bronze medal was stolen from the car of a friend parked at the White City, and a replacement had to be sourced.[67] Smythe's high profile was further celebrated in a 1957 *World Sports* front cover article that placed her alongside Emil Zatopek, Stanley Matthews and Denis Compton; stars of the previous decade.[68]

Queen Elizabeth also loaned her horse 'Countryman III' to the British team for the Three-Day Event, still often called 'The Military' informally today. 'Countryman III' was ridden by Albert 'Bertie' Hill, a West Country farmer and Devon's point to point champion. This was a first exciting team victory for Great Britain, including Frank Weldon astride 'Kilbarry'; Bertie Hill and Arthur Laurence Rook riding 'Wild Venture' ahead of line-ups from Germany and Canada. Weldon and his squad received their medals from the Marquess of Exeter. Petrus Kastenman, riding his horse 'Iluster', won the individual eventing gold medal for Sweden; ahead of August Lütke-Westhues, and his horse 'Trux von Kamax' for Germany, and Frank Weldon in third place. Britain's Laurence Rook took sixth and Bertie Hill was placed 12th individually to score for the team prize. This brought the entire British medal tally to a respectable one gold and two bronze medals in Stockholm; third overall behind Germany and Sweden.

The individual gold medal of the Grand Prix de Dressage went again to Henri St Cyr, of Sweden, second was Lis Hartel riding 'Jubilee' for Denmark and third, Germany's Liselott Linsenhoff on 'Adular'. This gave Sweden the team medal for the third consecutive time; followed by a German silver and a Swiss bronze.

In the official report, photographs show Princess Margaret looking more composed, perhaps disinterested and accessorised by an elegant cigarette holder, than her sister, who was animated by the proceedings.[69] On the day before the Eventing endurance test, Queen Elizabeth and Princess Margaret paid an informal visit to the Fäboda course, perhaps to offer some moral support, visiting several of the trickier hurdles. Elizabeth was featured several times in the official report, protected against the inclement weather by her favourite Hermès silk headscarf, and a Burberry trenchcoat.

Women were much in evidence in Stockholm, from the elite of Swedish Royalty (Princesses Margarethe, Désirée, Birgitta and Christina) to the Women's Auxiliary who provided the catering and the 'Etoile Rouge' a women's organisation that looked after wounded animals, and provided basic equestrian care. This was required in the very tough eventing class when a horse fell badly and was destroyed, creating some negative publicity. In the main Summer schedule later that year in Melbourne, *World Sports* also considered the Olympics and sport generally 'A Woman's World'.[70]

Of course, most of the British competitors in 1956 were at the Olympic Games in Melbourne, many travelling for the first time south of the Equator. Along with Australia, the USA and the Soviets, the British were among the four largest teams. Liverpool manufacturers, Jack Sharp Ltd, clothed the British team in 'Copdale' tracksuits, while Alec Brook Sports Equipment provided some competitors with Adidas sports shoes, blazers and trousers. A specially commissioned Panama hat distinguished the female representatives, as did their all-white parading uniform.

Elizabeth II was Patron of the Melbourne Olympics, featuring strongly in the official report, as did Prince Philip, as he opened the Games.[71] His Royal Highness the Duke of Edinburgh, oversaw a banquet for 500 guests, including the International Olympic Committee and the Australian Olympic Federation on the evening of 22 November, which coincided with the Opening Ceremony. Closing festivities were staged on 8 December 1956.

The Games cost around £8 million to stage amid international tensions and, in particular the Suez crisis, which was to have worldwide repercussions. The national teams of Spain, the Netherlands, Egypt, Iraq, the Lebanon, the People's Republic of China and Switzerland all stayed away, as did the Gold Coast, Guatemala, Malta and Panama. Hungarian athletes attended but must have felt compromised. Hungary had been controlled by Russia since 1945, however, the death of Stalin in 1953 led many Hungarians to campaign for independence. In July 1956, Rakosi, the 'Stalinist' Secretary of the Hungarian Communist Party, lost power, following protests in Hungary. In October 1956, Imre Nagy, a moderate westerniser became Hungary's Prime Minister. Those Hungarians who did travel were said to have been distracted by events back home, and yet wanted to represent their country on a world stage. Such personal conflicts reflected larger international relations contexts in the staging of Olympic Games.

The clear star of the women's track and field athletics was Betty Cuthbert who won both the 100-metres and 200-metres gold medal, with Christa Stubnick of Germany and Marlene Mathews of Australia taking the other medals in both races.[72] Cuthbert worked at a plant nursery run by her parents in Ermington, Paramatta, an outer suburb of Sydney and declared her hobbies to be breeding budgerigars and making her own clothes.[73] Betty had been spotted and coached by former Olympic sprinter June Mason, by then known under her married surname Ferguson, who worked as a physical education teacher in Paramatter.

Stubnick's story was one of the more extraordinary of the Melbourne Games because, having married the East German heavyweight boxing champion, she worked as a shorthand typist for the East German police and was coached by Max Schommeler of the Dynamo Sports Club in Berlin.[74] Selection for a combined East-West German team has therefore been based on Schommeler's chance sighting of Stubnick at a small sports meeting in 1952, and his subsequent work with her to Olympic level. Shirley de la Hunty took the gold in the 80-metres hurdles ahead of Gisela Kohler for Germany and Norma Thrower of Australia. Britain's Carole Quinton made it to the semi-finals but Pauline Threapleton-Wainwright was eliminated in the heats.[75]

For Britain, sprinters Heather Armitage and June Paul (née Foulds) would compete again in Melbourne in 1956 in the 100 metres, 200 metres and as part of the relay team. Their best individual placings across these events were, for Armitage sixth overall in the 100 metres, and for Paul fifth in the 200 metres. June had begun to diversify her sporting interests after marrying the amateur foil champion Raymond Paul, in 1953 and subsequently took exams under the direction of Mary Glen Haig.[76] Having initially retired from athletics after the birth of her son Steven, June reconsidered when it appeared likely that Raymond would be selected for the Melbourne Olympics, and she would not qualify to represent Britain in the fencing events. June had spent the intervening time working at the Paul dynasty fencing goods shop and, with Chad Varah, developing *The Eagle* children's magazine. Having decided to resume her athletic training, June was fortunate that the family flat was opposite Arsenal's Highbury ground, and due to her fame as an Olympian, Tom Whittaker would allow her to run around the pitch to get back into shape. It was only on this resumption of training that she undertook coaching advice, in this case from Charles Warner.[77]

Along with June Paul and Heather Armitage, Anne Pashley (who was eliminated in the 100-metres heats) would complete the British women's 4 × 100-metres relay team in Melbourne, along with Jean Scrivens (who was eliminated in the 200-metres heats). The British took the silver medal, behind Australia and ahead of the US team that featured a young Wilma Rudolf alongside Matthews, Fagg and Daniels. This was a considerable achievement for the British. In the final, both Paul and Armitage were ahead for Britain in their respective legs, only for Betty Cuthbert to put in a finishing sprint for a new world record time of 44.5 seconds.

Having been born in Ceylon, where her father was a policeman, Heather Armitage's family returned to Britain and she began to train as a physical education teacher at Lady Mary College, Yorkshire. Both parents were keen sporting amateurs and Armitage was a versatile athlete. She might not have made selection for the 1956 Olympic Games, as a hockey stick broke her knee-cap during a game in 1953 and a slipped disc kept her out for most of the

1955 track and field athletics season. It was only due to the process of recovery from these injuries that she took coaching advice from Jack Murphy, and improved her times as a result.[78] After the 1956 Olympics, Heather married Frank Young, a teacher of mathematics and went on to anchor the world record winning 4 × 100-metres relay team for England at the Empire and Commonwealth Games in Cardiff in 1958.

June Paul's reputation as a world-class athlete was also cemented by relay success at both the 1956 Olympic and the 1958 Empire and Commonwealth Games: she appeared on *Desert Island Discs* in November 1958 as the guest of Roy Plomley. More television and media work followed. Decades later, in 1993, Hunter Davies interviewed June as she prepared to buy the Everyman Cinema in Hampstead, North London as head of a company employing 40 people, and owner of several restaurants and food stalls, trading under the name *Huffs*.[79]

In the interview with Davies, June Paul outlined that a key life-lesson had been to learn to be resilient. Her maternal grandmother, from whom she learned to cook, had brought her up as her daughter. At the age of eight, June's elder sister died, but it was not until her maternal grandmother died, when she was aged 11, that she learned her sister, had, in fact, been her biological mother. The ability to reframe her perspective and move on, had helped her to focus in sport, with its many challenges and disappointments. After retiring for the second time from athletics and having two more children, June's marriage to Raymond Paul ended and she began a relationship with pop singer Ronnie Carroll. Two more children followed and, after a spell running a beach bar in Grenada, June and Ronnie separated. June's first business after the relationship ended was a food stall at Camden Lock market. After a brief third marriage, she expanded into a range of food-based businesses. The case indicates how much more work there is to do to understand the role of Olympic appearances in the life-course of women at this time.

Special mention should be also made at this point of how Ireland's Maeve Kyle would feel that a volunteer timekeeper had cost her a chance to win Olympic glory. Having run particularly well at the White City in 1956, Kyle ran in the same Olympic heats at Cuthbert, to be given a time a full three seconds slower at 26.5. What appeared to be an error in activating the stopwatch had led the official to estimate the time to cover his mistake, whereas at least two other timekeepers for Ireland had the figure at 24.8 seconds.[80] As an introduction to world class athletics, it was a crushing disappointment but Kyle would go on to compete again in both Rome and Tokyo, in the latter case reaching the semi-finals of the 400 metres and 800 metres. What this case, and several others, indicated was that electronic timing was absolutely necessary to be fair to the athletes involved.

In the fields events, America's Mildred McDaniel showed great superiority in the high jump as she went on alone to clear 1.76 metres, a new world and Olympic record. Britain's Thelma Hopkins tied with Mariya Pissareva of USSR for the silver medal, to become the only British woman to win an individual athletics medal in Melbourne.[81] Dorothy Tyler tied for 12th place for Britain and Audrey Bennett tied for 16th place. Hopkins had broken Tshudina's record with a 1.74-metres jump in 1956 but her athletic training for Melbourne had begun intensively only the Easter before and consisted of one or two hours, five or six times a week. Hopkins had relied on hockey and squash over the previous Winter months, she reported, to keep up her general fitness levels without wishing to specialise year-round in athletics.[82]

This was also the end of an amazing Olympic career for Tyler and had seen her adapt from the 'scissors kick' that she had used in the 1948 Olympics Games, to the 'western roll' technique for Helsinki in 1952.[83] Having become the only female track and field specialist to win medals before and after World War II, Tyler also demonstrated her longevity by winning two gold medals in British Empire Games in 1938 and 1950, and a silver medal in Vancouver in 1954.[84] She retired at a time when the high jump was becoming increasingly competitive. In 1957, Cheng Feng Yung, a student, bettered McDaniel's record with a 1.77 jump, at the Peking City Sports Meeting, making her the first woman from the People's Republic of China to hold a sporting world record.[85] However, since the PR of China did not compete in the Olympic Games between 1952 and 1984, Cheng was absent in 1956.

In the long jump, world record holder Elzbieta Krzesinska of Poland equalled her own record to take first place ahead of Willie White for the USA and Nadezhda Khnikina-Dvalishvili of the USSR. Both Thelma Hopkins and Sheila Hoskins were eliminated in the heats. In the shot, Tamara Tyshkevich and Galina Zybina won the top two spots for the Soviet Union and Marianne Werner third place for Germany. Suzanne Farmer-Allday came in 15th for Britain. Olga Fikotova of Czechoslovakia took gold in the discus, followed by Irina Beglyakova and Nina Romashkova-Ponomaryova for the USSR. Suzanne Farmer-Allday was eliminated in the qualifying rounds, which she would duplicate in both the shot and discus at the Rome Olympics as Britain's lone representative again. In the javelin, Inese Jaunzeme won and Nadezhda Konyayeva came third for the Soviet Union, split for the medals by Marlene Ahrens of Chile. The British journalist, Norris McWhirter, writing for *World Sports*, seemed particularly enamoured of all the female Russian athletes and posed the tantalising question 'Zybina: Strongest Woman in the World?'[86]

The 100-metres butterfly stroke was added to the women's Olympic programme from 1956, for a total of five individual events and the team relay.[87] Americans Shelley Mann, Nancy Ramey and Mary Sears provided the first three places in the women's butterfly race. Britain's Anne Morton did not make the final. The outstanding British female swimmers in Melbourne were Judy Grinham and Margaret Edwards who took gold and bronze in the 100-metres backstroke, respectively, with the silver claimed by Carine Cone of the USA.[88] Grinham and Edwards were rivals, not on the friendliest of terms, and this was much exaggerated by the newspapers.

> Women's swimming is no more full of cattiness than any other form of women's competition. The comparative restriction of the bath-side, the nearness of relatives and friends-these things conspire to create an atmosphere in which the camp followers have too much to say too audibly, and there is little the swimmers can do about it. The case of Margaret and I is one in point. In all our clashes in the water we never exchanged more than a handshake, a friendly smile and 'good luck.' Yet over-keen supporters did much to strain our relationship to breaking point.[89]

Julie Hoyle came in sixth place to make this Britain's best performance overall.[90] After briefly trying to change her competitive stroke to freestyle with some considerable success, Judy Grinham retired from sport at 20, pursued a very brief film and journalism career, then married and began a family before working for Dr Barnados.[91] Her autobiography is an interesting comparison to the upbeat nature of Pat Smythe's work, because the main theme is the extreme pressure of competing at such a level when so young. Grinham sought psychiatric help and received medication for her pre-competition nerves.

> A few days later, on the eve of my twentieth birthday, 5 March 1959, I officially retired. The following morning *The Daily Express* announced that I had joined their staff as a trainee journalist. This news came as a shock to most people, but I had a hankering to be a reporter for some time, though, like many others, I had been put off by not having the first idea how to break into the profession.[92]

There was little other good news for the British, as Grinham's gold and Edward's bronze medal were the only rewards for the whole swimming team. The journalist Pat Besford had forecast this dismal return and diagnosed lack of preparation as the cause.[93] The Amateur Swimming Association maintained the need to avoid 'staleness' or overtraining, however. Grinham's main complaint was lack of access to proper facilities and she emphasised that she trained amidst the public for her Olympic medals, although she also attended short-term preparatory training camps at Loughborough University.[94]

The lack of miles the British Olympians swam in the pool contrasted with a later feature in the same *World Sports* edition on Channel Swimming, which had become an enthusiasts' pursuit rather than just an elite event, by the mid-1950s. Of 24 swimmers from 13 countries to complete the Channel race in 1956, 21-year-old Eileen Fenton of Dewsbury, Yorkshire took home £1,000 prize money as the first woman home. Fenton had completed the crossing in

13 hours.[95] Away from the open water, Besford highlighted how Jan Stender of the Hilversum club in the Netherlands had young swimmers like Mary Kok train for five hours a day in the pool, supplemented by conditioning weights and training runs on a daily basis.[96]

In the women's 100-metres freestyle, the medals were an Australian clean sweep: Dawn Fraser, Lorraine Crapp and Faith Leech were all teenagers, aged between 19 and 15 years, respectively. Fearne Ewart and Frances Hogben for Britain were eliminated in the heats. In the 400-metres freestyle, Crapp led from Fraser and 14-year-old Sylvia Ruska of the United States for the medals, while Motherwell's Margaret Girvan finished well down the field.

The 200 metres breaststroke was without the world record holder, Ada den Haan, as the Netherlands had withdrawn from Melbourne in protest at the Russian invasion of Hungary. Without any strong contenders, the result was a German first and third for Ursula Happe and Eva-Maria Elsen, with Eva Székely of Hungary splitting the two. Elenor McKay (née Gordon) came sixth and 17-year-old Christine Gosden, from Croydon, came eighth overall for Britain.[97] Physically, the two were very different as McKay was petite, whereas Gosden was 1.8 metres tall and weighed 70 kilos.[98] This was also to be Elenor McKay's last major international tournament, as marriage and a family took precedence in her life. It cannot be over-estimated how much restrictive amateur rules limited the careers of the young swimmers, who were continually worried that they might be perceived as professionals for the slightest monetary gain. The rather mean-spirited Scottish Amateur Swimming Association considered McKay a professional for receiving £5 from the BBC for appearing on a programme to announce her retirement. Finally, the 4 × 100-metres freestyle relay was won by Australia, from the United States and South Africa with Britain's team (Hogben, Grinham, Girvan and Ewart) finishing in eighth place overall.

In the diving events, Britain's Anne Walsh was sixth and Charmain Welsh came 14th in the springboard, which was again dominated by Patricia McCormick from her compatriot Jeanne Stunyo and Canada's Irene MacDonald. From Hamilton, Ontario, MacDonald became only the second diver from outside the USA in 36 years to take a medal in this event, and she had moved to Los Angeles in 1954 to be coached by Pat McCormick and her husband, Glenn. Working in a Los Angeles bank during the day, MacDonald trained for at least three hours each evening with the McCormicks.[99]

The high dive saw Pat McCormick complete the double (as she had also won both events in Helsinki) only eight months after giving birth to her son. It was an American clean sweep with Juno Irwin and Paula Myers taking the remaining medals. Ann Long, the reigning Empire Games springboard champion and a bank typist from Essex, came in seventh and Charmian Welsh 12th.[100] Probably due to cost, this was the extent of the British female diving team at the Melbourne Games.

If swimming was a genuinely popular activity from which clubs could draw promising youngsters, the remaining Olympic women's sports like canoeing, diving, equestrianism, fencing, gymnastics and track and field athletics, depended on smaller cohorts of participants. In this, the British were not always alone.

Gillian Sheen took the women's foil gold medal for Great Britain in 1956, ahead of Olga Orban-Szabo of Hungary and Renée Garilhe of France.[101] Sheen had come to prominence by winning her first senior national title in 1949, before retaining the British Universities title for five consecutive years and securing the gold medal at the World Universities Championships in 1951.[102] Sheen had been eliminated early on in the 1952 Olympics, however. By winning gold in Melbourne, Sheen therefore obtained Britain's first fencing victory (male or female), and complemented three previous women's Olympic fencing silver medals (Gladys Davis in 1924; Muriel Freeman in 1928 and Judy Guinness in 1932).[103]

At the time of writing in 2016, Gillian Sheen remains Britain's only Olympic gold medal in fencing but, she has never been recognised, for example in the Queen's Honours List, in the same way that other victorious athletes have over the years. Sheen also won the British Empire and Commonwealth title in 1958, which included 20-year old Cardiff-born Meg Waters for Wales among the competitors. Like Sheen, Waters was a second-generation university medical student, so the class profile of fencing was often quite different from other Olympic sports and disciplines.

Sheen competed again in the Rome 1960 Olympics alongside Mary Glen Haig and Margaret Stafford in the individual women's foil competition. A female team foil event was added to the Olympic schedule in Rome, and Sheen made a four with Glen Haig, Jeanette Bailey and Shirley Netherway.[104] Sheen was to remain great rivals for the British senior women's championship with Glen Haig, as the latter was eight times runner-up to the former.

In 1960, Sheen won her 10th and final British national title under a newly inaugurated electronic points-scoring system, before marrying and moving to New York where, as Mrs Donaldson, she set up a dental practice with her husband. Sheen considered marrying an American as one of the key reasons why her achievements were not more celebrated in British public life. After her departure, Mary Glen Haig continued to compete against younger British opponents like Margaret Stafford, Eve Berry and Mildred Durne. Perhaps the ultimate British Olympic amateur administrator and competitor, Glen Haig also juggled a full-time job as a hospital administrator and part-time official duties with the Amateur Fencing Association.[105]

In the equestrian events at the Rome Olympics of 1960, it was Pat Smythe's turn to have a miserable time, to come 11th overall on 'Flanagan'. Smythe had survived a potentially career-ending fall at Badminton while training for the Olympics the April before.[106] The Queen had seen the fall and sent her condolences through the Duke of Beaufort, the host of Badminton.

Characteristically, both Smythe and 'Flanagan' were resilient and fully fit by the following September. The beautifully historic setting at Piazza di Siena, in the heart of Villa Borghese, was about 30 miles from the city. Many of the sporting competitions blended old and new staging, and events were telecast in Europe and North America, so Rome held considerable tourist appeal.

Four British show jumpers were selected, though only three were allowed to ride in the team contest.[107] Individually, David Broome on 'Sunsalve' took the bronze medal position behind Italy's Raimondo D'Inzeo, riding 'Posillipo' and his brother Piero, astride 'The Rock'. Smythe's protégé, Dawn Wofford (née Palethorpe), had come third in the individual event on Hollandia in the first round, but had a poor second round to finish in 20th place overall.[108]

Like Smythe, Wofford had openly admitted that, in 1955, her best year so far, she had won £1,200 in prize money. At the time, it was estimated that it cost between £5–7 per week to keep a thoroughbred in prime condition. Dawn Wofford had already followed Pat Smythe's lead by moving into writing, publishing *My Horses and I* in 1956, as well as encouraging young riders as an executive of the Pony Club, however she had not expected to be part of the show-jumping team event, and had not attended as many Olympic training sessions as Smythe.[109]

David Barker led the British show-jumping team event on 'Franco' but, with three refusals on a very difficult course, the squad was disqualified by 8 a.m. Only six of the 18 teams did complete the course. The Germans were victorious, ahead of the Americans and the Italians. Smythe was nevertheless required twice to jump round the course with 'Flanagan' to entertain the public, as the stadium was sold out. It was a dispiriting end to Olympic competition, passed over with considerable restraint in all Smythe's writing but there are many insights as to how badly prepared the British Olympic Association team were, even when hosting experienced and well-known competitors. For instance, Smythe was required to share a dormitory with the female fencing team, who had concluded their competition at 2 a.m. With crowded access to showers, basin and toilet facilities in the same room, Smythe had to be up at 4.30 a.m. to have time to eat and meet the rest of the equestrians at 5.30 a.m.[110]

However, this sparseness was uncharacteristic and by 1960, Smythe had begun to travel more widely as an international personality in her own right, and often did so in luxury. Smythe's influence on female equestrians, and British show jumping generally, was considerable, regardless of her Olympic appearances. She was also an international celebrity, much commented on in the society pages as the sporting press. As this overview of the career of Pat Smythe has indicated, women have had the most success in equestrian sport when they owned their own horses, had access to training facilities and could afford to enter events under their own control. As such, combined training competitions such as eventing, dressage or show jumping provided more opportunities than horse racing, on the flat or over hurdles because of the relative costs involved. Even so, any form of equestrianism was an aspirational sport and not open to the wider public at this time.

By the early 1960s, Smythe had established that both riding and writing were lucrative, prestigious and enjoyable work. With 11 books on the market and two more to be published in 1961, Smythe could afford to buy Sudgrove in the Cotswolds, with 150 acres and a pig farm. She then married Sam Koechlin, already father of three small children (Catherine, Sibylle and Dominick) from his first marriage, in September 1963, and the couple had two daughters of their own, Monica and Lucy. Such was the interest when Smythe was married that she created an elaborate plan, including a decoy car, to draw reporters away from the wedding venue.[111] She had already signed exclusive rights for photographs and coverage to the *Daily Express*, for whom she wrote on a number of topics. The revenues from public relations also added to her income streams.

Pat Koechlin-Smythe spent her time between Switzerland and Sudgrove and, having already joined the World Wildlife Fund in 1961, she used her international fame to draw attention to the need for conservation of animals and natural resources. In a very preliminary way, this focus on green issues was to foreshadow questions of sustainability and environmental impact that the Olympic Games has never fully reconciled in its own history.

Having spent from 1948 until 1963 in the elite of global sport, Pat Smythe was to dedicate the rest of her life to conservation projects until her death in 1996. She nevertheless continued her links with domestic equestrianism, and from 1983 to 1986, served as President of the British Show Jumping Association. Smythe was also active in The Riding for the Disabled Association (RDA incorporating Carriage Driving), established in 1969 to provide exercise, therapy and fun. Originally the Advisory Council on Riding for the Disabled in 1965, when membership had grown to 80 member groups it took on Association status. It remains one of the most successful of the sporting charities, with 18,000 volunteers facilitating 430,000 rides and drives for 28,000 participants in 2012. Sam died in 1986 and Pat moved back to the Cotswolds, before a heart condition, which she knew she had since childhood, caused her death in 1996.

In Pat Smythe's lifetime, the number of young people taking up horse riding more than tripled in Britain and many more would take lessons on an informal basis or watch *The Horse of the Year Show* on television. Both Elizabeth II and Princess Margaret attended these occasions and presented the cups personally.[112] Table-top and console television set manufacturers, like Cossor, used show jumping in their advertisements.[113] The Pony Club had a membership of 17,000 in 1947 and by 1962, this was over 30,000; in 1972 it was 40,000 and, after a peak of 43,000 in 1982, its current membership stands at around 32,000. Gibraltar became the first overseas branch of The Pony Club and, by 1964, the largest membership outside of Britain was Australia with 20,043.[114] Second, by a large margin, came the USA, with just under 6,000 affiliates. Smythe was not alone in promoting the various equestrian disciplines to women and young girls, as well as to a male audience, but she was an incredibly successful entrepreneur as a writer, equestrian, expert and transnational public figure before and after her Olympic medal. Readers could vicariously travel through her books, at a time when cheaper commercial flights and better roads made the possibility of touring more realistic.

Smythe's female co-competitors were also significant, whether they were, or were not, Olympians. Iris Kellett overcame a serious bout of tetanus to win the Dublin Grand Prix in 1948 and her career was to be subsequently affected by ill-health. However, the following year, she won the Princess Elizabeth Cup at the White City, London, on her horse 'Rusty' and came second the following year.[115] Pat Moss became part of the British show-jumping team in 1952, before representing the country in a number of international competitions. In 1953, she was presented to the Queen after winning the Queen Elizabeth Cup at White City. Smythe, Kellet and Moss represented the 'new Elizabethan' women of the era and were as popular in the media as on horseback. Moss in particular became better known later as an internationally successful rally driver. Such rivalry meant that horse riding developed a notable female following as a post-war sport.

Similarly, the literary associations of horse-breeding and in particular the spread of children's books relating pony ownership to travel and adventure, developed as a staple from this period onwards. This is a hugely under-researched area affecting how young readers could access commercial books that brought ponies into their living rooms, metaphorically at least, even if they could not own or have access to the real thing. Anne and Lieutenant Jack Bullen formed the Catherston Leweston Stud, near Bridport Dorset, in 1949, from where Anne trained many Dartmoor ponies for children, including gifting Prince Charles 'Juniper' in 1954.[116] As well as training horses, Anne would illustrate children's books with images of her children (Anthony, Charlie, Jane, Jennie, Michael and Sarah), riding their ponies in over 40 books, which she illustrated by writers such as Joanna Cannan, the Pullein-Thompson sisters, Monica Edwards and Violet Needham.[117] In addition, Anne wrote her own books about her first pony, *Darkie* (Country Life, 1950); as well as *Ponycraft* (Littlehampton Book Services, 1963) and *Showing Ponies* (J. A. Allen, 1964).

Although she died at the relatively young age of 52, in 1963, several of Anne's children went on to represent Britain in the Olympic Games, including Jennie Loriston-Clarke who competed in four Olympic Games in the individual and team dressage events, from 1972 to 1976 and again 1984 to 1988. Jennie Loriston-Clarke, MBE has been chairwoman of British Dressage since 2007, and has been chef d'equipe for many dressage teams and a judge at London in 2012. Michael Bullen would finish fourth on 'Cottage Romance', in the individual and team eventing course in Rome in 1960, the leading

British rider, narrowly missing a medal on a course that was so notoriously difficult as to cost two horses their lives. In 1964, Michael Bullen did not finish, in the first Three-Day Event open to mixed teams. His sister Jane, went on to win a gold medal in 1968.

Smythe, Kellet, Moss and the Bullens also helped to popularise equestrian television spectacles, involving female physical courage and elegance.[118] In spite, or perhaps because of, its upper-class associations, the rules of show jumping were relatively easy to understand and time-limits made the events exhilarating. Pat Smythe's glamour was of a somewhat down-to-earth, outdoorsy kind that nevertheless seemed to translate into lavish evening receptions wearing 'posh' frocks with ease. A homogenous upper class 'reading' of equestrian sport is therefore to be resisted, as the expanded middle class in Britain aspired to country-living and, particularly, an equestrian lifestyle which seemed to epitomise upwards mobility.

Conclusion

In some senses, the poem that best reflected much of the media's attitude to British sporting women of the 1950s and 1960s was Sir John Betjeman's *A Subaltern's Love Song*, with lines such as: 'The speed of a swallow, the grace of a boy, with carefullest carelessness, gaily you won... On the floor of her bedroom lie blazer and shorts, And the cream-coloured walls are be-trophied with sports'.[119] The subject of the poem, Miss Joan Hunter Dunn, was 'Furnish'd and burnish'd by Aldershot Sun' and the victor of a 'strenuous singles' tennis match against the poem's narrator. Joan Hunter Dunn was admiringly sexualised by the Subaltern as the poem's dominant force, before the engagement of the couple at the conclusion. The Subaltern in the title had a double meaning of the male writer as both a British army officer and of a lower status than Joan, even though the engagement signalled the heroine's conventional life-choice. Underneath the obvious anxiety of the poem, women were emerging as sports stars in British public life, often mythologised as an all-male club.

If the proverbial 'girl-next-door' could be made exotic, potent and statuesque by her will to win in sport, the same processes could be magnified when the British media considered overseas female Olympians. This was particularly pronounced in British coverage of Eastern European and North American athletes between 1952 and 1960. At the 1960 Rome Olympic Games, Britain finished a respectable eighth overall, courtesy of one gold medal each from athlete Don Thompson (in the 50-kilometre walk) and swimmer Anita Lonsbrough. The rest of the team brought home six silver medals and 12 bronzes. In comparison, the USSR had 43 golds, 29 silvers and 31 bronzes and the US haul was 34; 21; and 16, respectively. Germany, Italy, Australia, Hungary and Poland also won more honours, and so a narrative of a small country fighting gamely against larger rivals was frequently rehearsed in the British press. It did not escape the attention of the media that overseas female competitors were often more specialised, better prepared and had received more detailed coaching than their British counterparts, or that other countries were often prepared to fund more women contestants at Olympic Games.

In the track and field athletics events in Rome, America's Wilma Rudolph would take the 100 metres ahead of Dorothy Hyman for Britain and Giuseppina Leone for Italy. In the 200 metres, Rudolph took the second of her gold medals, ahead of Jutta Heine of the Unified Team of Germany and 19-year-old Hyman. Rudolph would lead the USA's 4 × 100-metres relay team to victory for her third gold medal, ahead of squads from Germany and Poland. Breaking three world records in the process, Rudolph was dubbed 'The Black Gazelle' by the European press for her speed, beauty and grace.[120] The intersection of gender and ethnicity was implicit in what was meant to be a complimentary nickname but which placed the African-American athlete as exotic and 'other'.

For Britain, Elizabeth Jenner was eliminated in the heats of the 100 metres and Jenny Smart came in sixth overall; an impressive result for a 17-year-old.[121] Smart would be eliminated in the heats of the 200 metres, with Jean Hiscock. The British 4 × 100-metres team (Carole Quinton, Dorothy Hyman, Jenny Smart and Mary Bignal) had initially won their heat, before being forced to withdraw in the final, but their qualifying time was over a second behind that recorded by the US team.

In the reinstated 800-metres race, Joy Jordan led the British contingent in sixth place, with both Diane Charles and Phyllis Perkins eliminated in the heats. Charles had come to prominence under her maiden name of Diane Leather, as the first woman to break the 5-minute barrier for the mile distance, just less than a month after Roger Bannister broke the 4-minute mile record in 1954.[122] Although she had won two important silver European championships in the 800 metres, in 1954 and 1958, against leading Soviet contenders, Charles was past her competitive best in Rome. It would not be until 1967 that the International Amateur Athletics Federation recognised a distance of a mile as an official women's event. Again, Diane Leather was ahead of her time and would otherwise, most likely, have become an Olympic medallist.

There were also important British competitors in middle-distance running competing with Leather, such as Phyllis Green, Enid Harding, Connie Slemon, Norah Smalley and Valerie Winn, suggesting strength in depth. Even so, Liudmyla Lysenko took the 800-metres gold medal for the USSR, ahead of Brenda Jones for Australia and Ulla Donath of Germany. It was another controversial finish, as Dixie Willis of Australia led until she stumbled in the home straight and was officially recorded as 'scratched' but does appear to have finished. The 80-metres hurdles was again a win for Russia, with Irina Press changing to the event rather than her usual pentathlon, as this was not yet available on the women's Olympic programme. Second and fourth came Britain's Carole Quinton and Mary Bignal split by Gisela Köhler-Birkemeyer of Germany. Aged 18, Pat Pryce would attend the first of three Olympics Games as an 80-metres hurdles contender, without making the finals.

In the field events, the overwhelming favourite for the high jump was Iolanda Balas of Romania, who beat Britain's Dorothy Shirley and Jarosława Jóźwiakowska-Bieda of Poland for the medals. Two Soviet athletes came in fourth and fifth: Galina Dolya and Taisiya Chenchik. A three-way tie in sixth involved Helen Frith of Australia, Frances Slaap of Great Britain and Inge-Britt Lorentzon of Sweden. Perhaps the biggest disappointment for the British domestic press came in the long jump, where Mary Bignal was expected to win. After doing well in the qualifiers, she seemed discomfited in the finals finishing ninth, 10 places ahead of her compatriot Christina Persighetti. The medals went to Vira Kalashnykova-Krepkina of the Soviet Union, Elżbieta Krzesińska-Duńska of Poland and Hildrun Laufer-Claus of Germany.

In the throwing events, the shot was won by Tamara Press of the Soviet Union ahead of Johanna Hübner-Lüttge for Germany and America's Earlene Brown. Brown therefore became the first American woman to medal in the shot and one of two women to finish in the track and field top three in Rome. Having represented the USA in both the discus and shot put at the Melbourne Olympics, she would go on to compete again in Tokyo and remained friendly with Wilma Rudolph and the Tennessee State University 'Tigerbelles'.[123] In the discus Tamara Press came second behind her compatriot, Nina Romashkova-Ponomaryova and Lia Manoliu of Romania in bronze medal position. The best throwing result for a British woman was Sue Platt's seventh place in the javelin, where Averil Williams was eliminated in qualifying. The medals went to two Russians, Elvīra Ozoliņa and Birutė Kalėdienė, in first and third, split by Dana Zátopková of Czechoslovakia.[124]

In the swimming, Natalie Steward, aged just 17, led the charge for the British in the 100-metres freestyle to win the bronze medal, with team-mate Diana Wilkinson eliminated in the heats. Wilkinson was just 16 years old, and this would be the first of two Olympic appearances, although in spite of being a big favourite with Pat Besford and *World Sports*, she did not win a medal.[125] Natalie Steward's third place was a great achievement, as the race was won by an in-form Dawn Fraser for Australia, with America's Chris von Saltza finishing second. Aged just 16, Nancy 'Nan' Rae, from Motherwell, also finished a creditable sixth overall in the 400-metre freestyle, ahead of Judy Samuel. By the age of 18, Nan Rae had retired from international competition, and so this was to be her only Olympic appearance. Chris von Saltza took the gold in the 400-metre freestyle from Jane Cederqvist of Sweden and Tineke Lagerberg of the Netherlands, with Dawn Fraser finishing in fifth place. The British team for the 4 × 100-metres freestyle relay (Beryl Noakes, Judy Samuel, Christine Harris and Natalie Steward) finished fifth behind the USA, Australia, Germany and Hungary.

In the 100-metres backstroke, the Olympic record holder, Judy Grinham, had retired from amateur sport after pioneering important internationals in Russia, China, South Africa, Australia and around the UK. American Lynn Burke, who won another gold medal as part of the relay team, won easily from Natalie Steward and Satoko Tanaka of Japan. Britain's Sylvia Lewis finished sixth overall, behind Laura Ranwell of South Africa and Rosy Piacentini of France. Lonsbrough's 200-metres backstroke medal was won in a new world and Olympic record time of 2.49.5, under regulations that prevented underwater swimming, and hence slightly slowed times. Wiltrud Urselmann and Barbara Göbel took the remaining medals for Germany, with Britain's Christine Gosden eliminated in the heats.[126] Sheila Watt narrowly missed out on a medal in the 100-metres butterfly, behind Carolyn Schuler of the USA, Marianne Heemskerk of the Netherlands and Australia's Jan Andrew. Jean Oldroyd failed to qualify from the heats. A new 4 × 100-metres medley relay saw Lewis, Lonsbrough, Oldroyd and Steward qualify first from their heat, with Watt replacing Oldroyd in the finals to take fifth overall behind the USA, Australia, Germany and the Netherlands.

In the 3-metre springboard diving event, Britain's Liz Ferris took the bronze medal behind Ingrid Krämer of Germany and Paula Jean Myers-Pope of the USA. Ann Long came in seventh overall. In the 10-metre high dive, Krämer won the gold, ahead of Myers-Pope and Ninel Krutova of Russia. Britain's Norma Thomas came sixth and Ann Long eighth overall.[127]

At the developing Paralympic Games, the number of Stoke Mandeville sports proliferated to netball, bowling, javelin, shot put and snooker. At an international Games inaugurated against Dutch competitors in 1952, Miss Ida Chilton and the four-strong women's archery team were frequently photographed and reported upon. By 1960, 350 men and women from 24 countries would contest what is now regarded as the first Paralympic Games, right after the Olympic closing ceremony in Rome.

Britain sent a 70-strong team, the logistics of which were considerable. Archer Margaret Maughan won the first gold medal for Britain in the Columbia round, having trained with the local toxophilite club in Preston prior to her selection.[128] Lady Susan Masham, who won three medals for swimming in Rome, remembered that she lost one while visiting the Trevi Fountain. Although it was reported in the Italian press that Masham had thrown it into the water, she had in fact tucked it into the side of her wheelchair and it had slipped out.[129] The village where the athletes stayed was built on stilts and the Italian army transported the athletes around, using vehicles and physical strength. After Rome, Paralympic events held in Olympic years remained quadrennial, but annual Stoke Mandeville International Games carried on during the remaining three years of an Olympiad cycle.

The International Games for the Deaf and Dumb, or 'Silent Olympics' were first staged in Paris in 1924, involving the British Deaf Amateur Sports Association and 14 other nations.[130] Sport became an increasingly medicalised as part of physical, emotional and psychological therapy and government funding improved significantly.[131] Organised by the Comité International des Sports Silencieux, and now known as the Deaflympics, these competitions also expanded to incorporate hearing disability and hearing and speech impaired competitors. Subsequent host cities included Amsterdam in 1928; Nuremberg in 1932; London in 1935; Stockholm in 1939; Copenhagen in 1949; Brussels in 1953; and Milan in 1957. In 1949, Seefeld in Austria hosted a 'Winter Silent Games' and subsequent editions were held in Oslo, Norway in 1953 and Oberammergau, West Germany in 1957. However, Britain does not appear to have sent a team to the Winter Silent Games until 1983 and then it was a trio of male skiers.

As with the Olympic Games themselves, women's tennis provided early British medal success in the Deaflympics. Having taken part in Amsterdam without distinguishing herself, British tennis player Marjorie Janet Durlacher would take home a full complement of medals from London in 1935, winning a gold for the mixed doubles tennis with Arthur 'Bill' Smith; a silver in the women's doubles with Lenore Dawson; and a bronze in the women's singles behind the Maere sisters, Antoine and Germaine, of Belgium. Florence Cox won a bronze with Margaret Scheptrand in the women's doubles in 1935, although this second British pairing finished fourth overall. Lenore Dawson had also competed in Amsterdam, and won two bronze medals in Nuremberg for the women's singles and women's doubles with Elsie May Mountain.

In Stockholm four years later, Joan Connew won a women's doubles silver medal with Lilian East and a bronze in the mixed doubles with Max Schrein. The gold medal for the mixed doubles went to Lilian East and Arthur 'Bill' Smith; the latter having a record of winning 12 gold and one silver medals between 1935 and 1957. Joan Connew took sixth place in the women's singles.

Jessie Florence Blanshard (married name Say) was among the first British women track and field athletes to compete in the Deaflympics, taking part in the 1935 London Games and winning a gold medal in the individual 100-metres sprint, and a second gold as part of the 4 × 100-metres relay team with G. Bowlingbroke, Betty Evelyn Shrine (née Gibbons) and Kathy Squires in a world record time of 57 seconds, ahead of Germany and France. Squires took the bronze in the individual 100 metres ahead of Sweden's Aina Kjellin and with Britain's J. Orr in sixth place. In 1939, Blanshard would come third in the individual 100-metres sprint. Doris Ball, Glenys Morgan and Betty Shrine also took part in the athletics.

In the swimming events in London 1935, Marjorie Booth won a bronze in the 100-metres freestyle, Anne Evans came fourth. Katharine Enid Allen was to win the bronze for the 100-metres freestyle in Amsterdam and come fifth in the 200-metres breaststroke final. However, many of the swimming disciplines were not contested by British athletes.

There were just 24 British in the reprised Deaflympics in Copenhagen in 1949, down from a previous record of 40 representatives. The female track and field athletes had a relatively successful meeting in Copenhagen, with Eileen Rose Dukes (née Hornegold) victorious in the 100 metres sprint. Christina Harrison (née Bicknall) was eliminated in the heats. In 1953, 33 members of the team selected and funded by the British Deaf Amateur Sports Association came third overall out of 14 nations, behind a much larger German contingent of 65 athletes and a 40-strong Swedish team. Diana Berman was not placed in the women's tennis in Copenhagen. Four years later in Brussels, Berman took a gold in the women's doubles with Jane Stryker, and a gold in the mixed doubles with Bill Smith. Stryker took the silver medal with John Corcoran. Berman came runner-up in the women's singles to Fredericque van Vyve of Belgium and ahead of Nancy Ann Milburn Paix of France, with Irene Brooker in fourth and Stryker in fifth place, respectively. British women track and field athletes and swimmers were noticeable by their absence.

At the 1957 Milan Deaflympics, 635 athletes from 25 nations competed in nine sports and 11 disciplines. Of the British team of 36, tennis players Margaret Brooker (married name Corcoran), Joan Turner and Joyce Matthews would come in second, third and fourth place, respectively in the women's singles behind Erna Frederiksen of Denmark. This was the beginning of an illustrious medal-winning streak for Brooker who took home the silver in the women's doubles with Joyce Matthews and another second place in the mixed doubles with John Corcoran, her husband. At the Helsinki Games in 1961, Margaret Brooker won a silver in the mixed doubles with her husband, and two bronzes (in the singles and doubles). In Washington, four years later, she won two more silver medals in the doubles events. Again, the women swimmers and track and field athletes were notably absent. There remains a wealth of material to research on this, in terms of where sport fitted into the lifestyle and life-courses of the individuals I have mentioned all-too briefly here. Now approaching its centenary, the Deaflympics are distinguished from all other IOC-sanctioned games because they are organised and run exclusively by members of the deaf community. Only deaf people are eligible to serve on the ICSD board and executive bodies.

The Winter Olympics between 1952 and 1960 were not particularly significant for the British. There was an evident shamateurism, in that men in the military service, and especially officers, often trained more or less full time for events like the bobsleigh and luge. Held from 26 January to 5 February 1956, the Winter Olympics in Italy cost a reported £3 million to stage and were predicted to lose money as a result.[132] A very small British team attended. In the Alpine skiing at the Winter Games Cortina D'Ampezzo in 1956, the women's giant slalom was won by Ossie Reichert for Germany, ahead of Josefine Frandl for Austria and her compatriot Dorothea Hochleitner.[133] The British team of Adeline Pryor, Susanne Holmes and Jocelyn Wardrop Moore finished well down the field with Jeanne Sandrop eliminated from the top 50 who actually got to contest the event. However, over 90 entries were received, requiring a draw to limit numbers, showing an increased popularity for skiing worldwide.

In the slalom, 89 entrants were reduced to 49 contestants in the draw. Britain's Zandra Nowell finished 25th; Sue Holmes and Jocelyn Wardrop Moore in 34th and 35th, respectively, and Addie Pryor was eliminated by the draw. Renée Colliard of Switzerland, Regina Schoepf of Austria and Evgeniya Sidorova of Slovenia took the medals. The downhill podium comprised Madeleine Berthod and Frieda Dånzer of Switzerland and Lucile Wheeler of Canada. Zandra Nowell did best of the British women, in 35th, with Sue Holmes and Jeanne Sandford in 41st and 43rd position, respectively. The inaugural Women's Cross-Country 10 kilometres and relay 3 × 5 kilometres had no British entrants.

Cortina, because of the compact nature of the site was considered to have been an exemplary event, and again figure skating was among some of the most popular events, with new levels of physical power, skill, and beauty. There were notably more triple jumps, and high speed spins, as well as better choreography. Only one young British man, Michael Booker aged 18, contested the men's singles to finish fifth. Aged 16, Joyce Coates partnered with Anthony Holles to come 10th in the mixed pairs, while Carolyn Krau was just 12 when she joined Rodney Ward, two years her senior, to finish in 11th place.

The most senior of the British women's singles contestants Erica Batchelor (aged 22), came in 11th place, while 16-year-old Dianne Peach managed 14th position. Also 16, Yvonne Sugden narrowly missed out on the medals and her fourth place achievement was to be Britain's top finish in Cortina.[134] Podium positions went instead to an All-American top three of Tenley Albright, Caro Heiss and Ingrid Wendl.[135] Krau also took part in the 1960 Winter Olympics in Squaw Valley, California with Patricia Pauley as the only two female British figure skaters of an entire team of four, along with Robin Jones, aged 16, and David Clements, aged 20, in the men's singles.[136]

The official report of Cortina is nevertheless a fascinating document for historians, since it details the ages, weights, heights and body composition of the athletes, by national group. Krau was not just the youngest, but the lightest and smallest of the contestants at just 80 pounds, as might be expected from her age. What is noticeable is the range of body types recorded here, and a growing fascination with medical measurement evidenced in Winter Sports.[137] Indeed, as a series of articles by Harold Abrahams writing as a 'sporting suffragist' in *World Sports* evidences, there were still debates raging about the medical benefits and challenges of women taking part in vigorous sports of all kinds.[138] This historical insight aside, Cortina had been a generally disappointing outcome for the British, who failed to make the medal table.

The 1960 Winter Olympics, held between 18 and 28 February, were even less significant to the historians of British women Olympians, probably because of the cost to the BOA of sending competitors to Squaw Valley in California. Until the Olympic festivities, all that had existed was a hotel with one ski-lift, so if Cortina was bijoux, Squaw Valley was positively obscure when selected to host the Winter Games in 1955. But not for long. Walt Disney, Chairman of the Pageantry Committee, oversaw the Opening Ceremony and he reimagined ancient marble statues as ice sculptures, dramatising Squaw Valley for a worldwide audience, with Vice President Nixon in attendance. In an Olympic first, IBM operated the first computer base to process greater volumes of data, more accurately than ever before and licensed television programmes were transmitted from a purpose-built facility; television broadcast rights increasingly appeared on IOC Executive Board agendas from 1957, as administrators grappled with the financial consequences of the new medium.[139]

There were no British competitors in either the inaugural 500-metres, 1,000-metres, 1,500-metres or 3,000-metres women's speed skating competitions. While Germany and the USSR shared the medals in the shorter sprints, in the longer runs, both the gold medals went to Lidija Skoblikova of USSR. Elwira Seroczynska and Helena Pilejczyk of Poland were podium finishers in the 1,500-metres event. Valentina Stenina (USSR) and Eevi Huttunen (Finland) took silver and bronze in the 3,000 metres.[140] Russia eventually took six of the 12 medals on offer in women's speed skating. In the individual figure skating event, America's 'Ice Queen' Carol Heiss and Barbara Roles split the medals with Sjoukje Dijkstra of the Netherlands. In the mixed pairs, Canadian team Barbara Wagner and Robert Paul gave an almost flawless performance to earn the gold medal. Marika Kilius and Hans Baumler of Germany took the silver medal and Nancy and Ronald Ludington of the USA captured the bronze.

In the Alpine skiing, British women were better represented but largely without distinction. In the downhill, Josephine Gibbs, Wendy Farrington and Susan Holmes finished in 25th place onwards. In the giant slalom, Gibbs was again strongest in 33rd position, with Holmes, Farrington and Scotland's Sonja McCaskie further down the field. In the women's slalom, Gibbs, of Worcestershire, again led the way in 27th place, ahead of Holmes and Yorkshire-born Farrington. The USA, Canada, Switzerland and Germany shared the majority of the women's Alpine medals. Again there were no British female cross-country competitors, where Russia and Sweden took top honours. Soviet skiers, led by Marija Gusakova, Liubov Baranova, Radia Eroshina and Alevtina Kolchina completely dominated the 10-km individual race, whereas the Swedish team won the relay, with Russia in second, followed by Finland. As the 1960 Winter and Summer Olympic concluded, the new decade would see a change in the nature of women's contribution to the Olympic Games more broadly.

To conclude this chapter then, equestrianism remained a popular Olympic and media spectacle for the rest of the twentieth century. Royal interest and the relatively rare sporting phenomenon of women competing against men in a dangerous display were undoubtedly part of the reason for its widening audience. This was not limited to Britain. In addition to her bronze and silver medals for the team and individual dressage in 1956, Liselott Linsenhoff took home a team gold for West Germany in 1968. Winning the individual dressage title in 1972, she also became the first ever woman gold medallist in this discipline. Linsenhoff was part of the West German silver-winning squad in 1972, making a total of five Olympic podiums, before her family moved to Switzerland and she retired from competitive sport.

Future British Olympic female riders included Marion Coakes, who won silver in 1968 to become the first British woman to win an individual medal in show jumping, also contributing to the team score. After marrying the jockey David Mould in 1969, Marion had such public success that she transcended sport to appear in an episode of *Monty Python's Flying Circus* in 1974, along with her horse 'Stroller'. Ann Moore on 'Psalm' won a silver medal in Munich in 1972 but retired in 1974 as the horse, by then 13, was passed his best. Aged 19, Wales' Debbie Johnsey became the youngest competitor in a show-jumping contest, riding 'Moxy' at Montreal in 1976, and narrowly missing out on a medal with fourth place. This earned her *The Daily Express* Sportswoman of the Year award in 1976. She married Gary Plumley, a goalkeeper who played for Newport County and Cardiff City; their daughter Gemma was also an Olympic equestrian hopeful in 2012.

On the one hand, equestrianism in the 1950s and 1960s was clearly a sport in which more girls and women participated than men and boys, estimated in an article of the time to be a ratio of about 20:1.[141] From an already wealthy background, Sheila Willcox (married name Waddington) would go on to win the Eventing trials at Badminton outright for three consecutive years from 1957 to 1959 on her horse, 'High and Mighty'.[142] After marrying a wealthy Lancashire cotton merchant, Waddington looked set to join the ranks of Britain's equestrian Olympians, but a terrible fall in 1971 left her partly paralysed and she had retired before Eventing opened as a mixed Olympic discipline to women in 1972.

On the other hand, elite level equestrianism was by no means a secure way of earning a living, as the survey of Pat Smythe's career has indicated. Lady Mary Rose Williams who, on 'Grey Skies', became the first woman to jump two clear rounds in a Nations Cup at Brussels (1953) and Ostend (1954) was perhaps Smythe's most obvious comparator in terms of international achievements.[143] But Williams' career was both shorter and more straightforward than Smythe's, as she had been born into a privileged family, and was the younger sister of the ninth Duke of Grafton. Williams had been gifted 'Grey Skies' by a friend, and took up equestrianism really seriously after the birth of her daughter, to regain fitness. She would not become an Olympian but was a judge, course builder and integral to the British Show Jumping Association, having also lectured internationally. Similarly, Lady Sarah Fitzalan-Howard would acquire a Smythe-trained stallion called 'Oberon', when she was 17 years old, without quite matching his competitive spirit.[144]

There were also many great British women contemporaries of Pat Smythe who would never compete in an Olympic Games because of the delay in incorporating female contestants into specific disciplines.[145] This was the subject of much contemporary debate, a great deal of it advocating opening the Olympic Three-Day Event to women.[146] There had been precedents outside of Olympic competition. The Badminton Three-Day Event was inaugurated in 1949, and each year had Royal endorsement in person from the Queen. In 1951 Jane Drummond-Hay of Seggieden, Perth, Scotland would place second, riding 'Happy Knight', in the tough Three-Day Event at Badminton, at the age of just 19.[147] In 1953, Badminton was the only FIA internationally-approved eventing competition outside of the Olympics, attracting crowds of over 60,000 people and promoting the sport in Britain, against a wider context where hunting was declining.[148] In comparison, Olympic rules at the Helsinki Three-Day Event effectively excluded women by stipulating that riders must weigh 75 kilos (165 pounds) including saddle and weight cloth.

By 1972, the Olympic weight restriction was lifted and Bridget Parker, riding 'Cornish Gold', would become part of the British gold medal winning Eventing team at the Munich Olympic Games, after being substituted for Debbie West when her horse, 'Baccarat', went lame. Like the other woman in the victorious side, Mary Gordon-Watson, riding 'Cornishman V', Bridget Parker remained on the British senior selection panel after retiring from competition and went on to breed several notable offspring of 'Cornish Gold'. Like other charismatic horses, 'Cornishman V' would briefly become a media star, appearing as himself in 1973 in the film *Dead Cert*, adapted from the Dick Francis novel of the same name.

There were other exclusions: the outstanding woman rider of her generation, Caroline Bradley, was not selected for the 1976 Olympics, having been ruled a professional for accepting prize money. Though recognised with an OBE, Bradley had eventually bought her grey horse, 'Tigre', for £12,000 in 1976, but was forced to sell him for eight times that amount five years later. In 1983, Bradley died of heart failure shortly after competing at a show, at the age of just 37, the condition generally considered to be the result of overwork, supporting herself and her horses.[149]

Four years later, the rules regarding professionalism were reclassified and equestrianism became an Open sport. Nevertheless, the wider participation of girls and women from the 1950s and 1960s onwards continued to reap benefits pioneered at the elite level. Equestrianism, thanks to its links with the Queen and the upper classes, was an aspirational sport and it continues to be an expensive hobby today, whether at Pony Club level or serious three-day eventing.

It is little surprise that it is the Queen's daughter, Anne, and her granddaughter, Zara, who became the family Olympians given this heritage. Princess Anne competed at the highest level since winning a gold medal at the European Eventing Championships in 1971, held at Burghley, and was voted the BBC Sports Personality of the Year; as was Zara, in 2006. At the European Eventing Championships in 1975, Princess Anne won two silver medals in the individual and team event, riding 'Doublet'. Princess Anne appeared at the Montreal Olympics in 1976 riding the Queen's horse, 'Goodwill'.

The first competitive appearance by a member of the royal family merited a good deal of comment in popular culture and Princess Anne seemed to relish this wider public role, becoming the first member of the Royal Family to appear as a contestant on a television quiz-show, when she competed on the BBC panel game *A Question of Sport* in February 1987 as a member of Emlyn Hughes' team after he had previously identified her as a male jockey in an earlier programme.[150] Although the BBC had sent a recording of Hughes' mistake as a courtesy in case she wanted to withdraw the excerpt, Princess Anne took the opportunity to make a joke at her own expense.

Retiring from active competition, The Princess Royal remained highly active in both the British Olympic Association and the International Olympic Committee, as well as holding the Presidency of the Fédération Équestre Internationale (FEI) from 1986 until 1994, in addition to many charity commitments, which also included riding and sport in a portfolio of over 200 aid organisations. Zara competed in the 2012 London Olympics riding 'High Kingdom', and won a silver medal in the team Eventing. Like the rest of the team, Zara received her medal from her mother, who was a member of the London Organising Committee for the Olympic Games and represented Great Britain and the International Olympic Committee at the 2014 Sochi Winter Olympics in Russia. In February 2015, the Princess Royal became one of the first female honorary members of the Royal and Ancient Golf Club of St Andrews when the organisation belatedly opened its doors to women members. Evidently, the spirit of pioneering New Elizabethanism continues into the twenty-first century.

Notes

1. Jean Williams 'The Immediate Legacy of Pat Smythe: The Pony-Mad Teenage Girl in Post-War British Culture' *New Elizabethans 1953–2013: Nation, Culture, and Modern Identity* 13 and 14 June 2013 University of London: Institute of English Studies.
2. Neville Cardus 'Let Our Cricketers Determine to Be New Elizabethans' *World Sports: The International Sports Magazine June 1952* London: Country and Sporting Publications, 1952 pp. 8–9.
3. Cecil Bear 'Sporting Drama: 1954' *World Sports: The International Sports Magazine December 1954* London: Country and Sporting Publications, 1954 p. 33.
4. Susan Noel 'Women in Sport' *World Sports: The International Sports Magazine January 1952* London: Country and Sporting Publications, 1952 pp. 34–35.

5 Cecil Bear 'Happy and Glorious' *World Sports: The International Sports Magazine May 1953* London: Country and Sporting Publications, 1953 p. 5.
6 Frank Lindley 'Look You' *World Sports: The International Sports Magazine April 1957* London: Country and Sporting Publications, 1957 p. 17.
7 Stephen Gundle *Glamour: A History* Oxford: Oxford University Press, 2008 pp. 207–208.
8 Sulo Kolkka (ed.) (translated by Alex Matson) *The Official Report of The Organising Committee For the Games of the XV Olympiad Helsinki 1952* Helsinki: Werner Söderström Osakeyhtiöm Porvoo, 1955 p. 541.
9 Otto Mayer 'Letter to Sandy Duncan 5 May 1956' IOC Archive, Lausanne p. 1.
10 Lieutenant Colonel Harry Llewellyn 'Story From Stockholm: The Equestrian Olympics' *World Sports: The International Sports Magazine July 1956* London: Country and Sporting Publications, 1956 p. 5.
11 Stephanie Daniels and Anita Tedder *A Proper Spectacle: Women Olympians 1900–1936* Dunstable, Bedfordshire: Priory Press, 2000 pp. 25–26.
12 Count Clary *Letter to IOC: Participation Des Amazones aux Jeux Equestres 13 May 1934 22 Avenue George Clemenceau Nice* IOC Archive Women and Sport File.
13 David Maraniss *Rome 1960: The Olympics That Changed the World* New York: Simon & Schuster, 2008 p. xiii.
14 Cecil Bear 'Russia Joins IOC: Vienna Congress Report' *World Sports: The International Sports Magazine July 1951* London: Country and Sporting Publications, 1951 p. 5.
15 International Olympic Committee *Executive Committee Minutes, Lausanne 3 May 1954 Committee* IOC Archive, Lausanne p. 2.
16 International Olympic Committee *Minutes of the 50th Session of the International Olympic Committee 18 June 1955* IOC Archive, Lausanne pp. 57–8.
17 Sulo Kolkka (ed.) *The Official Report Helsinki 1952* pp. 94–95.
18 Anon. 'Swedish Riders Triumph in the Olympics' *The Sunday Herald* 17 June 1956 p. 37 IOC Archive Women and Sport File.
19 Sulo Kolkka (ed.) *The Official Report Helsinki 1952* p. 519.
20 Cecil Bear 'The Blue Streak' *World Sports: Official Magazine of the British Olynmpic Association April 1950* London: Country and Sporting Publications, 1950 pp. 24–25.
21 Joe Galli 'Grand Finale: Shirley De La Hunty' *World Sports: Official Magazine of the British Olympic Association March 1955* London: Country and Sporting Publications, 1955 p. 7.
22 Cecil Bear 'Britain's Fastest 1950' *World Sports: Official Magazine of the British Olympic Association December 1950* London: Country and Sporting Publications, 1950 pp. 24–25.
23 Jack Crump 'Jean Desforges: Champion of Women's Rights' *World Sports: Official Magazine of the British Olympic Association March 1954* London: Country and Sporting Publications, 1954 pp. 22–23.
24 Susan Noel 'Some Talk of (Sheila) Alexander' *World Sports: Official Magazine of the British Olympic Association June 1951* London: Country and Sporting Publications, 1951 pp. 22–23.
25 Susan Noel "Women in Sport' *World Sports Official Magazine of the British Olympic Association February 1953* London: Country and Sporting Publications, 1953 pp. 13.
26 Malcolm Brodie 'Her Supreme Highness: World Record for Thelma' *World Sports Official Magazine of the British Olympic Association June 1956* London: Country and Sporting Publications, 1956 pp. 26–27.

27 Willy Meisl 'Spotlight on Soviet Sport' *World Sports: The International Sports Magazine August 1951* London: Country and Sporting Publications, 1951 pp. 12–13.
28 Emil Zatopek 'My Wife Dana: As Told in Interviews to Norris McWhirter' *World Sports: The International Sports Magazine December 1955* London: Country and Sporting Publications, 1955 p. 5.
29 Jack Crump 'Jack Crump's Gossip' *World Sports: The International Sports Magazine August 1954* London: Country and Sporting Publications, 1954 pp. 23–25.
30 Pat Besford 'Swim Chiefs Need Vision' *World Sports: The International Sports Magazine September 1955* London: Country and Sporting Publications, 1955 p. 42.
31 Pat Besford 'It's Warmer in Winter' *World Sports: The International Sports Magazine January 1952* London: Country and Sporting Publications, 1952 pp. 36–37.
32 Pat Besford 'A Lesson From Lillian' *World Sports: Official Magazine of the British Olympic Association May 1954* London: Country and Sporting Publications, 1954 p. 13.
33 Jeane Hoffman 'Everything's Just Pat: The Girl Who is America's 5 Star Diving Champion' *World Sports: The International Sports Magazine August 1951* London: Country and Sporting Publications, 1951 pp. 30–31.
34 Susan Noel 'Women in Sport' *World Sports: Official Magazine of the British Olympic Association October 1956* London: Country and Sporting Publications Ltd 1956 p. 30.
35 The Organizing Committee of the Games of the XVII Olympiad *The Official Report of the Organising Committee The Games of the XVII Olympiad Rome 1960 Volume 2* Rome: Carl Colombo Printing, 1960 pp. 269–270.
36 Sulo Kolkka *The Official Report Helsinki 1952* p. 440.
37 The Organizing Committee of the Games of the XVII Olympiad *The Official Report Rome 1960* pp. 423–433.
38 A. Anderson 'Letters to World Sports: 82 Lochlea Road Glasgow S3 Scotland' *World Sports: Official Magazine of the British Olynmpic Association September 1952* London: Country and Sporting Publications, 1952 p. 20.
39 J. P. W. Mallalieu MP 'Olympic Games: Should The Government Help? No' *World Sports: Official Magazine of the British Olympic Association February 1956* London: Country and Sporting Publications, 1956 p. 5; Dr Willy Meisl 'Olympic Games: Should The Government Help? Yes' *World Sports: Official Magazine of the British Olympic Association March 1956* London: Country and Sporting Publications, 1956 pp. 36–37.
40 Judy Grinham *Water Babe* London: Oldbourne Book Co. Ltd 1960 p. 181.
41 Raissa Kuts 'Kuts-by His Wife' *World Sports: Official Magazine of the British Olympic Association August1957* London: Country and Sporting Publications Ltd 1957 pp. 7–9.
42 Cecil Bear 'Round The World' *World Sports: Official Magazine of the British Olympic Association Octobr1956* London: Country and Sporting Publications Ltd 1956 p. 42.
43 Pat Smythe *Leaping Life's Fences* Wiltshire: The Sportsman's Press, 1992.
44 Pat Smythe *Leaping Life's Fences* p. 1.
45 The Pony Club 'History' www.pcuk.org/About-Us/History accessed 27 January 2016.
46 Horrace A. Laffaye *The Evolution of Polo* Jefferson: McFarland and Company, 2009 p. 114.
47 Guillermo MacLoughlin Bréard 'From Shepherds to Polo Players: Irish-Argentines from the First to the Last Chukker' *Irish Migration Studies in Latin America* 6: 1 March 2008 pp. 68–69.
48 Pat Smythe *Jump For Joy* Watford: The Companion Book Club, 1955 p. 42.

49 Fédération Équestre Internationale *History of Equestrian Events at the Games of the XV Olympiad: Factsheet* Lausanne: Fédération Équestre Internationale p. 1 http://history.fei.org/sites/default/files/1952_Helsinki.pdf accessed 11 August 2019.
50 Susan Noel 'Equal Play' *World Sports: The International Sports Magazine March 1953* London: Country and Sporting Publications, 1953 p. 31.
51 Cecil Bear 'Pageant in the Sun' *World Sports: The International Sports Magazine December 1951* London: Country and Sporting Publications, 1951 pp. 24–25.
52 Sulo Kolkka (ed.) *The Official Report Helsinki 1952* p. 534.
53 Harry Llewellyn *Foxhunter in Pictures* London: Hodder and Stoughton, 1953; Cecil Bear 'Foxhunter at Home' *World Sports Official Magazine of the British Olympic Association January1953* London: Country and Sporting Publications, 1953 pp. 24–25.
54 Tony Collings 'Horse Sense at Harringay' *World Sports Official Magazine of the British Olympic Association October 1953* London: Country and Sporting Publications, 1953 pp. 18–19.
55 Phyllis Hinton 'Horse With Perfect Manners' *World Sports: Official Magazine of the British Olympic Association July 1950* London: Country and Sporting Publications, 1950 pp. 26–27.
56 Cecil Bear 'Bannister: An Immortal' *World Sports February 1955* London: Country and Sporting Publications, 1955 p. 9.
57 Lucozade 'Pat Smythe…Another Lucozade Enthusiast' *World Sports September 1955* London: Country and Sporting Publications, 1955 p. 10.
58 Phil Pilley 'Bumbledom or Wisdom?' *World Sports: The International Sports Magazine December 1958* London: Country and Sporting Publications, 1958 p. 5.
59 Harold Abrahams 'The Writing and Broadcasting Case' *World Sports: Official Magazine of the British Olympic Association May 1957* London: Country and Sporting Publications, 1957 p. 34.
60 Jean Williams 'The Immediate Legacy Of Pat Smythe: The Pony-Mad Teenager in 1950s and 1960s Britain' in Dave Day (ed.) *Sporting Lives* Manchester: MMU Institute for Performance Research, 2011 pp. 16–29.
61 Deane McGowan 'Brasher Speaks as he Runs – In a Straight Line *The New York Times* 4 January 1957 p. 23.
62 Pat Smythe 'Pat Smythe Tells Her Own Story: Thrills, Spills, Anxiety' *World Sports: The International Sports Magazine July 1955* London: Country and Sporting Publications, 1955 pp. 5–8.
63 Cecil Bear 'Pirie-Sportsman of the Year' *World Sports: Official Magazine of the British Olympic Association February 1964* London: Country and Sporting Publications, 1956 p. 7.
64 Pat Smythe *Leaping Life's Fences* p. 67.
65 The Organizing Committee for the Equestrian Games *The Official Report of the Organizing Committee for the Equestrian Games of the XVIth Olympiad Stockholm 1956* Stockholm: Esselte Aktiebolag, 1959 p. 40.
66 The Organizing Committee for the Equestrian Games *The Official Report of the Equestrian Games Stockholm 1956* p. 246.
67 Pat Smythe *Leaping Life's Fences* p. 71.
68 Cecil Bear 'Stars of a Decade: Sports Ten Greatest Years' *World Sports: The International Sports Magazine December 1957* London: Country and Sporting Publications, 1957 Front Cover.
69 The Organizing Committee for the Equestrian Games *The Official Report of the Equestrian Games Stockholm 1956* p. 86.
70 Cecil Bear 'A Woman's World' *World Sports: Official Magazine of the British Olympic Association November 1956* London: Country and Sporting Publications, 1956 p. 56.

71 Edward A. Doyle (ed.) *The Official Report of the Organising Committee For the Games of the XVI Olympiad Melbourne 1956* Melbourne: W. M. Houston Government Printer, 1958 p. 2.
72 Edward A. Doyle (ed.) *The Official Report Melbourne 1956* pp. 347–349.
73 Joe Galli 'Our Fair Lady' *World Sports: The International Sports Magazine February 1958* London: Country and Sporting Publications, 1958 pp. 8–9.
74 Walter Wünsche 'Meet The Speed Typist: Christa Stubnick Germany' *World Sports: Official Magazine of the British Olympic Association June 1956* London: Country and Sporting Publications, 1956 pp. 36–37.
75 Ian Buchanan *British Olympians: A Hundred Years of Gold Medallists* London: Guinness Publishing, 1991 pp. 176–177.
76 C. L. de Beaumont 'The Fascination of Fencing' *World Sports: Official Magazine of the British Olympic Association February 1954* London: Country and Sporting Publications, 1954 p. 13.
77 Doug Gardner 'Fly-Away Paul Girl' *World Sports: Official Magazine of the British Olympic Association May 1957* London: Country and Sporting Publications, 1957 pp. 26–27.
78 A. R. Mills 'Now It May Be Hurdler Heather' *World Sports: The International Sports Magazine November 1958* London: Country and Sporting Publications, 1958 pp. 60–61.
79 Hunter Davies 'Interview: Still doing her personal best at 60' *The Independent* 7 December 1993 www.independent.co.uk/life-style/interview-still-doing-her-personal-best-at-60-in-the-fifties-june-paul-ran-like-the-wind-for-britain-1465983.html accessed 18 January 2015.
80 Sean Kyle 'A Timekeeper's Error Can Mean the Shattering of a Dream' *World Sports: Official Magazine of the British Olympic Association February 1957* London: Country and Sporting Publications, 1957 p. 36.
81 Malcolm Brodie 'Her Supreme Highness' *World Sports* pp. 26–27.
82 Thelma Hopkins 'Our Plans For Melbourne' *World Sports Official Magazine of the British Olympic Association April 1956* London: Country and Sporting Publications, 1956 p. 15.
83 Susan Noel 'Women in Sport: Let's Jump Back 20 Years' *World Sports Official Magazine of the British Olympic Association March 1956* London: Country and Sporting Publications, 1956 p. 38.
84 Cecil Bear 'Britain's Athletes For Olympics' *World Sports: The International Sports Magazine September 1956* London: Country and Sporting Publications, 1956 p. 26.
85 Liu Ping-Wen 'Champion From China' *World Sports: Official Magazine of the British Olympic Association February 1958* London: Country and Sporting Publications, 1958 p. 20.
86 Norris McWhirter 'Zybina: Strongest Woman in The World?' *World Sports: The International Sports Magazine January 1955* London: Country and Sporting Publications, 1955 pp. 26–7; Norris McWhirter 'Ballerina Nina' *World Sports: The International Sports Magazine September 1955* London: Country and Sporting Publications, 1955 pp. 30–31.
87 The Amateur Swimming Association *ASA Swimming Instruction* London: The Amateur Swimming Association and Educational Productions Ltd, revised edition 1963; first published in 1919 p. 100.
88 Pat Besford 'Margaret Edwards: Sweet Sixteen' *World Sports: The International Sports Magazine June 1955* London: Country and Sporting Publications, 1955 pp. 26–27.
89 Judy Grinham *Water Babe* p. 27.

90 International Olympic Committee *Swimming Medallists Melbourne/Stockholm 1956* www.olympic.org/content/results-and-medallists/gamesandsportsummary/ accessed 12 November 2015.
91 James Huntingdon-Whitely and Richard Holt *The Book of British Sporting Heroes* London: National Portrait Gallery, 1999.
92 Judy Grinham *Water Babe* London: Oldbourne Book Co. Ltd 1960 p. 181.
93 Pat Besford 'Stop the Caution and Go On Working' *World Sports: The International Sports Magazine April 1956* London: Country and Sporting Publications, 1956 p. 13.
94 Judy Grinham *Water Babe* p. 54.
95 Sam Rockett 'The Cruel Sea: Channel Swimming' *World Sports Official Magazine of the British Olympic Association April 1956* London: Country and Sporting Publications, 1956 pp. 40–41.
96 Pat Besford 'The Magician's Great Spell' *World Sports: Official Magazine of the British Olympic Association May 1956* London: Country and Sporting Publications, 1956 p. 17.
97 Graham Budd 'Lots 399 to 406: Eleanor (Helen Orr) Gordon 1948–1956' *Graham Budd Auction Catalogue GB21* London: Graham Budd Auctions, 2012 pp. 105–107.
98 Pat Besford 'The Gosden Girl' *World Sports: The International Sports Magazine August 1958* London: Country and Sporting Publications, 1958 p. 60.
99 Pat Besford 'She's States-Aided!' *World Sports: The International Sports Magazine April 1958* London: Country and Sporting Publications, 1958 p. 31.
100 Cecil Bear 'The Long Way Down' *World Sports: The International Sports Magazine November 1955* London: Country and Sporting Publications, 1955 pp. 24–25.
101 Frederick Kingley 'England Will Lead Them A Sword Dance' *World Sports: The International Sports Magazine July 1959* London: Country and Sporting Publications, 1959 p. 31.
102 C. L. de Beaumont 'Gillian Foils 'em!' *World Sports: Official Magazine of the British Olympic Association May 1954* London: Country and Sporting Publications, 1954 p. 27.
103 International Olympic Committee *Swimming Medallists Melbourne/Stockholm 1956* www.olympic.org/content/results-and-medallists/gamesandsportsummary/ accessed 12 November 2015.
104 International Olympic *Committee Executive Committee, National Olympic Committees, and International Sports Federations 7 and 8 June 1957* IOC Museum and Archive, Lausanne p. 10.
105 Doug Gardner 'When The Sheen Goes Off Our Fencing' *World Sports: The International Sports Magazine March 1959* London: Country and Sporting Publications, 1959 p. 27.
106 Lieutenant Colonel 'Mike' Ansell 'The Leap To Fame' *World Sports: The International Sports Magazine October 1955* London: Country and Sporting Publications, 1955 pp. 22–23.
107 The Organizing Committee of the Games of the XVII Olympiad *The Official Report Rome 1960* p. 445.
108 Dawn Palethorpe *My Horses and I* London: Country and Sporting Life Publications, 1956.
109 Dawn Palethorpe *My Horses and I*; Hylton Cleaver 'Books' *World Sports: Official Magazine of the British Olympic Association June 1956* London: Country and Sporting Publications, 1956 p. 40.
110 Pat Smythe *Jumping Around the World* p. 2.
111 Pat Smythe *Leaping Life's Fences* pp. 101–102.

112 Tony Collings 'High Sport of the Horseman's Year' *World Sports: The International Sports Magazine* July 1951 London: Country and Sporting Publications, 1951 p. 15.
113 Cossor 'Crystal Clear Cossor, Reception is So Realistic' *World Sports: The International Sports Magazine* July 1956 London: Country and Sporting Publications, 1956 p. 20.
114 Norman Fox 'Kindergarten of The Saddle' *World Sports: The International Sports Magazine* November 1964 London: Country and Sporting Publications, 1964 pp. 48–49.
115 Tony Collings 'High Spot of Horseman's Year' *World Sports* p. 15.
116 The Osborne Studio Gallery 'Anne Bullen' *The Osborne Studio Gallery London* www.osg.uk.com/artists/anne-bullen/ accessed 5 August 2017.
117 Anna Tyzack 'Life follows art for a pony-mad dynasty' *The Telegraph* 3 October 2012 www.telegraph.co.uk/lifestyle/9583938/Life-follows-art-for-a-pony-mad-dynasty.html accessed 3 October 2017.
118 Jeffrey Hill 'Patricia Rosemary Smythe (1928–1996)' *Oxford Dictionary of National Biography* Oxford University Press www.oxforddnb.com/view/article/62144 accessed 1 December 2015.
119 The Earl of Birkenhead (ed.) *John Betjeman's Collected Poems* London: John Murray 1962 pp. 105–107.
120 International Olympic Committee 'Wilma Rudolph Stormed to Gold: Rome 1960' www.olympic.org/videos/rome-1960-wilma-rudolph-stormed-to-gold accessed 25 August 2019.
121 The Organizing Committee of the Games of the XVII Olympiad *The Official Report Rome 1960* p. 184.
122 Jack Crump 'Jack Crump's Gossip' *World Sports: Official Magazine of the British Olympic Association* June 1954 London: Country and Sporting Publications, 1954 pp. 36–37.
123 Cecil Bear 'Off the Beaten Track: Earlene Brown' *World Sports: Official Magazine of the British Olympic Association* November 1956 London: Country and Sporting Publications, 1956 p. 67.
124 The Organizing Committee of the Games of the XVII Olympiad *The Official Report Rome 1960* pp. 211–212.
125 Pat Besford 'Diana-Blackpool Tower of Strength' *World Sports: The International Sports Magazine* September 1957 London: Country and Sporting Publications, 1957 pp. 21–23.
126 The Organizing Committee of the Games of the XVII Olympiad *The Official Report Rome 1960* pp. 591–592.
127 The Organizing Committee of the Games of the XVII Olympiad *The Official Report Rome 1960* pp. 603–605.
128 Mandeville Legacy *Margaret Maughan interview about Rome* 26 September 2013 www.youtube.com/watch?v=5PtL-RT7UOo accessed 11 August 2015.
129 Mandeville Legacy *Lady Susan Masham interview about Rome* 27 September 2013 www.youtube.com/watch?v=5PtL-RT7UOo accessed 11 August 2015.
130 P. G. Piley 'The Silent Games' *World Sports: Official Magazine of the British Olympic Association* December 1956 London: Country and Sporting Publications, 1956 p. 37.
131 Vanessa Heggie *A History of British Sports Medicine* Manchester: Manchester University Press, 2011 pp. 84–86.
132 Dr Willy Meisl 'Time Races On: Winter Olympics Report' *World Sports: Official Magazine of the British Olympic Association* March 1955 London: Country and Sporting Publications, 1955 pp. 20–21.

133 Comitato Olimpico Nazionale Italiano *The Official Report VII Giochi Olimpici Invernalivii: VII Olympic Winter Games Cortina d'Ampezzo 1956* Rome: Società Grafica Romana, 1956 p. 584.
134 Nigel Brown 'American Outlook-(Al) Bright!' *World Sports: The International Sports Magazine January 1956* London: Country and Sporting Publications, 1956 pp. 26–27.
135 Susan Noel Women in Sport' *World Sports: The International Sports Magazine January 1955* London: Country and Sporting Publications, 1955 p. 32.
136 Robert Rubin (ed.) *The Official Report of the VIII Winter Olympic Games Squaw Valley California 1960* Squaw Valley: California State Printing Office, 1960 pp. 147–148.
137 Comitato Olimpico Nazionale Italiano *The Official Report Cortina d'Ampezzo 1956* pp. 697–715.
138 Harold Abrahams 'These Doctors Talk Nonsense' *World Sports March 1955* London: Country and Sporting Publications, 1955 p. 28; Harold Abrahams 'Does This, Affect This-No!' *World Sports April 1955* London: Country and Sporting Publications, 1955 pp. 28–29.
139 International Olympic Committee 'Minutes of the Executive Committee 3 and 4 June 1957' IOC Archive, Lausanne p. 1.
140 Robert Rubin (ed.) *The Official Report Squaw Valley, California 1960* p. 154.
141 Captain C. E. G Hope 'Youth in The Saddle' *World Sports Official Magazine of the British Olympic Association February 1953* London: Country and Sporting Publications, 1953 p. 36.
142 Doug Gardner '£-S-D and the Saddle' *World Sports: The International Sports Magazine April 1959* London: Country and Sporting Publications, 1959 pp. 40–41.
143 Susan Noel 'Women in Sport' *World Sports: The International Sports Magazine June 1954* London: Country and Sporting Publications, 1954 p. 34.
144 George Rutherford 'Her Kingdom Is The Horse' *World Sports: The International Sports Magazine October 1958* London: Country and Sporting Publications, 1958 p. 25.
145 Hylton Cleaver 'Up The Spurs!' *World Sports: The International Sports Magazine October 1956* London: Country and Sporting Publications, 1956 p. 15.
146 Hylton Cleaver *They've Won Their Spurs* London: Robert Hale Limited, 1956.
147 Susan Noel 'Women in Sport' *World Sports: The International Sports Magazine July 1951* London: Country and Sporting Publications, 1951 pp. 29–30.
148 Tony Collings 'Three Red-Letter Days' *World Sports Official Magazine of the British Olympic Association April 1953* London: Country and Sporting Publications, 1953 pp. 16–17.
149 Gilliam Newsum (foreword by Pat Koechlin-Smythe) *Women and Horses* Hampshire: The Sportsman's Press, 1988 p. 18.
150 Carl Giles 'If HRH puts her horse down in that puddle once more, HRH is going to lose quite a lot of my goodwill' *Sunday Express* 29 October 1972.

Chapter 7

Britain's Olympic Golden Girls and the changing media industry 1964–1984

The decline of amateurism and the rise of sports medicine

Introduction: quasi-medical narratives questioning womanhood in sport

On 20 June 1984, the Royal Shakespeare Company (RSC) premiered *Golden Girls*, by playwright Louise Page at their smaller theatre, the Other Place, in Stratford-upon-Avon. Published in March 1985, *Golden Girls* featured a cast of three Black-British and two white female aspiring Olympic track and field athletes. The plot followed the selection process, whereby one of the five principal characters would be left out of a squad of four, who would go on to compete as the British women's 4 × 100-metres relay team at a fictional forthcoming Athens Olympic Games. The over-arching paradigm of the piece was the high personal cost of female ambition, and it was a critical success, moving to London's Barbican shortly after its debut. The subtext located Olympic sporting triumph as secondary to a female athlete's aspirations to motherhood and, in this, the play looked backwards as well as forwards, as this quotation shows: 'You sound like the fairy godmother in Adidas'.[1]

The drama also highlighted how important Black, Asian and ethnic minority women would be to Britain's Olympic history by the opening night of the play. As the chapter on Margaret Wellington has shown, there were important earlier examples of those with Jewish and mixed ethnic heritage who had represented Britain previously, but the number of female ethnic minority Olympians, especially among diverse black and Asian communities, would increase exponentially from the 1980s onwards.

This chapter, the longest in this book, analyses a 20-year timescale, which saw an unprecedented growth in the number of participants and sports codes at the Summer and Winter Olympic and Paralympic Games. It would be impossible to name all of the British female participants in diverse Olympic festivals over this time period, as the previous chapters have attempted to do, without becoming list-like and tedious for the reader. Appendix 1 details the British female contingent at the 1964 Olympic Games; Appendix 2 summarises the British Olympic women's team in 1968; Appendix 3 considers the squad in 1972 and Appendix 4 for 1976, Appendix 5 for 1980 and

Appendix 6 for 1984. By this time, the women's team would number over 100 across diverse sports and disciplines. The details are taken from the official reports, cross-referenced with BOA notes where possible and so should be read in conjunction with other works aiming to provide a complete overview, as new evidence becomes available.

Nor has the intention of the book been to register a definitive roll-call of female Olympians, even while seeking to acknowledge those who were part of successive British teams, as well as those who won medals. It was a conscious decision not to include the names of competitors at the Stoke Mandeville Games in appendices, since the period 1964 to 1984 marked a gradual and contested integration between several articulations of disability sport and the Olympic movement, which needs a focused treatment in itself, and there is not space to do that justice here. Indeed, by the time of Ludwig Guttmann's death in 1980, there had been something of a strain on whether international events could be called an Olympiad for the disabled. The compromise term 'Paralympic' was first used in Seoul in 1988. However, what follows does cover some key aspects of disability sport, and many of the significant female athletes are discussed. There are many statistical reference manuals on these and other topics. Alternatively, I have tried to show how ambiguity can nuance those statistical accounts.

While amateurism clearly shortened many individual women's sporting careers, and not necessarily by their own choice, the constant need for redefinition, in the face of sport-specific professionalism, continued throughout the twentieth century. What then, of important pioneers like Elaine Burton, Mary Rand, Dorothy Hyman and Dame Mary Glen Haig? Be they upper, middle or working class, these diverse women's sporting careers were shaped, at least in part, by amateur and voluntary ideals. What of professional and semi-professional women in Britain's Olympic tradition, such as Mary Peters who was suspected of shamateurism because she worked for a while in a local gymnasium? This chapter begins to answer those questions and argues that amateurism, heavily contested in the period between 1964 and 1984, had very personal effects on women's lives. What follows in this chapter are the key indicative changes during the 1964–1984 period as amateurism declined as a defining Olympic concept in the organisation of the Winter and Summer Games. Instead, by 1988, the IOC sought to host the pinnacle of several 'world championships' under the Olympic umbrella, 'Open', to professionals.

A separate, but related, aspect of the amateur debate, which dominated this period was the quasi-medicalisation of sex testing and quasi-scientific surveillance of women's bodies. This was ostensibly done to 'protect' female sport but it was often men who chose to define what it meant to be an 'essentially' female athlete. Gender binary is a construct that sport, more than any other industry, seeks to reinforce. This debate was heightened by Cold War tensions, mainly generated by tabloid media discourses.

There was a lot of respect between female athletes on either side of the East-West divide. But there was no doubt that the Cold War raised the profile of women's sport more than ever before. East Germany had to wait until 1956 to enter the Olympics as the junior partner in an all-German team, and it was not until 1964 that Eastern athletes outperformed their Western team colleagues.[2] Soon after, entering the Olympics for the first time as an independent team in Mexico City 1968, East Germany would outperform the Federal Republic of Germany (FRG) medal tally and would do so again at the Munich Olympics of 1972. By the 1976 Summer Olympic Games, East Germany ranked second and remained there in 1980 and 1988. By the end of the period discussed in this chapter, elite sport and particularly female track and field athletic records, would garner first recognition for the East German sport system involving a relatively small country of 17 million citizens and then infamy as the extent of State-condoned doping showed itself to have high human costs.[3] In 1980, 49 per cent of German Democratic Republic (GDR) medals were won by women, although they constituted 36.4 per cent of the team.[4]

Amidst these two major controversies, of amateurism and what constitutes a medically 'authentic' woman in sport, this chapter looks in depth, first, at the career of the Golden Girls in track and field athletics. It then considers the case study of 'all-rounder' and pentathlon gold medallist Mary Peters, and then in a subsequent section, the fencer Dame Mary Alison Glen-Haig, who became only the third woman to join the IOC Executive in 1982. The chapter concludes as amateurism gave way to the new 'Open era' and Olympic sport became tied more so than ever before with commercialism, popular culture, sponsorship and profit.

Depictions of characters in the *Golden Girls* play resonate with key themes that this chapter explores, and so are worth summarising here. Vivien Blackwood, the team doctor, had moved into medicine as a result of not being able to go to the Helsinki Olympic Games in 1952 because the longest track and field event was the 200 metres, and she was a middle-distance runner.[5] Black-British athletes Dorcas Ableman and Muriel Farr were coming towards the end of their athletic careers, and this is highlighted when they are joined by 17-year-old Janet Morris in the 4 × 100-metres relay team, along with Sue Kinder who is blonde and white. Having been dropped for a race at Gateshead, Dorcas begins to use Hydromel, a performance-enhancing drug and wins back her place in the British Olympic team at Crystal Palace. However, her return is at the expense of Pauline Peterson, a white athlete who struggles with her nerves on big competitive occasions but who runs 'clean'.

In the play, the most ambitious of the runners, Dorcas Ableman, is able to buy the banned substance Hydromel because Ortolan, a cosmetic company, sponsors the relay team with a line of hair products called 'Golden Girl'. There are some lines to suggest that Sue Kinder's hair colour suits the sponsors more than the other athletes, and there is ambivalence in the script about whether she is picked on athletic merit or to match the 'Golden Girl' image. After a disaster-ridden Olympic trial, all five sprinters choose to use what they think are performance-enhancing drugs, prescribed by Vivien Blackwood, and go on to win their gold medal in Athens. However, Blackwood had used psychology rather than stimulants, and had prescribed a placebo.

When the women's relay team beat the men's record for the same distance, Tom Billbow, a frustrated athlete who has since become a sports journalist, grows increasingly suspicious. Muriel Farr, concerned that her future children will be disabled by side-effects from what she is unaware is a placebo, gives him a scoop that the team has doped. After winning the Olympic 4 × 100-metres relay finals race in Athens, Dorcas is selected for drug testing and the play concludes just as the positive result has been confirmed to the media. Vivian Blackwood observes, 'If Dorcas is taking something it's nothing to do with me. It's something she's done on her own. She's always wanted to be brightest and best'.[6]

Although this seems a relatively mild assessment, the critique was at the heart of the complex of amateur superiority. While winning always *was* important to amateurs, it should be done 'in the right way'. Winning therefore was never the *only* thing that mattered to an amateur. Creeping professionalism and 'shamateurism' forced continual renegotiation of how a British Olympian should behave in both her preparation and post-athletic career.

In many respects, the play is quite conservative in its attitude towards female elite athletes, and women's assumed priorities while competing. Ultimately, the characters of *Golden Girls* find their professional focus on competitive sport is in opposition to their personal aspiration to become mothers at some undefined point in the future. Risking infertility for sporting glory is shown to be morally, and practically, dangerous for both mother and child. In spite of the lesson of Fanny Blankers-Koen's multiple victories in 1948, the furore over how competitive activity affects both potential mothers and their offspring remains. Blankers-Koen ran as an amateur, and without sophisticated medical preparation or training aids. Indeed a recent, rather expensive, IOC study tells us little beyond what the 'Flying Housewife' had already demonstrated in 1948.[7]

In spite of the persistence of myths on the issue, the focus on fertility makes some of the *Golden Girls'* plot implausible. A compressed timescale sees teacher Muriel Farr, who is a reserve as the team get on the plane to go to Athens, give the placebo capsule to the journalist soon after:

MURIEL: It's called hydro-something.
TOM: It's not cricket.
MURIEL: No. I don't want to stay in this game forever. Even if you want to your
    body starts to go and lets you down. I want to win here and then children.

(*About the drug.*) We're running as fast as some of the men. (TOM *takes it.*) It's not black market stuff. They come from the doctor.
TOM: Paid for by Ortolan?
MURIEL: I suppose so, in a manner of speaking. I thought you might have a way of finding out.

Given that she has been taking the placebo for considerably less than a year before Olympic competition, this seems unconvincing when, by the mid-1980s, the systemic nature of long-term East German doping regimes was well known. Similarly, the idea that the team doctor would suggest doping and then use a placebo appears somewhat tenuous. Similarly, the model, The Golden Girl, who is used to promote the shampoo, has none of the ambition or drive of the athletes. Given that women like Jean 'the Shrimp' Shrimpton and Lesley 'Twiggy' Lawson, had helped pioneer the new modelling profession for working class women up to this stage, this was perhaps a slight on models and their work ethic, with a new emphasis on 'slimness' rather than a muscular athletic body composition. Most interestingly, women's sport had passed into popular culture sufficiently that the RSC had thought it worthy of premiering the play. By 1985, women's sport, via Olympic competition, had become more integrated into the wider public and social life in Britain.

After the threatened and actual boycotts of the Melbourne Olympic Games, and the contested spectacle of Rome in 1960, Tokyo in 1964 provided iconic visual changes to Olympic festivals.[8] However, the next five Summer Olympic Games (Mexico 1968; Munich 1972, Montreal 1976, Moscow 1980 and Los Angeles 1984) would be the site of increasingly bitter national and international protest. Along with changing international relations, such as South Africa's role in the Olympic Games, and the 'Two China's' problem, diplomacy was required to keep the IOC intact.[9] As each issue has been written about extensively in its own right, the intention here is not to rehearse those arguments but to place British women's increasing participation in the Olympic Games against the wider politicised backdrop. Women's sport became more nationalistic as a result of increased rivalries, including the widespread questions about whether State-sponsored athletes in the USSR, Germany and Eastern Bloc countries were receiving undue assistance from unethical means.

We are unable to remember the Mexico Olympic Games without the student protests or the Tommie Smith and John Carlos Black Power salute; the Munich Games without the death of 11 Israeli athletes; the boycott of 29, mostly African, nations in Montreal; the US-led 65 nation boycott of Moscow in protest at the USSR invasion of Afghanistan and the resulting 13 nation USSR boycott of Los Angeles. However, behind these 'headline' moments that undoubtedly shaped the Games, there are individual accounts of participation, relatively neglected by the existing literature.

In some senses, the lone Golden Girl, or Golden Boy, appeared to stand for much older Olympic values than the increasingly politicised context of international competition, and so the paradigm had a nostalgic appeal. But, as the chapter argues, these were young women very much of their time, and the construct of their lives as 'Golden' a way of salvaging the old myth that politics and sport do not mix.

Across the timespan of the events covered by this chapter, medical testing for doping became more defined, and increasingly allied with sex testing, linking the two issues in the public mind. This chapter explores those changes and continuities. During the twentieth century, women's sport had repeatedly been reinvented as a voluntary, somewhat infantilised, activity for girls and young women before they took on the more serious adult business of dedicating themselves to a family. A well-known document written by practicing private physician Dr Franz Messerli, Secretary General of the Swiss Olympic Committee, advised the IOC in 1952:

> According to her constitution and as a future mother, woman can only go in for exercises intending to develop her physique and making her more supple, avoiding as a rule competitive events... It is wise therefore to curb her natural impulse which often leads her to overdo sports especially strenuous ones, thus restricting her accessibility to competitive performances. Any excess in sport may be injurious to herself and her descendants.[10]

Given that this ignored developments in strenuous female work during both the First and Second World Wars, and longer accounts of women's endurance in sport and leisure, this seems, at best, an ill-evidenced interpretation of medical history. As the medicalisation of gender in Olympic competition discussed above has shown, the idea of a limited amount of energy that, dissipated through sport, might harm female reproductive function, remained remarkably enduring into the twentieth century. Male sport, interpreted as evidence of virility, and so aiding procreative utility, also remained a persistent narrative. Both were contested, nevertheless.

There were other important voices in the 1950s and 1960s that were campaigning for more government support, and financial aid, for sport, both as an aid to the general health of the population but also increasingly to showcase British Olympic talent. The Wolfenden Committee was established in 1957, issuing the Wolfenden Report, which recommended the establishment of the Sports Development Council to distribute £5 million, annually, in grants to national governing bodies. A prototype Sports Council had been formed as a committee by 1959, and published another report *Leisure For Living*.

By 1963, Elaine Burton, who by then had been elevated to the peerage as Baroness of Coventry, introduced a Parliamentary Debate on Government

Encouragement of Sport, supported by The Marquess of Exeter, The Duke of Atholl, Lord Cornwallis and a number of other notable enthusiasts.[11] In asking for a dedicated Sports Minister, for £5 million funding to be distributed by the Sports Council and pointing out that basic facilities were problematic for most people, Burton and her colleagues detained the Lords for almost five hours. However, whether it was through lack of money, or an assumed moral superiority of the British amateur ideal, coherent and sustained State intervention remained something that other countries did for the time being, with even the proposal to raise money through a special edition Olympic stamp considered to be too radical by the Post Office.

However, Burton and her colleagues eventually carried the day, and she was appointed to the newly formed Sports Council (a precursor of the entity currently known as UK Sport) in 1965 and continued her campaign for increased government aid. In this way, the traditional role of the individual amateur, working towards representing Britain as best they might, given their personal circumstances, began gradually to change at the same time that meritocracy generally became a more widespread aspiration. Indirectly, this was to benefit some female athletes but a fundamental change in state support for Olympians was slow to be enacted. Similarly, in respect of wider international cooperation, The British Olympic Association retained its superior isolationist assumptions. The BOA declined an invitation in March 1966 to join a formal Association of National Olympic Committees, while proposing a series of rules under which the new organisation should operate.[12]

In moving on to look at the increased diversity of the women's programme of the Olympic Games from 1964 to 1984, the play *Golden Girls* provides a reminder that amateurism often used medical, as well as moral, justification for protecting women in sport from what were perceived corrupting influences. By contrast, in all-male Olympic sports like shooting, prize money was still awarded to amateur contestants since it was generally accepted that the cost of ammunition and related expenses far exceeded any cash return.[13] At the same time, Otto Mayer was moved to warn The Clay Pigeon Association that:

> If a competitor is paid for the use of his name or picture, or for a radio or television appearance, in connection with commercial advertising, it is capitalization of athletic fame as described above. Even if no payment is made, such practices are to be deplored, since in the minds of the many, particularly the youth, they undermine the exalted position rightly held by amateur competitors.[14]

It mattered little that a lot of the harm was more imagined than real. The hyperbole reflected what Olympic stalwarts actually thought was best for sport. The amateur declaration remained a separate form to the individual Olympic entry form, as the administration of the ethos grew with time.

What mattered more to the gentlemen of the international sporting federations and the IOC was that competitors were not judged to be able to act on their own best interests. In the case of women, this included imagined dangers to their planned, or unplanned, offspring.

The anxieties of the play *Golden Girls* were the freedoms and perils offered by professional sport, and this was to some extent a class-based concern, as well as gendered. Compared with middle class individuals like Pat Smythe, who evidently earned a living from sport, wider working class access to professional sporting opportunities was one of the moral panics of the day, and arguably remains so in 2020. It is worth saying though that 'sport for sport's sake' seems to have inspired many British Olympians women up until 1988, even while they may, on the one hand, have found the blazeratti over-officious and might, on the other, have received some modest financial compensation or gifts for related work. The large and complex issue of amateurism therefore requires us to move from the macro-level of institutions like the BOA and IOC to the micro-level of people's lives and the effect of ideas on lived experiences.

The Golden Girls generation 1964–1968: Mary Rand, Susan Masham and Jane Bullen

The whole British team for the Tokyo Summer Olympic Games in 1964 comprised 273 people; 160 male and 44 female athletes, plus associated coaches, administrators and representatives.[15] The previous January, at the Winter Olympics in Innsbruck, the British team had just nine women competitors (in the Alpine skiing and figure skating) and 27 men, returning two gold medals in the two-man bobsleigh brought home by Tony Nash and Robin Dixon. Anna Asheshov, Wendy Farrington, Divina Galica, Jane Gissing, Gina Hathorn and Tania Heald competed across three skiing events, the downhill, giant slalom and the slalom. Diane Clifton-Peach, Sally-Anne Stapleford and Carol-Ann Warner skated in the women's singles event.

Anita Lonsbrough carried the flag for the British team at the opening ceremony in Tokyo, in recognition of her outstanding performances since her Olympic gold medal in 1960 in the 200-metres breaststroke when she set the second of her four individual world records. Nationally, her eighth and last ASA victory came in the individual medley in 1964 and she preferred to contest the newer event at the Tokyo Olympics, rather than defend her breaststroke title. She reached the final in the individual medley, finishing seventh overall.

A veteran at 23, compared with many of the female swimmers who were still teenagers, Lonsbrough had been awarded an MBE in 1963 and retired after the 1964 Games. She married Hugh Porter, MBE, an Olympic cyclist who, on turning professional, became the only man to win the world pursuit championship four times. Anita followed Hugh into a career in journalism, mainly as the swimming correspondent for *The Telegraph*, before her retirement. Lonsbrough therefore became the first woman to carry the British flag for a Summer Olympics and only the second woman overall to carry the flag for a British team, since Mollie Phillips at the 1932 Winter Olympics in Lake Placid.

The British media had expected long jump specialist Mary Rand to win a gold medal at the Rome Olympic Games, and were unkind when she disappointed them.[16] Rand had been a gifted young athlete, born in Wells, Somerset, England, and was offered an athletics scholarship at the prestigious Millfield co-educational Independent school, with a record of preparing future Olympians in its 240 acres of grounds. Rand rewarded Millfield's investment with All-England Schools' titles, and in 1956, she was a guest of the Olympic squad at a training camp in Brighton, where she also excelled.[17]

Having won a silver medal in the 1958 Commonwealth Games in the long jump and achieving fifth in the high jump, Rand also came seventh in the European pentathlon championship. In the 1960 Olympics in Rome, she set a British record of 6.33 metres in the qualifying round of the long jump, which if repeated, would have won a silver in the final. However, she fouled two of the three jumps in the final and finished ninth. She also finished fourth in the 80-metres hurdles. Rand won a bronze medal in the European championship long jump in 1962 and, the same year, gave birth to her daughter Alison.

After being pronounced a 'flop, flop, flop' in Rome by the British newspapers, in spite of being the leading all-round track and field athlete of her generation, Rand trained with renewed intensity alongside her husband, Olympic rower Sid Rand, and other male athletic colleagues, for the Tokyo Games. Rand's three medals in 1964 were all the more remarkable since there were 22 events available for male track and field competitors, compared with 10 for women. One of the female events was new, and this changed British Olympic history. The pentathlon event, comprising the 80-metres hurdles, shot put, high jump, long jump and 200-metres sprint, was introduced for the 1964 Tokyo Games. Along with Mary Rand, Mary Peters and Ann Wilson were selected to compete. Also very good at putting the shot and long jump as events in themselves, Peters would set 25 British records between 1962 and 1972, but without Olympic success her reputation would not have been so stellar.

Mary Rand, along with Anne Packer, won Britain's first individual track and field athletic gold medals at the Tokyo Games in 1964. This would mean that women's track and field athletics became more important than ever before to the British medal tally; and therefore to the media. Rand won with a new world record, as she had forecast that she would like to achieve. Along with a photograph captioned 'This is it! Mary Rand leaping to Golden Glory', *The Evening Standard* reported the event in heavily sexist language, even for 1964:

> Mary Rand, Britain's pin-up girl athlete brought off her greatest triumph in the Tokyo Olympics today when she took the long jump gold medal, setting a new world record of 22 feet 2 inches. It was a fabulous performance by this 24-year-old Henley housewife and mother whose husband Sidney, a former Olympic oarsman who just missed selection for Tokyo, was among the first to congratulate her. She was a model of consistency.[18]

In fact, Rand was the British star in Tokyo overall, having brought home one medal of each colour, when she also took a silver in the pentathlon and won a bronze with the 4 × 100-metres relay team (along with Janet Simpson, Daphne Arden and Dorothy Hyman). Rand came second in the inaugural Olympic pentathlon in Tokyo to Russia's Irina Press, with Galina Bystrova, also of the USSR, in third. Rand therefore provided a significant role model for a young Mary Peters who came fourth overall. Although Peters finished in a disappointing ninth place in 1968, the two Olympic experiences helped her to a gold medal in the pentathlon in 1972.

This was soon complemented by Anne Packer's gold in the 800 metres and silver in the 400 metres. Packer's 800-metres campaign had started, it was reported, as a joke only six weeks before the Games when WAAA team manager, Marea Hartman had asked, 'How about having a bash at the 800 metres?' in what the Wilson government politicised as the 'most successful Olympics for 44 years'.

That it seemed to be a very modern moment, tells us something about the insularity of British sport, even while female international Olympic competition was over 60 years old. In Tokyo, two of Britain's four gold medals; two of the 12 silver medals and one of the two bronze medals won by the entire team were secured by female track and field contestants. Given the absence of medals won by other British female Olympic competitors in 1964, this made women's track and field the new populist focus. However, change was slow and although the Cold War intensified Olympic rivalry between the USA, Russia and Britain, the latter would not field an Olympic team including more than 100 women until 1984. Evidently, female track and field gold medals, especially those won by versatile athletes, represented comparatively good value for money.

Female Olympic success again made *The Evening Standard* headlines, when 'plucky little' Ann Packer also set a world record for the 800 metres to take gold in 2 minutes 1.1 seconds, having previously won silver in the 400 metres.[19] She retired soon after. Some years later, Lincoln Allison interviewed Ann Brightwell (née Packer) and husband Robbie Brightwell who both retired following the Tokyo Olympics, at which he also won a silver medal in the relay.[20] The reason they gave Allison for their retirement was to 'start a family'. While Robbie Brightwell went on to become Managing Director of Adidas UK, Le Coq Sportif UK and three fishing tackle companies, Anne went on to be 'principally a housewife and mother, working only part time' having three sons, two of whom went on to be professional footballers. Brightwell, and later, his compatriot Alan Pascoe would help pioneer the growing sporting apparel, sporting goods and sporting endorsement industries with attendant increased global competition. Once Onitsuka produced its own Tiger brand, along with Phil Knight's Nike, relatively neglected national markets for sportswear became more developed, especially where Adidas had failed to protect its own three stripe logo.[21]

As the Tokyo Games concluded, *The Evening Standard* featured both Rand and Packer under the headline 'A Royal Welcome', along with Ken Matthews, winner of the 20,000-metres walk and Lynn 'The Leap' Davies who had set a new long jump record in the men's event.[22] Rand won the BBC Sports Personality of the Year for 1964 and was awarded the MBE (Member of the Order of the British Empire) in the 1965 New Year's Honours List. Rolling Stones singer Mick Jagger, declared he would like to date Mary Rand, given half a chance. Desmond Hackett of *The Daily Express*, better known as 'the sportswriter in the brown bowler', was moved to turn women's sporting success into a human interest story, headlining, 'The way to Britain's medals has been paved with love' in an extended article on the subject, illustrated by photographs of both Packer and Rand kissing their medals and respective partners.[23]

A 'do it yourself' ethos was absolutely necessary to win Olympic medals if an athlete was British in 1964, but amateur status could be easily lost. The publication of a book, *Sprint to Fame* cost Dorothy Hyman her international amateur registration after she had helped Britain to win the bronze 4 × 100-metres relay medal in Tokyo in 1964 at the age of 23, even though journalist Phil Pilley had ghost-written the manuscript.[24] Having won the BBC Sports Personality of the Year in 1963, Hyman was thought to have been 'cashing-in' on her athletic achievements by issuing the ghosted autobiography after her second Olympic Games. This was the more ironic when domestic reinstatement as an amateur in national events in 1969 meant that she was to run faster times than she had when she won the 100-metres silver and 200-metres bronze at the 1960 Rome Olympics. Hyman had directly criticised amateur principles imposed by men like IOC President Avery Brundage, who could afford to amass a 35-million dollar collection of Jade objects d'art, while her family did not have an indoor bathroom.

Though dubbed by the media as one of the leading Golden Girls of her time, Hyman was from a coal-mining background and one of five children. She had taken two buses after work to train at a track eight miles away in preparation for her Olympic medals. Not only was there no nearer track of sufficient standard on which to practise, she had to go to a neighbour's house to wash after training. The strain of supporting her Olympic preparation meant that her father had risen at 4.30 in the morning to work down the mines, was back at 2.00 in the afternoon to rest briefly and eat, before he took Dorothy training at 6.30 in the evening. Her father died at Easter in 1961 at the age of 53 and so saw only her Rome Olympic medal-winning times. By publishing the book in 1964, Dorothy Hyman made it clear that she was burned out and fed up with British athletics. While there has been a sustained academic literature on State amateurism, such as practised in the United States Colleges, Soviet and Eastern European countries, the high human cost of the British system is evidently in need of more investigation by historians.

Strictly speaking, Dorothy Hyman could have been interpreted to have received payments (often called broken-time expenses) while on leave to compete internationally from the National Coal Board, where she worked as a planning technician, as did Mary Rand for post-room work at the Guinness brewery.[25] Hyman's lifelong commitment to athletics was nevertheless evident when she established the Dorothy Hyman Track Club in Barnsley and coached there for over 40 years. As Hyman's case indicates, the idea of the homely British amateur compared with her United States, German or Soviet Union competitor may have been a narrative used by the popular press but at least three other key factors also operated in this particular dynamic.

First, until the retirement of IOC President, Avery Brundage in 1972, it was in the interest of British women athletes to present themselves as 'ordinary' amateurs. As the case of Pat Smythe has indicated, a degree of media-awareness enabled female athletes from the 1950s to the 1980s to employ a range of strategies in dealing with the media: both Smythe (after she become nationally famous) and Mary Rand (before she won a gold medal in 1964, and again after she married her second husband, the American, Bill Toomey in 1969) played elaborate games of 'cat and mouse' with reporters keen to intrude on their marriage and honeymoon plans.[26] Personal agency and media awareness enabled leading stars, like Smythe and Rand, to exploit and control their sporting fame, and private lives, to a certain degree.

Second, there was a changing media-scape with which female athletes had to contend. Increasing objectification of the female 'other' was integral to the rise of tabloid journalism at this time, largely due to the role of the growing Rupert Murdoch empire.[27] Murdoch's company acquired a number of newspapers in Australia and New Zealand, before expanding into the UK in 1969, taking over *The News of the World*, then *The Sun*. In 1981, Murdoch bought *The Times*, his first British broadsheet, and moved into the US media market, television and film.

The tabloidisation of the mainstream media continued. Sexualised and sensationalised news was not novel: the media have long created the news, as well as reporting on events. But the degree of coverage dedicated to titillation and voyeurism in mainstream newspapers, across the BBC and into serious broadsheet journalism was innovative. Pat Smythe's case shows how respectfully she was venerated as a sporting star alongside her male contemporaries in the 1950s. This was to change, and the Golden Girls' nickname, which infantilised women, just as the Sex Discrimination Act came into being to reinforce feminist principles, reflected the bitter gender battles of the time. In tabloid vernacular, chauvinistic rumours that Irina and Tamara were nicknamed the 'Press Brothers' could be passed off as humour. For every reference to the masculine features of Tamara and Irina Press, there were 'leggy' blonde Russian athletes accompanied by photographs such as middle-distance runner Nina Otkalenko, or 'Ballerina Nina' as she was dubbed, by an enamoured Norris McWhirter.[28]

Third, by the 1950s and 1960s, the newspapers were not the only cheap media forming public or national opinion, and new printing techniques meant that photographs became more evident in the traditional press and in the many new colour magazines aimed at both adults and children. British television and radio had further diversified representation of the female sports star, both influenced by Hollywood production techniques.[29] So tabloid values did not go unchallenged and more women entered the media. By 1987, the Sports Writers' Association of Great Britain, which operated under the auspices of the Sports Council Press Unit, included stalwart of swimming journalism Pat Besford as Vice Chair and Alison Turnbull as running correspondent. When she became the first full-time Press Officer for the BOA, Caroline Searle was also co-opted to the 19 strong committee, led by Chair David Emery.[30] Sally Newman of the *Ealing Gazette* was commended for her weekly columns.[31]

When these three factors were taken into account, the autobiography became a staple way of British women Olympians replying to the critics, and a means by which they could author their own fame. Rand was not subtle, as her memoir was called *Mary Mary: Autobiography of an Olympic Champion*. In support of the cliché that there is an awful lot of failure in victory, Rand cited the bitter experience of media reaction in 1960, as integral to her motivation in her 1964 victory. As historians, reading the autobiographies and other personal, family and life-writing sources, we can evidence that many British women longed for more professional, less isolated and idiosyncratic training schedules, while at the same time being proud of their amateur careers.

At the heart of the British amateur system, from which Rand and Packer emerged, was the neglect of individual talent, and a piecemeal approach to preparation, compared with which the GDR showed quickly and clearly that talent identification, intense preparation and leading sports science research could produce world class athletes, male or female. With the introduction of volleyball as an Olympic sport in 1964, the home nation won the women's competition, and Japan again took the gold medal in 1976, but otherwise Soviet athletes and Eastern European countries dominated. Although doping was part of this story, other pioneering advances came to be an unintended consequence of 'progressive socialism'. The FRG also realised that administering anabolic steroids could enhance the performance of female athletes, particularly in throwing and strength-based disciplines. Amid the growing medicalisation of elite performance sport, the triumphs of British female athletes between 1964 and 1984 were driven by individual willpower and talent. In this, the Paralympic movement was no different than the Olympic movement.

The thirteenth Stoke Mandeville Games were held in Tokyo in 1964, with 375 competitors from 21 countries contesting nine sports. A 60-metres wheelchair race was added to the programme, won by Britain's Carol Bryant, who added a second gold medal in the slalom. Interviewed about this feat under her married name of Carol Walton, she pointed out: 'In the very early days of Paralympic sport, because there was so little finance... we had to do a number of different sports. If you didn't do more than one you just weren't selected'.[32] Carol Tetley also won a bronze medal in the Women's Columbia Round Archery, with Daphne Legge-Willis taking the silver. Walton was to go on to win 10 gold medals in all, in athletics, table tennis, swimming and fencing, before retiring in 1988, and later becoming a GB Paralympic team manager, also receiving an OBE for her services to disability sport. Foilist Sally Haynes, was conscious in 1964 of her diplomatic responsibility for Britain and disability sport:

> I remember Tokyo in 1964; the day before the ceremony the British team were all taken out onto the grass and Guttmann was addressing us all. He said our prime reasons for being here was as ambassadors for Great Britain and as pioneers of wheelchair sport. I think this was particularly important in Tokyo, because at the time the Japanese had this reputation for hiding all their disabled people away in remote homes on the tops of mountains, out of sight, out of mind. Whereas they saw us, the GB team, going out shopping, dining in restaurants and having friends.[33]

Gwen Buck and Susan Masham took another gold in the table tennis doubles in 1964, ahead an Italian pair and Britain's Sheelagh Jones and Carol Tetley, in third place. Susan Masham was another very gifted athlete, taking further silver medals in three swimming events and in the singles table tennis. Masham was injured as a 21-year-old equestrian, and gave a very forthright account of convincing Japanese authorities that a disabled person could also be married.[34] A committed member of the Riding for the Disabled movement, Masham was made a life Peer in the House of Lords and remains active in a number of health and disability charities. Similarly, Pauline Foulds, who won three swimming gold medals in 1964, was injured from the waist down in a riding accident. Overall, she would win five Paralympic gold medals.

The silver medallist in the Albion round of the archery, Valerie Forder, was a remarkably accomplished and versatile athlete, also winning one bronze medal in the discus and three silver medals in the wheelchair fencing and two swimming events, to compliment a gold medal in the 50-metres freestyle supine class. She would go on to do even better in Tel Aviv in 1968, entering nine events and winning gold in five, including one each in backstroke, freestyle and breaststroke events. Forder also won the 60-metres wheelchair sprint and the pentathlon in Tel Aviv, then married Scottish Commonwealth Games gold medallist John Robertson, before returning to compete as Valerie Robertson at the 1976 Stoke Mandeville Games, taking a further bronze medal.

When the Summer Olympic Games were held in Mexico City in 1968, financial and accessibility issues prevented the Paralympic organisers hosting the Stoke Mandeville Games there, so Tel Aviv was chosen instead. This time, the number of athletes more than doubled, with 774 athletes from 28 countries, competing in 10 sports, with lawn bowls added for the first time. The British team of 50 men and 24 women, won a total of 29 gold, 20 silver and 20 bronze medals. Janet Laughton took the inaugural lawn bowls gold medal with Gwen Buck, who also took the singles title.[35] Like several of those mentioned in this section, Laughton and Buck had already competed at the First Commonwealth Paraplegic Games in 1962 in Perth, Western Australia. Here, England had by far the largest team, but Pat Vizard competed for Northern Ireland; Gaynor Henry for Wales; and Maureen Taylor and Rose Harvey for Scotland. Again, a mix of identities could be experienced through different competition formats. Laughton won a silver medal in the freestyle in Tokyo, a bronze in the breaststroke and a further bronze in the club throwing event.

Though Vanessa Heggie has suggested that the 1968 Mexico City Summer Olympic Games marked a new era of scientific concern for the well-being of British competitors, the thesis really only works for the 175 male members of the team.[36] The 50 women in the British team were still largely dependent upon their own networks and expertise for training, although altitude did cause some panics about the time needed to acclimatise.[37] The IOC continued to struggle with the size of the schedule. Meanwhile, the International Shooting Union introduced another 'mixed' competition rather than an additional event confined to women, in order to limit the overall number of contestants.[38]

By 1967, concerns about various controversies meant that the official Olympic entry form became informally known as the 'Amateur/Sex/Dope' Certificate among officials and contained the ominously brief warning 'Female athletes maybe subjected to medical proof'.[39] The medicalisation of gender binary, and of surveillance for performance enhancing stimulants therefore became inextricably linked, with a signed declaration required:

> I, the undersigned, declare on my honour that I am an amateur and that I have read and comply with the Eligibility Code of the Olympic Games as specified on this form... Furthermore, I, the undersigned, declare that

> I enter as female/male athlete, that I do not indulge or have the intention of indulging in doping and that I agree to subject myself to any test or examination by qualified medical personnel appointed by Olympic authorities.[40]

Since the early drafts of these forms were so rushed as to lack definitions of what constituted doping, and then included alcohol, amphetamines, cocaine, vasodilators, opiates and cannabis in unspecified quantities, as well as anabolic steroids, the administration required considerable refinement. A specially-convened commission of the executive committee met with Doctor Thiebault in January to discuss the logistics of the increasing doping and sex-testing regimes, and concluded that tests should be quick, easy and cheap to administer, with the consensus that the burden should fall on the International Sporting Federations rather than the IOC.[41] Since the role of the medical commission was to become more important from this moment onwards, both the surveillance of women and the refinement of doping methods would continue to challenge the IOC. The scale of the logistical challenge alone meant an increasing need for full-time professional specialists.

These controversies aside, preparation by the WAAA for the Mexico Olympics included a number of 'athletic weekends' judged invaluable in getting a 'good team spirit' plus some sports-specific training at Lilleshall.[42] The entire female track and field team for 1968 comprised: Maureen Barton, Lillian Board, Mary Green, Barbara Inkpen, Della James, Pat Jones, Pat Lowe, Anita Neil, Joan Page, Val Peat, Mary Peters, Sue Platt, Pat Pryce, Sue Scott, Sheila Parkin-Sherwood, Dorothy Shirley, Janey Simpson, Sheila Taylor, Maureen Tranter and Ann Wilson.

In spite of the relatively unsystematic nature of preparation, many of these women made personal bests in Mexico. Sheila Parkin-Sherwood achieved a silver medal in the long jump, while Sue Scott came 10th overall. Val Peat, Della James and 16-year-old Anita Neil got through to the second round of the 100-metres sprints. Born in Wellingborough, Northamptonshire and a member of London Olympiades, Neil was a pioneer in the first generation of Black British female Olympic athletes. Often photographed and, more unusually, painted (by William Hubert Pack, now in Wellingborough Museum) Neil competed for Great Britain in Munich 1972, as well as in Mexico 1968, running in the Women's 100 metres and the 4 × 100-metres relay.[43] In 1969, Neil won a bronze medal in the 100 metres at the European Championships in Athens and at the following year's Commonwealth Games in Edinburgh, she won a silver medal as part of the 4 × 100-metres relay team.[44]

Unlike Ethel Scott in the 1930s, Neil had Black British contemporaries, like Marilyn Neufville, who had been born in Jamaica and moved to London when she was eight years old and initially represented Great Britain in the 1968 European Junior Games. However, in the 1970 Edinburgh

Commonwealth Games, Neufville competed for Jamaica, and continued to do so in an illustrious career up to, and including, the 1976 Olympic Games in Montreal.[45] Slight and lean, Neufville set new world records and illustrated that mixed heritage and a range of personal influences complicated issues of identity and national representation. While she seems to have been mistreated by a nationalistic British media, and her choice of Commonwealth Games affiliation undoubtedly caused controversy, Neufville felt that the support she received from Jamaica in attending a Californian university with a scholarship, more than merited representing the country of her father's heritage.[46]

Yvonne Saunders was also born in Jamaica and came to England, aged eight, settling in Greater Manchester. She took junior WAAA titles in the high jump in 1967; then the high jump and pentathlon in 1968. After moving to Canada in 1968, Saunders represented Jamaica at the 1970 Commonwealth Games and the 1971 Pan American Games, before obtaining Canadian citizenship and competing for her adopted nation at the 1974 Commonwealth and 1976 Olympic Games. Soon after, Kingston-born Lorna Boothe, who won the 100-metres hurdles for England at the 1978 Commonwealth Games, and who would appear for Great Britain in the 1976 and 1980 Olympic Games, made the transition to the British and International Athletics sporting establishment; explicitly raising diversity and equality issues as she did so. Evidently, this was an important and transitional period for British society's acceptance of the wider cultural heritage of Black British female athletes.

The star of the British Olympic track and field team in Mexico was undoubtedly South African-born Lillian Board. By 1968, a 20-year-old resident of Ealing, Lillian Board won silver in the 400 metres, having very narrowly missed the gold medal, to France's Collette Besson; Britain's Janet Simpson came fourth overall. Lillian Board was undoubtedly one of the Golden Girls, and another protégé of Rand at London Olympiades. In addition to her Olympic silver, Board won two individual gold medals at the European championships in 1968 and 1969. She also ran the anchor leg of the victorious gold medal 4 × 400-metres British female relay team, along with Rosemary Stirling, Pat Lowe and Janet Simpson, to win the European title. Known as 'Britain's favourite girl' and studying for a career in fashion, Board was awarded an MBE in the 1970 New Year's Honours and wanted to add the 1,500 metres to her portfolio, recording sub-5 minute miles in early races.[47] A national name, Board appeared in media programmes like *A Question of Sport* and *Desert Island Discs* in 1969. She was also training hard with a view to competing in the 800 metres at the Munich Olympics of 1972, when a diagnosis of bowel cancer rapidly declined her health and she died in a clinic in Germany on Boxing Day 1970, aged just 22.[48]

The overall British female star in Mexico was 20-year-old equestrian Jane Bullen, who had come to fame by winning the Badminton horse trials in 1968 on her horse 'Our Nobby', after working nightshift as a nurse. Nicknamed somewhat prosaically by the British press as 'The Galloping Nurse', Bullen won a gold in the mixed team Three-Day Event, with Derek Allhusen ('The Galloping Grandfather'), Richard Meade ('The Golden Wonder') and Ben Jones ('The Galloping Sergeant').[49] The rain caused problems on the course, and 'Our Nobby' was a pony-sized mount, which had to have several pain killing injections after the competition. Bullen was also left with two broken vertebrae. However she remembered:

> What was your best Olympic memory?
> Standing on the rostrum with all those boys. There were 11 men and me. There are a lot of reasons that was special. Seeing the Union Jack go up was something and hearing the national anthem. You felt you had done something for your country. It was the first Olympics that went into people's living rooms on the television. My family had specially got a colour television set to watch me compete in Mexico.[50]

After retiring 'Stroller' in 1971, she remained active in equestrian sport and won the 1976 Burghley Three-Day Event under her married name of Mrs Jane Holderness-Roddam, riding 'Warrior'.[51] Later appearing as the stunt double for Tatum O'Neill in *International Velvet* and a leading figure in the Riding for the Disabled charity, Holderness-Roddam received a CBE for services to equestrianism in 2004 and has gone on to write 25 books, in addition to owning West Kingston Stud, with her husband Tim.[52] Also a lady in waiting for Princess Anne for 25 years, Holderness-Roddam is today a past-President of British Eventing and previously Chair of the British Equestrian Federation. Show jumper Marion Coakes won silver on 'Stroller' in the individual event to complete the list of Britain's female medal winners in Mexico.

As proceedings from Mexico reduced, the WAAA began to think about the next Olympic Games in 1972. The balance sheet for the 1968 Olympic year read £1,574, 5 shillings and 10 pence. Almost one-third of the budget, £478, 18 shillings and 4 pence, had been spent on coaching.[53] As estimated by K. S. 'Sandy' Duncan four years later, on behalf of the BOA, the cost per head for competitors *and* team officials in Mexico was £420, lower than it had been for Tokyo in 1960 (£483 per person for a team of 273).[54] The costs of previous British teams was compared: Rome in 1960, £129 per head for a team of 338; Melbourne in 1956, £522 each for a Great Britain squad of 236; and Helsinki, £94 per individual for a party of 353 people. It is worth remembering that in the face of increased State-sponsored amateurism, preparations for the women were reliant upon voluntary public appeals, drawing in £70,436 in 1952; £147,273 in 1956; £74,370 in 1960; £182,920 in 1964 and £192,500 in 1968. As Sandy Duncan had been bitterly keen to point out in 1958:

> There is no Sports Lottery or Sport Toto in Great Britain helping sport as a whole. Lotteries are virtually illegal. There are Football Pools. These

however are controlled by private business and contribute virtually nothing to sport. The British Olympic Association therefore gets no finance from lotteries or Football Pools and must raise its funds by an appeal to the public.[55]

For some athletes, class was an important factor in their sporting opportunities. For instance, Gina Hawthorn was a star in skiing circles, and would become more so when narrowly missing out on a slalom bronze medal at the Winter Olympics in 1968, and competing again in 1972. With fellow Olympian Davina Galica, who had also taken part in the 1966 World Championships, and who had a dual career in motor sports, Hawthorn was recognised by the ski club of Great Britain with a Pery medal for services to competitive international skiing in 1972.[56] Hawthorn, in respect of her fame, carried the flag at the closing ceremony for the British team in Grenoble in 1968 before her marriage to Tommy Sopwith, and thereafter becoming a society figure.

There follows a short case study of how Mary Peters became an Olympian and sustained a high profile post-competition career in local politics. It shows how an Olympic profile can provide a degree of social mobility after an individual retires from sport.

Mary Peters: I wanted it more!

Mary Peters became a key figure in Britain's Olympic history in the late 1960s and remains so today. Historically, the WAAA had taken charge of selection for female track and field Olympians after its creation in 1922, comprised of the regional Northern Counties WAAA (Bury, Lancashire); Midland Counties WAAA (Birmingham); Southern Counties WAAA (Surrey) and Welsh WAAA (Glamorgan).[57] This organisation was an adjunct to the male-run AAA, formed in 1880, and affiliated through this connection to the IAAF.[58] By the late 1950s, especially without a female gold medal for either track or field athletics, WAAA officials had realised that the organisation had an English bias and that this was, in turn, southern-focused.

The WAAA was determined in 1958 to hold trials explicitly to encourage more Northern, Welsh, Scottish and Irish talent and this process found Mary Peters, born in Liverpool in 1939, who was very good at the long jump and the shot put.[59] Peters domestic co-competitors included experienced athletes like Suzanne Farmer (who was to marry the Hammer thrower Peter Allday) born in Shoreham by Sea, West Sussex in 1934. Affiliated to Brighton Ladies Athletic Club and the Spartan Ladies Athletic Club during her career, Farmer had represented Britain in the 1952 Helsinki and the 1956 Melbourne Games. Farmer won a discus gold medal in the 1958 British Empire and Commonwealth Games in Cardiff for England, the first in a field event and also took silver in the shot put. Sheila Hoskin, who had also been to the 1956 Games had won gold in the 1958 Commonwealth Games long jump and the 4 × 110-yards relay in a new world record time. But a particular favourite was Northern Ireland's Thelma Hopkins, 1956 Olympic high jump silver medallist and world record holder of whom Peter's wrote: 'Nice as she was an athlete of top class – it made me think there was something worthwhile in athletics'.[60]

The Peters family had moved to Ballymena from Liverpool when Mary was 11 years old and she went on to represent Great Britain in many international tournaments. Peters' autobiography details how her mother died when she was relatively young, and with athletics as her consolation, her father bought tonnes of sand for her 16th birthday to fill the long jump pit he had built nearby, also concreting a putting circle, and he made a shot in the foundry where he worked. Peters went on to represent Northern Ireland at every Commonwealth Games between 1958 and 1974; winning a silver medal in the shot put in 1966, a gold in the pentathlon and shot put in 1970 and retaining her pentathlon victory in 1974.

After her first two Olympic appearances, coming fourth in 1964; ninth in Mexico due to ankle injury in 1968, Peters took a year off her job as a qualified teacher for an even more intense period of training up to 1972, and worked at a Belfast gymnasium in addition to her job as a teacher. Investigations for professionalism did her public profile no harm whatsoever.[61] However, within two months of the competition, the Provisional IRA detonated 22 bombs in what became known as 'Bloody Friday', which killed nine people, and injured many more. She went on to win gold aged 33 in Munich 1972, with a world record score of 4,801 points to beat local heroine Heide Rosendahl, born 1947, in the North Rhine-Westphalia area of West Germany. This looked to be Peters last chance to take part in an Olympic Games. With athletes like Burglinde Pollak and Christine Bodner from East Germany competing under their own flag and anthem, East-West rivalry was intense. Pollack and Bodner would go on to take third and fourth place, respectively with Valentina Tikhomirova of the Soviet Union in fifth.

The West German women had upset previous predictions by winning four track and field events, so it looked like Rosendahl would be inspired, having already won a gold in the long jump, and Mary Peters would be consigned to the list of Olympic hopefuls who would not win a medal. This was a powerful rivalry, intensified by media interest, as both Rosendahl and Peters represented what had previously been unified countries that now had some divided national loyalties: each athlete seemed to want victory for more than just her own satisfaction.

Thanks to technology, the whole two-day competition is available on YouTube and ITN source. It is worth watching again because of the contrast between the relaxed elegance of Peters' body and the concentration of her facial expressions.[62] Mary Peters' story was arguably enhanced by the live colour television coverage of the event, even more so because she gave such an unselfconscious performance.[63] Having previously stated that she suffered from lack of ambition in big tournaments, Peters was very aware of who she considered the viewing public at home to be:

> It had to be gold or nothing. I wanted it for me. I wanted it for my coach, Buster McShane. Above all I wanted it for the people back home who would be watching me that day on television. I didn't mean the people of England [sic]. Back home was Belfast and Northern Ireland where it was long overdue for something good to happen. 'Mary P', I said, which is what all my close friends call me, 'you can't let those people down'.[64]

Peters set personal bests on day one in the hurdles, shot and high jump and the speed and lightness of her actions contrasted sharply with the sinewy look of determination she wore while competing. The first half of the competitions closed with a small points advantage to Peters, leaving Rosendahl to out-perform her on day two with a possible chance of gold. The 200-metres final race at the end of day two is one of the great set pieces of television and the start provided some outstanding still photography.

While Mary between events was smiling and hugging the other competitors, waving at the crowd, generally enjoying herself, the look of focus as she comes out of the blocks for the 200 metres is an intensity to behold. Winning a gold medal clearly mattered. It was Rosendahl's best event and she predictably came in first with Peters second. It then took some anticlimactic minutes for the calculations to confirm that Peters had done enough to win and she was congratulated by Rosendahl, who went on to win a consolation second gold medal in the 4 × 100-metres relay.

At our interview, Peters reminded me that she had told Rosendahl and her husband on day one: 'I needed it more!'[65] As one contemporary analyst described her victory:

> For her sport, Mary was a perfect example, a model champion, a girl without the gift of natural talent who won through without State support, the advantages of subsidies or the aid of artificial stimulants. She remained, even at her greatest moment, above all, a human being.[66]

The British could still win against the technocracy of state-amateurs of the North American colleges, the dual German systems and the Soviet bloc. But the rarity of such medals highlighted the lack of medical, psychological, tactical, technological and material support for female athletes in the UK.

The civic reception in Belfast for Mary Peters briefly united the city during the height of the sectarian troubles, and she won the BBC Sports Personality of the Year award by public vote, even though when returning home to Belfast, she could not move back into her flat for three months because of death threats. Viewers who respond to the Olympic clips often post comments like 'Ulster's finest'.[67] However, she perhaps became more of a symbolic figure for peace when Palestinians took hostage 11 Israeli athletes and officials two days later. In the rescue attempt, three of the captors and all nine remaining Israeli hostages then still alive, were shot by German police.

The games nevertheless continued, with Britain's Richard Meade leading the individual Three-Day Event, and the British team (Mark Phillips, Mary Gordon-Watson and Bridget Parker) also winning gold medals. Yachtsman Rodney Pattison retained his 'Flying Dutchman' title at Kiel with crewman Chris Davies aboard *Superdoso*. Britain's David Hemery won a silver in the men's 4 × 400-metres hurdles (along with Martin Reynolds, Alan Pascoe and David Jenkins) and bronze in the individual men's 400-metres hurdles. Further silver medals went to David Hunt and Alan Warren (sailing); Ann Moore (equestrianism); David Starbrook (judo) and David Wilkie (swimming).[68] The bronze medallists were Willi Moore, Ron Keeble and Mick Bennett (cycling); Angelo Parisi and Brian Jacks (judo); Ralph Evans, Alan Minter and George Turpin (boxing); John Kynoch (shooting) and Ian Stewart (athletics). While archery was reintroduced in 1972, there was also an expanded female canoeing programme, and diving schedule. Equestrianism remained significant too with Lorna Johnstone, Margaret Lawrence and Jennie Loriston-Clarke comprising the 'mixed' British dressage team, along with the three-day eventers and jumping competitors. At the Winter Olympics in Sapporo, cross country skiing for women was added to the schedule, but Frances Lütken was unable to distinguish herself, nor could Alpine skiers Carol Blackwood, Divina Galica, Gina Hathorn and Valentina Iliffe. Linda Connolly and Jean Scott skated in Sapporo but, like the rest of the British squad, returned no medals for their efforts.

However, perhaps because of the controversial nature of Avery Brundage's decision to continue with the Munich Olympic Games, both overseas golden boys and golden girls would resonate with the British public and press in 1972. The Californian swimmer Mark Spitz won seven events, and set seven world records; reported in the UK as the 'Golden Idol: Undimmed by tragedy, the Olympic Glories of Mark Spitz'.[69] The newspapers also enjoyed punning on the surname of Australia's Shane Gould, who won three gold medals in swimming events in world record times, a silver and a bronze.

But perhaps the most popular overseas competitor with the British press was Olga Korbut, who won three gold and one silver medal in the gymnastics at the age of 17. Allen Guttmann has claimed that during the 1972 Munich Games the 'graceful and womanly' Ludmilla Tourischeva was eclipsed by 'the sparrow from Minsk' because of Roone Arledge's mediatisation of Korbut on ABC-TV:

> Tourischeva, the reigning world champion, was the centre of attention until Korbut slipped and fell from the uneven parallel bars. The youngster

quickly remounted, continued her routine, dismounted and then burst into tears. Realizing instantly that he had the makings of a new heroine with attention-getting human interest, Arledge ordered the camera to focus on her, and a new era began in which 'pixies' displaced women and the sport of women's gymnastics was transformed into children's acrobatics.[70]

However, though only slightly older, Tourischeva had been born in Grozny in 1952, the year of the first Soviet participation in the Olympic Games. The Soviet media often referred to this and had established her reputation as captain of the Soviet gymnastics team as an unsmiling 'faithful Komosol – often almost appearing too solemn and distant'.[71] Olga Korbut was born in Hrodna in 1955 and was to become head coach of the Belarusian team on retiring from gymnastics in 1977.

British audiences were similarly fond of 'little Olga' and a Carl Giles cartoon for *The Sunday Express* in 1973 depicted an entire family unsuccessfully attempting to emulate some of her key moves to take 'their minds off the football' following Sunderland's shock defeat of Leeds United in the FA Cup Final.[72] Most of Britain's swimmers were younger than Korbut, with June Green just 13 years of age, and gymnasts Avril Lennox and Elain Willett aged 16. Tourischeva, 20 years old, the leader of the Soviet team and already a gold medallist from the Mexico Olympics, appeared to be an ideal Soviet citizen compared with the more dynamic personality from Belarus who was dubbed by the British press 'The Golden Girl Who Won the Hearts of Millions'.[73]

Korbut would go on to be called the 'mother of gymnastics' before winning a further gold and silver Olympic medal in 1976 and was the first to be inducted into the gymnastic Hall of Fame in 1988. Korbut was the long line of mediatised Olympic 'underdogs' who win moral victories and the affection of the public, whether they win a medal or not. Tourischeva had already been to Mexico in 1968 and would go to Montreal in 1976 to win four gold medals from three games.

Korbut was also unconventional. The National Soviet Sports Council had disapproved of her acrobatic self-promoting style of gymnastics (the Korbut flip, for example) in selection competitions before 1972, in addition to her emotional and impulsive character. It is worth re-listening to the British commentary which emphasised her late selection and unorthodox approach, typified by Alan Weeks' exclamation 'Isn't she marvellous?'[74] Korbut became the first person from the Eastern bloc to win the BBC's International Sports Personality of the Year Award in 1972.

After retiring from gymnastic competition, Tourischeva married Soviet sprint star Valeri Borzov, was honoured with the Order of Lenin for her achievements and served as delegate, coach and president of Soviet and Ukranian Gymnastics Federations until 2000. Korbut moved to the USA in 1991 and has since sold her medals, due to financial problems. As Olga Korbut modestly claims on her website 'She did more to ease the tensions of the Cold War than all the politicians and diplomats of the day put together. She made us all feel like part of one big family'.[75]

In contrast, since 1972, Mary Peters has translated her gold medal into sustained public service and high profile international appearances; travelling extensively as manager of the British women's athletics team (1979–84); is a member of the International Amateur Athletic Federation (1995–9); and President of the British Athletics Federation (1996–8). In recognition of her achievements, she was awarded the DBE in 2000. Though now of retirement age, Dame Mary Peters is active in the tourism industry for Northern Ireland and has represented the region in sports administration.

Peters also has a well-defined local presence, having worked in Belfast as a teacher, raising funds for the renovation of The Mary Peters Track and becoming the Lord Lieutenant of the city in 2009, a position she held for the London Olympics and Paralympic Games.[76] In 2013, a statue of her 1972 victory was unveiled at the track. She has clearly inspired many people and self-consciously sought to do so. Peters' continues to hold charitable and personal ties with the Liverpool area, so it would not be a surprise if more than one Lancastrian identified with her personal ethos of raw talent, hard work and easy good humour. Mary P's father and brother moved back after her mother's death in 1956, and since the male side of the family then emigrated to Australia, it would be interesting to know how she is viewed there, if there is a following at all. We could long debate the extent to which Olympic gold enabled Peters to draw attention to issues in Ireland and the degree to which it defined her as more loyal to the British crown.

And what of Mary Peters' legacy? By 1984, the five-part pentathlon would be changed to the seven discipline heptathlon, with the addition of the javelin and 800 metres. The enlarged event was first contested at the 1983 IAAF World Championships and then the 1984 Olympic Games in Los Angeles. In spite of these advances, women's relative weakness compared with men is still an important organising principle in competitive athletics. This compares with a men's decathlon event, which has been held since 1912 and which today includes four track and six field events: the 100-metres sprint, 110-metres hurdles, long jump, high jump, shot put, javelin, discus, pole vault, 400-metres and 1,500-metres races. The supposedly dangerous effect of the pole vault on women's reproductive system saw its delayed introduction in 2000 at Sydney, whereas the men's event has been part of Olympic competition since 1896.

That Peters helped to change attitudes to women's sport in Ireland is suggested by a 1982 article in *The Irish Times* referencing her success: 'How many potential women champions and record holders were completely lost to athletics in the Republic and to what extent did women in northern Ireland fail to reach their full potential through lack of competition?'[77] The article was accompanied by photographs of Frances Cryan, 'Ireland's first Olympic oarswoman'; the Leinster women's cricket team; Emily Dowling of the Dublin City Harriers selected to run for Ireland in the Osaka Women's Marathon and leading long-distance runner Carrie May. Cyril White had alerted the Council of Europe and the IOC, in the form of Monique Berlioux, that there had been not one woman on the Executive of the Irish Athletics Board (BLE) during the period 1955 to 1980.[78] When browsing various sites to look at Ireland's Olympians however, more reference is made to those born on the island, such as Bridget Robinson the javelin thrower, high jumper Thelma Hopkins and the sprinter and hockey player Maeve Kyle.[79]

A conversation over coffee or in the pub may well dispute whether Kyle or Peters is more accurately described as 'the mother of Irish athletics'. Unsurprisingly therefore, Mary Peters' public profile is quite unlike Maeve Kyle (née Shankey, born 6 October 1928, in County Kilkenny) who competed as an Irish Olympic athlete in 1956, 1960 and 1964, before becoming Chair of Coaching NI and awarded an honorary doctorate for the University of Ulster. Also a gifted hockey player, Kyle was awarded a lifetime achievement in respect of her work with the Ballymena and Antrim Athletics Club and made an OBE in 2008.

However, perhaps the defining aspect of Mary Peters' legacy is the role that she has played in raising awareness of women's sport to a wider public and in particular, using Olympic gold as a vehicle for public office. Her administrative leadership was also pioneering. In writing the foreword to a study of the physical characteristics of women finalists in Munich 1972 and Montreal 1976 Olympic Games, Mary Peters tried to motivate and encourage pragmatism in advising:

> The physical characteristics of 824 women finalists from each of the 47 Olympic events described here are of interest to potential finalists of the future. The importance of physique in relation to performance in specific events is well-recognised, for example champion endurance runners cannot become champion sprinters and vice versa. The authors have compiled useful tables to assist an aspiring girl to select those sporting events best suited at her age, height and weight and at which she is therefore, most likely to succeed in international competitions. I hope that this book will inspire anyone to take up a sport regardless of her size, but she will be well advised to select the most suitable one.[80]

As an example of the evidence to support my view of diversity in elite female Olympic athletes, the authors found it 'remarkable' to find an age variation of 14 (for a swimmer) to 45 (for an equestrian); a height variation of 140 cm (for a coxswain) to 210 cm (for a basketball player), and a weight differential between 38 kg (for a gymnast) and 117 kg (for a discus thrower). Although quasi-scientific and medical discourse had long tried to homogenise women, as similar to some notional 'average' female, one of the inspiring aspects of Olympic competition remains that diversity continues to be the main representation of female athletes.

From Munich to Montreal, Moscow and Los Angeles

Montreal was not a success for Britain's female Olympians: HRH Princess Anne was ceremoniously unseated by her horse 'Goodwill' in the Three-Day Event and finished well down the field. Of a total of 13 medals (three gold, five silver and five bronze), none was won by a woman athlete, although the British female team was relatively large with 70 competitors. However, there were advances for new female Olympic Summer sports, such as rowing, basketball and handball in 1976. There was no British female team in the basketball (won by Russia, over the USA and with Bulgaria in third place) or the handball (won by Russia over East Germany, with Hungary in third place).

Along with the World Rowing Federation, FISA (from the French, Fédération Internationale des Sociétés d'Aviron formed in 1892), the IOC had instigated a major survey on women's rowing in 1970. This found considerable variance, including a rather blunt note of opinion from Reg Blundstone of the Amateur Australian Rowing Council:

> The Australian Women's Rowing Council in my opinion is not a strong body... Their organisation is not affiliated to the Australian Amateur Rowing Council and among our Councillors is opposition to their Affiliation. The Australian Amateur Rowing Council does not foster women's rowing in Australia.[81]

However, the international picture was considerably more promising and this led to the introduction of the inaugural rowing competitions just six years later. The Coxless Pairs were contested by Beryl Mitchell of the Thames Trading Rowing Club and Linda Clark, while Pauline Wright Coxed the Fours team of Diana Bishop, Pauline Bird-Hart, Clare Grove and Gillian Webb.

The number of Black British track and field athletes continued to grow including Barbadian-born Jocelyn Hoyte-Smith, who trained at the Dorothy Hyman Track Club, and her compatriot Beverley Goddard-Callender. Other national stars included hurdler Shirley Strong and sprinter Donna Murray-Hartley. In many ways, Montreal was good experience for the Moscow Olympic Games in 1980, where the US boycott helped some of these sprinters to medals. At the 75th anniversary dinner of the British Olympic Association in November 1980, many of the athletes and administrators were recognised in a rather grand evening requiring a seating plan for over 55 tables.[82]

In the 1976 Winter Olympics, held in Innsbruck, John Curry was the British star in the men's singles figure skating, a title that Robin Cousins would take in 1980 in Lake Placid. With the women's Alpine skiing having been extended to three events since 1952 (downhill, giant slalom, slalom), sisters Valentina and Serena Iliffe joined the British team (both were born in New South Wales Australia). In 1980, brother and sister David and Moira Cargill, both represented Britain as skiers, along with Scotland's Kirstin Cairns, who was born on the Isle of Bute. The luge, a light toboggan for one or two people, had a female singles event in 1980, contested by Joanna Weaver and Anna Walker. Speed skating introduced female competitions at 1,000 metres; 1,500 metres and 3,000 metres, in which Mandy Horsepool and Kim Ferran took part for Britain.

Although Montreal had spent extravagant sums, in the region of $1.5 billion, to host the Olympic Games, the diplomatic row over Apartheid sport overshadowed these headlines. The Canadian government had changed its foreign policy regarding recognising the People's Republic of China (PRC) in 1970 and therefore challenged the diplomatic legitimacy of Taiwan, the Nationalist Republic of China (ROC). While the IOC seemed to dither between accepting a 'Two China's' policy or siding with one of these 'National' Olympic Committees, the Communist PRC and Nationalist ROC frequently lobbied for their own inclusion at the expense of the other.

In the event, neither participated in 1976 but that combined with a number of economic issues to draw attention from the fact that a more serious situation was developing involving the Supreme Council of Sport in Africa (SCSA). Though many other countries had sporting ties with South Africa, the SCSA used the symbolic power of rugby games between southern hemisphere teams to focus on the Springbok–All Blacks fixtures as an offence for which New Zealand should be barred from Montreal. Given the history of the Canadian–New Zealand national relationship, the fact that rugby was not an Olympic sport, the laissez faire attitude of the new IOC President Killanin, and the presence of athletes who had already travelled to Montreal, the situation seemed to confuse the Canadian government and the local organising committee.[83]

A total of 29 African national Olympic committees boycotted the Montreal Games; although some individuals tried to compete as independents. The Organisation of African Unity (OAU) resolved to boycott the games; as a result, Central African Republic, Gabon, Madagascar, Malawi, Sri Lanka, Tanzania, The Gambia and Zaire did not send teams. Algeria, Cameroon, Chad, Congo, Egypt, Ethiopia, Ghana, Guyana, Upper Volta (now Burkina Faso), Iraq, Kenya, Libya, Mali, Morocco, Niger, Nigeria, Sudan, Swaziland, Togo, Tunisia, Uganda and Zambia withdrew.[84] The sports mainly affected were athletics, boxing, football and hockey and therefore, not it was not so significant for the female Olympic programme at the time. But the general principle of Anti-Apartheid sport affected athletes and spectators alike. In

June 1977, 13 African nations threatened to pull out of the British Commonwealth Games, resulting in the Gleneagles Agreement to cease sporting exchanges with South Africa, although cricket and rugby tours continued to cause problems and the British government procrastinated.[85] Again, this is a complex issue with its own academic literature and with more space, it would have been interesting to have interviewed more women athletes about their thoughts on the wider political scene.[86]

There appears little evidence to support Alan Tomlinson's view that after the Second World War, the Olympic experience became commodified to such an extent that it became akin to the theme park or Disney experience with an emphasis on fun and fantasy.[87] The scale of the Montreal can be better understood by the media-reach of the Games and the debt that would not be repaid until 2006; an unwanted legacy effect which made subsequent potential bid cities nervous.

> In scarcely eighty years, the Olympic Games have grown from a fin-de siècle curiosity of regional interest to an international cultural performance of global proportion. Participants in the Olympic Games – athletes, coaches, officials, dignitaries, press, technicians, support personnel, as well as artists, performers, scientists and world youth campers attending ancillary events – now number in the tens of thousands, drawn from as many as 120 nations. Foreigners journeying to the host city number in the hundred thousands, total spectators in the millions and the broadcast audience in the billions. According to reasonable estimates, 1.5 billion people – or about one of every three persons then alive on the earth – watched or listened to part of the proceedings at Montreal through the broadcast media.[88]

If this was the situation in 1976, it seems safe to conclude that subsequent processes of representation have accelerated since and even categorised as post-Olympism.[89]

Disability sport also became more politicised as the 1970s progressed. The 1972 Paralympic Games were held at Heidelberg, as there was not enough accommodation in Munich. In 1976, the International Stoke Mandeville Games Federation (ISMGF) and the International Sports Organisation for the Disabled (ISOD) united. This meant that athletes who were blind or partially sighted and amputees could compete along with the wheelchair-based athletes. The 1976 Toronto Games were the first to use the title 'Olympiad for the Physically Disabled' but this would become contentious as the IOC sought to limit the use of the Olympic title. The first Winter Games followed at Örnsköldsvik in Sweden, called the Winter Olympics for the Disabled. However, this was only open to athletes who were blind or partially sighted or were amputees, competing in Nordic and Alpine skiing events. The 1980 Paralympics was hosted at the Papendal National Sports Centre in Arnhem, the Netherlands, having originally been due to take place in Russia; 42 countries took part with a total of 1,973 athletes.

The overall numbers of Olympic competitors were affected by the boycotts that affected Montreal in 1976, Moscow in 1980 and Los Angeles in 1984. In 1980, the USA boycotted the Moscow Games, joined by Canada, Chile, Congo, Israel, Japan, Kenya, Liberia, Norway, West Germany and several Islamic Asian and North African countries, in protest of the Soviet invasion of Afghanistan. Approximately 62 countries boycotted or did not attend the Moscow Games and around 81 (including the PRC) took part but it is difficult to be definitive, since some athletes marched under Olympic flags and further compromises.

With regard to the British team, the Steve Ovett and Seb Coe rivalry dominated the newspapers, each winning a gold medal in the 800 metres and 1,500 metres, respectively.[90] Coe also won a silver and Ovett a bronze.[91] Athletes Allan Wells and Daley Thompson, along with swimmer Duncan Goodhew added three more gold medals, with Wells also taking a silver. Freestyle swimmer June Croft helped the 4 × 100-metres relay team to a silver medal along with Helen Jameson, Maggie Kelly-Hohmann and Ann Osgerby. Another silver went to 400-metres individual medley competitor, Sharron Davies, who had previously gone to Montreal as a 13-year-old backstroke swimmer. The 4 × 400-metres relay team (June Croft, Sharron Davies, Kaye Lovatt and Jacquelene Willmott) also narrowly missed out on a bronze medal; more evidence of how the US boycott helped the British swimmers in Moscow.

Similarly, the track and field athletics team benefitted, with bronze medals for both the 4 × 100-metres relay team (Bev Goddard-Callender, Heather Hunte-Oakes, Sonia Lannaman and Kathy Smallwood-Cook) and the 4 × 400-metres relay team (Joslyn Hoyte-Smith, Linsey MacDonald, Donna Murray-Hartley and Michelle Probert-Scutt). While the British men did well with a silver and two bronze medals in the rowing events, Beryl Mitchell single sculled for Britain; while the double sculls combined German-born Astrid Ayling and Sue Hanscombe. Cox Sue Brown, led the Four squad comprised of Pauline Bird-Hart, Bridget Buckely, Jane Cross and Pauline Janson to sixth place overall and Pauline Wright coxed the Eights team (Nicola Boyes, Linda Clark, Rosemary Clugston, Beverley Jones, Gill Hodges, Elizabeth Paton, Penny Sweet and Joanna Toch) to fifth place. Many of these rowers would return to Los Angeles, where the coxed men's Four team would see the first of Steve Redgrave's gold medals.

At the 1984 Los Angeles Games, the Soviet Union and 16 allies stayed away, while 140 teams, including Romania, the People's Republic of China and 'Chinese Taipei' competed. Peter Uberroth, a Los Angeles businessman, created an organising committee of entrepreneurs branded as LA84, and television deals brought in $225 million. An overall profit of $223 million across this large and dispersed Olympic Games was reinvested and LA84 remains useful for academics, in terms of the online and hardback library available to researchers but has also funded several sports projects across California. The project was less about developing hard infrastructure and more about reinventing Los Angeles in popular culture, and Uberroth became *Time* magazine's man of the year in 1984. Having had official sponsors and suppliers in 1932, the upscaling of the business model for 1984 also incorporated reused and revamped venues, instead of costly new architecture.

Both the British track and field athletes and swimmers would benefit from the Soviet boycott in Los Angeles. As to the British women's team, the star was Jamaican-born Tessa Sanderson, with a gold medal in the javelin and a new Olympic record for the event. Becoming the first Black British female gold medallist in 1984, Sanderson would contest Olympic events spanning 20 years from 1976 to 1996, and was the first British woman to win a throwing event; in the context of Cold War rivalries, an immense achievement. Her rival Fatima Whitbread, who had Cypriot heritage, took the bronze medal on this occasion and would go one better in Seoul in 1988 to take the silver, after winning the World Championships in 1987.[92] Sanderson was awarded a CBE and created an academy to discover new talent in Newham ahead of London 2012, also serving as Vice Chair of Sport England from 1999–2005.

Wendy Smith-Sly took a silver medal in the 3,000 metres, where the hugely controversial representation of Zola Budd as the leading British contender, led to an intense rivalry with America's Mary Decker and ended with the latter falling on the track. Though approached by a number of universities in the USA, newspaper *The Daily Mail* had encouraged Zola Budd's parents to apply for British citizenship, as her grandfather was born in Britain, in order to allow the South African to compete while Anti-Apartheid rules were in place. She arrived in Britain on 24 March and was granted citizenship on 6 April. The furore surrounding the Decker fall took decades to die down and Budd would later return to, and compete for, South Africa at the 1992 Olympic Games. Wendy Smith-Sly was an English graduate of Loughborough University, later awarded an MBE for services to athletics.

Kathy Smallwood-Cook added to her bronze medal from 1980, with two further bronze medals in the 400-metres race and as part of the 4 × 100-metres relay team with Bev Goddard-Callender, Heather Hunte-Oakes and Simone Jacobs. Shirley Strong won a silver in the 100-metres hurdles. Sue Hearnshaw, the daughter of Muriel Pletts, who narrowly missed out of an Olympic medal in 1948 with the women's 4 × 100-metres relay team, came third in the long jump, much improving her placing from Moscow. Nawal El Moutawakel, a Moroccan hurdler, won the inaugural women's 400-metres hurdles, a pioneering win for female Muslim and Arabic athletes, and she has gone on to become an IOC member. Since becoming a Vice President of the IOC in 2012, El Moutawakel has maintained a high profile role in politics and sporting administration, promoting women in sport initiatives internationally.

Sarah Hardcastle, a 15-year-old British swimmer took a silver medal in the 400-metres freestyle event and a bronze in the 800-metres freestyle. Wigan swimmer, June Croft, added a bronze medal in the 400-metres freestyle to the silver she had already won in Moscow as part of the Medley Relay team. This medal tally would be matched by Maltese-born Virginia Holgate, who took a bronze in the individual Three-Day Event, and won a silver in the team competition with Lucinda Prior-Palmer, Diana Clapham and Ian Stark. Prior-Palmer carried the flag for the Opening ceremony. Holgate had broken her arm in 23 places in 1976, and considered amputation, and the equestrian team had not travelled to Moscow, so this was her first opportunity to win an Olympic medal.[93] In the mixed dressage event, Yorkshire's brother and sister team of Jane and Chris Bartle were joined by Jennie Loriston-Clarke, the sister of Jane and Michael Bullen.

Sarah Rowell, Joyce Smith and Priscilla Welch contested the first Olympic women's marathon, won by the inspirational Joan Benoit, from Grete Andersen-Waitz and Rosa Mota. With this seemingly a new era for women's distance running, pioneers like Violet Piercy who ran the distances in the 1920s and 1930s, and became famous as a result, were all but forgotten.[94] What is also frequently overlooked is that Katherine Switzer, who had run the Boston Marathon in 1967 as KV Switzer, had worked with the Avon cosmetics company since 1976 to launch international women's running events with an Atlanta Marathon in 1978, rapidly supplemented by others in 27 countries and on five continents. The Avon Championship London Marathon in 1980 was the first time that roads were closed for an athletic event, pre-dating the London Marathon by a year.[95]

Joyce Smith who had begun running in the 1950s and was the record holder for over 3,000 metres in 1971, was already a 46-year-old mother of two when she competed in Los Angeles, having established a fastest time of 2.30. 27. Smith, retired from the track to win the Tokyo marathon in 1979 and 1980, winning the first London Marathon in 2.29.57. By this time, 273 women aged 14–48, representing 25 countries ran a marathon in a world class time of 2.55 or faster.[96] Within 30 years of the first Olympic marathon, distance running would become one of the most popular fitness challenges for ordinary women and a highly professionalised activity, producing several female millionaire stars; most notably Paula Radcliffe.[97]

In 1984, in the newly introduced 'feminine' sport of synchronised swimming, Amanda Dodd, Caroline Holmyard and Carolyn Wilson contested the solo event. Holmyard and Wilson combined to take fourth place in the duet. In the rhythmic gymnastics, introduced for similar reasons, Jacqui Leavy and Lorraine Priest would make their debut for Britain. Although the shooting programme had provision for some mixed events like the trap and skeet, a new women's programme was introduced in which Carol Bartlett-Page and Adrienne Bennett competed in the women's sporting pistol, 25 metres. Meanwhile, Irene Daw and Sarah Cooper took part in both the women's air rifle, 10 metres and the women's small-bore rifle, three positions, 50 metres.

In the mixed sailing events Surrey's Cathy Foster partnered Peter Newlands in the mixed two-person dinghy class to take seventh place. This caused Mary Glen Haig to have a diplomatic hiccup in her role at the IOC, since Newlands had a passport issued by New Zealand, even though he had lived and worked in England for eight years. Foster held a UK passport and the bylaws to Rule 8, meant that team members could not hold passports issued by different countries. Appealing directly to Samaranch sorted the problem sooner than repeated requests to the New Zealand Olympic Committee.[98] By 1984, the International Yacht Racing Union (IYRU) would ask Hanne-Marie Bense, Chair of the Women's Sailing Committee, to present evidence to the IOC for the need for new women-only events to be inaugurated within the summer schedule.[99] Pointing out that there had been World Championships since 1977, Bense also made the case that this was an international sport, and a women's two person dinghy event would follow in 1988, in which Debbie Jarvis and Sue Hay-Carr competed.

In the newly inaugurated cycling women's road race, Maria Blower, Linda Gornall, Muriel Sharp and Catherine Swinnerton represented Britain. It would therefore be too late for Beryl Burton, perhaps the finest road cyclist of her generation, and her daughter Denise who had both represented Great Britain at World Championships in 1975.[100] There would be no women's Olympic judo until 1992, although the International Judo Federation had made representations for events to be inaugurated at Seoul in 1988 at least four years earlier.[101] The local organising committee in Seoul considered that it could not afford the expanded programme, but could host a demonstration event. Great Britain did not qualify for the 1984 women's hockey, since the women's field was based on the results of the 1983 World Cup, with the Netherlands, Canada, Australia, West Germany and New Zealand joining the USA as the host nation.

The headlines of the Winter Olympics in Sarajevo, in 1984, belonged to Jane Torvill and Christopher Dean, with a perfect score from all nine judges recorded for their ice dancing routine to Ravel's *Bolero*. They would go on to give an even better performance in the World Championships a month later in Ottawa to take their fourth title. After turning professional, they missed out on the 1988 Winter Games in Calgary and the 1992 Games in Albertville, before winning a bronze medal in 1994, by which time the IOC had continued a pattern of staging the Winter Olympics every four years, but with two years in between Winter and Summer Games. Only short track speed skating competitor Nicky Gooch would supplement the British medal table with another bronze medal in those 10 years, and the men's four-man bobsleigh team won another bronze four years later. In contrast to the perfection of Torvill and Dean, Eddie 'the Eagle' Edwards perhaps personified the British underdog when trying to compete in the ski jumping, for which he was the reigning, and only, British champion. Entirely self-funded, Edwards finished in Calgary last in both categories of jump and his lack of success endeared him to such an extent that the film *Eddie the Eagle* was released in 2016.

The choice of Seoul, South Korea for the 1988 Summer Olympic Games was highly controversial, given the recent Olympic boycotts and political tensions. However, this was a successful competition for the British with the men's hockey team winning a gold medal, their first since 1920, and the women's team narrowly missed out on a medal to finish fourth. Steve Redgrave and his partner, Andy Holmes, took a gold in the rowing, as did swimmer Adrian Moorhouse, Malcolm Cooper in the shooting and Bryn Vale in the sailing. Linford Christie won two silver medals in the sprinting events, made more controversial by the disqualification of Ben Johnson for steroid use, while Scot Ian Stark won silver in both the individual and team Three-Day Event with Virgina Holgate-Leng, Karen Straker-Dixon and Captain Mark Phillips. Holgate-Leng supplemented her team silver with an individual bronze medal.

On the track, the star was Liz McColgan who won a silver in the 10,000 metres and would go on to win two Commonwealth gold medals over the distance in 1986 and 1990. She achieved wider fame as a marathon runner, winning New York on her debut, and the World Championship in 1991, in recognition of which she was voted BBC Sports Personality of the Year. The signed running vest that she wore to victory in the Seoul Olympics was auctioned in 2012, with a reserve of just £200–250.[102] Although McColgan returned to the Olympics in 1992 and 1996, she could not regain her form in the increasingly professional context of Olympic distance running. McColgan's fellow Scot, Yvonne Murray, won a bronze medal in the 3,000 metres. Fighting a number of injuries and recovering from glandular fever, Fatima Whitbread won the silver medal in the javelin.

Tennis returned as a full medal event, with an individual and doubles title for women and men: Britain's Kathleen Godfree, then aged ninety-two, and France's John Borotra, aged ninety, were special guests having won medals sixty four years earlier at the last contested tournament in Paris.[103] Having previously been victorious in the demonstration event four years earlier at the age of just fifteen, Steffi Graf won the singles over Gabriela Sabatini of Argentina, and Pam Shriver and Zina Garrison took the Doubles for the United States. Graf was named 1988 BBC Overseas Sports Personality of the Year. Since the major tennis tournaments had been open to amateurs and professionals since 1968, the inclusion of a full medal sport in an Olympic schedule marked a point at which a new professional era was already underway. Shooting, canoeing, cycling and sailing moderately expanded the range of women's events with new specialisms like windsurfing.

The overall balance of the British team in Seoul was 220 men and 120 women, a much more even gender balance than in 1964. Patterns of women's participation have also to be read in the light of these international relations.

It is fair to expect that the boycotts between 1968 and 1984 will have proportionally affected male athletes more than women, though all the individuals concerned will have felt the loss of opportunity to compete keenly; certainly the women who wanted to become the first British female hockey squad in 1980 were frustrated by politics beyond their control. The expansion of the schedule, alongside newcomer, table tennis, at Seoul in 1988 meant that the inclusion of more team sports for women added to the longstanding tension of an ever-expanding Olympic programme.

Barcelona in 1992 was a new commercial era, with more athletes than ever before. Taking a longer view, we can also conclude that a disproportionate problem for women Olympians internationally would be illustrated in Atlanta 1996 where, of the 197 nations taking part, 26 had no female athletes, eight fewer than in 1992.[104] In contrast, two countries, Lebanon and Liechtenstein, sent women-only teams. Against the background of sporting participation, the chapter now turns to look at the career of a sporting administrator who helped to shape the newly commercial world of the Olympic Games.

Dame Mary Alison Glen Haig: women leaders in world sport

The message that women were quite capable of handling the sensitive political nature of international sport and diplomacy was a point acknowledged at the Executive Committee Board meeting in Tehran in 1967. Even Avery Brundage acknowledged that many of the existing members had died in office, or retired due to ill health, and there was a growing awareness that discrimination against women competitors was affecting the public image of the IOC.[105] A 1974 study initiated by Monique Berlioux, sought to assess the international scale of female involvement in National and International Olympic Committees and International Sporting Federations. The pace of change could be glacial, however. When Blondelle Thompson came to the fore in English track and field athletics in the 1974 season as a hurdles specialist, she was just 20 years old. A well-established career in sports law as a leading barrister would follow, as well as marriage and a family. But it would not be until 2011 that she was appointed to the Court of Arbitration for Sport in Lausanne.[106]

As has briefly been covered in previous chapters, Mary Alison Glen Haig (née Mary Alison James) was best known as a fencer and British Fencing Association official. She had been born on 12 July 1918 at 10 Alma Road, Islington, London, the only child of Captain William Charles James, an officer in the 1st/5th Norfolk Regiment, and his wife Mary Adelaide (née Bannochie).[107] Mary attended Dame Alice Owen's Girls' School, in Islington. Her father had been a competitor at the 1908 London Olympic Games and taught her the sport of fencing from the age of 14, as part of the inaugural Regent Street Polytechnic women's squad. Alison grew up at an exciting time for women's fencing in Britain. After regional competitions in 1937, Mary James also attended the world championship in France, and so was part of the early internationalisation of female competitions. This, in turn, helped her to obtain administrative experience, which mirrored her work in hospitals. She would go on to become better known under her married name after she wed Andrew Glen Haig at Christ Church, Highbury, on 29 December 1943, although the marriage itself was short-lived.[108]

The International Fencing Federation approved a foil event for women, at the 1924 Paris Olympic Games, and so the Olympic singles had some notable British role models in Mary Glen Haig's youth, including three silver medallists: Gladys Davis in 1924, Muriel Freeman in 1928 and Judy Guinness in 1932. Glen Haig contested the women's foil at four Olympic Games from 1948 to 1960, though without winning a medal. As the reigning British Ladies' foil champion in 1948, she made it to the final but finished eighth overall. She also became the British representative on the La Fédération Internationale d'Escrime (FIE), the International Fencing Federation.

Glen Haig's high profile undoubtedly helped promote the sport of fencing domestically and internationally, as glamorous and aspirational. In balancing this, she was aided by her professional career as an administrator, notably working at King's College Hospital in London from 1939 onwards. During the 1948 Olympics, she carried her own fencing gear from the hospital to the stadium. Having seen the horrors of war first hand during the London 'blitz' gave Glen Haig enormous composure under pressure and a sense of perspective in relation to sporting competition:

> When you've had a war and had ghastly things to contend with... On one occasion a nursery had been hit. Can you imagine? I'll never forget that day, mothers beside themselves, not knowing where to run to, not knowing if their child had been brought in. Things like winning medals, we didn't worry about things like that in those days.[109]

In addition to her British titles and Olympic appearances, Mary Glen-Haig's sporting reputation was cemented by her gold medals, first, at the British Empire Games in Auckland in 1950, then at the British Empire and Commonwealth Games in Vancouver in 1954 and, finally, by her bronze medal at the Cardiff Commonwealth Games in 1958. Women's fencing made a relatively early appearance at the British Empire Games, being a staple event, along with track and field athletics, diving and swimming. Although the general principle of women's participation was accepted at the Olympic Games, it was not until the 1996 Olympic Games in Atlanta that the women's épée became a recognised event, and not until the 2004 Games in Athens that the women's sabre would be introduced.

Alongside her sporting interests, she continued to work as a health administrator at King's College Hospital, then as assistant district administrator for South Hammersmith Health District, based at Charing Cross Hospital (1975–1982). After retiring, she served as chair of trustees of the Princess Christian Hospital, Windsor, from 1981 to 1994.

By the time of Mary Glen-Haig's retirement from Olympic competition, a new generation of British fencing talent had followed her lead, such as Jeanette Bailey; Judith Bain; Jeanette Bewley-Cathie (later Wardell-Yerburgh); Eva Davies; Julia Davis; Susan Green; Shirley Netherway; Thoresa Offredy; Shirley Parker; Joyce Pearce; Mary Stafford and Mary Watts-Tobin, to name but a few leading lights. Though the social mix of these athletes was not very diverse, the access of women to further and higher education can be read in the number able to take up such a specialised sport.

As early as 1948 Mary Glen-Haig had begun a parallel career as the consummate committee woman in relation to sport, which relied upon many amateur administrators rather than paid specialists. This committee work included holding office as: President of the Ladies Amateur Fencing Union (1964–1973) and of the Amateur Fencing Association (1973–1986); member of the Sports Council (1966–1982); Chair of the Central Council for Physical Recreation (1974–1980) and then Vice President (1982–1994) of the same organisation; President of the British Sports Association for the Disabled (1981–1991); Vice President of the Sports Aid Foundation from 1987; patron of the Women's Sports Foundation from 1998; and a long-serving Vice President of the British Schools Exploring Society.

Glen Haig was elected to the British Olympic Association and worked with some of the leading sporting administrators in Britain, such as Denis Follows, who was Secretary of the Football Association between 1962 and 1973 and became Chair of the BOA in 1977, until his death in 1983.[110] Denis Follows was internationally respected among IOC members and personally credited with minimising the international relations impact of the boycott of the Moscow Olympic Games, in so far as he was able.[111] Follows was succeeded as Chair by Charles Palmer, who continued to work closely with the President, the Princess Royal, even though he had been passed over as an IOC candidate to replace the Marquis of Exeter.[112] As Palmer had been Chair of the British Judo Association, his place was filled on the BOA National Committee by Gillian Keneally.

Glen Haig was also in good company at the BOA with the campaigning Eileen Gray, president of the Women's Cycle Racing Association in Britain, who had tried to get women's road cycling onto the Summer Olympic schedule since 1962, and had received short shrift from the IOC but nevertheless persevered. Also present by 1984, were Charlotte Russell-Vick OBE for the Great Britain Hockey Board; Elizabeth Anderson OBE for the National Skating Association of Great Britain, and as competitors' representative, Fatima Whitbread MBE.[113] In addition, Gray and Anderson, along with Glen-Haig, were on the General Purpose committee (of a total of 10) and the sub-committee chairs included Helen Bristow for physiotherapy. Gray was elected the Vice Chair of the BOA from 1988 for four years at the age of 72, when Sir Arthur Gold became Chair aged 75.

The first two co-opted female IOC members were Venezuelan Flor Isava-Fonseca and Norwegian Pirjo Häggman, both in 1981; in 1990, the latter would join the IOC Executive. In May 1982, Mary Glen-Haig became only the third woman elected to the International Olympic Committee (IOC) in its history, almost 100 years after its creation in 1894; she was personally endorsed by Sir Denis Follows and Prince Philip.[114]

> I understand from Sir Denis Follows that you are considering the appointment of either Mary Glen-Haig or Charles Palmer to succeed Lord Exeter as a member of the International Olympic Committee. I have known them both for many years and I can assure you that they are both whole-heartedly devoted to the development of amateur sport and to the Olympic ideal.
>
> I have had a particularly close working relationship with Mary Glen Haig as I am President of the Central Council for Physical Recreation and was its elected Chairman from 1975 to 1981 (sic). During that time she made a quite outstanding contribution to the administration of sports and recreation in an entirely voluntary capacity. I should add that by profession she is a hospital administrator in which capacity she had proved herself to be highly competent.[115]

Pressing Mary Glen Haig's case over Palmer, Philip had already conveyed his opinion by telephone message to Samaranch on 28 May 1982. Palmer would lead the fundraising efforts at the BOA, leaving it with reserves of over £3 million in 1988 but his abrasive manner alienated some, and he would be deselected in favour of Sir Arthur Gold by 15 votes to 18, as Chair of the BOA the same year.[116]

Glen Haig was joined as the British IOC representative in 1988 by the Princess Royal, who had taken over the Presidency of the BOA in 1983, in succession to the late Lord Rupert Neville.[117] Prince Philip had continued his enthusiasm for Olympic competition privately at least, even though he was obliged to absent himself formally from the chair and the debate, as the President of the International Equestrian Federation to save embarrassing Margaret Thatcher's government in 1980. Private comments attributed to Philip opposing any planned boycott of the Moscow Olympic Games were nevertheless widely reported.[118] Even though the British equestrian, fencing and hockey teams chose not to go to Moscow, Thatcher was one of the opposing voices in Princess Anne's appointment to the IOC, replacing Lord Luke. This was especially the case, given that the Princess Royal had already replaced her father as the President of the International Equestrian Federation. Nevertheless, the Princess Royal and Mary Glen-Haig remained powerful allies on a range of issues, from the bidding process to anti-doping. Their views on Thatcher are not known.

Marquise de Marino, Princess Nora of Liechtenstein joined the IOC in 1984, bringing with her a wealth of experience at the World Bank and International Institute for Environment and Development, as well as acting as President of Liechtenstein's National Olympic Committee from 1982 to 1992. Olympic bronze medal-winning rower Anita DeFrantz later became an IOC Executive member 1992–2001, and served a second term from 2013, also acting as IOC Vice-President from 1997 to 2001. DeFrantz used her professional experience as a lawyer to oppose the 1980 boycott of the Moscow Games by the US Organising Committee and has subsequently remained one of the highest-ranking African-Americans in world sport.[119]

Glen Haig therefore joined the IOC at a time when the organisation was becoming more aware that a lack of leading female sporting administrators was affecting its public image. Lord Killanin, the President from 1972 to 1980, had dedicated a chapter to the participation of women, but claimed that he was unable to appoint one to the IOC because he could not find a suitable female candidate at the right time in countries with vacant positions.[120] His successor, Juan Antonio Samaranch, would do better, although his fractious relationship with Monique Berlioux would see her leave the IOC in 1985, his embarrassment that she had said publicly in 1983 that he feared a Soviet boycott of the Los Angeles Games never forgiven. Françoise Zweifel took over as IOC Secretary General in 1985, having first begun to work with the Museum in 1982 and to where she would return in 1998, eventually leaving the IOC in 2003.

Glen Haig's appointment, like that of Princess Anne, provided the IOC with a unique diplomatic link between Britain's Commonwealth countries, epitomised by the Commonwealth Games, and the International Assembly of National Confederations of Sport (IANCS) chaired by Prince Philip. Losing no time since her appointment, in August 1982 Glen Haig wrote to Samaranch offering to broach greater integration of African nations with the developing role of IANCS, for instance, counter to the BOA's rather more isolationist approach.[121] Thus, by representing the IOC in Great Britain, Glen Haig helped to lead a change in British attitudes at the highest level in world sport. Nor was Philip immune to growing commercialism in sport, having inaugurated the FEI/Coca-Cola International jumping competition in 1982, opening the sport of equestrianism to unprecedented sponsorship and merchandising. Like Denis Follows before them, Glen-Haig, Prince Philip and the Princess Royal could all be characterised as conservative, pragmatic modernisers.

However, some of the problems that Glen-Haig faced seemed to be intractable. The whole issue of the relationship between the Paralympic Games and Olympic movement was one of these. Of course, Glen-Haig was highly committed to disability sport and had spent much of her professional life in hospital administration campaigning for disability recognition, resources and support. However, when trying to convene a conference on disability sport through the British Association of Disability Sport, with the support of the IOC in 1985, she ran into difficulty, since only the International Coordinating Committee of World Sports Organisations for the Disabled (ICC) had exclusive negotiating rights to the IOC and would not permit other organisations to seek support.[122] As President of the British Sports Association for the Disabled, and an IOC member, this obviously put Glen-Haig in a difficult position. Nevertheless, she presented the Olympic flag on behalf of the IOC at the next Stoke Mandeville Games in July 1986. When Glen-Haig was having a hip replacement operation in 1989, the Executive Board of the IOC considered requiring all bid cities to agree to stage the Paralympics in tandem with the Summer Olympic Games. Her advice was pessimistic:

> My view is that integration with their able bodies partners should take place when ever possible – it is not always possible or desirable – and, knowing the parlous state of the Paralympic International administration, would hope that the IOC do not become too involved at this stage with the proposal.[123]

The integration of women in the Olympic movement was another of Glen-Haig's campaign areas: again with partial success for her seemingly indefatigable efforts. There was a wider context. The United Nations had launched its Decade for Women on 1 January 1976, the goal of which was the promotion of equal rights and opportunities for women around the world. Monique Berlioux had spoken on the history of women at Olympic Games at what was termed, 'The First International Conference on Women in Sport', in London, held 4–6 December 1978, at The Y Hotel, London, sponsored by the Central Council of Physical Recreation and Langham Life Assurance.[124] Berlioux also invited Professor Betty Spears to contribute a chapter, 'Women in the Olympics: An Unresolved Problem', to a book entitled *The Modern Olympics*.[125]

Similarly, Vivian Barfield was making a case for a widespread social change in the way that sport was being done across the world at an international sport summit in Monaco.[126] By 1980, The New South Wales Women's Advisory Council was hosting an international symposium 'Women, Sport and Physical Recreation', to which Berlioux was invited to give a paper on the subject of sports organisations.[127] Ronald Reagan hosted a Women's Sports Foundation annual banquet in 1984, in which Olympic swimmer Donna de Varona outlined the challenges and the gradual changes brought about by Title IX amendments to US education laws, which produced contested advances in women's sport in America.[128] Diverse initiatives such as these culminated in 'The Brighton Declaration on Women and Sport', a legacy of the International World Conference on Women and Sport, organised in 1994 in Brighton, UK. Organised by the Sports Council and supported by the IOC, the conference brought together 280 delegates from over 80 countries to accelerate and advance gender equity in sport.

There were many inequalities to address. A survey presented in 1989, listed Princess Anne as the only female President of an International Federation, and two women Secretary Generals: for badminton, Veronica Rowan and for cycling, Carla Giuliani.[129] Out of the, then 167 National Olympic Committees, six had female Presidents: for Canada, Carol Anne Letheren (also the first chef de mission at the 1988 Olympic Games); for Fiji, Sophia Raddock; for Liechtenstein, Princess Nora; for Romania, Lia Manoliu; for Tonga, Princess Salote Mafile'o Pilolevu Tuita; and for Czechoslovakia, Vera Caslava. National Olympic Committee Secretary Generals included: for El Salvador, Myriam Margarita Quezada de Rodriguez; for Sweden, Gunilla Lindberg; for Syria, Nour El Houda Karfoul; and for the British Virgin Islands, Eileen Parsons. As well as uneven development, there were reversals. When French fencer Brigitte Gapais-Dumont won a silver medal in the women's team foil event at the 1976 Summer Olympics, she was invited to become the chef de mission for the team to Moscow but protests from male colleagues meant that she stood down to second, so that a man could lead the squad.

As well as these developments campaigning for the inclusion of more women in the organisation of world sports, a survey undertaken by Berlioux in 1974, yielded some impressive individuals: from Argentina (Berta Silbergbeg De Tula and Maria Alicia Sklenar De Klega); Cameroon (Elizabeth Manyongha Nyongha); Finland (Jane Erkko, Elli Kahila, Hilkka Kujala, Liisa Orko and Inkeri Soininen); Nigeria (Modupe Akibo; Victoria Alalade; Dr Simi Johnson; Amelia Okpaloka and Charlotte Omiyale); Panama (Diana Arosemena, Maria Del Rosario Correa and Adela Mitil).[130] However, by far the most frequent response was a nil return to the survey.

Mary Glen-Haig continued to fence until her late 70s, so she saw some radical changes in attitudes to women's sport in her lifetime and was active in pioneering some key initiatives in her sport of choice, first along with Charles de Beaumont, and later, Professor Philip Bruce, President of the British Academy of Fencing. Glen Haig played an important part in the 1976 cheating exposé of modern pentathlon star Boris Onischenko, when a modified sword registered hits electronically, even when no contact had been made. After insisting that the equipment be inspected 'Disonischenko' as he was dubbed by the British press, was disqualified and banned from sport for life. The British team who had so far not distinguished themselves in Montreal went on to win gold in the modern pentathlon event.

Later, as an Olympic administrator, Glen-Haig would not accept expensive gifts from cities wishing to host Olympic Games, and was critical of overt commercialism. Glen-Haig remained in the post until 1993, and served on the IOC Medical Commission (1983–1993) and on Olympic bid committees for both Birmingham and Manchester.[131] She also held several positions within the British Olympic Association, including serving on the Medical Trust. As the IOC's representative, she supervised the first Women's Islamic Games in Tehran in 1993.

Glen Haig was appointed an MBE in 1971, a CBE in 1977, and in the 1993 New Year's honours list was made a DBE. She lived for many years with Joyce Pearce until the latter's death in 2011. Pearce, also a leading international fencing competitor in the 1960s and a British Empire and Commonwealth Games gold medallist in 1966, accompanied Glen-Haig to the various social events that coincided with her many sporting commitments, and which they enjoyed enormously.[132] In 1994, Glen-Haig became an honorary member of the IOC, and awarded the Olympic Order. She was made an honorary member of the FIE, the international fencing federation, in 1999.[133] Glen Haig died at the age of 96 on 15 November 2014. A memorial service, attended by the Princess Royal, was held at St Martin-in-the-Fields on 24 June 2015. A response to one of the many tributes and obituaries that were written perhaps provides an insight into Glen-Haig's personality:

> Ann Hawker writes: The fine obituary of the Olympic fencer and sports administrator Dame Mary Glen-Haig referred to her full time work as a hospital administrator. I first encountered her in that capacity at the Royal National Orthopaedic hospital in Stanmore, north-west London. Mrs Glen-Haig, as she was then, gave me a job there when I needed one badly and would have appeared, on the surface, to be a really dicey bet. I didn't let her down. I don't think anyone did, or could have let her down, not Mrs Glen-Haig.[134]

Conclusion

Definitions of amateurism have largely changed over time, to preserve a shaky consensus on how *not* to be a professional. The binary of 'men' and 'women' is no less constructed than ideas of amateurism and professionalism, which nevertheless take gendered forms. Modern sports are marked by many such irrational demarcations. Their legitimacy draws from a heritage that seems longstanding and deep-rooted, organised and rational. The quasi-medicalisation of sport from 1964 to 1984 placed female athletes under surveillance regimes as intrusive as they were conservative. The legacy of those testing regimes, including the buccal smear mouth swab, visual and physical checks of a female athlete's anatomy, and testosterone tests remains with us still.

More widely, access to sport has been part of international instruments and documents, which the United Nations and others approved and promoted in the 1970s and 1980s as a human right. Women consequently became more evident in the last third of the twentieth century in sport in general. The International Olympic Committee, International Federations (IFs) and National Olympic Committees (NOCs) have shared a legitimacy crisis facing other international governing bodies of sport, such as the Federation Internationale de Football Association (FIFA), as they have grown wealthy, developed an increased public profile and their ability to self-regulate has been called into question in the public domain.

Anxiety about the effects of sport on the female physique, mind and character is very much part of the longer view of Olympic history, which takes different forms over time. This chapter has shown that there is not a simple narrative of female assimilation or of acculturation by the IOC. As can be indicated by the court case in Los Angeles brought by the International Runner's Committee to have a 5,000-metres race and a 10,000-metres race included in the women's schedule for 1984, the schedule for women was still restricted at the same time that new middle- and distance-events were included.[135] The long-term effect of 1949s Rule 32 of the IOC Olympic Charter designed to limit the overall expansion of the Summer Games schedule often meant that women's athletics were affected disproportionately. It also means that where women's events are expanded, male events have to be sacrificed and this has caused gender-based antagonism; most notably across sports like wrestling, triathlon, cycling, judo and boxing. So the individual examples within sports, nuance the overall trends.

For some sports involving distance and endurance (the triathlon was included as an Olympic event in 2000), strength (weightlifting in 2000) and contact (women's football in 1996 and boxing in 2012), the change has been slower than others. There is a need to resist the view that inclusion of a particular sport for women was, in itself, a success. For instance, two specifically 'feminine events were included in the Los Angeles Olympic Games, in the form of rhythmic gymnastics and synchronised swimming. So, as the survey has tried to indicate, it is the programme of events that more often contains the detail of how Olympic participation has been gendered, along with individual differences experienced by each person. Hence, the in-depth case studies of two very different individuals, Mary Peters and Mary Glen-Haig, in this chapter. Danger remains contentious. In track and field athletics, the discipline of pole vaulting was not introduced until the 2000 Olympics because there were fears that it could upset a delicate female reproductive cycle. It was not until the Winter Olympics in Sochi 2014 that a women's ski jump discipline was added. The battle for parity and equity remains an on-going campaign.

The chapter has asked readers to consider how, and why, Mary Peters was perceived to the public in Ireland, Britain, Australia and in a unified Germany? There are unionist calls for the name Team GB and Britain to be changed to Team UK, to raise awareness of the fact that the squad draws members from Northern Ireland, as well as Scotland, Wales, England and a number of related smaller dependencies such as Jersey, Guernsey and the Isle of Man. Over the timescale of this chapter, the question of British Sovereignty and Devolution became more of a feature of British political life at home and overseas.

The chapter has responded to questions put by Mark Dyreson for the attention of historians to focus on women, as the twentieth century progressed, being international figures 'increasingly enmeshed in the process of making national identity through sport'.[136] Transnational comparisons helped to define the British women medallists, in a technocratic Cold War atmosphere that increasingly saw athletics as work. However, the chronology presented here resists the orthodox view that women's representation on an international sporting stage has been a 'recent change'.

In addition to discussions of amateurism, with both medical and moral concerns around participation, the chapter highlights that there remains a lot of work to be done on the place on gender in the globalisation of sport. My different reaction to the Korbut-Tourischeva rivalry from that of Allen Guttmann may be due to my nationality, age (I was eight in 1972), the British media's liking for an underdog and a different political view. Korbut became popular in Britain as part of a more global profile, while Tourischeva could be argued to be a more locally-popular heroine. It would be interesting to read accounts of Russian academics of the rivalry. While it is not possible to look at Korbut as innocently now, and know the difficulty she endured then, she also pioneered technically-advanced moves, which developed gymnastics as a sport. Along the way, she inspired millions of young women. Whatever the case, globalisation accelerated the rate of an athlete's fame across this period as television and broadcasting rights expanded.

The question of equality and diversity in sport became more important across the timespan covered in this chapter. The 1984 Summer Paralympic Games were shared between New York and Stoke Mandeville and over 2,000 athletes from 54 countries, competed in 903 events in 18 sports. The Great Britain team of 156 men and 68 women won a total of 107 gold, 112 silver and 112 bronze medals. Having long been associated with Stoke Mandeville, the 1988 Summer Games in Seoul were the first in 24 years to take place in the same city as the Olympic Games, and was the first time the term 'Paralympic' was officially used to describe the programme. However, the Paralympic Games had grown way beyond wheelchair sport. Stars like archery gold medallists Wilma Anic and Joan Cooper; swimmers Dianne Barr, Janice Burton, Louise Byles and Tara Flood, combined with shooting specialists like Deanna Coates, Gill Middleton and athletes like Tanni Grey (now Dame Tanni Grey-Thompson), in the British team. Unlike the 1964 Stoke Mandeville Games, where generalists were rewarded with medals across sports, most participants would specialise in one sport, and most would not win a medal for their participation. In this, the Paralympic Games mirrored the Olympic Games, as disability sport became more professional in organisation. In 1989, the newly established International Paralympic Committee coordinated all future the Paralympic Games and Barcelona in 1992 would become pivotal for public perceptions of the commercial viability of disability sport.

In 1991, the Women's Amateur Athletic Association had agreed to merge with the Amateur Athletic Association of England, with Marea Hartman as its President. The British Athletic Federation was also formed bringing together all clubs in the UK under a single umbrella organisation. In 1992, Sally Gunnell, the 400-metres hurdles gold winner at the Barcelona Olympics would become the first British woman to win a track race in 28 years, as the amateur era gave way to professional dedication. Captain of the British women's Olympic team, Gunnell was made an MBE in the New Year's Honours list, the same time that Mary Glen-Haig was elevated from OBE to Dame. Although aged 75, and therefore required to retire from the IOC in 1993, Glen-Haig had used her connections to advocate on behalf of individuals and diverse communities hoping her honour would be 'good for sport, and particularly women in sport'.[137]

Joining Gunnell and Glen-Haig in the honours list was Tanni Grey and Chris Holmes, both made MBEs, who had won four wheelchair gold medals, and six in the swimming pool, respectively.[138] Chris Boardman had an even more telling Olympic win, as his was the first British win in an individual cycling event for 84 years. Rowers Matthew Pinsent, Greg Searle, Jonny Searle, Garry Herbert, and swimmers Nick Gillingham and Sharron Davies were also recognised. Linford Christie, who had won the 100 metres in Barcelona, had already been recognised with an honour after his silver medal in Seoul.

Jane Sixsmith led the women's hockey team in Barcelona to a bronze medal, appearing four times at the Olympics in all and was awarded an MBE. Sharon Randle, who had competed in the women's judo demonstration event in 1988, won a bronze medal in 1992, as did Kate Howey, while Nicola Fairbrother went one better, to win a silver.

Although all three had less success in Atlanta four years later, Howey would return to Sydney to take a silver medal and therefore become the first female British judo multiple medallist and now works in talent identification and coaching. Britain would have to wait until 2012 for their next female Olympic judo medals: Gemma Gibbons took silver and Karina Bryant bronze. The other outstanding female British success in 1996, was Denise Lewis taking bronze in the heptathlon, a feat she would improve upon to take gold in 2000. Although it seemed incongruous by 2000, the modern pentathlon for women was finally placed on the Olympic schedule. Nevertheless, women had competed at the modern pentathlon World Championships since 1978. Britain's Steph Cook and Kate Allenby won gold and bronze medals, respectively, supplemented by a gold for Shirley Robinson in the Europe sailing class.

As a nation lacking Alpine mountain ranges, the British have traditionally been less well represented at the Winter Olympic Games, however, the addition of new disciplines to the schedule has changed the profile of female representatives quite recently. At the Salt Lake City Winter Olympics, the Scottish 'housewives' Janice Rankin, Fiona MacDonald, Debbie Knox and Margaret Morton, led by team captain Rhona Martin would win Britain's first female curling gold medal, and Alex Coomber took a bronze in the inaugural skeleton event.[139] Followed by a silver medal winning performance by Shelley Rudman in Turin 2006, and gold medals for Amy Williams and Lizzy Yarnold, respectively in 2010 and 2014, the female skeleton appears to be something in which Britain can lead the world in marked contrast to the male competition and the question remains of why that should be. Into the twenty-first century, Britain's representatives, and the tiny elite of medal winners, have continued to diversify. It is a topic that the chapter has explored but there are many points for further examination of a complex range of identities.

Finally, the chapter has debated the role of individual agency and national pride based on representing a nation. Some athletes have chosen to stay away because of their conscience on different matters and others have been prevented from going to the Games by local circumstances and national policy. Princess Anne has contributed to the narrative that the more nationalistic aspects of teams marching en masse at the Opening Ceremonies behind flags could be replaced with more celebratory festivities.

Her Highness' response to the question, 'What is the value of the Games in a professional era?' was equally pragmatic:

> They have a huge value in potential to professionals and those who want to make a career in sport, and a medal will enormously enhance their earning ability. Whether that's right or wrong I am not sure, certainly it would be wrong to have a direct reward for winning. Obviously in the old days there was no scope for earning money and it was forbidden, but nowadays with greater leisure time activities this is one of the world's growing industries, where sports is available to more and more people and a proportion of those want to do very well. I wouldn't argue that this is a perfectly reasonable ambition.[140]

Notes

1. Louise Page *Golden Girls* London: Methuen, 1985 p. 4.
2. Mike Dennis and Jonathan Grix *Sport Under Communism: Behind the East German 'Miracle'* Basingstoke: Palgrave Macmillan, 2012 pp. 29–30.
3. Paul Dimeo 'Good Versus Evil? Drugs, Sport and the Cold War' in Stephen Wagg and David Andrews (eds.) *East Plays West: Sport and the Cold War* London: Routledge, 2007 p. 158.
4. Mike Dennis and Jonathan Grix *Sport Under Communism* pp. 49–50.
5. Louise Page 'Act One Scene One' *Golden Girls* p. 5.
6. Louise Page 'Act Two Scene Five' *Golden Girls* p. 104.
7. International Olympic Committee 'International Olympic Committee Drives Discussion on Pregnancy and Elite Athletes' International Olympic Committee www.olympic.org/news/ioc-drives-discussions-on-pregnancy-and-elite-athletes accessed 8 June 2016.
8. John Hughson *The Friendly Games*—The 'Official' IOC Film of the 1956 Melbourne Olympics as Historical Record *Historical Journal of Film, Radio and Television* 30: 4 pp. 529–542.

9. J. W. Westerhoff *Letter to KS Duncan re: South Africa in the Olympic Games 25 March 1968* p. 1 BOA Archive, London.
10. Dr Franz M. Messerli *Women's Participation to the Modern Olympic Game. Report to the International Olympic Committee* Lausanne: International Olympic Committee, 1952 p. 16 IOC Archive, Lausanne.
11. Hansard *House of Lords Parliamentary Debates Official Report* Vol 25 No 88 22 May 1963 London: Her Majesty's Stationery Office, 1963 pp. 287–387.
12. Sandy Duncan *Letter to Signor Onesti re: National Olympic Committees 10 March 1966* BOA Archive, London p. 2.
13. Sandy Duncan *IOC/NOC Session 17 June 1961* BOA Archive, London, p. 2.
14. Otto Mayer *Letter to A.P. Page The Clay Pigeon Shooting Association 13 February 1961* Lausanne: International Olympic Committee p. 1 IOC Archive, Lausanne.
15. K. S. Duncan British Olympic Association *Table of Costs and Appeal Income 6 March 1972* BOA Archive, London.
16. Mary Rand *Mary, Mary: An Autobiography* London: Hodder & Stoughton, 1969 p. 25.
17. Mary Rand *Mary Mary* p. 20.
18. Harold Palmer 'A Gold For Mary: She Breaks World Record' *Evening Standard* 14 October 1964 front page.
19. Harold Palmer 'Tears of Joy For Golden Girl Ann: She Shatters World 800 Metres Record in Olympic Triumph' *Evening Standard* 20 October 1964 front page.
20. Lincoln Allison 'Chapter 7 First Family' in *Amateurism in Sport: An Analysis and a Defence* London: Frank Cass, 2001 pp. 118–122.
21. J. B Strasser and Laurie Becklund *Swoosh: the Unauthorised Story of Nike and the Men Who Played There* San Diego: Harcourt Brace Jovanovich, 1991.
22. Harold Palmer 'Tokyo 1964: A Royal Welcome' *Evening Standard* 24 October 1964 front page.
23. Desmond Hackett '…That Brings Them Victory' *The Daily Express* 20 October 1964 p. 11.
24. Dorothy Hyman *Sprint to Fame* London: Stanley Paul, 1964.
25. Mary Rand *Mary, Mary* p. 26.
26. Pat Koechlin-Smythe *Leaping Life's Fences: an autobiography* London: The Sportsman's Press, 1992 pp. 100–104; Mary Rand *Mary Mary* pp. 61–64. The *Daily Express* was to get exclusive photographs and stories by pre-arrangement in both cases; Smythe already wrote for the paper on show jumping and skiing.
27. Yorgo Pasadeos and Paula Renfro 'An Appraisal of Murdoch and the U.S. Daily Press' *Newspaper Research Journal* 18: 2 1997 pp. 33–35.
28. Norris McWhirter ' "Ballerina" Nina' *World Sports: International Sports Magazine* September 1955 London: Country and Sporting Publications, 1955 pp. 30–31.
29. Jeffrey Richards *Cinema and Radio in Britain and America 1920–1960* Manchester University Press, 2010 p. 53.
30. David Emery 'Olympic Job Goes to Our Member' *Sports Writers' Association Bulletin July 1987* p. 1 BOA Archive, London.
31. Sports Writers' Association of Great Britain 'Accreditation Notes' The Sports Council Press Unit 16 Upper Woburn Place London BOA Archive, London.
32. Caz Walton *Caz Walton Remembers Winning Gold at the Tokyo Games* www.paralympicheritage.org.uk/content/sports/wheelchair-racing/caz-walton-remembers-gold-medal-tokyo-1964 accessed 23 August 2017.
33. Sally Haynes *Sally Haynes on being urged to set an example at the Tokyo Games* www.paralympicheritage.org.uk/content/stories/paralympians/haynes-sally/sally-haynes-urged-set-example-tokyo-games accessed 23 August 2017.

34 Susan Baroness Masham of Ilton *Tokyo Games* www.paralympicheritage.org.uk/content/stories/paralympians/cunliffe-lister-susan/lady-susan-masham-tokyo-games accessed 23 August 2017.
35 Jackie Ward *Early sports and recreation* www.paralympicheritage.org.uk/content/topics/stoke-mandeville/early-sports-and-recreation accessed 23 August 2017.
36 Vanessa Heggie ' "Only the British Appear to be Making a Fuss": The Science of Success and the Myth of Amateurism at the Mexico Olympiad, 1968' *Sport In History* 28: 2 2008 pp. 213–235.
37 Doug Gardner 'Dangers of Mexico 1968' *World Sports: The Official Magazine of the British Olympic Association* London: Country and Sporting Publications Ltd., November 1964.
38 J. W. Westerhoff *Letter to KS Duncan Re: IOC Newletter No 1* 25 October 1967 p. 1 IOC Archive, Lausanne.
39 J. W. Westerhoff *Letter to Sandy Duncan re: IOC Entry forms* 19 December 1967 p. 1 IOC Archive, Lausanne.
40 K. S Duncan *Letter to Avery Brundage Re: International Olympic Committee Entry Form (Standard Text)* 27 December 1967 p. 1 IOC Archive, Lausanne.
41 International Olympic Committee *Minutes of the International Olympic Committee Executive Commission on Sex Tests and Doping* Grenoble 30 January 1968 pp. 24–28 IOC Archive, Lausanne.
42 WAAA *Report of the Honorary Secretary* 1967/8 p. 5 Special Collections WAAA Box 1 Birmingham University.
43 Anon. 'The Girls Who Seek to Strike Gold: They'll carry Britain's hopes at the Mexico Olympics' *The Evening News* 5 September 1968 p. 15.
44 Mel Watman The Official History of the Women's Amateur Athletic Association 1922–2012 Cheltenham: Sports Books Ltd, 2012 p. 114.
45 Mel Watman The Official History of the Women's Amateur Athletic Association p. 115.
46 Brian Oliver *The Commonwealth Games: Extraordinary Stories Behind the Medals* London: Bloomsbury, 2014 p. 60.
47 Frank Taylor 'Golden Girl! Lillian Board Gallops Away with the European 800 metre title' *The Sun* 19 September 1969 p. 11.
48 Nigel Benson and Bill Wigmore 'Lillian Board Gravely Ill: Track Star for Bavarian Clinic' *Daily Sketch* 7 November 1970 Headline.
49 Greg Struthers 'Best and Worst: Jane Bullen' *The Sunday Times* 15 January 2012 www.thetimes.co.uk/article/best-and-worst-jane-bullen-pbx3dksrzpl accessed 5 August 2012.
50 Greg Struthers 'Best and Worst: Jane Bullen'.
51 Land Rover Burghley Horse Trials 'Three Day Event: Past Winners' Land Rover Burghley Horse Trials www.burghley-horse.co.uk/three-day-event/past-winners/ accessed 5 August 2017.
52 Anna Tyzack 'Life follows art for a pony-mad dynasty' *The Telegraph* 3 October 2012 www.telegraph.co.uk/lifestyle/9583938/Life-follows-art-for-a-pony-mad-dynasty.html accessed 5 August 2017.
53 WAAA *Report of the Honorary Secretary* 1967/8 p. 5 Special Collections WAAA Box 1 Birmingham University.
54 K. S. Duncan British Olympic Association *Table of Costs and Appeal Income*.
55 Sandy Duncan *Letter to Otto Mayer* 21 October 1958 BOA Archive, London p. 2.
56 The Ski Club of Great Britain 'The Pery Medal: 1972 Miss Davina Galica and Miss Gina Hawthorn' www.skiclub.co.uk/news-and-events/inspire-awards/the-pery-medal accessed 7 August 2017.

57. The Minutes of the WAAA for the five years 1922–1927 have been lost so the information is based on a history of the main events during that time compiled by the following founder members Mr Joe Palmer, Major W. B. Marchant, Mr E. H. Knowles and Mrs F. Millichip (née Birchenough) and Mrs V. Searle (née Palmer) Birmingham: Special Collections University of Birmingham, Box Two WAAA Files.
58. Mel Watman *The Official History of the AAA 1880–2010* Cheltenham: Sports Books Ltd, 2011 p. 5.
59. WAAA *Minutes of Annual General Meeting 1st February 1958 Polytechnic Regent Street London 7 February 1959* Birmingham: Special Collections University of Birmingham, Box Two WAAA Files p. 3.
60. Neil Wilson 'Mary Peters' *British Sport 1972–3* London: The Sportswriters Association of Great Britain, 1973 p. 39.
61. Mary Peters with Ian Woolridge *Mary P.: Autobiography* London: Stanley Paul, 1974 pp. 33–34.
62. Deanocity08 'Mary Peters 1972 Olympic victory' YouTube www.youtube.com accessed 2 February 2017.
63. Though the 1936 Berlin Games had been televised and live colour TV was available from Mexico City in 1968.
64. Mary Peters *Mary P.* Prologue.
65. Mary Peters *Mary Peters: Oral History Interview with Jean Williams* London: Heathrow Airport, 4 August 2010.
66. Neil Wilson 'Mary Peters' p. 39.
67. Captain Beecher 'Go on Mary Girl, Ulster's Finest' YouTube www.youtube.com accessed 2 February 2017.
68. Brian Giles 'How Britain Keeps One Jump Ahead…' *The Daily Mail* 9 September 1972 p. 12.
69. John Smith 'Golden Idol: Undimmed by tragedy, the Olympic Glories of Mark Spitz' *Sunday Mirror* 10 September 1972 p. 2.
70. Allen Guttmann *Women's Sports: A History* New York: Columbia University Press, 1991 p. 137.
71. Evelyn Mertin 'Presenting Heroes: Athletes as Role Models for the New Soviet Person' *The International Journal of the History of Sport* 26: 4 March 2009 pp. 477–9.
72. Carl Giles 'Thank Little Olga for Taking Their Minds Off Football' *The Sunday Express* 6 May 1973 p. 5.
73. Clive Bolton 'The Golden Girl Who Won the Heart of Millions' *The Sun* 2 September 1972 p. 5.
74. BBC 2 'Olga Korbut – The Gymnast, Her Coach, Her Rival And The President' 24 August 2017. Other footage available at www.itnsource/ accessed 2 February 2017.
75. Olga Korbut www.olgakorbut.com/korbut accessed 2 February 2010.
76. Mary Peters *Mary Peters: Oral History Interview*.
77. Joan Lombard 'Sin on the Sportsfield, or what's kept women sidetracked' *The Irish Times* 3 October 1982 p. 24.
78. Cyril White 'Opportunities for Women in Sport' *Council of Europe Committee for the Development of Sport Seminar on the Greater Involvement of Women in Sport* Dublin Castle, 30 September to 3 October 1980 p. 1 IOC Archive, Lausanne. The Bord Luthchleas na hEireann (BLE) was the Gaelic name of the Irish athletic association.
79. Denis O'Hara *The Remarkable Kyles* Belfast: O'Hara Publications, 2006.
80. Mary Peters 'Foreword' in Triloke Khosla and Valerie McBroom *Physique of Female Olympic Finalists: Standards on age, height and weight of 824 finalists from 47 events* Penarth: Welsh National School of Medicine, 1984.

81 Reg Blundstone *Letter to Charles Riolo Honorary Secretary FISA* 27 January 1970 IOC Archive, Lausanne.
82 British Olympic Association *Guest List and Seating Plan: 75th Anniversary Dinner, Piccadilly Hotel London* 21 November 1980 BOA Archive, London.
83 Lord Killanin *Letter to All Members of the IOC Regarding Future Policy* 16 August 1976 IOC Archive, Lausanne.
84 IOC Executive Board *Report on NOCs Withdrawal Olympic Games Montreal* 6 October 1976 IOC Archive, Lausanne.
85 Danielle Griffin *Sport and Canadian Anti-Apartheid Policy: a political and diplomatic history c.1968–c.1980* unpublished PhD thesis, De Montfort University 2012.
86 The National Archives *Government policy on 1980 Games following Soviet invasion of Afghanistan* AT 60/185, AT 60/187, AT 60/188, AT 60/191 www.nationalarchives.gov.uk/olympics/timeline.htm#&panel1-22 accessed 20 August 2017.
87 Alan Tomlinson 'The Disneyfication of the Olympics? Freak Shows of the body' in John Bale and M Christiansen (eds) *Post-Olympism? Questioning Sport in the Twenty-First Century* Oxford: Berg, 2004 pp. 147–163.
88 John MacAloon *This Great Symbol: Pierre de Coubertin and the Origins of the Modern Olympic Games* Chicago: University of Chicago Press, 1981. See also John J. MacAloon *Brides of Victory: Nationalism and Gender in Olympic Ritual* London: Berg, 1997, for an ethnographic reading of the place of females in Olympic victory ceremonies.
89 John Bale and Mette Krogh Christensen (eds.) *Post-Olympism?: Questioning Sport in the Twenty-First Century* Oxford: Berg, 2004 pp. 13–32.
90 Ian Woolridge 'Ecstasy: Magnificent Coe runs the race of a lifetime to win Olympic Gold' *The Daily Mail* 2 August 1980 p. 1.
91 Neil Wilson 'The World Beaters: Victory for Britain: Ovett and Coe smash records' *The Daily Mail* 2 July 1980 p. 1.
92 Colin Hart 'Thanks God For Fatima: A Gold At Last' *Sun Sport* 7 September 1987 p. 1.
93 Virginia Holgate *Ginny-An Autobiography* London: Hutchinson, 1986 pp. 15–16.
94 Peter Lovesey *The First Lady: The Mystery of Violet Piercy, Marathon Pioneer* unpublished paper, BOA Archive, London.
95 Michael Coleman 'This Girl Will Stop the London Traffic' *The Times* 1 August 1980 p. 74.
96 Elizabeth Ferris 'Attitudes to Women's Sport: Towards a Sociological Theory' *Council of Europe Seminar The Greater Involvement of Women in Sport Dublin Castle Ireland* 30 September to 3 October 1980 IOC Archive, Lausanne p. 11.
97 Paula Radcliffe *Paula: My Story So Far* London: Simon and Schuster, 2004.
98 Mary Glen-Haig *Letter to Juan Antonio Samaranch regarding Kathy Foster and Peter Newlands* 14 December 1983 BOA Offices London Mary Glen-Haig File IOC Archive, Lausanne.
99 Hanne-Marie Bense *International Yacht Racing Union: Organisation of Women's Sailing Throughout The World* Women and Sport File IOC Archive, Lausanne.
100 Beryl Burton *Personal Best: The Autobiography of Beryl Burton* Huddersfield: Springfield Books, 1986 pp. 130–131.
101 Monique Berlioux *Letter to Mary Glen Haig regarding the introduction of women's judo to the Summer Olympic programme* 5 December 1984 BOA Offices London Mary Glen Haig File IOC Archive, Lausanne.
102 Graham Budd Auctions 'Liz McColgan's signed running vest worn during her silver medal winning performance in the 10,000 metres at the Seoul Olympics' *Olympic Memorabilia* 24 July 2012 London: Sotheby's, 2012 p. 139.

103 Alan Little *Tennis and the Olympic Games* London: Wimbledon Lawn Tennis Museum, 2009 p. 56.
104 Stephanie Daniels *Women and the Olympics* unpublished MA thesis Leicester: De Montfort University, 1997 pp. 52–53.
105 International Olympic Committee Minutes of the Executive Board of the IOC Royal Tehran Hilton 2–8 May 1967 p. 4 IOC Archive, Lausanne.
106 Mel Watman *The Official History of the Women's Amateur Athletic Association* p. 127.
107 Ancestry UK 'James, William Charles' *England and Wales National Probate Calendar 1955* www.Ancestry.co.uk accessed 31 January 2017.
108 General Register Office *Certified Copy of an Entry of Marriage: Andrew Glen Haig and Mary Alison James 29 December 1943* General Register Office England application number 7099199-32.
109 Anon. 'Dame Mary Glen Haig – Obituary' *The Telegraph* 26 November 2014 www.telegraph.co.uk/news/obituaries/11255904/Dame-Mary-Glen Haig-obituary.html accessed 7 August 2017.
110 British Olympic Association *Minutes of the BOA Committee 1 Malet Street London 3 May 1977* BOA Archive, London p. 1.
111 Juan Antonio Samaranch *Letter of Condolence to Richard Palmer Secretary General of the BOA 20 September 1983* Mary Glen Haig File IOC Archive, Lausanne.
112 David Millner 'David Millner's Olympic Diary' *The Times* 11 February 1984 Mary Glen-Haig File IOC Museum and Archive, Lausanne.
113 British Olympic Association *Minutes of National Olympic Committee 8 October 1884 Mander Hall, Mabledon Place, London* Mary Glen-Haig File IOC Archive, Lausanne.
114 Sir Denis Follows *Letter to Juan Antonio Samaranch regarding Mary Glen Haig's election to the IOC 15 June 1982 BOA Offices London* Mary Glen Haig File IOC Archive, Lausanne.
115 Prince Philip *Letter to Juan Antonio Samaranch regarding Mary Glen Haig's election to the IOC 3 June 1982 Buckingham Palace, London* Mary Glen Haig File IOC Archive, Lausanne.
116 John Goodbody 'Officials Return to Dark Age' *The Times* 28 October 1988 p. 8.
117 Sandy Duncan *Letter to Monique Berlioux regarding HRH Princess Anne's election as President of the BOA 8 August 1983* Women and Sport File IOC Archive, Lausanne.
118 John Rodda 'Princess Anne Set for Place on the IOC' *The Guardian* 10 February 1988 p. 34.
119 Anita DeFrantz http://anitadefrantz.net accessed 2 February 2017.
120 Michael Morris Baron Killanin *My Olympic Years: President of the International Olympic Committee 1972–1980* London: Secker and Warburg, 1983 pp. 63–65.
121 Mary Glen Haig *Letter to Juan Antonio Samaranch regarding African Nations and International Assembly of National Confederations of Sport (IANCS) 2 August 1982* Mary Glen Haig File IOC Archive, Lausanne.
122 Robert Price *Letter to Mary Glen Haig Regarding a proposed International Conference on Sport for the Disabled 7 August 1985 British Sports Association for the Disabled Offices London* Mary Glen Haig File IOC Archive, Lausanne.
123 Mary Glen Haig *Letter to Juan Antonio Samaranch regarding Executive Board Minutes 10 October 1989* Mary Glen Haig File IOC Archive, Lausanne.
124 Monique Berlioux 'Women in the Olympic Context' *First International Conference on Women in Sport 4–6 December 1978, The "Y" Hotel, London; sponsored by the CCPR and the Langham Life Assurance Co., Ltd* Women and Sport File IOC Archive, Lausanne.

125 Betty Spears 'Women in Olympics: an unresolved problem' in Peter Graham, and Horst Ueberhorst (eds.) *The Modern Olympics* New York, Leisure Press, 1976 pp. 62–82.
126 Vivian Barfield 'Women in the International Sports Scene' *International Sport Summit Monte Carlo Monaco 5–12 March 1978 Women and Sport File* IOC Archive, Lausanne.
127 Barbara Wertheim *Letter to Monica Berlioux: Invitation to speak at Women, Sport and Physical Recreation Conference, Sydney Australia 20–23 January 1980 Women and Sport File* IOC Archive, Lausanne.
128 Donna de Varona 'Women's Fight for Sport Equality Begins Again' *The New York Times* 18 March 1984 p. 5.
129 Monique Berlioux 'Women and the Olympic Movement' *Women and Sport File* IOC Archive, Lausanne p. 2.
130 Monique Berlioux *Letter introducing IOC Survey on Lady Members in the International Olympic Committee, International Federations, and National Olympic Committees 7 January 1974 Women and Sport File* IOC Archive, Lausanne.
131 Mary Glen Haig *Letter to Juan Antonio Samaranch regarding Mary Glen Haig's invitation to join the IOC Medical Committee 10 April 1983 BOA Offices London Mary Glen Haig File* IOC Archive, Lausanne.
132 Peter Nichols 'Dame Mary Glen Haig obituary' *The Guardian* 2 December 2014 www.theguardian.com/sport/2014/dec/02/dame-mary-Glen Haig accessed 7 August 2017.
133 International Olympic Committee 'Death of Dame Mary Alison Glen Haig DBE: IOC Member Honorary Member in Great Britain' *Olympic News* www.olympic.org/news/death-ofdame-mary-alison-Glen Haig-dbe-ioc-honorary-member-in-great-britain accessed 26 July 2017.
134 Ann Hawker 'Letter Dame Mary Glen Haig' *The Guardian* 5 December 2014.
135 International Runners' Committee 'The Flame Will Burn Less Brightly' *International Runners' Committee Press Release July 1984 Los Angeles Women and Sport File* IOC Archive, Lausanne.
136 Mark Dyreson Icons of Liberty or Objects of Desire? American Women Olympians and the Politics of Consumption' *Journal of Contemporary History* 38: 3 2004 p. 435.
137 Mary Glen Haig *Letter to Juan Antonio Samaranch regarding congratulations from the IOC on being awarded my DBE 12 January 1993 Mary Glen Haig File* IOC Archive, Lausanne.
138 David Powell 'Olympic Winners are Honoured' *The Times* 31 December 1992 p. 5.
139 Nick Yapp *Chasing Gold: Centenary of the British Olympic Association* London: Getty Images, 2005 pp. 162–163.
140 David Miller 'End All Team Sports At the Olympics' *The Times* 8 June 1984 pp. 5–6.

Chapter 8

Olympic legacies
Lottery funding, professional sport, diversity and fame

The Langham Life First International Conference on Women in Sport, was held in 1978 in a collaboration between Dame Mary Glen Haig, as Chair of the Central Council for Physical Recreation (CCPR) and HRH Princess Anne, who was prompted to say:

> A lot of people find it difficult to understand what drives so many sportswomen to reach that pinnacle as it seems to mean so much hardship and so many sacrifices. I'm afraid the only answer is to go to the Olympic Games – no other sporting occasion has the same effect. That is the top – but it all has to start somewhere and it must be remembered that the reason for any woman taking up a sport is that a) she *wants* to do it and b) she *can* do it.
>
> For at the end of the day it is natural talent, inclination and opportunity that encourages anybody to take up a sport at all. Women in sport is not a new thing but is obviously growing in popularity both for participators and spectators.[1]

It was not the first International Conference on women's sport, as this work has shown in relation to the pioneering work of Alice Milliat in the 1920s, and the organisation of the WAAA at the London 1934 Women's World Games, but it was an important milestone in the British sporting establishment recognising that it had neglected this topic. It would take someone of the standing of Princess Anne and Mary Glen Haig to effect this change, and it highlighted more continuity than transformation.

How then can we make links between the absolute penury, and hardship of Britain's women amateurs in the Golden Girls generation, suggested by Hyman's quotation below and today's professional athletes? Although Dorothy Hyman had been Sports Personality of the Year in 1963, she clearly had little physical, or psychological help with her preparation for major titles, as she made clear in her autobiography:

> Sometimes the wind has blown bitter cold through my track-suit, or the clinging mud has dragged on my leg muscles. I've trained wearing a

raincoat in weather not fit for a dog to be out in. I've been sick through my efforts, then gone on training. Now I'm giving it up: I've retired. Athletics has taken more out of me than most of you may imagine. The Press once christened me 'Miss Poker Face' because of my nerveless appearance in Olympic Games and European championships. But I've never been just a running machine... In short, running – the training and the competition – has often been a strain. It's not always been easy on the cash side, either, for I'm not from a wealthy family.[2]

To make links between the generation of Olympians such as Hyman, Rand and Packer and the athletes we today laud as Olympians, such as Denise Lewis, Kelly Holmes, Christine Ohurugo and Dina Asher-Smith, the twin themes of this conclusion are continuity and change.

Using two case studies, of rower Sarah Winckless MBE and footballer Eniola Aluko, the conclusion will highlight what the legacy of National Lottery Funding for Olympic athletes has been in the more recent period, as well as the continuities faced by women who wish to earn a living from sport, even for a relatively short period of their young lives.

Obviously, the main change is that The National Lottery, and the Exchequer has funded UK Sport, at an arm's length from the government, since 1997. Decisions are made on a four-year basis but now have an eight-year performance development model. Around 70 per cent of the money is distributed, first, to National Governing Bodies, for the World Class Performance programme and, second, directly to athletes themselves, called an Athlete Performance Award (APA). The longstanding arguments about whether the UK government should fund Olympic and Paralympic athletes has then been resolved as integral to national prestige, and with dramatic effect for a collection of small countries on a world stage. As one of 12 beneficiaries from the National Lottery, UK Sport had funded 4,600 athletes, with a return of 633 Olympic and Paralympic medals, as at 1 January 2020.

It should though be noted that some of our most famous and wealthy athletes, such as the distance specialist Paula Radcliffe, who has won the London marathon three times, and New York marathon three times, as well as Chicago, have other avenues of revenue available to them, for which Lottery Funding is but one small source of income. A former, world, European, Commonwealth champion over marathon, half marathon and cross-country distances, Radcliffe was also a talented track distance runner. A millionaire, living in Monte Carlo, Radcliffe's greatest distinctions did not come at Olympic events and in spite of representing Britain four times at the Games, she did not win a medal. The great-niece of Olympic silver medallist swimmer Charlotte Radcliffe, Paula Radcliffe has a high profile in the media at major events and is a prominent anti-doping campaigner.

At the first Olympic Games to benefit from lottery funding in the approach to develop the British team in Sydney in 2000, almost £60 million in National Lottery Heritage funding garnered 11 gold, 10 silver and seven bronze medals. Denise Lewis won gold in the women's heptathlon; Shirley Robinson in the Europe sailing class; and Steph Cook in the women's modern pentathlon. The judoka, Kate Howey MBE, would take silver in the under 70 kilogram event, and therefore beat her bronze from Barcelona in 1992, going on to compete in four Games all-told, and carrying the British flag in 2004 at the opening ceremony. As well as the first women's rowing silver medal for Britain in the quadruple sculls, Jeanette Law and Pippa Funnell took silver in the mixed Eventing with Leslie Law and Ian Stark. Yvonne McGregor took a bronze in the cycling, as did Katherine Merry and Kelly Holmes in the athletics, and Kate Allenby in the modern pentathlon. Along with badminton partner, Simon Archer, Joanne Goode completed the women's medal-haul. By Beijing, in 2008, the British would finish fourth in the medal table, and has continued to improve with a third place behind the USA and China in 2012 and a second place in 2016, with 67 medals. Across five consecutive games the medal tally, and the Lottery Funding, has continued to increase.

According to an IOC magazine, *Olympic Review*, Great Britain had sent 835 women competitors to Games of the Olympiad, or Summer Olympic Games, and 131 to Olympic Winter Games from 1900 to 1998. This placed Britain second only to the USA at Games of the Olympiad, with a total of 1,183 women competitors.[3] The USA also topped the chart of the Olympic Winter Games, with 309 competitors, leaving Britain in seventh spot, behind the likes of Canada, Germany, Austria, Japan and Sweden. Perhaps Britain's lack of an Alpine tradition was a factor here. However, at the Summer Games, almost a century of competition had seen Britain's enthusiastic amateurs outnumber Germany (East, West and unified teams), Canada, Russia (including Soviet Union teams), Australia, Japan, France, the Netherlands and Italy.

In spite of the obvious enthusiasm of British women for the Olympic Games, one of the main continuities throughout the twentieth century was that Britain's finest sportswomen would not become Olympians because there was no event, either at sporting or discipline level, for women in which they might compete. The greats that would miss out included campaigning boxers such as Jane Crouch; cricket celebrities, including Rachael Heyoe Flint; generations of pioneering cyclists such as Eileen Sheridan, Marguerite Wilson and Beryl Burton; football players like the great Gill Coultard; hockey players like Mary Russell Vick; golfers from the era of Cecil Leitch and Joyce Wethered, to Laura Davies; rowers like Amy Gentry; table tennis and Wimbledon tennis stars including Ann Jones, Christine Truman, Betty Nuthall, Dorothy Round, Sue Barker and Virginia Wade, as well as a host of others who featured prominently in the daily news. Of course, not all men's sporting events are included in the Olympic programme but the incremental and uneven nature of growth of the women's programme meant that many women who featured in the annual Sports Personality of the Year awards made their names outside the Games.

This said, it is also clear that British women have helped to pioneer key aspects of the Olympic Movement as athletes and leaders. There are now more opportunities in the twenty-first century and the profile of our decorated Olympians includes more women sailors, rowers, cyclists, boxers, football players, snowboarders and martial arts specialists, changing the nature of our perceptions of who, and what, the Olympics and Paralympic movement represents. As more women make their name in the Olympic and Paralympic Games, they can use this to move to a career either in politics and public life such as Baroness Tanni Grey-Thompson, or onto board leadership positions, as Anne Panter, a bronze medal winning hockey player, has done at UK sport.

In spite of this, it was still much harder for a woman to compete in an Olympic tournament in the twentieth century, due to less events being available, than it became in the twenty-first century. Women made up 34 per cent of competitors for the 1996 Games of the Olympiad, and 36 per cent of the 1998 Olympic Winter Games contestants. By London 2012, this was almost 45 per cent of competitors, although Donnelly et al. identified the persistence of fewer medal opportunities for women in what was identified by Jacques Rogge as 'a major boost for gender equality'.[4] British flyweight Nicola Adams made Olympic history in 2012 winning gold, as boxing was open to both sexes, and she won again in 2016 before a short professional career, from which she retired due to a torn pupil in her right eye, in 2019.

Although, generally, women can now compete in more sports, the available disciplines are far fewer, for example, in women's boxing, the five weight ratios for women's events (51 kg, 57 kg, 60 kg, 69 kg and 75 kg) mean fewer medal opportunities and none above middleweight. The men's programme has varied between as few as five weight classes in 1908, and 12 in 2000. The Winter Olympics finally opened ski jumping to women in Sochi, Russia, in 2014. Softball, traditionally a women's version of baseball, was included and dropped again after Beijing in 2008. Judging the overall number of competitors requires nuance, as rules are often different in men's and women's events, as football evidences with the Olympic Games effectively an 'Under 23' tournament, with three over aged 23 players able to play! Gender verification, for instance, has never been part of the men's Olympic programme. Some sports have been better placed to respond to these changes in lottery funding than others, and the conclusion uses the traditionally upper class sport of rowing, and what has often been described as the more working class 'the people's game' of football, as its two case studies. The examples are nuanced, by ideas of elite performance, education, health and well-being, education, class and social change, particularly in the case of Eniola Aluko, around the increasing numbers of Black and minority ethnic British Olympians, and the diversity of their heritage.

Sarah Winckless and rowing: continuity and change

In 1996, Matthew Pinsent and Steve Redgrave in the Men's Coxless Pairs Rowing class, won the only gold return for Great Britain won at the Olympic Games in Atlanta. Along with eight silver medals all won by men, there were six bronze medals, among which Denise Lewis was the only woman to win in the heptathlon, and Britain was just 36th in the medal table. However, along with Pinsent and Redgrave's gold medal, Tim Foster, Rupert Obholzer, Greg Searle and Jonny Searle, rowing also won a bronze in the men's Coxless Four class. These combined results gave British Rowing UK Sport money, which had been allocated on the basis of setting targets for attainment and reaching, or surpassing those set for each Olympic medal place. This was made possible by the distribution of National Lottery Funding. Rowing had always been a male Olympic sport, until 1976 when a distance of 1,000 metres was introduced. The first International Rowing Federation (FISA) women's international races were introduced at the 1951 European Rowing Championships as test events. These became official FISA championships at the 1954 European Rowing Championships. The Olympic races were extended to 2,000 metres from 1984 onwards at world championship level, and from 1988 at the Summer Olympics. However, even in 1996, there were seven men's rowing classes, compared with three events for women.

Like men's rowing, most women would develop their sport while at university and there was historically a distinctive class profile to the sport, which had previously been pioneered in the UK by Amy Gentry OBE, forming the Women's Amateur Rowing Association in 1923.[5] In fact, 75 years later, because of this combination of social class, education and a newly professional generation, women could extend their university training as rowers into a career as full-time athletes, and women's rowing became increasingly important to British Olympic tradition. At the 2000 Summer Olympics in the quadruple scull class, sisters Guin and Miriam Batten, Gillian Lindsay and Katherine Grainger won a silver medal. This was not just an important first for Britain, it was also the first of Grainger's four silver medals, the last of which she won in 2016, to which she added a gold medal in 2012 in the double sculls, with Anna Watkins. Grainger completed a PhD at King's College, London in 2012. Now honoured as Dame Katherine Grainger, she is currently Chair of UK Sport and Britain's most decorated Olympian, showing how a sport like rowing has benefited from the National Lottery and UK Sport system of allocating funds, and providing new opportunities for women, especially those who meet the physical and educational profile of the sport. However, in 1996, there was no national training centre that women could access, and so Longridge, in Marlow became an impromptu base but so much more developed than for the generation before Lottery funding became available.

How then did Sarah Winckless join this newly professional set up? First of all, Sarah's father, Robert (or Bob), had been university educated, graduating in Natural Sciences at Fitzwilliam College Cambridge in 1966 and was a keen rower.[6] Bob was a Cambridge Blue, also a member of Leander and Henley Rowing Club and a well-known rowing coach, working with Cambridge University Eights. This would later influence her choice of university and college, also studying Natural Sciences, at Fitzwilliam from 1993 onwards. Although in our 2012 interview she said that she considered her background to be 'normal' and very down-to-earth, traditionally in the twentieth century, fewer than 10 per cent of state educated schoolchildren went on to an undergraduate place at Oxford or Cambridge. Though this has recently changed significantly, with the appointment of Louise Richardson as vice-chancellor of Oxford in 2016, the number of British medal winners at London 2012 who were privately educated or from an Oxbridge background, makes this still a significant factor.

Winckless was born in Henley in 1973 and lived in Hamilton Avenue with her brother Charlie and mother Valerie. Educated at Rupert House School and then the selective Tiffins Girls' School (now a Grammar Academy), she enjoyed sport and science, and took up rowing while at university. In the meantime, Valerie had remarried Mike Hart, an Olympic silver medallist and had two children of their own, John and Imogen. Mike Hart competed at the 1972 and 1976 Olympics, and while at Peterhouse college, rowed in the winning Cambridge boat in the 1972 and 1973 Boat Races. Although rowing was very much in the family, Sarah was more concerned to excel at netball and athletics, specifically throwing the discus, than to replicate this success. Winning a scholarship to Millfield to study her A levels, the independent coeducational school that Mary Rand also attended, Sarah found both the sports facilities and the academic curriculum to be of the highest level.

Having initially focused on being a sprint athlete, Winckless gradually developed both her strength and stamina. Sarah was also the right height for rowing, at six foot three inches (1.9 metres). The Talent Identification consensus for rowing is that a woman has to have reached at least five feet 10 inches (1.6 metres), by the age of 22 years. Having learnt the discipline of elite training, Sarah was selected for the 1995 development crew for Cambridge for the Boat Race at Henley, which, against the odds, they won. However, shortly after her mother had been diagnosed with Huntington's disease, a hereditary condition of progressive brain damage, Sarah also tested positive. Understandably coming to terms with this threw her future as an elite athlete into doubt, at the same time as she was studying for her finals, and was president of the university boat club.

Graduating in 1997, a promised college grant to enable her to train was not forthcoming and Winckless worked in marketing at a rowing firm to fund herself, finding the move from working in an '8' to '4' and '2', a challenge as well as the more strenuous training regime, and intense days of rowing. The world championships in Cologne in 2008 were inauspicious, and just six weeks before the 2000 Olympic Games, where she was part of the quadruple scull Four, a stress fracture to her ribs saw her replaced and the squad went on to win silver. Winckless and Sarah Houghton competed in the double scull, finishing last. The fracture was attributed to over training, with an average of five sessions a day. Continued overtraining in an effort to overcome the disappointment, led her to miss most of the 2001 season.

Reasonable world championship results and more endurance saw Winckless selected for the 2004 Athens Olympics, with Elise Laverick in the double sculls, winning bronze. As part of the quad boat with Rebecca Romero, Frances Houghton and Katherine Grainger, Winckless won the World Championships in 2005, and once Romero left rowing to pursue her cycling ambitions, they retained the title at Eton Dorney in 2006 with Debbie Flood, Frances Houghton and Katherine Grainger in 2006. It is worth also saying here that Rebecca Romero, at 1.82 metres and 73 kilos, made the transition from being a rowing world champion and Olympian to becoming a cycling world champion and gold medal winning Olympian, in Beijing. She is only the second woman to win medals in different sports at the Olympic Games. The individual pursuit event for women was dropped from the 2012 Olympic Games, preventing her from defending her Olympic title.

Injury ruled Sarah Winckless out of competition in 2007, and after a disappointing 2008 Olympics, she retired in 2009. Focussing on leadership and good governance since then, Winckless was Chair of the BOA Athletes Commission and on the Board of UK Anti-Doping. She was the first woman to be appointed a Boat Race Umpire, and is set to umpire the men's Boat Race in 2020 if it goes ahead. Winckless has diversified her leadership and consultancy roles, acting as Chef de Mission for the British team at the Youth Olympic Games and is active across several Huntington's charities. A public and motivational speaker, with a company called 'Women Ahead', Winckless was awarded an MBE for services to sport and charity in 2015. It is possible to see from this, that, as the backroom functions around sport become more specialised and also provide public platforms for more women in post-competition careers, Winckless has been able to use her Olympic and world championship fame to become an umpire, an entrepreneur, a leadership coach, and a philanthropist in a variety of roles.

Eniola Aluko and women's football: people will ask 'what did she stand for?'

Born in Lagos, Nigeria in 1987, Aluko moved with her parents Sileola and Daniel to Birmingham, as an infant.[7] Aluko's British-Nigerian identity, and British-African identity is a key theme of her memoirs.[8] While Daniel returned to Nigeria to pursue a career in politics, Sileola worked as a nurse and then for a pharmaceutical company. From an upper-middle class family, the move nevertheless placed the family on an inner-city estate, and Aluko has been vocal about the place of her family values, and her faith in overcoming the challenges that she faced. She grew up playing football and other sports with her brother Sone Aluko, who went on to a professional career. Aluko started her career at Leafield Athletic Ladies – many women's football teams still call themselves 'Ladies' rather than 'women's' teams – and she subsequently played for Birmingham City Ladies with future England team-mate, Karen Carney. A strong forward player, Aluko scored on her Birmingham team debut, aged 14. By 2003, Aluko was named Young Player of the Year at the FA Women's Football Awards, before moving to play for Charlton between 2004 and 2007, and when that team folded, Chelsea 2007–2009. In the meantime, she graduated from Brunel University in London, with a first class degree in law and continued her training as a lawyer. She has since continued with a Masters degree in sporting management and has considerably expanded her portfolio of skills.

The FA had taken full control over women's football in 1993, when the financial problems of the, mainly volunteer, Women's Football Association (WFA), which could only finance one full-time employee, Linda Whitehead, as secretary, became too complicated to resolve. The WFA had run women's football since 1969, on behalf of the FA, in much the same way that County Associations did in the regions. Aluko therefore joined women's football in England at a time when new forms of semi-professional and professional careers were now possible, with the Women's FA Premier League the top flight available to women from 1991 to 2011 when the FA Women's Super League was launched.

In the USA, several British players had obtained athletic scholarships to play football full time, including the leading player of her generation Kelly Smith at Seton Hall. This could lead to lucrative and prestigious coaching and professional contracts when professional women's leagues were set, following the success of the 1999 Women's World Cup in Los Angeles, where 93,000 spectators watched the final in the Rose Bowl, proving a market for women's football. Women's Professional Soccer (WPS) was one of the iterations of professional leagues, established in 2009 and Eniola Aluko was signed to St Louis Athletica, then Atlanta Beat and Sky Blue FC, illustrating how precarious the team finances and league structures could be. Aluko returned to Birmingham briefly, before her second spell at Chelsea, until 2018, where her score rate, was matched by her assists. Her final club football was at Juventus in the 2018–2019 season, after which she retired to work in the media, including on 'Match of the Day', and in the USA, covering men's and women's World Cups, and as a Sporting Director of Aston Villa Women's FC. Other roles include mentoring elite athletes transitioning to a post-competitive working life, and as a motivational speaker, as well as writing for *The Guardian*.

Having chosen to play for England, and working her way through the talent identification system, and youth squads, her senior debut came with England in 2004.

Aluko went on to win 102 caps in her England career, mainly under longtime coach Hope Powell, herself a former international with over 50 caps and one of the first Black British women to play for an England women's team, along with Brenda Sempare. That women like Powell were changing the traditional look of British football is clear from her autobiography, where she covers her Jamaican heritage, her working class childhood in 1970s London, and how in 1998 'In one fell swoop, England got its first black manager, its first woman manager, and its first gay manager'.[9]

Again, this was a time of key change in world football's attitude to women. The first Women's World Cup had taken place in China in 1991, followed by England women's first qualification for the second Women's World Cup in 1995 in Sweden. Thereafter, women's football became part of the Olympic Games in Atlanta in 1996, but as a Great Britain squad, there has always been problems of whether the home nations should supply a joint squad for the tournament. Fearing that it could change qualification rights for men's World Cups, traditionally this has been resisted. In the 18-person squad for the 2012 Olympics women's football tournament, only two Scots, Kim Little and Ifeoma Dieke, were selected for the Games, with Wales and Northern Ireland not represented at all by coach Hope Powell. Although the Women's World Cup and the Olympic tournament have a complimentary qualification system between the two events, it took a historic decision to promote British women's football, through the London 2012 Olympics, for Aluko and her team-mates to appear. Women's football was an important curtain raiser for the entire Games and therefore appeared to showcase the more diverse range of Olympic sports on offer.

However, after the Olympic Games, and the disastrous 2013 Women's Euro campaign, Powell's 15-year term of management came to an end. When Aluko became the first British-African to win a 100th cap for England it was under manager Mark Sampson, an inexperienced coach with no international playing expertise or top-management qualifications. Although the 100th cap was achieved, it was under muted circumstances, as Aluko was substituted into the game in the second half and was hastily handed the armband to mark a brief captaincy. Two matches later, she was dropped from the England squad for 'Un-Lioness Behaviour', which later led to a hearing of the Department for Culture Media and Sport, which showed the levels of casual racism under Sampson's management, ending the career of both Lianne Sanderson, who had over 50 caps until that point, and Aluko.

The calm, clear and professional manner in which Aluko conducted herself, was in marked contrast to the officers of the FA who appeared confused over what exactly had happened, and at what point. Although Aluko has written about forgiveness as a positive decision, and remains gracious, in her account of the situation, there is the wider problem of the lack of diversity in the FA as an institution, and in British football generally, with racist and homophobic attitudes still constantly being challenged.

The wider issue from the case study, beyond how the athlete themselves can choose to change their life chances as determinedly and wisely as Aluko, is that she was ultimately dependent for her Olympic place on the structural forces of the world governing body of football, FIFA, and the IOC on being willing and able to make changes to their rules to allow a women's Team GB squad to play in London 2012, and also dependent upon the FA, and its choice of Team GB manager for her selection, based not just on her club performances, but her fit with the wider England squad. That a Black British, gay, woman coach who had also been an international player of the highest calibre would give Aluko her Team GB opportunity and that an inexperienced male, white, coach who lacked the sophistication to understand her heritage would end her England career, tells us much about the continuities of British sport at organisational and governance levels.

Even in sports which now seem to be Olympic medal staples, gendered systems of coaching and governance have seen a 'culture of fear' without the systems of complaint and whistleblowing that Aluko used to formally progress her complaint against Sampson. Jess Varnish's omission from the elite cycling programme, after she raised concerns formally at British Cycling, inevitably raise parallels with Aluko's case. Although this appears to have been solely based on gender, the wider problems of duty of care to athletes also reached UK Sport, as the ultimate funder of British Cycling. The considerable resources of large sporting organisations can therefore be used against individual women, whose careers in sport can be cut short by the institutional sexism widespread in world sport.

What is an encouraging note on which to end, in what should be a celebration of how women have changed the Olympic and Paralympic Games in the last 120 years, is that the likes of Aluko and Winckless are able to effect change at the highest level in world sport and, in the case of Aluko, having a legal background has always been a good route into high-level positions at FIFA. So could the patrimony of the IOC and FIFA be changed by more of these young women in future years, from the current situation where relatively modest gender quotas set as increased targets for more women leaders since 2000 have still not been met? I look forward to seeing the first female IOC President, and the first woman President of FIFA. There is a rich history of women at the Olympic Games, which I have only scratched the surface of here, on which to build.

Notes

1 HRH Princess Anne 'Patron's Report of the Langham Life First International Conference on Women in Sport' *The Langham Life First International Conference on Women in Sport* The Central Council of Physical Recreation 4–6 December 1978 The Y Hotel, Great Russell Street London WC 1, British Library Collections, London.
2 Dorothy Hyman with Phil Pilley *Sprint to Fame* London: Stanley Paul, 1964 p. 11.

3 Fékrou Kidane (ed.) Olympic Review XXVI–31 March 2000 IOC Archive, Lausanne 2000 p. 51.
4 Peter Donnelly and Michelle Donnelly The London 2012 Games: A Gender Equality Audit Centre for Sport Policy Studies Research Report. Toronto: Centre for Sport Policy Studies, Faculty of Kinesiology and Physical Education, University of Toronto, 2013.
5 Jean Williams A Contemporary History of Women's Sport, Part One: Sporting Women, 1850–1960 Oxon: Routledge, 2014 p. 224.
6 Sarah Winckless interview with the author, Leicester 5 June 2012.
7 Eniola Aluko interview with the author, London 12 November 2012.
8 Eniola Aluko with Josie Le Blond They Don't Teach This London: Yellow Jersey Press, 2019.
9 Hope Powell with Marvin Close Hope: My Life in Football London: Bloomsbury, 2016 p. 69.

Appendix 1

Great Britain's female team at the 1964 Winter Olympics in Innsbruck, Austria and the 1964 Summer Olympic Games, Tokyo[1]

Winter Olympics Innsbruck, Austria 29 January–9 February 1964

Alpine Skiing

Women's Downhill

Gina Hathorn
Divina Galica
Tania Heald
Anna Asheshov

Women's Giant Slalom

Divina Galica
Jane Gissing
Gina Hathorn
Wendy Farrington

Women's Slalom

Jane Gissing
Tania Heald
Gina Hathorn
Divina Galica

Figure Skating

Women's Singles

Sally-Anne Stapleford
Carol-Ann Warner
Diana Clifton-Peach

Summer Olympic Games Tokyo, Japan 10–24 October 1964

Canoeing

Women's Kayak Singles, 500 metres

Marianne Tucker

Diving

Women's Platform

Frances Cramp
Joy Newman

Equestrianism

Mixed Dressage, Individual

Johanna Hall

Fencing

Women's Foil: Individual

Mary Watts-Tobin
Shirley Netherway
Janet Bewley-Cathie-Wardell-Yerburgh

Women's Team Foil

Shirley Netherway
Theresa Offredy
Janet Bewley-Cathie-Wardell-Yerburgh
Mary Watts-Tobin

Gymnastics

Women's Individual All-Around

Denise Goddard
Monica Rutherford

Women's Floor Exercise

Monica Rutherford
Denise Goddard

Women's Horse Vault

Monica Rutherford
Denise Goddard

Women's Uneven Bars

Denise Goddard
Monica Rutherford

Women's Balance Beam

Denise Goddard
Monica Rutherford

Swimming

Women's 100m Freestyle Individual

Sandra Keen
Diana Wilkinson
Linda Amos

Women's 4 × 100m Freestyle Relay

Sandra Keen
Pauline Sillett
Liz Long
Diana Wilkinson

Women's 100m Backstroke Individual

Linda Ludgrove
Jill Norfolk
Sylvia Lewis

Women's 200m Breaststroke Individual

Stella Mitchell
Jill Slattery
Jacqueline Enfield

Women's 100m Butterfly Individual

Glenda Phillips

Mary Anne Cotterill
Judy Gegan

Women's 400-metres Individual Medley

Anita Lonsbrough
Pamela Johnson

Women's 4 × 100-metres Medley Relay

Jill Norfolk
Stella Mitchell
Mary Anne Cotterill
Liz Long
Linda Ludgrove

Track and Field Athletics

Women's 100 metres

Dorothy Hyman
Daphne Arden
Madeleine Cobb

Women's 200 metres

Janet Simpson
Daphne Arden
Dorothy Hyman

Women's 400 metres

Ann Packer, silver medallist
Joy Grieveson
Pat Kippax

Women's 800 metres

Ann Packer, gold medallist
Anne Smith
Mary Hodson

Women's 80 metres Hurdles

Pat Pryce-Nutting

Women's 4 × 100-metres Relay – bronze medallists

Janet Simpson
Mary Bignal Rand
Daphne Arden
Dorothy Hyman

Women's High Jump

Frances Slaap
Gwenda Matthews
Linda Knowles

Women's Long Jump

Mary Bignal Rand, gold medallist
Sheila Parkin-Sherwood
Alix Jamieson

Women's Shot Put

Mary Peters

Women's Javelin Throw

Sue Platt

Women's Pentathlon

Mary Bignal Rand, silver medallist
Mary Peters

Note

1 Compiled from the Organizing Committee for the Games of the XVIII Olympiad, Tokyo *The Games of the XVIII Olympiad, Tokyo 1964: The Official Report of the Organizing Committee* Tokyo: Kyodo Printing Co Ltd, 1966; and Friedl Wolfgang und Bertl Neumann *Offizieller Bericht der IX.Olympischen Winterspiele Innsbruck 1964* Vienna: Unterricht, Wissenschaft and Kunst, 1967. Subsequent appendices complied from sources taken from the respective official reports.

Appendix 2

Great Britain's Olympic women's team at the 1968 Mexico Summer Olympic Games and the Grenoble Winter Games

Summer Olympic Games in Mexico City
12–27 October

Canoeing

Women's Kayak Singles, 500 metres

Sylvia Jackson

Women's Kayak Doubles, 500 metres

Lesley Oliver
Barbara Mean

Diving

Women's Springboard

Kathy Rowlatt

Women's Platform

Mandi Haswell

Equestrianism

Mixed Dressage, Individual

Margaret Lawrence
Lorna Johnstone
Johanna Hall

Mixed Dressage, Team

Margaret Lawrence
Lorna Johnstone
Johanna Hall

Mixed Jumping, Individual

Marion Coakes, silver medallist

Mixed Jumping, Team

Marion Coakes

Mixed Three-Day Event, Individual

Jane Bullen

Mixed Three-Day Event, Team

Jane Bullen Gold (with Derek Allhusen, Ben Jones and Richard Meade)

Fencing

Women's Foil, Individual

Janet Bewley-Cathie-Wardell-Yerburgh
Sue Green
Margaret Bain

Women's Foil, Team

Margaret Bain
Janet Bewley-Cathie-Wardell-Yerburgh
Sue Green
Julia Davis
Eve Davies

Gymnastics

Women's Individual All-Around

Margaret Bell
Mary Prestidge

Women's Floor Exercise

Mary Prestidge
Margaret Bell

Women's Horse Vault

Margaret Bell
Mary Prestidge

Women's Uneven Bars

Margaret Bell
Mary Prestidge

Women's Balance Beam

Margaret Bell
Mary Prestidge

Swimming

Women's 100-metres Freestyle

Alexandra Jackson
Fiona Kellock
Gillian Treers

Women's 200-metres Freestyle

Susan Williams
Alexandra Jackson
Sally Davison

Women's 400-metres Freestyle

Sheila Clayton
Sally Davison
Susan Williams

Women's 800-metres Freestyle

Susan Williams

Women's 4 × 100-metres Freestyle Relay

Shelagh Ratcliffe
Fiona Kellock
Susan Williams
Alexandra Jackson

Women's 100-metres Backstroke

Jacqueline Brown
Wendy Burrell

Women's 200-metres Backstroke

Wendy Burrell
Jacqueline Brown

Women's 100-metres Breaststroke

Dorothy Harrison
Jill Slattery
Diana Harris

Women's 200-metres Breaststroke

Jill Slattery
Dorothy Harrison
Diana Harris

Women's 100-metres Butterfly

Margaret Auton
Gillian Treers

Women's 200-metres Butterfly

Margaret Auton

Women's 200-metres Individual Medley

Shelagh Ratcliffe

Women's 400-metres Individual Medley

Shelagh Ratcliffe

Women's 4 × 100-metres Medley Relay

Wendy Burrell
Dorothy Harrison
Margaret Auton
Alexandra Jackson

Track and Field Athletics

Women's 100 metres

Della James-Pascoe
Val Peat
Anita Neil

Women's 200 metres

Lillian Board
Maureen Tranter

Women's 400 metres

Lillian Board, silver medallist
Janet Simpson
Mary Green

Women's 800 metres

Sheila Taylor-Carey
Pat Lowe-Cropper
Joan Page-Allison

Women's 80-metres Hurdles

Pat Jones
Ann Wilson
Pat Pryce-Nutting

Women's 4 × 100-metres Relay

Anita Neil
Maureen Tranter
Janet Simpson
Lillian Board

Women's High Jump

Barbara Inkpen
Dorothy Shirley

Women's Long Jump

Sheila Parkin-Sherwood, silver medallist
Maureen Barton-Chitty
Ann Wilson

Women's Javelin Throw

Sue Platt

Women's Pentathlon

Mary Peters
Sue Scott-Reeve
Ann Wilson

Winter Olympic Games in Grenoble
9–17 February 1968

Alpine skiing

Women's Downhill

Felicity Field
Gina Hathorn
Helen Jamieson
Divina Galica

Women's Giant Slalom

Divina Galica
Felicity Field
Gina Hathorn
Helen Jamieson

Women's Slalom

Gina Hathorn
Felicity Field
Diana Tomkinson
Divina Galica

Figure Skating

Mixed Pairs

Linda Bernard (with Ray Wilson)

Women's Singles

Sally-Anne Stapleford
Patricia Dodd
Frances Waghorn

Speed Skating

Women's 1,000 metres

Trish Tipper

Women's 3,000 metres

Trish Tipper

Appendix 3

Great Britain's female team at the 1972 Summer Olympic Games in Munich, West Germany and the 1972 Winter Olympics in Sapporo, Japan

Summer Olympic Games Munich 26 August to 11 September 1972

Archery

Women's Individual

Pauline Edwards
Lynne Evans
Carol Sykes

Canoeing

Women's Kayak Singles, 500 metres

Jane Rouse

Women's Kayak Doubles, 500 metres

Pamela Renshaw
Helen Woodhouse

Women's Kayak Singles, Slalom

Victoria Brown
Heather Goodman
Pauline Goodwin

Diving

Women's Springboard

Alison Drake
Helen Koppell

Women's Platform

Helen Koppell
Beverly Williams

Equestrianism

Mixed Dressage, Individual

Lorna Johnstone
Margaret Lawrence
Jennie Loriston-Clarke

Mixed Dressage, Team

Lorna Johnstone
Margaret Lawrence
Jennie Loriston-Clarke

Mixed Jumping, Individual

Ann Moore, silver medallist

Mixed Jumping, Team

Ann Moore

Mixed Three-Day Event, Individual

Mary Gordon-Watson
Bridget Parker

Mixed Three-Day Event, Team

Mary Gordon-Watson and Bridget Parker, gold medallists
With Richard Meade and Mark Phillips

Fencing

Women's Foil: Individual

Janet Bewley-Cathie-Wardell-Yerburgh
Sue Green
Clare Henley-Halsted

Women's Foil, Team

Janet Bewley-Cathie-Wardell-Yerburgh
Sue Green

Clare Henley-Halsted
Sally Anne Littlejohns
Susan Wrigglesworth

Gymnastics

Women's Individual All-Around

Barbara Alred
Pamela Hopkins
Pamela Hutchinson
Avril Lennox
Yvonne Mugridge
Elaine Willett

Women's Team All-Around

Barbara Alred
Pamela Hopkins
Pamela Hutchinson
Avril Lennox
Yvonne Mugridge
Elaine Willett

Women's Floor Exercise

Barbara Alred
Pamela Hopkins
Pamela Hutchinson
Avril Lennox
Yvonne Mugridge
Elaine Willett

Women's Horse Vault

Barbara Alred
Pamela Hopkins
Pamela Hutchinson
Avril Lennox
Yvonne Mugridge
Elaine Willett

Women's Uneven Bars

Barbara Alred
Pamela Hopkins

Pamela Hutchinson
Avril Lennox
Yvonne Mugridge
Elaine Willett

Women's Balance Beam

Barbara Alred
Pamela Hopkins
Pamela Hutchinson
Avril Lennox
Yvonne Mugridge
Elaine Willett

Swimming

Women's 100-metres Freestyle

Lesley Allardice
Susan Edmondson
Diane Walker

Women's 200-metres Freestyle

Lesley Allardice
Susan Edmondson
Diane Walker

Women's 400-metres Freestyle

Susan Edmondson
June Green
Diana Sutherland

Women's 800-metres Freestyle

June Green
Susan Jones
Avis Willington

Women's 4 × 100-metres Freestyle Relay

Lesley Allardice
Susan Edmondson

Judith Sirs
Diana Sutherland

Women's 100-metres Backstroke

Diana Ashton
Jacqueline Brown
Diana Sutherland

Women's 200-metres Backstroke

Diana Ashton
Pamela Bairstow
Diana Sutherland

Women's 100-metres Breaststroke

Diana Harris
Dorothy Harrison
Christine Jarvis

Women's 200-metres Breaststroke

Pat Beavan
Christine Jarvis
Amanda Radnage

Women's 100-metres Butterfly

Jean Jeavons

Women's 200-metres Butterfly

Jean Jeavons
Moira Brown

Women's 200-metres Individual Medley

Shelagh Ratcliffe
Susan Richardson
Avis Willington

Women's 400-metres Individual Medley

Shelagh Ratcliffe
Susan Richardson
Diane Walker

Women's 4 × 100-metres Medley Relay

Lesley Allardice
Pamela Bairstow
Dorothy Harrison
Jean Jeavons

Track and Field Athletics

Women's 100 metres

Sonia Lannaman
Andrea Lynch
Anita Neil

Women's 200 metres

Margaret Critchley
Della James-Pascoe
Donna Murray-Hartley

Women's 400 metres

Verona Bernard-Elder
Janette Roscoe
Janet Simpson

Women's 800 metres

Margaret Coomber
Pat Lowe-Cropper
Rosemary Stirling

Women's 1,500 metres

Joan Page-Allison
Joyce Smith
Sheila Taylor-Carey

Women's 100-metres Hurdles

Judy Vernon
Ann Wilson

Women's 4 × 100-metres Relay

Della James-Pascoe
Andrea Lynch

Anita Neil
Judy Vernon

Women's 4 × 400-metres Relay

Verona Bernard-Elder
Janette Roscoe
Janet Simpson
Rosemary Stirling

Women's High Jump

Penelope Dimmock
Ros Few
Barbara Inkpen

Women's Long Jump

Maureen Barton-Chitty
Ruth Martin-Jones
Sheila Parkin-Sherwood

Women's Discus Throw

Rosemary Payne

Women's Pentathlon

Mary Peters Gold Medallist
Ann Wilson

Winter Olympics Sapporo, Japan 3–13 February 1972

Alpine Skiing

Women's Downhill

Carol Blackwood
Divina Galica
Gina Hathorn
Valentina Iliffe

Women's Giant Slalom

Carol Blackwood
Divina Galica

Gina Hathorn
Valentina Iliffe

Women's Slalom

Carol Blackwood
Divina Galica
Gina Hathorn
Valentina Iliffe

Cross-Country Skiing

Women's 5 kilometres

Frances Lütken

Women's 10 kilometres

Frances Lütken

Figure Skating

Mixed Pairs

Linda Connolly with Colin Taylforth

Women's Singles

Jean Scott

Appendix 4

Great Britain's female team at the 1976 Summer Olympic Games in Montréal, Canada and the 1976 Winter Olympics in Innsbruck, Austria

Summer Olympic Games Montréal 17 July to 1 August 1976

Archery

Women's Individual

Pat Conway
Rachel Fenwick

Canoeing

Women's Kayak Singles, 500 metres

Sheila Burnett

Women's Kayak Doubles, 500 metres

Pauline Goodwin
Hilary Peacock

Diving

Women's Springboard

Helen Koppell

Equestrian

Mixed Dressage, Individual

Jennie Loriston-Clarke
Diana Mason
Sarah Whitmore

Mixed Dressage, Team

Jennie Loriston-Clarke
Diana Mason
Sarah Whitmore

Mixed Jumping, Individual

Debbie Johnsey

Mixed Jumping, Team

Debbie Johnsey with Rowland Fernyhough, Graham Fletcher and Peter Robeson

Mixed Three-Day Event, Individual

HRH Princess Anne
Lucinda Prior-Palmer-Green

Mixed Three-Day Event, Team

RH Princess Anne and Lucinda Prior-Palmer-Green with Richard Meade and Hugh Thomas

Fencing

Women's Foil, Individual

Wendy Ager-Grant
Clare Henley-Halsted
Susan Wrigglesworth

Women's Foil, Team

Wendy Ager-Grant
Hilary Cawthorne
Sue Green
Clare Henley-Halsted
Susan Wrigglesworth

Gymnastics

Women's Individual All-Around

Susan Cheesebrough
Avril Lennox
Barbara Slater

Women's Floor Exercise

Susan Cheesebrough
Avril Lennox
Barbara Slater

Women's Horse Vault

Susan Cheesebrough
Avril Lennox
Barbara Slater

Women's Uneven Bars

Susan Cheesebrough
Avril Lennox
Barbara Slater

Women's Balance Beam

Susan Cheesebrough
Avril Lennox
Barbara Slater

Rowing

Women's Coxless Pairs

Linda Clark
Beryl Mitchell

Women's Coxed Fours

Pauline Bird-Hart
Diana Bishop
Clare Grove
Gillian Webb
Pauline Wright

Swimming

Women's 100-metres Freestyle

Susan Edmondson
Elaine Gray

Women's 200-metres Freestyle

Susan Barnard
Ann Bradshaw
Susan Edmondson

Women's 400-metres Freestyle

Susan Barnard
Susan Edmondson

Women's 4 × 100-metres Freestyle Relay

Ann Bradshaw
Susan Edmondson
Elaine Gray
Debbie Hill

Women's 100-metres Backstroke

Amanda James
Joy Beasley

Women's 200-metres Backstroke

Joy Beasley
Sharron Davies
Kim Wilkinson

Women's 100-metres Breaststroke

Helen Burnham
Christine Jarvis
Maggie Kelly-Hohmann

Women's 200-metres Breaststroke

Christine Jarvis
Maggie Kelly-Hohmann
Debbie Rudd

Women's 100-metres Butterfly

Jane Alexander
Joanne Atkinson
Sue Jenner

302   Appendix 4

Women's 200-metres Butterfly

Anne Adams
Jane Alexander
Joanne Atkinson

Women's 400-metres Individual Medley

Anne Adams
Ann Bradshaw
Susan Richardson

Women's 4 × 100-metres Medley Relay

Joy Beasley
Debbie Hill
Sue Jenner
Maggie Kelly-Hohmann

Track and Field Athletics

Women's 100 metres

Sharon Colyear-Danville
Andrea Lynch

Women's 200 metres

Bev Goddard-Callender
Helen Golden

Women's 400 metres

Verona Bernard-Elder
Donna Murray-Hartley
Gladys Taylor

Women's 800 metres

Liz Barnes
Angela Creamer
Chris McMeekin

Women's 1,500 metres

Mary Stewart
Penny Yule

Women's 100-metres Hurdles

Lorna Boothe
Sharon Colyear-Danville

Women's 4 × 100-metres Relay

Wendy Clarke
Sharon Colyear-Danville
Andrea Lynch
Denise Ramsden

Women's 4 × 400-metres Relay

Liz Barnes
Verona Bernard-Elder
Donna Murray-Hartley
Gladys Taylor

Women's High Jump

Denise Brown
Moira Walls

Women's Long Jump

Myra Nimmo
Sue Scott-Reeve

Women's Javelin Throw

Tessa Sanderson

Women's Pentathlon

Sue Longden

Winter Olympics in Innsbruck, Austria 5–10 February 1976

Alpine Skiing

Women's Downhill

Fiona Easdale
Hazel Hutcheon

Valentina Iliffe
Theresa Wallis

Women's Giant Slalom

Fiona Easdale
Hazel Hutcheon
Serena Iliffe
Valentina Iliffe
Theresa Wallis

Women's Slalom

Fiona Easdale
Hazel Hutcheon
Valentina Iliffe
Theresa Wallis
Anne Robb

Figure Skating

Mixed Pairs

Erika Taylforth and Colin Taylforth

Mixed Ice Dancing

Kay Barsdell and Kenneth Foster
Hilary Green and Glyn Watts
Janet Thompson and Warren Maxwell

Women's Singles

Karena Richardson

Appendix 5

Great Britain's female team at the 1980 Summer Olympic Games in Moscow, USSR and the 1980 Winter Olympics in Lake Placid, USA

Summer Olympic Games in Moscow, USSR
19 July–3 August 1980

Archery

Women's Individual

Christine Harris
Gillian Patterson

Canoeing

Women's Kayak Singles, 500 metres

Lucy Perrett

Women's Kayak Doubles, 500 metres

Lesley Smither
Frances Wetherall

Diving

Women's Springboard

Alison Drake
Deborah Jay

Women's Platform

Lindsey Fraser
Marion Saunders

Fencing

Women's Foil, Individual

Ann Brannon
Linda Ann Martin
Susan Wrigglesworth

Women's Foil, Team

Wendy Ager-Grant
Ann Brannon
Hilary Cawthorne
Linda Ann Martin
Susan Wrigglesworth

Gymnastics

Women's Individual All-Around

Suzanne Dando
Susan Cheesebrough
Denise Jones

Women's Floor Exercise

Suzanne Dando
Susan Cheesebrough
Denise Jones

Women's Horse Vault

Suzanne Dando
Susan Cheesebrough
Denise Jones

Women's Uneven Bars

Suzanne Dando
Susan Cheesebrough
Denise Jones

Women's Balance Beam

Suzanne Dando
Susan Cheesebrough
Denise Jones

Rowing

Women's Single Sculls

Beryl Mitchell

Women's Double Sculls

Astrid Ayling
Sue Handscombe

Women's Coxed Fours

Pauline Bird-Hart
Sue Brown
Bridget Buckley
Jane Cross
Pauline Janson

Women's Coxed Eights

Nicola Boyes
Linda Clark
Rosemary Clugston
Gill Hodges
Beverly Jones
Elizabeth Paton
Penny Sweet
Joanna Toch
Pauline Wright

Swimming

Women's 100-metres Freestyle

June Croft
Jacquelene Willmott

Women's 200-metres Freestyle

June Croft
Jacquelene Willmott

Women's 400-metres Freestyle

Sharron Davies
Jacquelene Willmott

Women's 800-metres Freestyle

Jacquelene Willmott

Women's 4 × 100-metres Freestyle Relay

June Croft
Sharron Davies
Kaye Lovatt
Jacquelene Willmott

Women's 100-metres Backstroke

Joy Beasley
Helen Jameson

Women's 200-metres Backstroke

Jane Admans
Helen Jameson

Women's 100-metres Breaststroke

Suki Brownsdon
Maggie Kelly-Hohmann

Women's 200-metres Breaststroke

Debbie Rudd
Maggie Kelly-Hohmann

Women's 100-metres Butterfly

Susan Cooper
Ann Osgerby
Janet Osgerby

Women's 200-metres Butterfly

Ann Osgerby
Janet Osgerby

Women's 400-metres Individual Medley

Sharron Davies, silver medallist
Sarah Kerswell

Women's 4 × 100-metres Medley Relay

June Croft, Helen Jameson, Maggie Kelly-Hohmann and Ann Osgerby, silver medallists

Track and Field Athletics

Women's 100 metres

Heather Hunte-Oakes
Sonia Lannaman
Kathy Smallwood-Cook

Women's 200 metres

Bev Goddard-Callender
Sonia Lannaman
Kathy Smallwood-Cook

Women's 400 metres

Joslyn Hoyte-Smith
Linsey MacDonald
Michelle Probert-Scutt

Women's 800 metres

Christina Boxer-Cahill

Women's 1,500 metres

Janet Marlow

Women's 100-metres Hurdles

Lorna Boothe
Shirley Strong

Women's 4 × 100-metres Relay

Bev Goddard-Callender, Heather Hunte-Oakes, Sonia Lannaman and Kathy Smallwood-Cook, bronze medallists

Women's 4 × 400-metres Relay

Joslyn Hoyte-Smith, Linsey MacDonald, Donna Murray-Hartley, Michelle Probert-Scutt

Women's High Jump

Louise Miller

Women's Long Jump

Sue Hearnshaw
Sue Scott-Reeve

Women's Shot Put

Angela Littlewood

Women's Discus Throw

Meg Ritchie

Women's Javelin Throw

Tessa Sanderson
Fatima Whitbread

Women's Pentathlon

Judy Livermore-Simpson
Sue Longden
Yvette Wray

Winter Olympic Games Lake Placid 13–24 February 1980

Alpine Skiing

Women's Downhill

Moira Cargill
Valentina Iliffe

Women's Giant Slalom

Valentina Iliffe
Anne Robb

Women's Slalom

Kirstin Cairns
Valentina Iliffe
Anne Robb

Figure Skating

Mixed Pairs

Susy Garland and Robert Daw

Mixed Ice Dancing

Karen Barber and Nicky Slater
Jayne Torvill and Christopher Dean

Women's Singles

Karena Richardson

Luge

Women's Singles

Joanna Weaver
Avril Walker

Speed Skating

Women's 500 metres

Kim Ferran

Women's 1,000 metres

Kim Ferran
Mandy Horsepool

Women's 1,500 metres

Kim Ferran
Mandy Horsepool

Women's 3,000 metres

Mandy Horsepool

Appendix 6

Great Britain's female team at the 1984 Summer Olympic Games in Los Angeles, USA and the 1984 Winter Olympics

**Summer Olympic Games in Los Angeles, USA
28 July–12 August 1984**

Archery

Women's Individual

Eileen Robinson
Angela Goodall
Susan Willcox

Canoeing

Women's Kayak Singles, 500 metres

Lesley Smither

Women's Kayak Doubles, 500 metres

Lucy Perrett
Lesley Smither

Women's Kayak Fours, 500 metres

Janine Lawler
Lucy Perrett
Lesley Smither
Deborah Watson

Cycling

Women's Road Race, Individual

Catherine Swinnerton
Linda Gornall

Maria Blower
Muriel Sharp

Diving

Women's Springboard

Alison Childs

Women's Platform

Carolyn Roscoe
Lindsey Fraser

Equestrianism

Mixed Dressage, Individual

Jane Bartle-Wilson
Jennie Loriston-Clarke

Mixed Dressage, Team

Jane Bartle-Wilson
Jennie Loriston-Clarke
With Christopher Bartle

Mixed Three-Day Event, Individual

Diana Clapham
Virginia Holgate-Leng Bronze medallist
Lucinda Prior-Palmer-Green

Mixed Three-Day Event, Team

Diana Clapham
Virginia Holgate-Leng Silver medallists
Lucinda Prior-Palmer-Green
With Ian Stark

Fencing

Women's Foil, Individual

Linda Ann Martin
Fiona McIntosh
Liz Thurley

Women's Foil, Team

Katie Arup
Ann Brannon
Linda Ann Martin
Fiona McIntosh
Liz Thurley

Gymnastics

Women's Individual All-Around

Natalie Davies
Amanda Harrison
Sally Larner
Hayley Price
Kathy Williams
Lisa Young

Women's Team All-Around

Natalie Davies
Amanda Harrison
Sally Larner
Hayley Price
Kathy Williams
Lisa Young

Women's Floor Exercise

Natalie Davies
Amanda Harrison
Sally Larner
Hayley Price
Kathy Williams
Lisa Young

Women's Horse Vault

Natalie Davies
Amanda Harrison
Sally Larner
Hayley Price
Kathy Williams
Lisa Young

Women's Uneven Bars

Natalie Davies
Amanda Harrison
Sally Larner
Hayley Price
Kathy Williams
Lisa Young

Women's Balance Beam

Natalie Davies
Amanda Harrison
Sally Larner
Hayley Price
Kathy Williams
Lisa Young

Rhythmic Gymnastics

Women's Individual

Lorraine Priest
Jacquie Leavy

Rowing

Women's Single Sculls

Beryl Mitchell

Women's Double Sculls

Sally Bloomfield
Eleanor Ray

Women's Coxless Pairs

Ruth Howe
Kate Panter

Women's Coxed Fours

Katie Ball
Jean Genchi
Teresa Millar

Kathy Talbot
Joanna Toch

Women's Coxed Eights

Astrid Ayling
Sue Bailey
Ann Callaway
Alexa Forbes
Gill Hodges
Belinda Holmes
Kate Holroyd
Sarah Hunter-Jones
Kate McNicol

Sailing

Mixed Two Person Dinghy

Cathy Foster with Peter Newlands

Shooting

Women's Sporting Pistol, 25 metres

Carol Bartlett-Page
Adrienne Bennett

Women's Air Rifle, 10 metres

Sarah Cooper
Irene Daw

Women's Small-Bore Rifle, Three Positions, 50 metres

Sarah Cooper
Irene Daw

Swimming

Women's 100-metres Freestyle

June Croft
Nikki Fibbens

Women's 200 metres Freestyle

Annabelle Cripps
June Croft

Women's 400-metres Freestyle

June Croft, bronze medallist
Sarah Hardcastle, silver medallist

Women's 800-metres Freestyle

Annabelle Cripps
Sarah Hardcastle, bronze medallist

Women's 4 × 100-metres Freestyle Relay

Annabelle Cripps
June Croft
Nikki Fibbens
Debra Gore

Women's 100-metres Backstroke

Beverley Rose
Catherine White

Women's 200-metres Backstroke

Kathy Read
Catherine White

Women's 100-metres Breaststroke

Sandra Bowman
Jean Hill

Women's 200-metres Breaststroke

Suki Brownsdon
Gaynor Stanley

Women's 100-metres Butterfly

Nikki Fibbens
Ann Osgerby

Women's 200-metres Butterfly

Ann Osgerby
Samantha Purvis

Women's 200-metres Individual Medley

Zara Long
Gaynor Stanley

Women's 400-metres Individual Medley

Sarah Hardcastle
Gaynor Stanley

Women's 4 × 100-metres Medley Relay

June Croft
Nikki Fibbens
Jean Hill
Beverley Rose

Synchronised Swimming

Women's Solo

Amanda Dodd
Caroline Holmyard
Carolyn Wilson

Women's Duet

Caroline Holmyard
Carolyn Wilson

Track and Field Athletics

Women's 100 metres

Heather Hunte-Oakes
Shirley Thomas

Women's 200 metres

Joan Baptiste
Kathy Smallwood-Cook
Sandra Whittaker

Women's 400 metres

Helen Barnett-Burkart
Michelle Probert-Scutt
Kathy Smallwood-Cook

Women's 800 metres

Lorraine Baker

Women's 1,500 metres

Chris Benning
Christina Boxer-Cahill
Lynne MacDougall

Women's 3,000 metres

Zola Budd-Pieterse
Jane Furniss-Shields
Wendy Sly Silver medallist

Women's Marathon

Joyce Smith
Sarah Rowell
Priscilla Welch

Women's 100-metres Hurdles

Sharon Colyear-Danville
Shirley Strong Silver medallist

Women's 400-metres Hurdles

Sue Morley
Gladys Taylor

Women's 4 × 100-metres Relay

Bev Goddard-Callender Bronze medallists
Simone Jacobs
Heather Hunte-Oakes
Kathy Smallwood-Cook

Women's 4 × 400-metres Relay

Helen Barnett-Burkart
Joslyn Hoyte-Smith
Michelle Probert-Scutt
Gladys Taylor

Women's High Jump

Diana Elliott-Davies
Judy Livermore-Simpson

Women's Long Jump

Sue Hearnshaw, bronze medallist

Women's Shot Put

Venissa Head
Judy Oakes

Women's Discus Throw

Venissa Head
Meg Ritchie

Women's Javelin Throw

Sharon Gibson
Tessa Sanderson, gold medallist
Fatima Whitbread, bronze medallist

Women's Heptathlon

Kim Hagger
Judy Livermore-Simpson

Winter Olympic Games Sarajevo, Yugoslavia 8–19 February 1984

Alpine skiing

Women's Downhill

Clare Booth

Women's Slalom

Lesley Beck

Cross-Country Skiing

Women's 5 kilometres

Carolina Brittan
Ros Coats
Nicola Lavery
Doris Trueman

Women's 10 kilometres

Ros Coats
Lauren Jeffrey
Nicola Lavery
Doris Trueman

Women's 20 kilometres

Ros Coats
Nicola Lavery

Women's 4 × 5-kilometres Relay

Ros Coats
Lauren Jeffrey
Nicola Lavery
Doris Trueman

Figure Skating

Mixed Pairs

Susy Garland with Ian Jenkins

Mixed Ice Dancing

Karen Barber with Nicky Slater
Wendy Sessions with Stephen Williams
Jayne Torvill with Christopher Dean, gold medallists

Women's Singles

Susan Jackson

Luge

Women's Singles

Claire Sherred

Bibliography

Primary sources

Archival sources

Amateur Swimming Association Archive, British Swimming Loughborough

Amateur Swimming Association Handbooks 1902–1948; contemporary publications; Olympic memorabilia, clothing and numismatics relating to swimming and diving disciplines.

British Olympic Association Archive, Wandsworth London

Minutes of British Olympic Council Meetings 20 December 1904–1988; National Olympic Committee Correspondence Files 1900–1988; British Olympic Association Yearbooks 1906–1984; Desborough Press Clippings File; Official Reports 1908–1988; Women and Sport Files 1900–1988.

David Hewitt Collection, Sutton on Sea, Lincolnshire

Collection related to the life and career of David's mother Gladys Hewitt (née Carson), including clothing and Olympic memorabilia, scrapbooks, press cuttings and recordings of radio interviews.

Graham Budd Auctions (ed.) Auction Catalogue: Olympic Memorabilia London: Graham Budd Auctions and Sotheby's, London 24–26 July 2012

The auction catalogue and preview included a range of Olympic material, including personal collections; swimmers Jennie Fletcher and Eleanor Gordon, and internationally focused ephemera such as artwork by, and about, the American tennis player Helen Wills, and a wide range of Olympic clothing, numismatics and philately.

International Olympic Committee Museum and Archive, Lausanne

Correspondence of the National Olympic Committee of Great Britain Files 1900–1988; Fédération Sportive Féminine Internationale and IOC correspondence; Mary Glen Haig File; Publications of the NOC of Great Britain 1906–1988; Women and Sport Files reference DGI 2049641900–1988; national organising committee reports, later called Local Organising Committee for the Olympic Games, or LOCOG from 1900–1988.

Leicestershire County Record Office, Wigston

Kelly's Directory of Leicestershire and Rutland 1896–1936; contemporary local history publications.

Leicester County Museum Store, Barrow Upon Soar

Corah's of Leicester Files; Jantzen license plans; swimsuits and labels 1890–1936.

Lesley Restorick Collection, London

Collection related to the life and career of Lesley's mother, Margaret Restorick (née Wellington), including several scrapbooks, clothing, Olympic memorabilia, press cuttings and medals. Also contact information for Helen Yate and personal letters.

London Metropolitan University: The Women's Library

Autograph Letter Collection: Female Educationalists File 1850–1951; All England Women's Lacrosse Association Files 1912–1993.

The National Football Museum, Preston

Preston North End Board Minute Books 1900–1920; Dick, Kerr Ladies FC memorabilia; women's football artefacts 1869–present, including items related to the England women's team since 1972 and Team GB in 2012 and Eniola Aluko artefacts.

University of Bath Special Collections

Richard Bowen and British Judo collections, including Sarah Mayer letters; All England Women's Hockey Association files 1894–1980.
All England Women's Hockey Association (AEWHA) Files 1895–1998; International Federation of Women's Hockey Associations (IFWHA) Files 1930–1983; individual player files and tour diaries.

University of Birmingham Special Collections

Fédération Sportive Féminine Internationale papers 1920–1934 WAAA files, Box 2; Harold Abrahams Collection: Women's Amateur Athletics Association Files Boxes 1, 2, 3, 4 covering 1922–1988.

Contemporary publications and artefacts

Abrahams, Harold *Fifty Years of the Amateur Athletic Association Championships* London: Carborundum, 1961.

Amateur Swimming Association *ASA Swimming Instruction* London: The Amateur Swimming Association and Educational Productions Ltd, revised edition 1963; first published in 1919.

Anon. 'French Exhibition Tournament' *Lawn Tennis The Official Organ of the Lawn Tennis Association and Croquet (including Badminton)* 5: 25 April 1900 to 3 April 1901 Inclusive London: Lawn Tennis and Croquet, 1901.

Anon. 'Eunice Shriver: Obituary' *The Sunday Times* News Review 16 August 2009.

Anon. 'Miss Lines' *Daily News* 28 April 1921.

Anon. 'Pong Sik Pak: The Competitor from Korea' *Picture Post: Special Olympic Souvenir Issue July 1948* London: Picture Post, 1948.

Anon 'The Paris International Exhibition Tournament' *Lawn Tennis The Official Organ of the Lawn Tennis Association and Croquet (including Badminton)* 5: 25 April 1900 to 3 April 1901 inclusive London: Lawn Tennis 1901.

Anon. 'Speed Typist: Dorothy Manley Strides to Victory' *Sunday Pictorial* 1 August 1948, personal collection of the author.

Associated Newspapers Ltd. *The Royal Jubilee Book 1910–1935: Telling in Pictures the Story of 25 Momentous Years in the Reign of Their Majesties King George V and Queen Mary* London: Associated Newspapers Ltd, 1935.

Avé, Albert, Charles Denis and Georges Bourdon (eds.) *Comité Olympique Français Les Jeux de La VIIIE Olympiade Paris 1924: Rapport Official* Titre I, II, III and IV Paris: La Librairie de France, 1924.

Barfield, Vivian 'Women in the International Sports Scene' *International Sport Summit Monte Carlo Monaco 5–12 March 1978* IOC Archive, Lausanne.

Bear, Cecil 'Star Sprinter: Sylvia Cheeseman' *World Sports: The International Sports Magazine* July 1950 London: Country and Sporting Publications, 1950.

Bear, Cecil 'Jeanette Altwegg: World, European and British Figure Skating Champion' *World Sports Official Magazine of the British Olympic Association* February 1952 London: Country and Sporting Publications, 1952.

Bear, Cecil 'Happy and Glorious' *World Sports: The International Sports Magazine* 19: 5 May 1953 London: Country and Sporting Publications, 1953.

Bear, Cecil 'Sporting Drama: 1954' *World Sports: The International Sports Magazine* December 1954 London: Country and Sporting Publications, 1954.

Bear, Cecil 'Off the Beaten Track' *World Sports Official Magazine of the British Olympic Association* April 1956 London: Country and Sporting Publications, 1956.

Bear, Cecil 'Greta 1948, Greta 1957' *World Sports: The International Sports Magazine* October 1957 London: Country and Sporting Publications, 1957.

Bear, Cecil 'Matthews – A Sporting Name Lives On' *World Sports: Official Magazine of the British Olympic Association* February 1958 London: Country and Sporting Publications, 1958.

Beaumont, C. L de 'Empire Fencing Champion' *World Sports: Official Magazine of the British Olympic Association* October 1950 London: Country and Sporting Publications, 1950.

Bergvall, Eric (translated by Edward Adams-Ray) *The Fifth Olympiad: The Official Report of the Olympic Games of Stockholm 1912* Stockholm: Wahlström & Widstrand, 1912.

Berlioux, Monique 'Women in the Olympic Context' *First International Conference on Women in Sport 4–6 December 1978, The 'Y' Hotel, London; sponsored by the CCPR and the Langham Life Assurance Co., Ltd* IOC Archive, Lausanne.

Besford, Pat 'Helsinki to Hove' *World Sports: The International Sports Magazine September 1952* London: Country and Sporting Publications, 1952.

Besford, Pat 'A Lesson From Lillian' *World Sports: Official Magazine of the British Olympic Association May 1954* London: Country and Sporting Publications, 1954.

Besford, Pat 'Swim Chiefs Need Vision' *World Sports: The International Sports Magazine September 1955* London: Country and Sporting Publications, 1955.

Blankers-Koen, Mrs Francina 'Foreword' in George Pallet *Women's Athletics* London: The Normal Press, 1955.

Blankers-Koen, Fanny 'It's Fun When You Are An Unknown' *World Sports: Official Magazine of the British Olympic Association November 1956* London: Country and Sporting Publications, 1956.

Boxer, Christina 'Olympic Athlete' *The Sunday Times* 16 August 2009.

British Olympic Association *The British Olympic Association and the Olympic Games* Surrey: G. Donald and Co. Ltd, 1987.

British Olympic Council *Olympic Games of 1908: Programme, Rules and Conditions of Competition for Swimming, Diving and Water Polo* London: British Olympic Council, 1909.

Brodie, Malcolm 'Her Supreme Highness' *World Sports: Official Magazine of the British Olympic Association June 1956* London: Country and Sporting Publications, 1956.

Brown, Dr Whitcombe 'A Chat with a Lady Champion' *Lawn Tennis The Official Organ of the Lawn Tennis Association and Croquet Vol. 3 27 April to 5 October 1898 inclusive* London: Lawn Tennis, 1898 pp. 229–230.

Brundle, Fred 'Can Heather Bring Us Luck?' *World Sports: The International Sports Magazine March 1957* London: Country and Sporting Publications, 1957.

Burton, Beryl with Colin Kirby *Personal Best: The Autobiography of Beryl Burton* Huddersfield: Springfield Books, 1986.

Cardus, Neville 'Let Our Cricketers Determine to Be New Elizabethans' *World Sports: The International Sports Magazine June 1952* London: Country and Sporting Publications, 1952.

Collings, Captain Tony 'High Spot of Horseman's Year' *World Sports: The International Sports Magazine July 1951* London: Country and Sporting Publications, 1951.

Comitato Olimpico Nazionale Italiano *The Official Report VII Giochi Olimpici Invernalivii: VII Olympic Winter Games Cortina d'Ampezzo 1956* Rome: Società Grafica Romana, 1956.

Comité Olympique Suisse Secrétariat *Général Rapport Général Sur Les Ves Olympiques D'Hiver St-Moritz 1948* Lausanne: Comité Olympique Suisse Secrétariat Général, 1948.

Cossor 'Crystal Clear Cossor, Reception is So Realistic' *World Sports: The International Sports Magazine July 1956* London: Country and Sporting Publications, 1956.

Court, Audrey and Cynthia Walton *Birmingham Made a Difference: The Birmingham Women's Welfare Centre and the Family Planning Association 1926–1991* Birmingham: Barn Books, 2001.

Crump, Jack 'Dorothy Manley's Big Day' *World Sports: Official Magazine of the British Olympic Association July 1949* London: Country and Sporting Publications, 1949.

Crump, Jack 'The Real Result of the London Olympic Games' *Bulletin Du Comité International Olympique* 19 January 1950.
Crump, Jack 'Women's Athletics' in Carolyn Dingle (ed.) *News Chronicle: Sport for Girls* London: News Chronicle Publications Department, 1951.
Crump, Jack 'Never Say Die Dorothy' *World Sports: The International Sports Magazine September 1951* London: Country and Sporting Publications, 1951.
Crump, Jack 'Jean Desforges: Champion of Women's Rights' *World Sports: Official Magazine of the British Olympic Association* March 1954 London: Country and Sporting Publications, 1954.
Dod, Lottie 'Foreword' Denis Foster *Improve Your Tennis* London: Findon Publications 1950.
Dod, Lottie 'Lawn Tennis for Ladies' in J. M. Heathcote (eds.) *Tennis, Lawn Tennis, Badminton, Fives: The Badminton Library of Sports and Pastimes* London: Longmans, Green and Company, 1890.
Doust, Stanley 'Lawn Tennis' in James Rivers (ed.) *The Sports Book* London: MacDonald and Company, 1946.
Doyle, Edward A. (ed.) *The Official Report of the Organising Committee For the Games of the XVI Olympiad Melbourne 1956* (Melbourne: W. M. Houston Government Printer 1958).
Dyson, Geoffrey 'A Tribute From the Chief National Coach' in H. Palfreman and A. Grant *Pole Vaulting For Beginners* Hull, London and Northampton: English Schools Athletic Association with A. Brown and Sons, 1953.
Dyson, Maureen 'Over My Shoulder' *World Sports: Official Magazine of the British Olympic Association August 1952* London: Country and Sporting Publications, 1952.
Dyson, Maureen 'We are winning!' in Carolyn Dingle (ed.) *News Chronicle: Sport for Girls* London: News Chronicle Publications Department, 1951.
Eliott-Lynn, Sophie C. *Athletics for Women and Girls: How To Be An Athlete And Why* London: Robert Scott, 1925.
Fédération Sportive Féminine Internationale *Jeux Féminins Mondiaux Londres 1934* (Paris: 3 Rue De Varenne, 1934).
Fédération Sportive Féminine Internationale *Fourth Womens World Games Official Programme Thursday-Saturday 9–11 August 1934* White City Stadium London. London: Fleetway, 1934.
From Our Geneva Correspondent 'Olympic Games and Women: Ban Likely' *Manchester Guardian* 12 April 1929.
Gallagher, Linda M. '1st Female Olympic Medallist is SC Native' *The State* unpaginated c.1922.
Gamages Ltd, A. W. 'The Sports House of the West' *Golf, Programme and Regulations: Olympic Games of London 1908* London: British Olympic Council, 1908.
Gardner, Graham Limited 'Maureen Gardner Shorts' *World Sports: The International Sports Magazine* 19: 5 May 1953.
Gillmeister, Heiner *Olympisches Tennis: Die Geschichte der Olympischen Tennisturniere 1896–1992* Berlin: Sankt Augustin, 1993.
Grinham, Judy *Water Babe* London: Oldbourne Book Co Ltd, 1960.
Guttmann, Ludwig 'Olympic Games for the Disabled' *World Sports: Official Magazine of the British Olympic Association* October 1952 London: Country and Sporting Publications, 1952.

Gymphlex 'Maureen Gardner Looking After Women's Interests' *World Sports Official Magazine of the British Olympic Association* January 1952 London: Country and Sporting Publications, 1952.

Harding, Aileen 'There's Fun In Fencing' in Carolyn Dingle (ed.) *News Chronicle: Sport For Girls* London: News Chronicle Publications Department, 1951.

Heckescher, Dan 'Jeux Olympiques de 1924-Fleuret, Les Finalists du Championnat' Paris: Dan Heckescher, 1924 www.olympic.org/photos/paris-1924/fencing accessed 4 February 2019.

Henry, Alan 'Pat Moss: Obituary' *The Guradian* 27 October 2008.

Hitler, Adolf in Organisationskomitee Für Die XI Olympiade Berlin 1936 E. V. *The XITH Olympic Games Berlin, 1936 Official Report Volume 1* Berlin: Wilhelm Limpert, 1937.

Hoffman, Jeane 'Stella Walsh, 47 – And She Still Won 100 Events Last Year' *World Sports: The International Magazine* June 1959 London: Country and Sporting Publications, 1959.

Holgate, Virginia *Ginny-An Autobiography* London: Hutchinson, 1986.

Hopkinson, Tom (ed.) *Picture Post: Olympic Games Special 40: 7 14 August 1948* London: Hulton Press Ltd, 1948.

Howcroft, W. J. 'Swimming' in James Rivers (ed.) *The Sports Book 2* London: MacDonald and Company, 1948.

Howcraft, W.J. 'She Ruled the Waves-But Never Waived the Rules' *World Sports: The International Sports Magazine June 1950* London: Country and Sporting Publications, 1950.

Hyman, Dorothy *Sprint to Fame* London: Stanley Paul, 1964.

Jarvis, John Arthur *The Art of Swimming: with Notes on Polo and Aids to Life Saving* London: Hutchinson and Co, 1902.

Jeanneau, Georges (translated by Kate Huang) *Golf and the Olympic Games* Paris: Fédération Française de Golf, 2003.

Joubert, Edgar 'Madame Ostermeyer: Top Notch Athlete, Top Note Pianist' *World Sports: The International Sports Magazine* July 1949 London: Country and Sporting Publications, 1949.

Kellermann, Annette *How to Swim* London: George H. Doran Company, 1918.

Killanin, Michael Morris Baron *My Olympic Years: President of the International Olympic Committee 1972–1980* London: Secker and Warburg, 1983.

Kolkka, Sulo (ed.) *The Official Report of The Organising Committee For the Games of the XV Olympiad Helsinki 1952* Helsinki: The Organising Committee, 1952.

Kyle, Sean 'A Timekeeper's Error Can Mean the Shattering of a Dream' *World Sports: Official Magazine of the British Olympic Association February 1957* London: Country and Sporting Publications, 1957.

Kuts, Raissa 'Kuts – by His Wife' *World Sports: Official Magazine of the British Olympic Association August1957* London: Country and Sporting Publications Ltd 1957.

Lambert-Chambers, Dorothea (Lady Champion 1903, 1904, 1906) *Lawn Tennis for Ladies* London: Methuen & Co. Ltd, 1910.

Lattimer, George M. (ed.) *III Olympic Winter Games: Official Report Lake Placid 1932* Lake Placid and New York: III Olympic Winter Games Committee, 1932.

Legh, Alice 'Ladies' Archery' in C. J. Longman and H. Walrond (eds.) *Archery: The Badminton Library of Sports and Pastimes* London: Longmans, Green and Company, 1894.

Lenglen, Suzanne and Eustance E. White (ed.) *Lawn Tennis for Girls* New York: American Sports Publishing Co., 1920.
Lindley, Frank 'Look You' *World Sports: The International Sports Magazine* April 1957 London: Country and Sporting Publications, 1957.
Llewellyn, Lieutenant Colonel Harry 'Story From Stockholm: The Equestrian Olympics' *World Sports: The International Sports Magazine* July 1956 London: Country and Sporting Publications, 1956.
Lowther, Toupie 'Ladies' Play' in Reginald Frank and Hugh Lawrence Doherty *Lawn Tennis* New York: The Baker and Taylor Company, 1903.
Lucas, Charles P. (ed.) *The Olympic Games 1904* St Louis: Woodward and Tiernan Printing Co. 1905.
Lucozade 'Pat Smythe ... Another Lucozade Enthusiast' *World Sports* September 1955 London: Country and Sporting Publications, 1955.
McGhee, Joe and Jean Scrivens 'Two More Athletes Disclose "Our Plans for Melbourne"' *World Sports: Official Magazine of the British Olympic Association* May 1956 London: Country and Sporting Publications, 1956.
McKelvie, Roy 'Table Tennis' in James Rivers (ed.) *The Sports Book* London: MacDonald and Company, 1946.
McWhirter, Norris '"Ballerina" Nina' *World Sports: International Sports Magazine* September 1955 London: Country and Sporting Publications, 1955.
Mathiot, Ginette *La Cuisine Pour Tous* Paris: Albert Michel, 1932.
Meisl, Dr Willy 'Sonja-Pavlova of the Ice' *World Sports: Official Magazine of the British Olympic Association* February 1954 London: Country and Sporting Publications, 1954.
Meisl, Dr Willy '"The Babe": A Genius With An Infinite Capacity For Taking Pains' *World Sports: Official Magazine of the British Olympic Association* November 1956 London: Country and Sporting Publications, 1956.
Meisl, Dr Willy 'Happy Birthday Wimbledon: The Crowning Glory' *World Sports* June 1957 London: Country and Sporting Publications, 1957.
Mérillon, M. D. (ed.) *Expostition Universelle Internationale de 1900 À Paris: Concours Internationaux D'Exercices Physiques et de Sports* Part One and Part Two Paris: Ministére Du Commerce, De L'Industrie Des Postes et Des Télégraphes, 1901.
Messerli, Dr F. M. *La Participation Fèminine Aux Jeux Olympiques Modernes* (Édité par le Comité International Olympique Lausanne: An 1 de la XVme Olympide, 1952.
Messerli, Dr Franz M. *Women's Participation to the Modern Olympic Games: report to the International Olympic Committee* Lausanne: IO C, 1952.
Milhado, Albert 'My Friend Fanny' *World Sports: Official Magazine of the British Olympic Association December 1950* London: Country and Sporting Publications, 1950.
Miller, David *Official History of the Olympic Games and the IOC* London: Mainstream Publishing, 2012.
Montgomery, Viscount 'Amateurism and the Olympic Games' *World Sports: The International Sports Magazine* March 1952 London: Country and Sporting Publications, 1952.
Moran, Gussy 'Making A Job of It' in Carolyn Dingle (ed.) *News Chronicle: Sport For Girls* London: News Chronicle Publications Department, 1951.
Noel, Susan 'Women in Sport' *World Sports: Official Magazine of the British Olympic Association* September 1949(London: County and Sporting Publications, 1949.
Noel, Susan 'Women in Sport' *World Sports Official Magazine of the British Olympic Association January 1950* London: Country and Sporting Publications, 1950.

Noel, Susan 'Women in Sport' *World Sports: The International Sports Magazine* January 1952 London: Country and Sporting Publications, 1952.
Noel, Susan 'Women in Sport: Let's Jump Back 20 Years' *World Sports Official Magazine of the British Olympic Association March 1955* London: Country and Sporting Publications, 1955.
Obituaries 'Dr Arthur Wint' *Olympic Review* 303 January to February 1993.
Olliff, John 'What's Wrong With British Tennis?' *World Sports Magazine* May 1951 London: Country and Sporting Publications, 1951.
Organisationskomitee Für Die XI Olympiade Berlin 1936 E. V. *The XITH Olympic Games Berlin, 1936 Official Report* Volume 1 and 2 Berlin: Wilhelm Limpert, 1937.
Organising Committee for the XIV Olympiad *The Official Report of the Organising Committee for the XIV Olympiad* Parts One and Two London: Organising Committee for the XIV Olympiad, 1948.
Ovaltine 'Leading Athletes Drink Ovaltine' *World Sports: Official Magazine of the British Olympic Association May 1956* London: Country and Sporting Publications, 1956.
Page, Louise *Golden Girls* London: Methuen, 1985.
Palethorpe, Dawn *My Horses and I* London: Country Life, 1956.
Pember, Doloranda *Mercedes Gleitze: A Sea Career* unpublished manuscript, 2014 personal communication to the author 2 May 2014.
Peters, Mary with Ian Woolridge *Mary P.: Autobiography* London: Stanley Paul, 1974.
Petersen, Rolf (ed.) (translated by Margaret Wold) *VI Olympiske Vinterleker: The Olympic Winter Games: Oslo 1952* Oslo: Utgitt Av Organisasjonskomiteen [The Organising Committee] 1952.
Photogravure Section 'Olympic girls' *Chicago Tribune* 16 July 1922.
Picture Post *Picture Post: Hulton's National Weekly Olympic Games Souvenir Special 14 August 1948* 40: 7 London; Hulton Press, 1948.
Piley, P. G. 'The Silent Games' *World Sports: Official Magazine of the British Olympic Association* December 1956 London: Country and Sporting Publications, 1956.
Ping-Wen, Liu 'Champion From China' *World Sports: Official Magazine of the British Olympic Association February 1958* London: Country and Sporting Publications, 1958.
Pollard, Marjorie *Fifty Years of Women's Hockey: The Story Of The Foundation and Development Of The All England Women's Hockey Association 1895–1945* Letchworth: St Christopher Press, 1945.
Radcliffe, Paula *Paula: My Story So Far* London: Simon and Schuster, 2004.
Rand, Mary *Mary Mary: Autobiography of an Olympic Champion* London: Hodder and Stoughton, 1969.
Rivers, James (ed.) *The Sports Book 2* London: MacDonald and Company, 1948.
Rockett, Sam 'The Cruel Sea: Channel Swimming' *World Sports Official Magazine of the British Olympic Association April 1956* London: Country and Sporting Publications, 1956.
Roukhadzè, Marie-Hélène 'The Small Beginnings of the Secretariat: An Interview with Lydie Zanchi' *Olympic Review* 1986.
Rowe, Diane and Rosalind 'Table Tennis Twins' in Carolyn Dingle (ed.) *News Chronicle: Sport For Girls* London: News Chronicle Publications Department, 1951.
Rubin, Robert (ed.) *The Official Report of the VIII Winter Olympic Games Squaw Valley California 1960* Squaw Valley: California State Printing Office, 1960.

Rudd, Bevil 'Athletics' in James Rivers (ed.) *The Sports Book* London: MacDonald and Company, 1946.

Sheridan, Eileen *Wonder Wheels: The Autobiography of Eileen Sheridan* London: Nicholas Kaye, 1956.

Sheridan, Eileen 'The Greatest Woman Cyclist Britain has Produced' *World Sports: Official Magazine of the British Olympic Association* June 1956 London: Country and Sporting Publications, 1956.

Smythe, Patricia *Jump for Joy* Watford: The Companion Book Club, 1955.

Smythe, Patricia *Jumping Round the World* London: Cassell, 1962.

Somers, Florence A. *Principles of Women's Athletics* New York: A. S. Barnes and Company, 1930.

Spears, Betty 'Women in Olympics: an unresolved problem' in Peter Graham and Horst Ueberhorst (eds.) *The Modern Olympics* New York, Leisure Press, 1976.

Sterry, Mrs Charlotte 'My Most Memorable Match' in Mrs Lambert Chambers *Lawn Tennis for Ladies* London: Methuen & Company Ltd, 1910.

Svenson, Sten '15,000 Gymnasts in Swedish Festival' *World Sports: The International Sports Magazine* July 1949 London: Country and Sporting Publications, 1949.

Tenth Olympiade Committee (eds.) *Official Report: The Tenth Olympiad 'Los Angeles 1932'* Parts One, Two Three and Four. Los Angeles: Tenth Olympiade Committee Official 'Los Angeles 1932' Ltd, 1932.

The Earl of Birkenhead (ed.) *John Betjeman's Collected Poems* London: John Murray 1962.

The Organizing Committee for the Equestrian Games *The Official Report of the Organizing Committee for the Equestrian Games of the XVIth Olympiad Stockholm 1956* Stockholm: Esselte Aktiebolag, 1959.

The Organizing Committee of the Games of the XVII Olympiad *The Official Report of the Organising Committee The Games of the XVII Olympiad Rome 1960* Volume 1 and 2. Rome: Carl Colombo Printing, 1960.

The British Travel Association 'Britain: Land of Sport' *World Sports Official Magazine of the British Olympic Association* March 1952. London: Country and Sporting Publications, 1952.

The Sporting Life 'Olympic Games of London 1908: A Complete Record with Photographs of Winners of the Olympic Games held at the Stadium, Shepherd's Bush London July 13–25' London: *The Sporting Life*, 1908.

The Daily Express *These Tremendous Years 1919–1938: A History in Photographs of Life and Events, Big and Little, in Britain and the World Since the War* London: Daily Express Publications, 1938.

The Sports Council *Women and Sport: A Consultation Document* London: Sports Council 1992.

The Sports Council *Women and Sport: Policy and Frameworks for Action* London: Sports Council, 1993.

Time Magazine 'Helen Newington Wills' *Time Magazine* 1 July 1929 www.time.com/time/covers/ accessed 20 August 2010.

Underwood & Underwood *Mercedes Gleitz Postcard* 26 June 1928 National Portrait Gallery NPGx136729 www.npg.org.uk/collections/search/person/mp58662/mercedes-gleitze accessed 3 July 2019.

Van Rossem, G. (ed.) on behalf of The Netherlands Olympic Committee *The Ninth Olympiad Being the Official Report of the Olympic Games of 1928 Celebrated at Amsterdam* Parts One, and Two. Amsterdam: J. H. De Bussy Ltd, 1928.

Voight, C. A. 'Letter concerning The Paris International Exhibition Tournament dated 27 April 1900' *Lawn Tennis The Official Organ of the Lawn Tennis Association and Croquet (including Badminton)* 5: 25 April 1900 to 3 April 1901 inclusive London.

Walrond, Colonel H. 'Archery: The Royal Toxophilite Society' *British Olympic Association Yearbook 1914* London: British Olympic Association, 1914.

Webster, F. A. M. *Athletics of To-day for Women: History Development and Training* London: Frederick Warne, 1930.

Webster, F. A. M. (ed.) *World Sports: the Official Organ of the British Olympic Association* 1 London: British Olympic Association, 1936.

Wellington, Margaret 'Swimming to be a Champion-7 Days a Week' in Carolyn Dingle (ed.) *News Chronicle: Sport For Girls* London: News Chronicle Publications Department, 1951.

White, Cyril 'Opportunities for Women in Sport' *Council of Europe Committee for the Development of Sport Seminar on the Greater Involvement of Women in Sport* Dublin Castle, 30 September to 3 October 1980.

Wills, Helen *Self Portrait* (Los Angeles: Olympic Arts Competition and Exhibition, 1932) featured in Graham Budd (ed.) *Olympic Memorabilia* London: Graham Budd Auctions and Sotheby's, 24–26 July 2012.

Wills, Helen *Tennis* New York and London: Charles Scribner and Son, 1928.

Wills, Helen *Fifteen, Thirty: The Story of a Tennis Player* New York and London: Charles Scribner and Son, 1938.

Women's Amateur Athletics Association *Fifteenth Annual Coronation Championships Programme, White City Stadium Shepherds Bush 7 August 1937* London: Women's Amateur Athletics Association, 1937.

Women's Cross Country and Road Walking Association *The Grange Farm, Winton Worsley Women's Senior Cross County Championship Programme 5 March 1949* Birmingham: Women's Cross Country and Road Walking Association, 1949.

Women's Amateur Athletics Association *International Athletic Match Programme White City Stadium London 20 August 1949* London: Women's Amateur Athletics Association, 1949.

Women's Amateur Athletics Association *WAAA and Women's National Cross County Championship (under WAA rules) Programme Parliament Hill Secondary School Hampstead 4 March 1950* London: Women's Amateur Athletics Association, 1950.

Women's Amateur Athletics Association *Junior and Intermediate Track and Field Championships Programme The Alexander Sports Ground Perry Barr Birmingham 9 July 1955* London: Women's Amateur Athletics Association, 1955.

Yeaden, T. M. (ed.) *ASA Handbook 1913 Containing a List of English Swimming Clubs; Laws of Swimming and Rules of Water Polo; Past and Present Champions and Programme for the Year* London: Hanbury, Tomsett & Co., 1913.

Zaharias, 'Babe' Didrikson *This Life I've Led: The Autobiography of 'Babe' Didrikson Zaharias* London: Robert Hale, 1956.

Zatopek, Emil 'My Wife Dana: As Told in Interviews to Norris McWhirter' *World Sports: The International Sports Magazine* December 1955 London: Country and Sporting Publications, 1955.

Secondary sources

Adams, Carly 'Fighting For Acceptance: Sigfrid Edström and Avery Brundage: Their Efforts to Shape and Control Women's Participation in the Olympic Games' in Kevin B. Wamsley, Robert K. Barney and Scott G. Martyn (eds.) *Global Nexus Engaged: Sixth International Symposium for Olympic Research 2002* International Centre for Olympic Studies: University of Western Ontario Canada, 2002.

Adams, Mary Louise *Artistic Impressions: Figure Skating, Masculinity and The Limits of Sport* Toronto, Buffalo and London: University of Toronto Press, 2011.

Allison, Lincoln *Amateurism in Sport: An Analysis and a Defence* London: Frank Cass, 2001.

Andrassy, Hannah 'Spinning a Golden Thread: The Introduction of Elastic into Swimwear' *Things* 5 (Winter 1996–1997) pp. 59–85.

Arnold, Rebecca *The American Look: Sportswear, Fashion and The Image of Women In 1930s and 1940s New York* London & New York: I. B. Tauris, 2009.

Bailey, Steve 'A Noble Ally and Olympic Disciple: The Reverend Robert S. de Courcy Laffan, Coubertin's 'Man' in England' *Olympika Volume VI – 1997* pp. 51–64.

Bale, John Mette K. Christensen and Gertrude Pfister (eds.) *Writing Lives in Sport: Biographies, Life-Histories and Methods* Langelandsgade: Aarhus, 2004.

Bancroft, James 'Sybil Fenton 'Queenie' Newall 1854–1929' *Oxford Dictionary of National Biography* Oxford University Press www.oxforddnb.com accessed 24 April 2019.

Bandy, Susan and Anne Darden *Crossing Boundaries: An International Anthology Women Experiences In Sport* Champaign, Illinois : Human Kinetics, 1999.

Bannister, Roger *The First Four Minutes* Stroud: Putnam, 1955 reprinted 2004.

Barney, Robert K. 'The Olympic Games in Modern Times: An Overview' in Gerald P. Schaus and Stephen R. Wenn (eds.) *Onward to the Olympics: Historical Perspectives on The Olympic Games* Waterloo, Ontario: Wilfred Laurier University Press, 2007.

Barney, Robert K. 'The Genesis of Sacred Fire in Olympic Ceremony: A New Interpretation' in Hai Ren, Lamartine Da Costa, Ana Miragaya and Niu Jing (eds.) *Olympic Studies Reader 1* Beijing, China and Rio De Janeiro, Brazil: Beijing Sport University and Universidade Gama Filho, 2009.

Barrett, John and Alan Little *Wimbledon: Ladies' Singles Champions 1884–2004* London: Wimbledon Lawn Tennis Museum, 2005.

Bartlett, Robert 'Failed Bids and Losing Cities: Adelaide's Failure to Secure the 1962 British Empire and Commonwealth Games' *Sporting Traditions* 15: 2 May 1999.

Beamish, Rob 'Totalitarian Regimes and Cold War Sport' in Stephen Wagg and David L. Andrews (eds.) *East Plays West: Sport and the Cold War* London and New York: Routledge, 2006.

Beazley, Ben *Peelers to Pandas: An Illustrated History of the Leicester City Police* Leicester: Breedon Books, 2001.

Beck, Peter J. 'Britain and The Olympic Games: London 1908, 1948, 2012' *Journal of Sport and History* 39: 1 2012.

Bennett, Victoria *Invisible women/Hidden Voices: Women Writing On Sport In The Twentieth Century* unpublished PhD thesis, De Montfort University, Leicester 2003.

Berlioux, Monique 'Managing a Gentleman's Club' *Journal of Olympic History* 23: 1 2015.

Biddle-Perry, Geraldine 'The Rise of 'The World's Largest Sport and Athletic Outfitter': A Study of Gamage's of Holborn, 1878–1913' *Sport in History: Special*

Issue: Sport's Relationship with Other Leisure Industries. Part I: Sites of Interaction 34: 2 2014 pp. 295–317.

Bier, Lisa *Fighting the Current: The Rise of American Women's Swimming 1870–1926* New York: McFarland and Company, 2011.

Bijkerk, Anthony 'Xenia Stad-De Jong (1922–2012): Obituary' *Journal of Olympic History* 20: 2 2012.

Bilsborough, Peter 'John Arthur Jarvis (1872–1933)' *Oxford Dictionary of National Biography* www.oxforddnb.com/view/article/65070 accessed 15 October 2019.

Boddy, Kasia *Boxing: A Cultural History* London: Reaktion Books, 2008.

Bowen, Richard 'Koizumi, Gunji (1885–1965)' *Oxford Dictionary of National Biography* Oxford University Press www.oxforddnb.com/view/article/75932 accessed 4 September 2019.

Boyce, D. George 'Alfred Charles William Harmsworth, Viscount Northcliffe (1865–1922)' *Oxford Dictionary of National Biography* Oxford University Press www.oxforddnb.com/view/article/33717 accessed 9 January 2019.

Brace, Reginald 'Slazenger's Centenary' in John Barrett and Lance Tinjay (eds.) *Slazenger's World of Tennis 1981: The Official Yearbook of the International Tennis Federation* London: Slazenger's/Queen Anne Press, 1981.

Bradbury, Jonathan 'Dame Enid Mary Russell-Smith (1903–1989)' *Oxford Dictionary of National Biography* Oxford University Press www.oxforddnb.com/view/article/65870 accessed 4 September 2019.

Brittain, Ian *From Stoke Mandeville to Sochi: A History of the Summer and Winter Paralympic Games* Champaign, Illinois: Common Ground Publishing, 2014.

British Olympic Association *Chasing Gold: Centenary of the British Olympic Association* London: Getty Images, 2005.

Bryant, M. A. 'Albert George Hill (1889–1969)' *Oxford Dictionary of National Biography* Oxford University Press www.oxforddnb.com/view/article/65170 accessed 22 October 2019.

Buchanan, Ian *British Olympians: A Hundred Years of Gold Medallists* London: Guinness Publishing, 1991.

Buchanan, Ian 'Kinuye Hitomi: Asia's First Female Olympian' *Journal of Olympic History* 8: 3 2000.

Buchanan, Ian and Wolf, Lyberg 'The Biographies of all IOC Members Part XI' *Journal of Olympic History* 20: 2 2012.

Budd, Graham 'Lots 399 to 417: Helen Orr Gordon 1948–1956' *Graham Budd Auction Catalogue GB21* (London: Graham Budd Auctions, 2012).

Calder, Angus 'Nancy Anderson Long Riach (1927–1947)' *Oxford Dictionary of National Biography* Oxford University Press www.oxforddnb.com/view/article/65073 accessed 17 November 2019.

Campbell Warner, Patricia *When the Girls Came Out to Play* Amerhurst and Boston: University of Massachusetts Press, 2006.

Carpentier, Florence and Pierre Lefèvre 'The Modern Olympic Movement, Women's Sport and the Social Order During the Inter-war Period' *The International Journal of the History of Sport* 23: 7 2006.

Chambers, Ciara 'An Advertiser's Dream: The Construction of the "Consumptionist" Cinematic Persona of Mercedes Gleitze' *Alphaville Journal of Film and Screen Media* 6: 2 Winter 2013 pp. 10–11 www.alphavillejournal.com/Issue6.html accessed 31 July 2019.

Collins, Sandra *The 1940 Tokyo Games: The Missing Olympics: Japan, the Asian Olympics and the Olympic Movement* London, Routledge, 2007.

Cowe, Eric *Early Women's Athletics: Statistics and History, Volume One* Bingley, Eric Cowe Publications, 1999.

Cronin, Mike 'Arthur Elvin and the Dogs of Wembley' *The Sports Historian* 22: 1 2002.

Cronin, Mike and Richard Holt 'The Globalisation of Sport' *History Today* 53: 7 July 2003.

Curthoys, Mark C. 'Maureen Angela Jane Gardner (1928–1974)' *Oxford Dictionary of National Biography* Oxford University Press www.oxforddnb.com/view/article/104312 accessed 6 November 2012.

Daniels, Stephanie and Anita Tedder *'A Proper Spectacle': Women Olympians 1900–1936* Bedford: Zee Na Na Press, 2000.

Davenport, Joanna 'Monique Berlioux: Her Association with Three IOC Presidents' *Citius, Altius, Fortius* (became *Journal of Olympic History* in 1997) 4: 3 1996.

Dawson, Michael 'Acting Global, Thinking Local: "Liquid Imperialism" and the Multiple Meanings of the 1954 British Empire & Commonwealth Games' *The International Journal of the History of Sport* 23: 1 February 2006.

De Coubertin, Pierre *Olympic Memoirs* Lausanne: IOC, 1997).

Dee, David ' "Nothing Specifically Jewish in Athletics?": Sport, Physical Recreation and the Jewish Youth Movement in London 1895–1914' *The London Journal* 34: 2 2010.

De Frantz, Anita 'Women's participation in the Olympic Games: Lessons and Challenges For the Future' in International Olympic Committee *Final Report of the International Olympic Committee's 2nd IOC Conference on Women and Sport: New perspectives for the XXI century* Paris: International Olympic Committee, 2000.

Doughan, David 'Muriel Lilah Matters-Porter (1877–1969)' *Oxford Dictionary of National Biography* Oxford University Press www.oxforddnb.com/view/article/63878 accessed 9 January 2013.

Douglas, Ed 'Eileen Healey: Obituary 1921–2010' *The Guardian* 22 November 2010.

Drevon, André *Alice Milliat: La Pasionaria du Sport Feminine* Paris: Vuibert, 2005.

Duval, Lynne 'The Development of Women's Track and Field in England: The Role of the Athletic Club, 1920s-1950s' *The Sports Historian* 21: 1 2001.

Dyhouse, Carol *Students: A Gendered History* London: Routledge, 2006.

Dyhouse, Carol *Glamour: Women, History, Feminism* London and New York: Zed Books, 2010.

Dyreson, Mark 'Icons of Liberty or Objects of Desire? American Women Olympians and the Politics of Consumption' *Journal of Contemporary History* 38: 3 2004.

Dyreson, Mark 'The Republic of Consumption at the Olympic Games: Globalization, Americanization, and Californization' *Journal of Global History* 8: 2 2013.

Edelman, Robert *Serious Fun: A History of Spectator Sport in the USSR* New York: Oxford University Press, 1993.

Edgerley, David 'How About Volunteering At The 1948 Olympics?' *Journal of Olympic History* 20: 1 2012.

Edwards, Owen Dudley 'Sir Arthur Ignatius Conan Doyle (1859–1930)' *Oxford Dictionary of National Biography* Oxford University Press www.oxforddnb.com/view/article/32887 accessed 9 January 2019.

Emery, Lynne 'An Examination of the 1928 Olympic 800m race for women' *NASSH Proceedings 1985* p. 30 www.la84foundation.org accessed 10 July 2019.

Evans, Richard 'Gussie Moran: Obituary' *The Guardian* 20 January 2013.
Gardiner, Juliet *The Thirties: An Intimate History* London: Harper Press, 2010.
Gold, John and Margaret M. Gold 'Future Indefinite? London 2012, The Spectre of Retrenchment and The Challenge of Olympic Sports Legacy' *The London Journal* 34: 2 July 2009.
Green, Kathleen '1948 Olympians: Dorothy Parlett and Dorothy Tyler (Athletics)' *London, Oral History and Publication* www.katherinegreen.co.uk/1948-olympians/ accessed 29 May 2019.
Griffin, Danielle *Sport and Canadian Anti-Apartheid Policy: a political and diplomatic history c.1968–c.1980* Unpublished PhD thesis, De Montfort University 2012.
Gundle, Stephen *Glamour: A History* Oxford: Oxford University Press, 2008.
Guttmann, Allen *Women's Sports: A History* New York: Columbia University Press, 1991.
Halberstam, Judith *Female Masculinity* Durham, North Carolina: Duke University Press, 1998.
Hall, M. Ann *The Grads Are Playing Tonight: The Story of the Edmonton Commercial Graduates Basketball Club* Edmonton: The University of Alberta Press, 2011.
Hampton, Janie *London Olympics, 1908 and 1948* London: Shire, 2011.
Hampton, Janie *The Austerity Olympics: When the Games Came to London in 1948* London: Aurum Press, 2012.
Hardy, Stephen 'Entrepreneurs, Organizations and the Sports Marketplace' in S. W. Pope (ed.) *The New American Sport History: Recent Approaches and Perspectives* Urbana and Chicago: University of Illinois Press, 1997.
Hargreaves, Jennifer 'Women and the Olympic Phenomenon' in Alan Tomlinson and Gary Whannel (eds.) *Five Ring Circus: Money, Power and Politics at the Olympic Games* London: Pluto Press, 1984.
Hargreaves, Roger and Bill Deedes *Daily Encounters: Photographs From Fleet Street* London: National Portrait Gallery, 2007.
Hayes, Win 'Lucy Morton [married name Heaton] (1898–1980)' *Oxford Dictionary of National Biography* www.oxforddnb.com/view/article/92814 accessed 14 July 2019.
Heggie, Vanessa *A History of British Sports Medicine* Manchester: Manchester University Press, 2011.
Henderson, Jon *The Last Champion: A Life of Fred Perry* London: Yellow Jersey, 2010.
Hewitt-Soar, Hugh D. 'Alice Blanche Legh (1856–1948)' *Oxford Dictionary of National Biography* Oxford University Press www.oxforddnb.com accessed 24 May 2019.
Hill, Jeffrey *Sport, Leisure and Culture in Twentieth Century Britain* Basingstoke: Palgrave Macmillan, 2002.
Hill, Jeffrey 'Patricia Rosemary Smythe (1928–1996)' *Oxford Dictionary of National Biography* Oxford University Press www.oxforddnb.com/view/article/62144 accessed 1 December 2019.
Hilton, Christopher 'Amazing tale of man called Hermann who finished fourth in women's high jump' *The Independent* 20 July 2008 www.independent.co.uk/sport/general/athletics/amazing-tale-of-man-called-hermann-who-finished-fourth-in-womens-high-jump-872322.html accessed 22 July 2019.
Hines, James R. 'Cecilia (Magdalena) Colledge 1920–2008' in Lawrence Goldman (ed.) *The Oxford Dictionary of National Biography* Oxford: Oxford University Press, 2008.
Holloway, Gerry *Women and Work in Britain Since 1840* London and New York: Routledge, 2005.

Holt, Richard '(Arthur) Godfrey Kilner Brown (1915–1995)' *Oxford Dictionary of National Biography*, Oxford University Press, 2004 www.oxforddnb.com/view/article/59785 accessed 20 July 2019.

Holt, Richard 'Audrey Kathleen Court [née Brown] (1913–2005)' *Oxford Dictionary of National Biography* Oxford University Press www.oxforddnb.com/view/article/96973 accessed 17 August 2019.

Horn, Pamela *Women in the 1920s* Stroud: Amberley, 2010 first published 1995.

Horrall, Andrew *Popular Culture in London, c.1890–1918* Manchester: Manchester University Press, 2001.

Hudson, Hugh *Chariots of Fire* Allied Stars/Enigma Productions, 1981.

Hughson, John 'An Invitation to "Modern" Melbourne The Historical Significance of Richard Beck's Olympic Poster Design' *Journal of Design History* 25: 3 2012.

Hult, Joan S. 'The Story of Women's Athletics: Manipulating a Dream 1890–1985' in D. Margaret Costa and Sharon R Guthrie (eds.) *Women and Sport: Interdisciplinary Perspectives* Champaign, Illinois: Human Kinetics, 1994.

Hunt, Peter 'Kenneth Grahame (1859–1932)' *Oxford Dictionary of National Biography* Oxford University Press www.oxforddnb.com/view/article/33511 accessed 18 May 2012.

Huntingdon-Whitely, James and Richard Holt *The Book of British Sporting Heroes* London: National Portrait Gallery, 1999.

Jeffreys, Kevin 'The Heyday of Amateurism in Modern Lawn Tennis' *International Journal of the History of Sport* 26: 15 2009.

Jenkins, Rebecca *The First London Olympics 1908* London: Piaktus, 2008.

Jensen, Erik *Body By Weimar: Athletes, Gender, and German Modernity* New York: OUP USA, 2010.

Johnsey, Debbie *Sport Horses* www.johnseysporthorses.com/index.html accessed 1 December 2019.

Keil, Ian and Don Wix *In the Swim: The History of the Amateur Swimming Association from 1869 to 1994* Loughborough: Swimming Times Publications Ltd, 1996.

Kennedy, Sarah *The Swimsuit: A Fashion History From 1920s Biarritz and The Birth of The Bikini to Sportswear Styles and Catwalk Trends* London: Carlton Books, 2007.

Keys, Barbara *Globalising Sport: National Rivalry and International Community in the 1930s* Cambridge, Massachusetts and London: Harvard University Press, 2006.

Kidd, Bruce 'Missing: Women From Sports Halls of Fame' *CAAWS Action Bulletin* Winter, 1995 www.caaws.ca/e/milestones/women_history/missing accessed 3 January 2019.

Koishihara, Miho 'The Emergence of The 'Sporting Girls' in Japanese Girls' Magazines: Descriptions and Visual Images of The Female Athlete in Japanese Culture of The 1920s and 1930s' *Fourth Meeting of the Transnational Scholars for the Study of Gender and Sport* Pädagogische Hochscule Ludwigsburg 27–30 November 2008.

Krüger, Arnd 'What's The Difference Between Propaganda For Tourism or For A Political Regime?: Was The 1936 Olympics The First Postmodern Spectacle?' in John Bale and Mette Krogh Christensen *Post-Olympism? Questioning Sport in the Twenty-First Century* Oxford and New York: Berg, 2004.

Kushner, Tony *Anglo-Jewry Since 1066: Place Locality and Memory* Manchester: Manchester University Press, 2009.

Kynaston, David *Austerity Britain 1945–1951* London: Bloomsbury, 2007.

Lambie, James *The Story of Your Life: A History of The Sporting Life Newspaper, 1859–1998* Leicester: Matador, 2010.

Leigh, Mary H. and Thérèse M. Bonin 'The Pioneering Role of Madame Alice Milliat and the FSFI in Establishing International Track and Field Competition for Women' *Journal of Sport History* 4: 1 1977.

Leigh, Mary H. 'The Enigma of Avery Brundage and Women Athletes' *Arena Review* 4: 2 May 1980.

Lennartz, Karl 'Two Women Ran the Marathon in 1896' *Citius, Altius, Fortius* 2: 1 1994 pp. 11–12.

Lennartz, Karl 'The Story of the Rings' *Journal of Olympic History* 10: 3 2002 pp. 29–61.

Lennartz, Karl 'The Story of the Rings Part II' *Journal of Olympic History* 11: 2 2003 pp. 33–37.

Lennartz, Karl 'The IOC During World War Two' *Journal of Olympic History* 20: 1 2012.

Lewis, Peter N. 'Joyce Wethered [married name Joyce Heathcoat-Amory, Lady Heathcoat-Amory] (1901–1997)' *Oxford Dictionary of National Biography* Oxford University Press www.oxforddnb.com/view/article/68365 accessed 15 January 2019.

Litsky, Frank 'Aileen Riggin Soule, Olympic Diver and Swimmer, Dies at 96' *The New York Times* 21 October 2002 www.nytimes.com/2002/10/21/sports/aileen-riggin-soule-olympic-diver-and-swimmer-dies-at-96.html accessed 28 July 2019.

Little, Alan *Suzanne Lenglen: Tennis Idol of the Twenties* London: Wimbledon Lawn Tennis Museum, 2005.

Love, Christopher 'Social Class and the Swimming World: Amateurs and Professionals' *International Journal of the History of Sport* 24:5 2007.

Lovesey, Peter 'Conan Doyle and The Olympics' *Journal of Olympic History* 10 December 2001.

Lovesey, Peter 'Violet Piercy (b. 1889?)' *Oxford Dictionary of National Biography* Oxford University Press www.oxforddnb.com/view/article/103698 accessed 17 August 2019.

Lowerson, J. R. 'Ralph Slazenger (1845–1910)' *Oxford Dictionary of National Biography* Oxford University Press www.oxforddnb.com/view/article/39048 accessed 28 June 2019.

Lucas, Shelley 'Women's Cycle Racing: Enduring Meanings' *Journal of Sport History* 39: 2 Summer 2012.

Lykke Poulson. Anne 'Women's Gymnastics and citizenship in Denmark in the Early Twentieth Century' *Women's History Magazine* 59 2008 Oxford: Women's History Network 2008.

MacAloon, John J. *This Great Symbol: Pierre de Coubertin and the Origins of the Modern Olympic Games* Chicago: University of Chicago Press, 1981.

MacAloon, John J. *Brides of Victory: Nationalism and Gender in Olympic Ritual* London: Berg, 1997.

Mair, Lewine *One Hundred Years of Women's Golf* Edinburgh: Mainstream Publishing in conjunction with the Ladies Golf Union, 1993.

Malies, Jeremy 'Charlotte [Lottie] Dod (1871–1960)' *Oxford Dictionary of National Biography* Oxford University Press www.oxforddnb.com/view/article/37363 accessed 7 January 2013.

Mallon, Bill 'The First Two Women Olympians' *Citius, Altius, Fortius* (became *Journal of Olympic History* in 1997) 3: 3 1995.

Mallon, Bill *The 1900 Olympic Games: Results for All Competitors in All Events, with commentary* Jefferson, North Carolina: McFarland and Co., 1998.

Mallon, Bill *The 1904 Olympic Games: Results for All Competitors in All Events, with commentary* Jefferson, North Carolina: McFarland & Co., 1999.

Mallon, Bill & Ian Buchanan *The 1908 Olympic Games: Results for All Competitors in All Events, with Commentary* Jefferson, North Carolina: McFarland & Co., 2000.

Maragaya, Ana Maria *The Process of Inclusion of Women in the Olympic Games* unpublished PhD thesis Universidade Gama Filho, Rio De Janeiro 2006.

Maraniss, David *Rome 1960: The Olympics That Changed the World* New York: Simon & Schuster, 2008.

Maughan, Robert J. (ed.) *The Encyclopaedia of Sports Medicine: An IOC Medical Commission Publication* Chichester: Wiley-Blackwell Publishing, 2009.

Mason, Tony 'Geoffrey Harry George Dyson (1914–1981)' *Oxford Dictionary of National Biography* Oxford University Press www.oxforddnb.com/view/article/100477 accessed 6 November 2019.

Nead, Lynda *The Haunted Gallery: Painting, Photography and Film c1900* New Haven and London: Yale University Press, 2007.

Newsum, Gillian *Women and Horses* London: The Sportsman's Press, 1988.

Obituary 'Fanny Blankers-Koen' *The Times* 26 January 2004.

Obituaries 'Cecilia Colledge: Champion figure skater' *The Independent* 21 April 2008 www.independent.co.uk/news/obituaries/cecilia-colledge-champion-figure-skater-812673.html accessed 14 May 2019.

O'Hara, Denis *The Remarkable Kyles* Belfast: O'Hara Publications, 2006.

Oliver, Brian 'Sir Ralph Kilner Brown Obituary' *The Telegraph* 20 June 2003 www.telegraph.co.uk/news/obituaries/1433497/Sir-Ralph-Kilner-Brown.html accessed 20 July 2019.

Oliver, Brian 'Dorothy Tyler Obituatry' *The Guardian* 28 September 2014 www.theguardian.com/sport/2014/sep/28/dorothy-tyler accessed 20 July 2019.

O'Sullivan, Tim 'Television and The Austerity Games: London 1948' in Jeffrey Hill, Kevin Moore and Jason Wood (eds.) *Sport, History and Heritage: Studies in Public Representation* Woodbridge, Suffolk: Boydell and Brewer Ltd, 2012.

Parks, Jennifer 'Verbal Gymnastics: Sports, Bureaucracy, and The Soviet Unions' Entrance Into the Olympic Games 1946–1952' in Stephen Wagg and David L. Andrews (eds.) *East Plays West: Sport and the Cold War* (London and New York: Routledge, 2007) pp. 27–44.

Parr, Susie *The Story of Swimming* Stockport: Dewi Lewis Media, 2011.

Pearson, Jeffrey *Lottie Dod: Champion of Champions, The Story of an Athlete* Wirral, Merseyside: Countyvise, 1988.

Pérez, Alberto Aragón 'Royalty and the Olympic Games: From Ancient Greece to the Present' *Journal of Olympic History* 23: 2 2015.

Perrone, Fernanda Helen 'Constance Mary Katherine Applebee (1873–1981)' *Oxford Dictionary of National Biography* Oxford University Press www.oxforddnb.com/view/article/102441 accessed 11 July 2019.

Phillips, Bob *The 1948 Olympics: How London Rescued the Games* London: Sports Pages, 2007.

Pottle, Mark 'Dorothea Katharine Lambert Chambers [née Douglass] (1878–1960)' *Oxford Dictionary of National Biography* Oxford University Press www.oxforddnb.com/view/article/32353 accessed 23 April 2019.

Pottle, Mark 'Sophie Catherine Theresa Mary Heath, Lady Heath (1896–1939) *Oxford Dictionary of National Biography* Oxford University Press www.oxforddnb.com/view/article/67141 accessed 10 August 2019.

Quintillan, Ghislane 'Alice Milliat and the Women's Games' *Olympic Review* 36: 31 2000 pp. 27–28 Lausanne: IOC, 2000 www.la84foundation.org/OlympicInformation Center/OlympicReview/2000 accessed 12 August 2012.

Richards, Jeffrey *Cinema and Radio in Britain and America 1920–1960* Manchester: Manchester University Press, 2010.

Ridley, Jane and Clayre Percy 'Ethel Anne Priscilla Grenfell, Lady Desborough (1867–1952)' *Oxford Dictionary of National Biography* Oxford University Press www.oxforddnb.com/view/article/40733 accessed 4 January 2019.

Robinson, Lynne *Tripping Daintily Into the Arena: A Social History of English Women's Athletics 1921–1960* unpublished PhD thesis, Warwick University, 1997.

Roche, Maurice *Mega-Events and Modernity: Olympics and Expos in the Growth of Global Culture* London: Routledge, 2000.

Rodda, John 'Sydney Wooderson: Obituary' *The Guardian* Wednesday 3 January 2007. www.guardian.co.uk/news/2007/jan/03/guardianobituaries.athletics accessed 5 November 2019.

Ruffin, Raymond *La Diablesse: La Véritable Histoire de Violette Morris* Paris: Pygmalion, 1989.

Ruffin, Raymond *Violette Morris: La Hyène de la Gestap* Paris: Le Cherche Midi, 2004.

Ryan, Mark *Running with Fire: The True Story of 'Chariots of Fire' hero Harold Abrahams* London: JR Books, 2011.

Ryan, Mark 'Muriel Robb (1878–1907): A Little-Known Wimbledon Singles Champion' *Tennis Forum* www.tennisforum.com accessed 24 April 2019.

Ryan, Mark 'Ethel Warneford Larcombe [née Thomson] (1879–1965)' *Oxford Dictionary of National Biography* Oxford University Press www.oxforddnb.com accessed 15 May 2019.

Schoenfeld, Bruce *The Match: Althea Gibson & Angela Buxton* New York: Harper Collins, 2004.

Schweinbenz, Amanda and Alexandria Cronk 'Femininity Control at the Olympic Games' *Thirdspace: A Journal of Feminist Theory & Culture: Special Edition Gender, Sport and the Olympics* 9: 2 2010.

Silver, J. R. *The Role of Sport in the Rehabilitation of Patients with Spinal Injuries* Stoke Mandeville: National Spine Injuries Centre, 2004.

Smith, Martin (ed.) *The Daily Telegraph of Sports Obituaries* London: Pan Books, 2001.

Smyth, J. G. 'Charlotte Renaigle Sterry (née Cooper) 1870–1966' *Oxford Dictionary of National Biography* Oxford University Press www.oxforddnb.com accessed 30 October 2019.

Sutherland, Duncan '(Frances) Elaine Burton, Baroness Burton of Coventry 1904–1991' *Oxford Dictionary of National Biography* Oxford University Press www.oxforddnb.com/view/article/49597 accessed 18 December 2019.

Terret, Thierry 'From Alice Milliat to Marie-Thérèse Eyquem: Revisiting Women's Sport in France (1920s–1960s)' *The International Journal of the History of Sport* 27: 7 2010.

Timmers, Margaret *A Century of Olympic Posters* London: V & A Publishing 2012.

Tomlinson, Alan 'Olympic survivals: The Olympic Games as a Global Phenomenon' in Lincoln Allison (ed.) *The Global Politics of Sport: The Role of Global Institutions in Sport* Oxon: Routledge, 2005 pp. 46–62.

Vamplew, Wray 'Muriel Amy Cornell (1906–1996)' *Oxford Dictionary of National Biography* Oxford University Press www.oxforddnb.com/view/article/62157 accessed 17 August 2019.
Vamplew, Wray 'Sir Arthur Abraham Gold (1917–2002)' *Oxford Dictionary of National Biography* Oxford University Press www.oxforddnb.com/view/article/76890 accessed 6 November 2019.
Van Someren, Janine *Women's Sporting Lives: A Biographical Study of Elite Amateur Tennis Players at Wimbledon* unpublished PhD thesis, University of Southampton, 2012.
Vertinsky, Patricia *The Eternally Wounded Woman: Women, Doctors and Exercise in the Late Nineteenth Century* Manchester: Manchester University Press, 1990.
Vertinsky, Patricia and Christiane Job 'Celebrating Gertrudes: Women of Influence' in Annette R. Hofmann and Else Trangbaek (eds.) *International Perspectives on Sporting Women in Past and Present* Denmark: Institute of Exercise and Social Sciences University of Copenhagen, 2005.
Walker, Graham 'Nancy Riach and The Motherwell Swimming Phenomenon' in Grant Jarvie and Graham Walker (eds.) *Scottish Sport In The Making of The Nation: Ninety-Minute Patriots?* Leicester: Leicester University Press, 1994.
Walmsley Kevin B. 'Laying Olympism to Rest' in John Bale and Mette Krogh Christensen *Post-Olympism? Questioning Sport in the Twenty-First Century* Oxford and New York: Berg, 2004.
Walmsley, Kevin 'Womanizing Olympic Athletes: Policy and Practice during the Avery Brundage Era' in Stephen R. Wenn, Gerald P. Schaus (eds.) *Onward to the Olympics: Historical Perspectives on the Olympic Games* Ontario: Wilfred Laurier University Press and the Canadian Institute in Greece, 2007.
Watman, Mel *The Official History Of The AAA: The Story Of The World's Oldest Athletic Association* London: Sportsbooks, 2011.
Watman, Mel *The Official History of the Women's Amateur Athletic Association (WAAA) 1922–2012* Cheltenham: Sports Books Ltd, 2012.
Watman, Mel 'Women athletes between the world wars 1919–1939' *Oxford Dictionary of National Biography* Oxford University Press www.oxforddnb.com/view/article/103699 accessed 18 December 2019.
Welch, Paula 'Search for Margaret Abbott' *Olympic Review* 1982 p. 753 http://library.la84.org/OlympicInformationCenter/OlympicReview/1982/ore182/ORE182s.pdf accessed 30 July 2019.
Welch, Paula and Margaret Costa 'A Century of Olympic Competition' in Margaret Costa and Sharon Guthrie (eds.) *Women and Sport: Interdisciplinary Perspectives* Champaign, Illinois: Human Kinetics, 1994.
Wilcock, Bob *The London 1948 Olympic Games: A Collector's Guide* London: The Society of Olympic Collectors, 2012.
Williams, Elizabeth 'Walter Whitmore Jones 1831–1872' *Oxford Dictionary of National Biography* Oxford University Press www.oxforddnb.com/view/article/100464 accessed 15 May 2019.
Williams, Jean *A Game For Rough Girls: A History of Women's Football in England* London: Routledge, 2003.
Williams, Jean *A Beautiful Game: International Perspectives on Women's Football* London: Berg 2007.

Williams, Jean 'The Curious Mystery of the "Olimpick Games": Did Shakespeare Know Dover... and Does It Matter?' in Jeff Hill and Jean Williams (eds.) *Sport and Literature: A Special Edition of Sport in History* 29: 2 June 2009.

Williams, Jean 'The Immediate Legacy Of Pat Smythe: The Pony-Mad Teenager In 1950s and 1960s Britain' in Dave Day (ed.) *Sporting Lives* Manchester: MMU Institute for Performance Research, 2011.

Williams Jean 'Aquadynamics and the Athletocracy: Jennie Fletcher and the British Women's 4×100 metre Freestyle Relay Team at the 1912 Stockholm Olympic Games' in John Hughson (ed.) *Costume* 46: 2 Summer 2012.

Williams Jean 'The Most Important Photograph in the History of Women's Olympic Participation: Jennie Fletcher and the British 4×100 Freestyle relay team at the Stockholm 1912 Games' in Martin Polley (ed.) *Sport in History, Special Issue: Britain, Britons and the Olympic Games* 32: 2 Summer 2012.

Williams, Jean *A Contemporary History of Women's Sport, Part One Sporting Women, 1850–1960* London and New York: Routledge, 2014.

Williams 'Given the Boot: Reading the Ambiguities of British and Continental Football Boot Design' in Jean Williams (ed.) *Sport in History Special Issue Kit: Fashioning the Sporting Body* 25: 1 2014.

Williams, Jean 'Jane 'Jennie' Fletcher (1890–1968)' *Oxford Dictionary of National Biography* Oxford University Press www.oxforddnb.com/view/article/102443 accessed 8 January 2019.

Williams, Linda 'Sportswomen in Black and White: Sports History from an Afro American Perspective' in Pamela J. Creedon *Women Media and Sport: Challenging Gender Values* London: Sage, 1994.

Williams, Owen rev. Anita McConnell 'Sir Arthur James Elvin (1899–1957)' *Oxford Dictionary of National Biography* Oxford University Press www.oxforddnb.com/view/article/33017 accessed 6 November 2019.

Wilson Elizabeth *Fashion and Modernity* London: I. B. Tauris and Co. Ltd 2003; first published by Virago 1985.

Wilson, Judith 'Florence Madeline 'Madge' Syers [née Cave] 1881–1917' *Oxford Dictionary of National Biography* Oxford University Press www.oxforddnb.com accessed 24 April 2019.

Yapp, Nick (ed.) *Chasing Gold: Centenary if the British Olympic Association* London: British Olympic Association, 2005.

Yeomans, Patricia Henry 'Hazel Wightman and Helen Wills: Tennis At The 1924 Paris Olympic Games' *Journal of Olympic History* 11: 2 2003.

Zagha, Muriel 'Ban the Bolt!' *World of Interiors* 9 January London: Condé Nast Publications, 2015.

Websites

British Broadcasting Company 'BBC Sports Personality of The Year' www.bbc.co.uk/pressoffice/keyfacts/stories/spoty.shtml accessed 19 October 2019.

British Pathé moving images www.britishpathe.com accessed 29 June 2019 including.

Margaret Wellington: Mermaid in the City 1946 film no. 1388.02 www.britishpathe.com/video/mermaid-in-the-city accessed 29 June 2019.

Nancy Riach Funeral, 1947 film no. 2168.10 www.britishpathe.com/video/stills/nancy-riach-funeral accessed 29 May 2019.

Fédération Équestre Internationale *History of Equestrian Events at the Games of the XV Olympiad: Factsheet* Lausanne: Fédération Équestre Internationale p. 1 http://history.fei.org/sites/default/files/1952_Helsinki.pdf accessed 11 August 2019.

International Olympic Committee *Olympic.Org: Official Website of the Olympic Movement* www.olympic.org/medallists accessed 23 April 2019.

International Olympic Committee 'Paris 1924–4 May-27 July' www.olympic.org/paris-1924-summer-olympics accessed 15 July 2019.

International Olympic Committee 'Audrey Mickey Patterson 29 July 1948' *London 1948* www.olympic.org/news/audrey-mickey-patterson-athletics/179793 accessed 29 May 2019.

International Olympic Committee 'Wilma Rudolph Stormed to Gold: Rome 1960' www.olympic.org/videos/rome-1960-wilma-rudolph-stormed-to-gold accessed 25 August 2019.

International Swimming Hall of Fame www.ishof.org/honorees/ accessed 15 October 2019.

International Tennis Hall of Fame 'Suzanne Lenglen' International Tennis Hall of Fame www.tennisfame.com/hall-of-famers/suzanne-lenglen accessed 29 July 2019.

International Table Tennis Federation Museum *World Championships Women's Singles 1927–2011* www.ittf.com/museum/WorldChWSingles.pdf accessed 21 August 2012.

ITN Source collections at www.itnsource.com accessed 29 June 2019.

Lyons, J. & Company online archive www.kzwp.com/lyons/index.htm accessed 10 August 2019.

Mandeville Legacy Margaret Maughan interview about Rome 26 September 2013 www.youtube.com/watch?v=5PtL-RT7UOo accessed 11 August 2019.

Mandeville Legacy Lady Susan Masham interview about Rome 27 September 2013 www.youtube.com/watch?v=5PtL-RT7UOo accessed 11 August 2019.

National Portrait Gallery, collections www.npg.org.uk accessed 15 September 2019.

Paralympic Heritage Caz Walton *Caz Walton Remembers Winning Gold at the Tokyo Games* www.paralympicheritage.org.uk/content/sports/wheelchair-racing/caz-walton-remembers-gold-medal-tokyo-1964 accessed 23 August 2017.

Paralympic Heritage Sally Haynes *Sally Haynes on being urged to set an example at the Tokyo Games* www.paralympicheritage.org.uk/content/stories/paralympians/haynes-sally/sally-haynes-urged-set-example-tokyo-games accessed 23 August 2017.

Paralympic Heritage Susan Baroness Masham of Ilton *Tokyo Games* www.paralympicheritage.org.uk/content/stories/paralympians/cunliffe-lister-susan/lady-susan-masham-tokyo-games accessed 23 August 2017.

Riding for the Disabled www.riding-for-disabled.org.uk/about-us/ accessed 27 January 2019.

Sport Australia 'Frank Beaurepaire' *Sport Australia Hall of Fame* www.sahof.org.au/hall-of-fame/ accessed 14 July 2019.

Sport Scotland 'Isabella 'Belle' Mary Moore (1894–1975)' *Scottish Sports Hall of Fame* Sport Scotland www.sportscotland.org.uk/sshf/Isabella_Mary_Moore accessed 8 December 2019.

The British Library *Nineteenth Century British Library Newspapers Database* http://newspapers.bl.uk/blcs/ accessed 19 June 2019.

The British Library *Oral History of British Athletics* including: Cutler, Rachel 'Audrey Court (Brown) 1913–2005' *Oral History of British Athletics* catalogue no: C790/02–4 London: The British Library 1996 http://sounds.bl.uk/Oral-history/Sport/021M-C0790X0002XX-0100V0 accessed 19 May 2015

The National Archives Foreign Office Files including: British Non-Sectarian Anti-Nazi Council *Agitation against holding the Olympic Games in Germany in 1936; suggestion from British Non-Sectarian Anti-Nazi Council* FO 371/19940/306 www.nationalarchives.gov.uk/olympics/1936.htm accessed 19 May 2019.

General Post Office 'Transmission of press telegrams between the United Kingdom and Sweden, Denmark and Norway: transmission of telegrams respecting the Olympic Games, Stockholm 11 April 1913' record T 1/11533, The National Archives, Kew www.nationalarchives.gov.uk accessed 16 May 2019.

Sir E. Phipps 'Olympic Games to be held in Germany 1936; German Chancellor's interest, fears of Germany that United States would withdraw, inclusion of Jewish woman in fencing team' FO 371/18884/7552 *The National Archives* www.nationalarchives.gov.uk/olympics/1936.htm accessed 19 May 2019

The National Spinal Injuries Centre (NSIC) 'Our History' The National Spinal Injuries Centre (NSIC), Stoke Mandeville Hospital www.buckshealthcare.nhs.uk/NSIC%20Home/About%20us/nsic-history.htm accessed 5 August 2019.

The Pony Club www.pcuk.org/About-Us/History accessed 17 January 2019.

The Royal Academy of Arts 'Our Story: Women at the Royal Academy' *The Royal Academy of Arts* www.royalacademy.org.uk/about-the-ra#our-story accessed 11 May 2019.

The Ski Club of Great Britain 'The Pery Medal: 1972 Miss Davina Galica and Miss Gina Hawthorn' www.skiclub.co.uk/news-and-events/inspire-awards/the-pery-medal accessed 7 August 2017.

Wimbledon Lawn Tennis Museum *Roll of Honour* http://aeltc2011.wimbledon.com/players/rolls-of-honour/ladies-singles accessed 14 June 2019.

Index

Page numbers in *italics* denote figures.

30-year anniversary Olympic Games 70

Abbott, Margaret 20–1
Aberdare, Lord 106, 121, 172
Ableman, Dorcas 219–20
Abrahams, Harold 63, 132, 135, 186, 205
Adamson, Percy 84
Aitchison, Helen 47–8
Alfred Hutton Memorial Cup 105
All England Club 24
All England Women's Hockey Association 8, 34, 324
all-female British team: Garmisch-Partenkirchen (1936) 106–8; Lake Placid and Los Angeles (1932) 100–6; St Moritz and Amsterdam (1928) 95–100
Allison, Lincoln 14, 16, 226
Altwegg, Jeanette 4, 161–3, 165
Aluko, Eniola 271; birth of 274; coaching and professional contracts 275; complaint against Sampson 277; dropped from the England squad 276; early life and career 274; Leafield Athletic Ladies 275; participation in professional leagues 275; professional career 275; racism under Sampson's management 276; as winner of 102 caps in her England career 276; and women's football 274–7
Amateur Athletic Association (AAA) 3–4, 28, 53, 63, 66, 127, 132, 180, 259
Amateur Athletic Union 27, 104
Amateur Fencing Association 4, 16, 65, 86, 103, 195, 252
Amateur Fencing Council 38

Amateur Football Association 5, 39
amateurism: 'Amateur/Sex/Dope' Certificate 231; British amateur system 113, 229; controversies of 219; decline of 218; definition of 13, 257; female 15; justification for protecting women in sport 223; Olympic entry form 223; pseudo-amateurs 185; spiteful aspects of 14; sporting 17; and voluntarism 17–48; and women's sporting careers 218
'Amateur/Sex/Dope' Certificate 231
amateur sport 25, 95, 153, 161, 202; British 158; development of 12, 253; Dod's views on 15; Olympic voluntarism and 18
Amateur Swimming Association (ASA) 4, 8, 13, 17, 39, 44, 53, 72, 77, 80, 103, 141, 148, 193, 194
American Broadcasting Company (ABC) 88
American Hatred and British Folly 38
Amsterdam Summer Olympic Games (1928) 89, 95–100; costs associated with 100; rent and administrative expenses 100
anabolic steroids, use of 229, 232
Andersen, Greta 150
Anglo–American rivalry 38
Anglo–Soviet rivalries, in Olympic Games 180
Anne, Princess 234, 254, 261, 268; appointment to the IOC 253; birth of 173; gold medal at the European Eventing Championships (1971) 209; horse 'Goodwill' 209, 242; media

Index

Anne, Princess *continued*
  profile of 8; Montreal Olympics (1976) 209; as only female President of an International Federation 256
Anti-Apartheid sport, principle of 243
Antwerp Olympic Game (1920) 62–4; and British Olympic Association 64–9
Arbuthnot, Betty 105, 129
Armitage, Heather 50, 176–7, 190
Arnold, Thomas 2
Association of National Olympic Committees 223
Athens Olympiad (1896) 12, 217
Athens Olympics (2004) 274
Athlete Performance Award (APA) 269
athletic competition, moral benefits of 16
athletic scholarships 275
athletic weekends 232
A.& W. Gamage Ltd 70

Badcock, Joyce 98–9
Band of German Maidens 129
Barfield, Vivian 255
Barker, David 196
Barker, Florence 71, 81
Batter, Doris 156
BBC Sports Personality of the Year: Anne, Princess 8, 209; Hyman, Dorothy 227; McColgan, Liz 249; Packer, Ann 207; Peters, Mary 237; Phillips, Zara 8, 209; Rand, Mary 207
Beaurepaire, Frank 74
Bergère, Folies 77, 184
Berlin Olympic Game (1936) 95, 106, 113–35, 183; Brown, Audrey 113–35; Hitler, Adolf 113; 'Nazi' Olympics 114; opening of 113; Owens, Jesse 113
Berlioux, Monique 3, 241, 250, 255, 256
Besford, Pat 9, 180, 193–4, 201, 229
Billbow, Tom 220
Birchenough, Florence Ethel 120
Black British female athletes, cultural heritage of 233
Blackwood, Carol 238
Blackwood, Vivien 219–20
Blankers-Koen, Fanny 220; female athlete of the twentieth century 161; as Flying Housewife 155; in London Olympic Games (1948) 155–60; long jump and high jump world records 155; Olympic achievements of 155; Taher Pacha Trophy by the IOC 161

Blanshard, Jessie Florence 203
Bloody Friday 236
Board, Lillian 232–3
Bogen, Erna 105
Bolt, The (1931) 115
Borzov, Valeri 239
Bowden, Harold 102
Bradford Textile Company 70
Brasher, Chris 180, 186
British Amateur Athletic Association 3
British Amateur Athletic Board 120
British Amateur Fencing Association 65, 86
British Association of Disability Sport 255
British Athletics Federation 240
British Broadcasting Company (BBC) 88; Sports Personality of the Year *see* BBC Sports Personality of the Year
British Commonwealth Games 244; African threat of pulling out of 244
British Cycling 277
British Deaf Amateur Sports Association 202, 204
British Empire 172, 251
British Empire Games 98, 105–6, 135, 152, 159, 172, 192, 251
British Equestrian Federation 234
British Equestrian Fund 185
British female Olympians: in diverse sports and disciplines 218; ethnic minority 217; from Munich to Montreal, Moscow and Los Angeles 242–50; preparation and post-athletic career 220; priorities while competing 220; sport-specific professionalism 218; success of 226
British Ice Hockey Association 101
British nationalism 140
British Olympic Association (BOA) 62, 95, 102, 173, 223; Antwerp 1920 and 64–9; campaign against continuing use of Entertainment Tax 69; *Chasing Gold* 4; consciousness of international rivalry 95; financial concerns of 86; formation of 4, 16–17; fundraising campaign 69, 86, 235, 253; impact on the IOC 16–17; on improving Britain's sporting culture 100; life membership of 39; objects of 17; Paris Olympics of 1924 and 69–85; response to international rivalries in women's sport 179;

Revenue Account 63; Thorpe's medals issue 14; *World Sports: International Sports Magazine* 172
British Olympic Council 4, 17, 39, 40, 65, 100, 107
British Olympic Journal 100
British Schools Exploring Society 252
British Show Jumping Association (BSJA) 173, 208
British Sports Association 69
British Sports Association for the Disabled 252, 255
'broken time' payments 102
Brouwer, Bertha 176
Brown, Audrey 113, 132; case study of 113–35; early life in India 114; representation of Britain in Berlin Olympics (1936) 114, 122–30
Brown, Godfrey 116, 127
Brown, Ralph Kilner 127–8
Bruce, Philip 256
Brundage, Avery 3, 131, 142, 165, 175, 185, 227–8, 238, 250
Bryant, Carol 230
buccal smear mouth swab 257
Buck, Gwen 230, 231
Bullen, Jane 224–42, 233–4
bungalow village scheme 103
bureaucratisation, of Olympic Games 89
Burghley, Lord 106, 142, 209
Burke, Barbara 124, 126, 202
Burlford, Thomas Rugby 38
Burton, Elaine 114, 218, 222–3, 248, 259, 270
Butler, Maude 'Peggy' 98, 105, 107
Button, Dick 162

Cardiff Commonwealth Games (1958) 172, 251
Carson, Connie 71, 74, 83, 200
Carson, Gladys 7, 64, 71, 79; Breaststroke Championship of All England, Kent (1921) 76; controversial photograph of 81; first job as a secondary state school domestic science teacher 77; head and shoulders photograph portrait 75; headstone showing the Olympic rings 84; life-saving exhibition at a gala 76; Paris Olympic Games (1924) 69–85; retirement from competitive swimming 83; swimming career 72; training regime of 76; transnational sporting success 71
Carson, Olive 74, 87
Cecil, David 142
Central Council for Physical Recreation (CCPR) 252–3, 268
ceremonial and sporting uniforms, of British teams 66
Chair of the Central Council for Physical Recreation 252, 268
Chariots of Fire (film) 63–4
Charles, Prince 173, 198
Cheeseman, Sylvia 152, 157, 176–7
Chicago Columbian Exposition (1893) 18
Chicago Tribune 83, 87
Christchurch Centenary Celebration Games (1951) 153
Christie, Linford 249, 260
Clarke, Harold 82
Coakes, Marion 207, 234
Coe, Seb 245
Cold War rivalry, in Helsinki Olympic Games (1952) 174–99
Columbia Broadcasting System (CBS) 88
Comité International des Sports Silencieux 203
Connall, Kathleen 127
Cook, Theodore 38
Cooper, Charlotte 'Chattie' 14; birth of 22; club tennis at Ealing Lawn Tennis Club 24; as first British female Olympic prize winner 22; first Olympic mixed doubles title 22; five singles successes at Wimbledon 24; Paris Olympic Games (1900) 18–26; as part of the amateur sporting establishment 25
Cooper, John Astley 2
Cooper, Joyce 98, 105
Cornell, Muriel 107, 120–1, 132
Court, Audrey *see* Brown, Audrey
Court of Arbitration for Sport 1, 250
Cripps, Winsome 176
Croft, June 245, 247
Curwen, Daisy 44, 46
Cuthbert, Betty 189–91
cycling programme: British Cycling 277; Varnish's omission from 277

Daily Mail, The 29, 53, 74, 100, 103, 182, 246
Daily Sketch, The 97

Daniell, Gladys 71, 98
Davies, Lynn 'The Leap' 227
Davies, Sharron 7
Dawson, Lenore 203
Dean, Christopher 248
de Beaumont, Charles 256
de Coubertin, Pierre 2–3, 12, 22, 28, 116, 174
DeFrantz, Anita 254
de Fredy, Pierre 2
de Marino, Marquise 254
Dennis, Clare 105, 162
de Paleologu, Jean 19
Desforges, Jean 176–7
Dewar, Thomas 43
Didrikson, Babe 104, 155, 161
Didrikson, Mildred Ella 104
disability sports 230; key aspects of 218; politicisation of 244
Dix, Joan 101
Dod, Lottie 13; from Paris 1900 to London 1908 38–9; sporting life 50; views on amateur sport 15
Doherty, Reginald 22, 26, 48
'do it yourself' ethos 227
doping: in East Germany 221; link with sex testing 222; medical testing for 222; State-condoned 219
Douglass, Dorothea 24–6, 37, 49, 54, 85
Dowling, Emily 241
Downham, Lord 65
Doyle, Arthur Conan 39–40, 53
drug testing 220
Duke of Edinburgh 173, 189
Duke of Westminster's Olympic Games Fund 53
Du Louvre, Magasins 78, 79
Duncan, K.S. 'Sandy' 86, 156, 173, 234, 245
Durack, Fanny 41–2, 44–6
duty of care, to athletes 277
Dyehouse, Carol 114
Dyreson, Mark 82, 258
Dyson, Geoff 165–6

Ealing Gazette 229
East German athletes: anabolic steroids, use of 229; doping regimes 221; performance of 219
East-West divide 180, 219, 236
Edelman, Robert 140
Edström, Sigfrid 3, 116, 142
Egan, Cornelia 174

electronic points-scoring system 195
Eliott-Lynn, Sophie 115, 119
elite sports 219
Elizabeth II, Queen 171–3; and British Royal family 173; 'Countryman III' horse 188; equestrian skill 172; fascination of racing 174; as first Queen Regnant to attend a cricket match at Lord 173; Honours List 195; and Olympic movement 173; as Patron of the Melbourne Olympics 189; Royal Life Saving Society's Junior Resuscitation Badge 141; sporting enthusiasm 174; visit to the Fäboda course 188
English rural sports 2–3
Entertainment Tax, BOA campaign against use of 69
equestrian professionalisation, business of 182
espirit de corps 69
Essex Ladies' Athletic Club 156
European Athletics Championship (1938) 133
European pentathlon championship 225
European Rowing Championships 272
Evening Standard, The 226–7
Exposition Universelle 12

Fairlie, F. 71
fancy-swimming Christmas pantomimes 75
Farr, Muriel 219–20
Fauvannat, Marie-Louise 142
Fédération Équestre Internationale (FEI) 173, 209
Federation Internationale de Football Association (FIFA) 257, 277
Fédération Sportive Féminine Internationale (FSFI) 117, 120
female amateurism 15
female athletes: amateur athletes 42; international resurgence of 97–8; visual and physical checks of anatomy of 257
female competitions: internationalisation of 251; in speed skating 243
female employment 106
female 'other,' objectification of 228
female sports stars, media representation of 229
Festival of Britain 173

Fleischer, Tilly 104, 127, 129
Fletcher, Jennie 14–15, 42; career of 50; on joy of learning to swim 43; moment of fame 42; retirement of 44; Stockholm Olympic Games (1912) 39–48; swimming career 43; Swimming Hall of Fame 45; as world's champion swimmer 44
Follows, Denis 252–4
Forder, Valerie 230–1
Foulds, Pauline 230
Freeman, Muriel 71, 98, 195, 251
Free Trade policies 18
French Olympic Committee 65, 69, 78–9
Fry, C.B. 4, 50

gala socials 75
Galica, Davina 224, 235, 238
Gardner, Maureen 157–8, 161, 165
Garmisch-Partenkirchen Olympic Game (1936), Germany 106–8
gender binary 218, 231, 257; medicalisation of 231
gender equity, in sport 255
gender quotas 277
gender verification and testing 132
Gentry, Amy 270, 272
George VI, King 140
Geraghty, Agnes 80
German Olympic Committee 106
Gerschwiler, Jacques 102
Gibson, Cathie 145–50
Gilbert, Irene 71, 80, 82
Glasgow Corporation 46
Gleneagles Agreement 244
Glen-Haig, Dame Mary Alison 195, 219, 250–7, 253, 268; award of Olympic Order 257; birth of 250; as British IOC representative 253; campaign to integrate women in Olympic movement 255; competition against younger British opponents 195; election to British Olympic Association 252; election to International Olympic Committee (IOC) 253–4; as fencer and British Fencing Association official 250; on growing commercialism in sport 254; as honorary member of the IOC 257; on integration of African nations with IANCS 254; on integration of women in the Olympic movement 255; promotion of sport of fencing 251; retirement from Olympic competition 252; sporting reputation 251; work as a health administrator 251
Glover, Ted 172
Golden Girls (1984) 217, 223; depictions of characters in 219–20; on freedoms and perils offered by professional sport 224
Golden Girls generation (1964–1968) 7, 224–42
Gordon, Elenor 150, 152, 159, 178
Gothenburg Women's World Games (1926) 120
Grainger, Dame Katherine 272, 274
Grand Festival of Paraplegic Sport 160
Great British female team: at Grenoble Winter Olympic Games (1968) 289; at Innsbruck Winter Olympics, Austria (1964) 279; at Innsbruck Winter Olympics, Austria (1976) 303–4; at Lake Placid Winter Olympics (1980) 310–11; at Los Angeles Olympic Games, USA (1984) 312–20; at Mexico City Olympic Games (1968) 284–8; at Montréal Olympic Games, Canada (1976) 298–303; at Moscow Olympic Games, USSR (1980) 305–10; at Munich Olympic Games, Germany (1972) 290–6; at Sapporo Winter Olympic Games, Japan (1972) 296–7; at Sarajevo Winter Olympic Games, Yugoslavia (1984) 320–2; at Tokyo Olympic Games, Japan (1964) 280–3
Great Exhibition of the Industry of All Nations, The (1851) 18
Greek Olympic Games (1910) 39
Grenoble Winter Olympic Games (1968) 289
Grinham, Judy 164, 171, 180, 192–3, 202
Guerra, Elvira 20, 174
Guinness, Heather Seymour 98, 104–5
Gundle, Stephen 172
Gunnell, Sally 4, 7, 260
Guttmann, Ludwig 159–60, 218, 230
Gyarmati, Olga 159

Hackett, Desmond 227
Halstead, Nellie 103–4, 120
Hamilton, Laetitia 174
Hannam, Edith 47–8
Hardcastle, Sarah 247

Harding, Phyllis 71, 81, 105, 128
Hartel, Lis 175–6, 187–8
Hartman, Marea 226, 259
Hart, Mike 273
Hatt, Hilda 119
Hawthorn, Gina 235
Haynes, Sally 230
health and disability charities 230
Heggie, Vanessa 231
Hellenic Olympic tradition 12
Helsinki Olympic Games (1952) 140, 171, 219; accommodation for female competitors 175; Britain's changing political relations 175; Cold War rivalry 174–99; dominance of Australian sprinters 176; female track and field athletics programme 174; new women's sports events 175; performance of USSR in 176–8
Henie, Sonja 70, 95, 102, 108
Herbert, Charles 3–4
Hewitt, David 64, 76, 83, 85, 238
Hewitt, Gladys 62, 71, 85
Hiscock, Eileen 103, 120–1, 124, 126–7
Hitler, Adolf 113, 125–6
Hitler Youth (Nazi Party youth movement) 129
Hitomi, Kinuye 97, 120
HMS Vanguard 172
Holderness-Roddam, Jane 234
Holman, Edith Dorothy 67
Holt, Richard 50
Hope Brothers 70
Hopkins, Thelma 177, 192, 236, 241
horse-breeding 198
horse riding events, in Olympic Games 183
Hoskin, Sheila 192, 235
Houghton, Sarah 274
House of Lords 230
Hoyle, Julie 193
Hyman, Dorothy 200, 218, 226–8, 268–9

Île de Puteaux Club, Paris 22
Innsbruck Winter Olympics, Austria (1964) 279
Innsbruck Winter Olympics, Austria (1976) 303–4
International Amateur Athletics Federation (IAAF) 97, 116, 142
International Assembly of National Confederations of Sport (IANCS) 254

International Athletic Congress 12, 17
International Federations (IFs) 256–7
International Fencing Federation 251, 257
International Foundation for the Olympic Truce 1
International Games for the Deaf and Dumb 202
International Judo Federation 248
International Lawn Tennis Federation 25
International Olympic Committee (IOC) 1, 3, 12, 62, 106, 253, 257, 277; admission of USSR into 175; establishment of 63; impact of BOA on 16–17; Rule 32 of Olympic Charter 258
International Paralympic Committee 1, 259
International Rowing Federation (FISA): women's international races 272
International Shooting Union 231
International Skating Union (ISU) 38
International Sporting Federations 224, 232, 250
international sporting tournaments 15
International Sports Organisation for the Disabled (ISOD) 244
International Stoke Mandeville Games Federation (ISMGF) 244
International Tennis Hall of Fame 67
International Week of Winter Sport 69
International World Conference on Women and Sport 255
International Yacht Racing Union (IYRU) 248
IOC Olympic Charter, Rule 32 of 257
Irish Times, The 240

Jackson, Marjorie 176
James, Mary 251
Jarvis, Jack 43, 51, 72–3
Jeans, Constance 67, 71, 81
Johnson, Ben 249
Johnson, Ethel 103, 104, 120
Johnson, Phyllis 38, 69–70
Johnstone, Lorna 1, 187, 238
Jones, Marion 22
Jones, Sheelagh 230
Journal of Olympic Studies 18
Justice of the Peace 108

Kastenman, Petrus 188
Kauffman, Angelica 99
Kellerman, Annette 44

Kellett, Iris 198
Kendall, Pat 149
Kensington Athletic Club, London 115
Killanin, Lord 142, 243, 254
King, Ellen 98
Knight, Laura 99–100
Knipe, G.T. 142
Koechlin-Smythe, Pat 197
Korbut, Olga 239–40; rivalry with Tourischeva 259
Koubkova, Zdenka 132
Krzesinska, Elzbieta 192
Kuts, Raisa 180
Kyle, Maeve 191, 241
Kynaston, David 140

Ladies Amateur Fencing Union 252
La Fédération Internationale d'Escrime (FIE) 87, 251
Laffan, Robert Stuart de Courcy 5, 16, 28, 63
Lake Placid Winter Olympics (1932) 95, 100–6; British all-female team at 95, 101; women's speed skating 101
Lake Placid Winter Olympics (1980) 310–11
Lambert Chambers, Dorothy *see* Douglass, Dorothea
Langham Life First International Conference on Women in Sport (1978) 268
Laughton, Janet 231
Lawn Tennis 21; Olympic tennis tournament 22; Wimbledon Championships 22
Lawn Tennis for Ladies (1910) 21–2, 25
League of German Girls, The 129
Leaping Life's Fences (1992) 181, 186
Legh, Alice Blanche 50
Leicester Ladies Swimming Club 43, 72, 85
Leicester Ladies Water Polo Team 74
Leicester Mercury, The 83
Lenglen, Suzanne 49, 67, 88, 108
Lennartz, Karl 12
Lewis, Denise 260, 269, 270, 272
Liddell, Eric 63
Lines, Mary 117–19
Linsenhoff, Liselott 187–8, 207
Llewellyn, Harry 183–5
Lock, Betty 130
London Olympiades 117, 232–3

London Olympic Games (1908) 98, 140, 250
London Olympic Games (1948) 172, 179; Blankers-Koen, Fanny 155–60; domestic media coverage of 140; number of contestants in 140; Opening Ceremony of 143, 160; shadow of a scandal 183; technological innovation 143; Wellington, Margaret 144–54
London Woollen Company 70
Lonsbrough, Anita 4, 199, 202, 224–5
Lonsdale, Lord 173
Los Angeles Olympic Games, USA (1932) 98, 100–6
Los Angeles Olympic Games, USA (1984) 258, 312–20
Lovett, Kathleen 95
Lunn, Gladys 121–2

McCormick, Pat 178, 194
McDaniel, Mildred 191–2
McKane, Kathleen 'Kitty' 67, 85, 88
McNair, Winifred 67
McShane, Buster 237
McWhirter, Norris 192, 229
Mahoney, Harold 23–5
Maillart, Ella 87
Maison, Madame 20
Mallon, Bill 19–20, 28
Manley, Dorothy 156, 158
Mary Mary: Autobiography of an Olympic Champion 229
Masham, Susan 202, 224–42, 230
mass tourism 16
Mathiot, Ginette 79
Matthews, Bernard 7
Matthews, Stanley 165
Mayer, Otto 142, 173, 223
media representation, of sportswomen 19, 229
medicalisation, of elite performance sport 230
medically 'authentic' woman, in sport 219
Mejzlikova, Marie 119
Melbourne Olympic Games (1956) 172; boycott of 221; Elizabeth II as Patron of 189
Messerli, Franz 222
Messrs T.H. Downing & Co. Ltd 66
Mexico City Olympic Games (1968) 219, 231, 284–8

Middlesex Ladies' Athletic Club 115
Milhado, Albert 155
Milliat, Alice 8, 116–17, 120, 122, 133, 268
Mitcham Athletics Club scholarships 127
Mitchell, Jean 129, 143
modern sport, codification of 14
Molesworth, Doris 82–3
Monte Carlo European Championships (1947) 178
Montréal Olympic Games, Canada (1976) 298–303; boycott of 243, 245; Canadian–New Zealand national relationship 243; diplomatic row over Apartheid sport 243; Springbok–All Blacks fixtures 243
Monty Python's Flying Circus (1974) 207
Moore, Isabella McAlpine 46; gold medal in the 4 × 100-metres freestyle relay 46
Morton, Lucy 40, 62, 71, 76, 79, 80, 83, 88
Moscow Olympic Games, USSR (1980) 253, 305–10; boycott of 254
Moser, Mary 99
Mould, David 207
Muckelt, Ethel 70, 95
Munich Olympic Games, Germany (1972) 208, 238, 290–6
Murdoch, Rupert 10, 228
Murphy, Jack 191

Nadezda, Hnykina 176
National Broadcasting Company (NBC) 88
National Discount Committee 106
National Discount Company 100
National Governing Bodies 222, 257, 269
National Hunt Racing 174
National Lottery Funding, for Olympic athletes 269
National Lottery Heritage 270, 272
National Olympic Committees (NOCs) 63, 257
National Organising Committee (NOC) 4
National Playing Fields Association 100
National Soviet Sports Council 239
'Nazi' Summer Olympics 7
Neufville, Marilyn 232–3
Neville, Rupert 253
Newall, Queenie 30, 32, 50

'new' Elizabethan era, in British history and popular culture 171–4; media's coverage of 172
Newman, Sally 229
Newman, Verrall 77, 82, 100
New South Wales Women's Advisory Council 255
New York News 83, 87
New Zealand Olympic Committee 248
Nicks, John 162
Nielsen, Patricia 147, 149–50
Noel, Susan 9, 180
Noon, Joan 'Bunty' 160
Northcliffe, Lord 29, 53
Nuremberg trials 99

Olney, Violet 124, 126
Olympiad for the Physically Disabled 244
Olympic entry form 223; 'Amateur/Sex/Dope' Certificate 231
Olympic festivities 206
Olympic Games: British women's participation in 15; bureaucratisation of 89; commercialization of 13, 15; as cultural 'bond of unity' 15; eligibility code of 231; equestrian events 173; international expansion of 89; modern revival of 15–16; 'new' Elizabethan era 171; objective of 15; philosophy of 2; popularity of 40; as representative of modern sporting contests 13; South Africa's role in 221; 'Two China's' problem 221
Olympic Games BC776–AD1896; The 12
Olympic inter-war revival: Antwerp in 1920 to Paris 1924 62–4; British Olympic Association and 64–9; Paris Olympics of 1924 and 69–85
Olympic Journal 100, 103
Olympic movement 1–2, 18, 230; effect of social democracy and feminism on 18; Elizabeth II, Queen 173; during the Great War 63; integration of women in 255
Olympic rivalry, between the USA, Russia and Britain 226
Olympic voluntarism, benefits of 18
Opening Ceremony parade uniform 40
Organisation of African Unity (OAU) 243
'ornamental' swimming displays 75
Osaka Women's Marathon 241

Ostermeyer, Micheline 158
Otkalenko, Nina 229
Ovett, Steve 95, 245
Owens, Jesse 113

Pacha, H.E. Mohammed Taher 161
Packer, Anne 4, 225–7, 269
Page, Louise 217
paid journalism 181
Palmer, Charles 252–3
Palmer, Vera 115
Panter, Anne 271
Paralympic Games 202, 217, 240, 244, 254, 259, 271, 277
Paralympic movement 135, 230, 271
Paris Exposition (1889) 18–19
Paris Olympic Game (1900) 16; Charlotte 'Chattie' Cooper and 18–26; fencing competition 19; inclusion of female athletes in 18; *Journal of Olympic Studies* 18; market-based exhibition movement 18
Paris Olympic Games (1924) 7, 62–4, 251; Gladys Carson and 69–85
Parton, Mabel 47
Pashley, Anne 190
Paterson, Audrey 'Mickey' 157
Pattison, Rodney 238
Paul, June 191
Peelers to Pandas 75
performance enhancing stimulants, surveillance for 231
Persson, Gehnäll 183
Peters, Mary 4, 7, 218–19, 225–6, 232, 235–42, 258
Peterson, Pauline 219
Philadelphia World's Fair (1876) 18
Philip, Prince 189, 253
Phillips, Bob 140
Phillips, Mollie 101, 107–8, 225
physique in relation to performance, importance of 241
Pilley, Phil 227
Pinsent, Matthew 260, 272
politicisation of sport 171
Ponomaryeva, Nina 180
Pony Club 182, 196–7, 208
Porter, Gwendoline 103, 120
Porter, Hugh 224
portrayals, of athletic women 89
Powell, Hope 276
Pratt, Daria 21
Preis, Ellen 105, 129

Prevost, André 23
Prevost, Hélèn 22–3
Pritchard, Winifred 143
Prix de la ville de Compiègne (championnat de dames) 20
professionalism: antithesis of 14; rules regarding 208
progressive socialism 229
propaganda culture 19
protection of women in sport, justification for 223
pseudo-amateurs 185
public entertainment and sport 185
public role of women, in post-war Britain 171
Punchestown Races 174

Radcliffe, Paula 68, 247, 269
Radio Leicester 62, 64, 80, 83
Radke, Linda 97–8, 120
Rand, Mary 224–42, 225
Reagan, Ronald 255
Redgrave, Steve 245, 249, 272
Restorick, Basil 153, 163
Richardson, Louise 273
Riding for the Disabled Association (RDA) 176, 197
Riding for the Disabled movement 230
Riggin, Aileen 81–2, 88, 108
rivalries, in Olympic Games: between Britain and US 38; between Britain and USSR 180; between East and West 180
Robb, Muriel 26
Robinson, Elizabeth 'Betty' 97, 126
Rogge, Jacques 3, 271
Rosendahl, Heide 236–7
Rothermere, Lord 100, 102, 103
rowing: Boat Race at Henley 273; European Rowing Championships 272; International Rowing Federation (FISA) 272; Talent Identification consensus for 273; Women's Amateur Rowing Association 272; world championships in Cologne (2008) 273
Royal Shakespeare Company (RSC): *Golden Girls* (1984) 217, 219
Royal Toxophilite Society 4, 17, 30
Rudman, Shelley 261
rugby games 243

Sandell, Florence 50–1
Sanderson, Tessa 7, 246, 276

Sandow, Eugen 39
Sapporo Winter Olympic Games, Japan (1972) 238, 296–7
Sarajevo Winter Olympic Games, Yugoslavia (1984) 248, 320–2
Saunders, Yvonne 233
Scott, Edburga Clementina 120
Scott, Ethel 232
Scottish Amateur Athletic Association 39, 63
Seaborne, Pamela 176
selection process, of women athletes 217
Selfridges Ltd 70
Seoul Summer Olympic Games (1988) 249
Sex Discrimination Act 229
sex testing, quasi-medicalisation of 218, 222
sexualised and sensationalised news, tabloidisation of 228
shamateur, notion of 14, 104, 204, 218, 220
Shaw, Kathleen 70, 95
Sheen, Gillian 105, 159, 195
Shostakovich, Dmitri 115
Silent Olympics 202
Slazenger, Albert 39
Smallwood-Cook, Kathy 246
Smith, Joyce 247
Smythe, Monique 182
Smythe, Patricia Rosemary 165, 171, 193; achievements of 183–4; birth of 181; books and other paid writings of 186; as Britain's greatest and best-loved horsewoman 181–99; British women contemporaries of 208; career of 181; case study of 181–99; *Daily Express* Sportswoman of the Year (1952) 185; dominance in national championships 184; endorsement of commercial products 185; entrepreneurial activities 171; equestrian career 171; family life of 181; female co-competitors 198; 'feminine courage' by competing alongside men 172; financial problem 185; Horse of the Year duel 184; *Leaping Life's Fences* (1992) 181; life story of 171; link with breeders and traders of horses and ponies 182; opportunity to become an Olympian 180; performance at the first International Horse Show 183; promoting of equestrian disciplines 198; public image of 186; reputation in Europe 184; *Sporting Records* Sportswoman of the Year (1955) 186; success at the International Show 188; win at the 1949 Grand Prix in Brussels 184; as world's leading equestrians 186
Sochi Winter Olympics (2014) 209, 271
social democracy 18
social mix, of athletes 252
social mobility 7, 235
Somers, Florence A. 97
South Africa: role in Olympic Games 221
Speirs, Annie Coupe 40–1, 46
Speirs, Jessie 44
sporting amateurism 17
sporting appeasement 141
sporting couples, of Britain 116
sporting print journalism, growth in 180
Sports Aid Foundation 252
Sports Business Houses 70
Sportschuhfabrik Gebrüder Dassler 98
Sports Council 222–3, 229, 239, 252, 255
Sports Council Press Unit 229
Sports Development Council: establishment of 222
sports science research 229
sportswomen, media representation of 19
Sports Writers' Association of Great Britain 229
Sprint to Fame 227
Stafford, Margaret 195, 252
Steer, Irene 40–1, 44, 46
Stender, Jan 194
Stephens, Helen 126, 133
Sterry, Alfred 25
Sterry, Charlotte 18, 24–6, 37, 48
St Moritz Winter Olympic Games (1928) 95
Stockholm Olympic Games (1912) 12, 14, 39, 68; Jennie Fletcher and 39–48; women's events at 40
Stoke Mandeville Games 160, 218, 230, 231, 244, 255, 259
Stubnick, Christa 189–90
Suez crisis 189
Sunday Herald, The 175
Supreme Council of Sport in Africa (SCSA) 243
Swedish Olympic Committee 40, 174

Syers, Madge 38, 163
synchronised swimming, 'feminine' sport of 247, 258

tabloid journalism 163, 228
talent identification system 53, 275
Tamara and Irina Press 229
Tanner, Iris 81, 98
Taylor, Megan 27, 101, 107, 108
Telegraph, The 225
tennis competitions 21, 26, 85
testosterone tests 257
Tetley, Carol 230
Thatcher, Margaret 253
Third Reich 99
Thompson, Blondelle 250
Thorpe, Jim 14
Tikhomirova, Valentina 236
Time magazine 172, 246
Tokyo Olympic Games, Japan (1964) 280–3
Tomlinson, Alan 244
Toronto Games (1976) 244
Torvill, Jane 248
Tourischeva, Ludmilla 238–9; rivalry with Korbut 259
transnational global movement 16
'Two China's' problem 221, 243
Tyler, Dorothy 127, 158, 161, 177, 192

Uberroth, Peter 245–6
UK Sport system 223, 269, 271, 272, 277
'Under 23' tournament 271
United States Olympic Association (USOA) 67

Vancouver Commonwealth Games (1954) 172, 251
Vanity Fair 19
Varah, Chad 190
Varnish, Jess 277
Voorhees, Nancy 119
voyeurism, in mainstream newspapers 228

Walsh, Anne 194
Walsh, Stella 133
Waters, Meg 195
Webb, Violet 103–4, 116, 120, 127
Webster, F.A.M. 103, 106, 165
Weissmuller, Johnny 82–3
Wellington, Margaret 7, 141, 217; appetite for increased training 147; birth of 144; British Empire Games in New Zealand (1950) 152; career of 165; case study of 144–54; coaching tips for the *Daily Graphic* 163; end of her competitive swimming career 154; *History of Beckenham Swimming Club, A* 163; at London Olympic Games (1948) 144; as part of an ASA English national team 148; personality of 148; swimming costumes of 164; training regimes of 146; transnational fame 144
Weston, Mark Edward Louis 132
Weston, Mary 132
wheelchair-based athletes 244
Whitbread, Fatima 246, 249, 252
Whitehead, Linda 275
Whitehead, Sue 186
White, Isabella Mary 47
Wilkinson, Emily 42
Willcox, Sheila 207
Williamson, Audrey 156–7
Wimbledon Lawn Tennis Club 25
Winckless, Sarah: appointment as Boat Race Umpire 274; award of MBE for services to sport and charity 274; birth of 273; on Board of UK Anti-Doping 274; as Chair of the BOA Athletes Commission 274; as Chef de Mission for the British team 274; injuries and retirement 274; rowing championships 272–4; selection for the 2004 Athens Olympics 274
Windsor, Elizabeth *see* Elizabeth II, Queen
winning 'in the right way' 220
Winter Olympics for the Disabled 244
Winter Silent Games 203
Wofford, Dawn 196
Wolfenden Committee (1957): *Leisure For Living* report (1959) 222; Wolfenden Report (1957) 222
womanhood in sport: female athlete's aspirations to 217; *Golden Girls* (1984) 217; quasi-medical narratives on 217–24; sex testing 218; surveillance of women's bodies 218
Women Ahead 274
women leaders, in world sport 250–7
Women's Amateur Athletic Association (WAAA) 97, 103, 107, 114, 121, 176, 259; first generation pioneers 114–22
Women's Amateur Rowing Association 272

Women's Army Auxiliary Corps (WAAC) 115
women's athletics, developments in 97, 103, 114, 115, 117, 119
women's bodies, quasi-scientific surveillance of 218
women's endurance, in sport and leisure 222
Women's FA Premier League 275
women's football: Olympic Games 276; Women's World Cup 276
Women's Football Association (WFA) 275
Women's Football World Cup: in China 276; in Sweden 276
Women's Olympic Games 117, 165
Women's Professional Soccer (WPS) 275
women's road cycling 252
women's speed skating 101, 206
women's sport: in America 255; changes in attitudes to 256; impact of Cold War on 219; integration into public and social life in Britain 221; International Conference on 268; international rivalries in 179; in Ireland 240; transnational aspects of 16, 18–19
women's sporting careers, impact of amateurism on 218
Women's Sports Foundation 252, 255
women's track and field athletics, structures of 64, 97, 103, 114, 120, 127, 129, 132, 134, 176, 189, 225
Women's World Games 8, 117, 120–1, 133, 268
Woosnam, Maxwell 67
World Anti-Doping Agency 1
World Class Performance programme 269
World Figure Skating Championships (1902) 38, 107
World Sports: International Sports Magazine 9, 172, 176
Wright, Dorothy 69
Wylie, Mina 41–2, 45

Zanchi, Lydie 141–2
Zweifel, Françoise 3, 254